Story Time Sampler

Story Time Sampler

Read Alouds, Booktalks, and Activities for Children

Paula Gaj Sitarz

1997
Libraries Unlimited, Inc.
Englewood, Colorado

LIBRARIES UNLIMITED, INC.
P.O. Box 6633
Englewood, CO 80155-6633
1-800-237-6124

Production Editor: Kay Mariea
Copy Editor: Susan Brown
Proofreader: Suzanne Hawkins Burke
Interior Design and Typesetting: Judy Gay Matthews

Illustrations by Donna Rowe

Library of Congress Cataloging-in-Publication Data

Sitarz, Paula Gaj, 1955-
    Story time sampler : read alouds, booktalks, and activities for children / by Paula Gaj Sitarz.
        xii, 309 p. 17x25 cm.
        Includes bibliographical references and index.
        ISBN 1-56308-464-3
        1. Storytelling. 2. Children--Books and reading. 3. Tales--Study and teaching (Primary) 4. Fairy tales--Study and teaching (Primary)
    I. Title
    LB1042.S58   1997
    372.64'2--DC20   96-34602
                                                                CIP

To my family:
Michael, Andrew, and Kate with love

To my friends:
Alison and Lori

To the dedicated teachers
at the Joseph P. DeMello Elementary School
in Dartmouth, Massachusetts,
who have brought literature to life for my children.

Contents

Preface

While I was a children's librarian in Quincy, Massachusetts, the children's staff struggled to find a program format that would appeal to children in kindergarten through grade three. We needed appealing programs to attract young, school-age children throughout the summer, during school break periods, after school, and during class visits from nearby schools. The other children's librarians and I tried showing feature films. We received a mediocre response. Short films interspersed with booktalks related to the subject matter of the movies didn't work either.

Often while doing a picture-book story hour for preschoolers during a vacation week or during the summer, I noticed that older children gravitated to the program area but hung back just enough to look as though they weren't interested. However, they couldn't hide their expressions. They were watching and listening intently to these picture books, including the modern classics *Corduroy* by Don Freeman and *Curious George* by H. A. Rey.

I realized, too, that often children graduate directly from picture books to chapter books. Many of these youngsters are ready for a longer, more complex text, but they miss the illustrations they enjoyed in the picture books. I noticed that numerous, longer picture books and illustrated books, too long to share with preschoolers, were passed over by young elementary school-age children as being babyish. Many of them, however, were perfect for this age group. There are so many well-written folktales and fairy tales with pleasing language, original and satisfying story lines, and text sophisticated enough to share with these same youngsters who appreciate books full of exquisite and visually appealing illustrations.

Doing these programs with school-age children is exciting. It allows you to use illustrated stories, classic picture books, poetry, nonfiction, collections of stories, short fiction—a whole range of books and materials. Whether you're sharing literature in the classroom or doing a storytime at the library, you're almost guaranteed to find something to please even the most reluctant reader or young library visitor.

Acknowledgments

Special thanks to the individuals and institutions that were helpful and supportive, especially Candida Desjardins for working "computer magic" on my manuscript and the staffs of the North Dartmouth Library (especially Carol Flanagan), North Dartmouth, Massachusetts; Southworth Library, South Dartmouth, Massachusetts; Fall River Public Library, Fall River, Massachusetts; and the New Bedford Free Public Library, New Bedford, Massachusetts.

Introduction

I have included program material on 21 subjects and themes ranging from birds, cooks and cookery, and magic, to tall tales, fractured fairy tales, and word play. You'll find a chapter on an author, "Meet Hans Christian Andersen"; several on ethnic groups, including "Native American Tales"; thematic programs, such as "Rags to Riches"; and programs for holiday seasons, including "Pumpkins" and "Scary Tales."

For each subject, titles and activities are listed alphabetically with bibliographic information and annotations under the following headings: "Read Alouds," "Booktalks," "Poetry," "Songs," and "Demonstration/Participation Activities."

In "Read Alouds" I have listed individual illustrated stories, folktales, and fairy tales; individual and multiple stories from collections; excerpts from books; and other material appropriate to read aloud or tell.

Next are comprehensive "Booktalks" on titles related to the given subject. These are books and stories that are too long to share in one sitting, chapter books, nonfiction titles, and books that might not appeal to a general audience, such as a love story that would make many of the boys restless or a poetic or mood piece that would appeal to a limited number of children.

Under "Poetry" and "Songs" you'll find individual poems and songs, and poems and songs in collections that will appeal to children.

You'll find in "Demonstration/Participation Activities" (some I've created and tested) a list of craft and activity ideas related to the topic. I indicate whether the activity or craft is best demonstrated to the children or done with them.

Sometimes it was difficult to place a title in only one chapter because it applied to two or more subjects. Most of the time a title fit obviously in one chapter, but sometimes I placed it in more than one. For example, many "How-and-Why Stories" are also in "Native American Tales." Many trickster tales are also found in "Native American Tales." When I annotated a title in more than one chapter, I emphasized in each chapter what makes it specifically appropriate to that subject.

You will find many recent titles in this bibliography, but you'll also find some older titles. Some of the older books are classics and readily available. Unlike picture books that get much use, many of these illustrated books and folktales have a longer "shelf life" because they aren't used as much, and they are easy to locate. Many titles go out of print and then come back into print or are reissued as paperbacks. Stories I shared in collections dating to the 1970s have recently been published in new collections.

The length of your program depends on your audience and when you are using the program. I know librarians who do half-hour after-school programs for school-age children. Other librarians do hour-long programs during the summer. How much literature you use and how much time is spent on a craft depends on what your main purpose is in doing the program. I like making literature the focus of the program.

Chapter 1

Meet
Hans Christian Andersen

Read Alouds

Andersen, Hans Christian. **The Emperor's New Clothes.** Retold by
  Riki Levinson. Illus. by Robert Byrd. New York: Dutton Children's
  Books, 1991.

Delightful, full-color illustrations, rich with detail and full of lively animal
characters complement this impressive version of Andersen's classic tale. Here the
emperor is a lion, the royal minister is a bear, and the lord high chamberlain is an
old goat. Levinson provides much humor, especially in depicting the chain of
command in the royal household (passing the buck). Levinson's wit is most evident
in the scenes in which the weavers, two foxes, fawn over the emperor and with
great fanfare present him with each article of clothing that no one can see.

Andersen, Hans Christian. **The Emperor's New Clothes.** Adapted
  and illus. by Janet Stevens. New York: Holiday House, 1985.

Stevens' version of this funny tale combines an amusing, well-told story with
illustrations in brilliant colors. Her characters are perfect—the emperor is a pink
pig; the weavers are two sly foxes; the prime minister is a camel; and the councilor
is a walrus. The foxes trick the emperor into supplying them with money, fine silk,
and gold thread to weave magic cloth they say can only be seen by smart people
who are good at what they do. The foxes weave nothing, but no one will admit to
seeing nothing, certainly not the emperor. He wears the "outfit" in a royal proces-
sion, and in this retelling, a little bear shouts that the emperor isn't wearing any
clothes. The emperor continues walking, very pink and naked.

Andersen, Hans Christian. **The Emperor's New Clothes.** Retold by
  Eric Metaxas. Illus. by Robert Van Nutt. Westport, CT: Rabbit
  Ears Productions, 1991.

Author Metaxas has retold this story with rich language. He develops the
characters well; pokes fun in a sophisticated, subtle way at the wealthy; and
captures the slyness of the knaves. Although the illustrations aren't as fine as
the telling, there are moments when the shock, surprise, and embarrassment
on the faces of the characters is amusingly rendered.

Andersen, Hans Christian. **The Emperor's New Clothes.** Retold and
  illus. by Nadine Bernard Westcott. Boston: Little, Brown, 1984.

Nadine Westcott has blended language that zips along with wild and zany
illustrations full of detail, action, and humor to create a lively, short retelling.
Westcott emphasizes the emperor's love of clothes and the overwhelming task
for the maids and butlers to keep his garments clean and pressed. The emperor's clothes are shown hanging on a line over the banquet table, and in one
picture the butler's head peers from between the legs of flowered bloomers. The
emperor is obsessed by clothes and constantly worries about wearing the
appropriate outfit to create the right image, which he never does. This is a
perfect setup for the two swindlers who promise the emperor an outfit only the
wise can see. One of the funniest illustrations depicts the swindlers threading
nothing on a needle and hanging nothing on a hangar. When the emperor is
dressed in his "new outfit," the tricksters go through an elaborate pantomime
checking for loose threads.

Andersen, Hans Christian. **The Nightingale.** Trans. by Naomi Lewis. Illus. by Josef Palaček. New York: North-South Books, 1990.

Translator Lewis includes an introduction that offers insight into Andersen's life and what he put of himself in his books. Palaček's illustrations are full-color, muted paintings that complement this gentle tale.

Young listeners are taken to China long ago where the emperor hears of a nightingale who sings beautifully. A poor kitchen maid brings the nightingale to the emperor, who is delighted by its songs. The emperor keeps the nightingale and only lets it out three times a day at the end of a silk ribbon tied to its leg and accompanied by 12 attendants. One day the emperor of Japan sends the emperor of China a mechanical bird of gold and silver that sings the same tune anytime night or day. The mechanical bird is revered; the real nightingale flies away. Ultimately the mechanical bird wears down and can only sing once a year.

Five years later the emperor is deathly ill. It is then that the real nightingale returns, the emperor gets well, and the nightingale promises to return evenings to sing to him.

Andersen, Hans Christian. **The Princess and the Pea.** Illus. by Dorothée Duntze. New York: North-South Books, 1984.

This is one of Andersen's best known and most appealing tales about a prince in search of a real princess. The queen tests potential wives for the prince by placing a pea on a bed and then putting 20 mattresses and 20 blankets atop the pea. A true princess will feel the pea through the many layers of bedding.

Duntze's version is simply but beautifully told, adhering closely to the original text. In this large format book the sophisticated illustrations are soft, rendered in warm shades of colored pencil and wash, particularly pale purples and pinks. Duntze's art-nouveau style suggests an old European setting, especially in the costumes.

Andersen, Hans Christian. **The Tinderbox.** Illus. by Warwick Hutton. New York: Margaret K. McElderry Books/Macmillan, 1988.

Children in grades one and up will enjoy this classic tale, well written and illustrated in soft, muted watercolors that suit the text.

An old witch asks a soldier on his way home from the wars to go into the trunk of a hollow tree where he will find three rooms, each with a chest of coins guarded by dogs. The soldier can take what he wants as long as he brings her the tinderbox her grandmother left there. The soldier meets a dog with eyes as big as teacups guarding copper coins, a dog with eyes as big as mill wheels guarding silver coins, and a dog with eyes as big as the "Round Tower" guarding gold coins. By placing each dog on a magic apron, the soldier is able to get the money. Later, he refuses to give the witch the tinderbox and gets rid of her.

The soldier's adventure continues in the next town when, having squandered his wealth, he learns that if he strikes the tinderbox he can summon the dogs and have his wishes granted. Wealth isn't enough for the soldier. He wants to see the princess who is kept under guard. Several times he gets the dogs to bring her to him. Finally the soldier is caught and condemned to die by hanging. The soldier, however, has one more stroke of luck. The dogs assist him again, and ultimately he marries the princess and becomes king.

Andersen, Hans Christian. **The Tinderbox.** Adapted and illus. by
Barry Moser. Boston: Little, Brown, 1990.

Barry Moser has written a captivating adaptation of **The Tinderbox,**
setting the tale in the post-Civil War South, rather than in Europe. The hero is a
Confederate soldier named Yoder Ott. Instead of meeting a witch on the way home
from the Civil War, he meets an old man who makes him climb a mountain, crawl
down a hole, and retrieve copper, silver, and gold coins guarded by three dogs.
When the task is completed, the man and soldier tussle for the box, and the old
man falls off the mountain. As in the original tale, the soldier squanders his money,
discovers that striking the flint across the tinderbox will summon the dogs, and
regains his wealth. Again, not satisfied, he has the dogs bring the mayor's daughter
Elvira Abernathy to him and is ultimately caught, scheduled to be hanged, but
able to use the tinderbox to summon the dogs to save him.

Andersen, Hans Christian. **The Tinderbox.** Retold by Peggy Thomson.
Illus. by James Warhola. New York: Simon & Schuster, 1991.

Thomson has retold **The Tinderbox** with colorful language (e.g., the witch
has a chin so long it "jiggled" as she spoke), in a text that moves along with
sprightliness. Illustrator Warhola's rich watercolors perfectly complement the
text. The big pug dogs' faces are as expressive as the people's faces. The witch has
a huge hooked nose with warts, a crooked mouth, hairy feet, and clawlike fingers.

In this version, the soldier doesn't kill the witch; he drops her into the
hollow tree trunk, and at the tale's end the dogs don't eat the king and queen
but instead release the royal couple.

Andersen, Hans Christian. **The Ugly Duckling.** Retold and illus. by
Troy Howell. New York: G. P. Putnam's Sons, 1990.

Youngsters will enjoy this touching story of a duckling who is different
and perceived as ugly. His mother is kind to him, but the duckling is treated
cruelly and indifferently by other animals. The duckling flees and survives on
his own. He faces many hardships: He gets stuck in the frozen pond in the
winter, is rescued by a farmer, turns things topsy-turvy in the farmer's household and is thrown out, and survives alone until spring arrives. He sees the
swans once again, with whom he felt an affinity, and assumes they will beat
him. When he is welcomed by the swans, he looks down in the pond and is
surprised to see his reflection and learn that *he* is a handsome swan.

The telling is so sensitive that children will feel the duckling's joys and
sorrows. They'll enjoy the beautiful paintings, which capture each season to
create beautiful landscapes.

Andersen, Hans Christian. **The Ugly Duckling.** Retold by Marianna
Mayer. Illus. by Thomas Locker. New York: Macmillan, 1987.

Author Mayer captivates youngsters with literary but approachable and
touching language to create emotion and build tension, and illustrator Locker
has rendered breathtakingly beautiful oil paintings to fashion an exquisite
version of this tale. The plot holds children's interest; they feel sympathetic to
the duckling, who faces rejection by his siblings, the threat of a hunting dog,
and a harsh winter before he turns into a swan. Youngsters will savor the
paintings, including a wide view of a crumbling castle wall with the play of sun
in the background casting shadows, and the full-page illustration of the duckling,

now a swan, looking majestic. Each illustration is a lovely painting that enhances the text but could stand alone.

Calmenson, Stephanie. **The Principal's New Clothes.** Illus. by Denise Brunkus. New York: Scholastic, 1989.

Children will appreciate this modern, hilarious retelling of **The Emperor's New Clothes,** especially if you share it after reading a traditional version of the story. In this revision Mr. Bundy, the principal of P.S. 88, is a sharp dresser who is visited one day by Moe and Ivy, who present themselves as tailors. The swindlers convince Mr. Bundy that they can make him a suit with special powers that will be invisible to anyone who is stupid or no good at his job. In this version, the vice principal and Roger, a bright student, are sent to check on the progress of the suit. Neither sees anything, and neither will admit to it. The invisible suit is brought in plastic, and so Mr. Bundy enters the school auditorium in underwear, socks, and shoes. A kindergarten child shouts what everyone knows, but the children and teachers pass clothing to Mr. Bundy and decide that he is still smart and good at his job.

The richly colored illustrations have a wonderful sense of movement, and Moe and Ivy are excellent caricatures.

Campbell, Ann. **Once upon a Princess and a Pea.** Illus. by Kathy Osborn Young. New York: Stewart, Tabori & Chang, 1993.

Children familiar with Andersen's **The Princess and the Pea** will find this a clever reinterpretation of the original. The illustrations offer a unique, bold, sophisticated style with sharp angles and crisp colors.

Princess Esmerelda has run away from home to avoid marrying King Frobius, who is old and almost toothless. Prince Hector is driving in the rain, disappointed with the princesses he has met, when he comes upon a bedraggled Princess Esmerelda. When Prince Hector brings Esmerelda home, the queen puts her to the test: 20 mattresses, 50 quilts, 100 blankets, and a pea under all. The next day Esmerelda recounts her miserable night's sleep, everyone realizes she is a real princess, and Hector is happy because he had found Esmerelda very nice and hoped she was a princess.

Johnston, Tony. **The Cowboy and the Black-Eyed Pea.** Illus. by Warren Ludwig. New York: G. P. Putnam's Sons, 1992.

Johnston has written a clever twist on **The Princess and the Pea.** He sets the story in Texas and introduces Farethee Well as her dying father tells her that once he's gone, many men will want to marry her to get her wealth. She, however, can tell the real cowboy who will love her for herself with a sensitivity test. Each suitor must ride the range with a tiny black-eyed pea hidden in his saddle blanket. Only one cowboy can't recover from the pain of that pea.

Booktalks

Andersen, Hans Christian. **The Little Mermaid.** Illus. by Michael Hague. New York: Henry Holt, 1981.

The real story of **The Little Mermaid** is different from the movie versions. It is a long story, full of description, sensitivity, and religious overtones, that will appeal to special readers and listeners. Hague's beautiful paintings are rich and detailed.

Longing to be human, the little sea princess trades her mermaid's tail for feet that hurt when she walks. The prince that she rescues marries the girl who first saw him lying on shore. The mermaid can save herself by killing the prince, but she doesn't. For this act she is taken up in the heavens with the other daughters of the air to do good deeds and ultimately earn an immortal soul.

Andersen, Hans Christian. **The Nightingale.** Trans. by Anthea Bell. Illus. by Lisbeth Zwerger. Natick, MA: Picture Book Studio, 1984.

The Nightingale is a beautiful story (also see version on page 3 translated by Naomi Lewis), and this is a lovely telling. It is better shared one-on-one than in a group, however, because the left pages are solid blocks of text and the illustrations on the right pages are muted, soft watercolors, serene and pale in their shades of light blues, browns, grays, and peaches.

Andersen, Hans Christian. **The Snow Queen.** Illus. by Mary Engelbreit. New York: Workman, 1993.

Like many of Andersen's tales, **The Snow Queen** is long but worth recommending to children to read or share at home in one or several sittings. Andersen's beautiful writing style and his precise language is underscored in this version. It is immensely readable and gentle and flows well.

When we meet young friends Kay and Gerda we know that goblins have dropped a mirror with magic powers, and if someone gets a speck of the mirror in the eye and heart, he will see only the bad in everything. This happens to young Kay, who is suddenly cruel to Gerda and easily taken from his home by the cold-hearted snow queen.

Determined and feisty Gerda's quest to rescue Kay takes her to a flamboyant old conjure woman who wants to keep her, to a talking crow who leads her to a prince and princess, to a robber girl, to Lapland, to a Finmark woman, by reindeer to the snow queen's castle, and ultimately to free Kay. Everyone helps Gerda because she is so innocent, kind, and good.

Engelbreit's illustrations are warm, full of glorious, full-color detail; she makes you feel the closeness between Kay and Gerda. Children and adults will savor the expressive paintings: for example, rosy-cheeked Kay, listless in the arms of the snow queen dressed in her blue-white iciness and flashing her long tapered fingernails; or the ancient crone who Gerda visits, with her purple eye shadow and excess rouge. The Finmark woman is quite a character, depicted with one dangling earring and glasses perched on the bridge of her nose.

Andersen, Hans Christian. **The Snow Queen.** Trans. by Naomi Lewis. Illus. by Angela Barrett. Cambridge, MA: Candlewick Press, 1993.

Noted translator Naomi Lewis's text is perfectly complemented by Angela Barrett's watercolor and pencil illustrations, which capture each mood and setting perfectly, from the soft arch of flowers that link Kay and Gerda's homes to the frost and heartlessness of the snow queen's domain.

Andersen, Hans Christian. **The Steadfast Tin Soldier.** Retold by Tor Seidler. Illus. by Fred Marcellino. New York: Michael Di Capua Books/Harper Collins, 1992.

This is a touching but sad tale of a tin soldier with one leg, the last of 25 soldiers to be cast, whom a little boy receives for Christmas. The most impressive toy the boy receives is a huge castle that has a ballerina standing on one leg in the doorway. To the soldier she looks like she has only one leg and would be the perfect wife for him. Another fate, however, awaits the soldier. Left on a windowsill the next day he is blown out and down three stories by a gust of wind. The soldier lands upside down, stuck by his bayonet. After a rainstorm two street urchins place him in a newspaper boat and sail him down the rain-filled gutter. The soldier remains at attention even when the boat is swept under a plank and a water rat approaches. Eventually the boat sinks, the soldier is swallowed by a large fish, and the fish is caught by the family he belongs to. The fish is opened and the soldier found.

Later, for no apparent reason, one boy picks up the soldier and throws him in the stove. The soldier burns but remains steadfast. A door opens, creating a gust of wind that blows the paper ballerina into the fire next to the soldier. Much later when the ashes are emptied, the soldier's remains are found in the shape of a heart. All that is left of the dancer is her spangle, burned black as coal.

A sophisticated youngster will appreciate this fairy tale. Marcellino's soft paintings have a European, turn-of-the-century flavor.

Andersen, Hans Christian. **The Steadfast Tin Soldier.** Trans. by Naomi Lewis. Illus. by P. J. Lynch. New York: Gulliver Books/Harcourt Brace Jovanovich, 1991.

Lewis does an admirable job of translating Andersen's beautiful language. Illustrator P. J. Lynch offers detailed, old-fashioned paintings in a variety of fascinating perspectives. The soldier is seen from above, falling to the sidewalk below. It's a dizzying sight. When the soldier is in the tunnel with the rat, Lynch uses shades of blue and gray to convey a sense of darkness and rushing water.

Andersen, Hans Christian. **The Swineherd.** Trans. by Anthea Bell. Illus. by Lisbeth Zwerger. New York: William Morrow, 1982.

Translator Bell adheres to Andersen's charming, literary language and captures the humor and satire of one of my favorite Andersen tales. Illustrator Zwerger uses ink and wash in a light palette of colors to create an old-world look in her paintings.

A poor prince who wishes to marry the emperor's daughter sends her two precious gifts, a rose from a tree that blooms once every five years and a nightingale that sings the most beautiful music in the world. The proud and silly princess is disappointed in the gifts; she'd prefer artificial flowers and a mechanical nightingale.

Undaunted, the prince dresses as an unkempt fellow, presents himself at the castle, and gets a job as the court swineherd. While there he makes toys: a pan with bells that, when used properly, will allow a person to smell what is being cooked in every house and a rattle that plays many tunes. When giving the princess these toys, the swineherd asks for a kiss as payment. When the emperor catches the princess kissing the swineherd, he banishes them. The princess now wishes she had married the handsome prince. The swineherd transforms himself back to a prince and tells the princess that he despises her, for she wouldn't marry an honest prince but she'd kiss a swineherd for a toy.

Andersen, Hans Christian. **Thumbelina.** Retold by Amy Ehrlich. Illus.
by Susan Jeffers. New York: Dial Press, 1979.
This is another long but sensitively and finely written tale by Andersen.
Jeffers's full-color illustrations are breathtaking in this oversized book. She draws
the reader into the setting and the story and captures the colors of each season.
A woman who has longed for a child is given a seed by a witch and told to
plant it in a flowerpot, water it, and guard it. A flower springs up, the woman
kisses the petals, the flower opens, and a tiny girl appears. Their happy life is
disrupted when a frog sees Thumbelina, decides she'd be the perfect bride for
his son, takes her, and sets her on a lily pad. Fish and then a butterfly help her
escape. When winter arrives a mouse rescues her but decides she'd be the
perfect wife for an unpleasant mole. On her wedding day Thumbelina is rescued
by a swallow she had nursed to health. The swallow sets her on a flower where
she meets a young man her size, king of the small people who live in the flowers.
Thumbelina becomes his queen.

Andersen, Hans Christian. **Thumbeline.** Trans. by Anthea Bell. Illus.
by Lisbeth Zwerger. Natick, MA: Picture Book Studio, 1985.
Noted translator Bell captures well the rich, sophisticated, gentle, precise
literary quality and evocative imagery of Andersen's writing, and illustrator
Zwerger lends an old-world, European flavor to the paintings. The human and
animal characters are soft, delicate, and expressive and stand out against the
varying shades of brown backgrounds.

Andersen, Hans Christian. **Twelve Tales.** Selected, trans., and illus. by
Erik Blegvad. New York: Margaret K. McElderry Books/Macmillan,
1994.
Children in grades three and up can read these tales, whereas younger
children can listen to an adult read these stories aloud. Youngsters will
particularly like **The Steadfast Tin Soldier,** full of emotion and action; **The
Princess on the Pea; The Tinderbox,** rich with excitement; **The Swineherd,** sophisticated, featuring a nice prince and a spoiled and haughty princess
who ultimately gets what she deserves; and **The Emperor's New Clothes.**
Translator Blegvad is Danish, so these tellings are as close as you'll get to
Andersen's original text. Blegvad's watercolors are interspersed throughout
the book and offer much detail, capturing personality traits in small faces and
gestures.

Bellville, Cheryl Walsh. **Theater Magic: Behind the Scenes at a
Children's Theater.** Photos by author. Illus. by Nancy Ekholm
Burkert. Minneapolis, MN: Carolrhoda Books, 1986.
This book is worth a brief mention for youngsters interested in seeing how
one of Andersen's stories is brought to life on stage. The author explains how
the Minneapolis Children's Theatre Company produced an adaptation of Andersen's *The Nightingale.* Bellville explains the plot of the story, and then
children learn through her concise text and varied and interesting full-color
photographs how the tale, as illustrated by Nancy Ekholm Burkert, was turned
into a play. Youngsters will see how the nightingale puppets were made. They'll
follow the development of the play from production meetings to designing and
building of the set, and staging of the final production.

Burch, Joann Johansen. **A Fairy-Tale Life: A Story about Hans Christian Andersen.** Illus. by Liz Monson. Minneapolis, MN: Carolrhoda Books, 1994.

Any child interested in learning more about the personal life of Hans Christian Andersen will enjoy Burch's book. The text is also useful for adults presenting a program of Andersen's books. It will give you insight into how Andersen incorporated his own life into his works. The original artwork, a mixture of painting and paper cutting, is appropriate since cutting figures from paper was one of Andersen's favorite pastimes. Burch immediately hooks the reader into feeling sympathetic for Andersen, who was taunted by neighborhood boys and classmates. He overcame poverty, great hardships, and constant rejection to ultimately become a revered storyteller and author of fairy tales. This is a gripping story that second graders and up can enjoy alone. The text includes a booklist and bibliography.

Fleischman, Paul. **Shadow Play.** Illus. by Eric Beddows. New York: Harper & Row, 1990.

Join a brother and sister at a country fair as they watch a shadow puppet show presentation of **Beauty and the Beast.** After the children watch the action-packed play they are invited backstage, where they see that although the characters looked like real performers, they are shadow puppets. The siblings see the rods and string in the puppets' backs, and they meet the man who manipulated the puppets.

Shadow Play, with illustrations in black, white, and gray, gives young people a clear, visually striking view of shadow play and a feel for intricate cut-outs similar to the paper cutouts Andersen created throughout his life. The book also provides a glimpse of the type of plays Andersen produced.

Greene, Carol. **Hans Christian Andersen: Prince of Storytellers.** Chicago: Childrens Press, 1991.

Greene's text is not great literature, but it is immensely readable and interesting with a good balance of information and anecdotes. The book provides a fine overview of Andersen's life for children in kindergarten through grade three.

Most of the illustrative material consists of line drawings, photographs, and illustrations from some of Andersen's books. The artwork is varied and visually appealing.

Demonstration/Participation Activities

Bauer, Caroline Feller. "Fold-and-Cut Stories," pp. 306-309, in **Handbook for Storytellers.** Illus. by Kevin Royt. Chicago: American Library Association, 1977.

Present these short rhymes with accompanying cut-paper designs as a change-of-pace between stories during your program. Some, like the pumpkin that results after telling "Peter, Peter, Pumpkin Eater" and the eggs that appear at the end of "Hickety, Pickety, My Black Hen" are easy to do. Bauer suggests what type of paper to use and how to prepare the paper before the program.

Brust, Beth Wagner. **The Amazing Paper Cutting of Hans Christian Andersen.** New York: Ticknor & Fields Books for Young Readers, 1994.

Brust provides a wealth of information about Andersen's life, especially his youth, and she concentrates on his artistry at paper cutting. Show children examples of Andersen's paper cutting from this book (there are many) as an introduction to a craft demonstration or participation activity on the art.

Children will find it interesting that Andersen usually made his delicate paper cuttings using an enormous pair of scissors in his big hands while telling one of his fairy tales. He didn't use the cutouts to illustrate his stories but to hold his audience's attention. They'd want to know how his story would end and also see what the cutting would look like. Andersen's cuttings were made for children but were often confiscated by adults. About 250 of his cuttings have survived.

Guerrier, Charlie. **A Collage of Crafts.** Photos by Marc Schwartz. New York: Ticknor & Fields, 1994.

Share examples of Hans Christian Andersen's paper cuttings on page 39 of Guerrier's book. They are quite stunning.

Kohl, MaryAnn F. "Cut Paper Design," p. 20, in **Scribble Art: Independent Creative Art Experiences for Children.** Illus. by Judy McCoy. Bellingham, WA: Bright Ring, 1994.

Few materials are needed to make these cut-paper snowflakes. The process is explained concisely, and suggestions for variations on the snowflakes are provided.

Milord, Susan. "Clip Art," pp. 21-22, in **Adventures in Art: Art and Craft Experiences for 7- to 14-Year Olds.** Illus. by author. Charlotte, VT: Williamson, 1990.

This activity is a basic introduction to cut-paper designs. A list of materials and clear instructions are included.

Rich, Chris. **The Book of Paper Cutting: A Complete Guide to All the Techniques with More Than 100 Project Ideas.** New York: Sterling, 1993.

Show children one of Andersen's cut-paper designs on page 14 and then share the photographs of children's cut work on page 121. Pages 32 and 33 contain clear instructions with accompanying photographs on how to make simple cut-paper patterns. With a bit of help, even kindergartners can do the basic heart design shown.

Chapter 2

Birds

Read Alouds

Aardema, Verna. **How the Ostrich Got Its Long Neck.** Illus. by
  Marcia Brown. New York: Scholastic, 1995.
Renowned storyteller Aardema offers this appealing and amusing folktale from the Akamba people of Kenya. Caldecott medalist Brown complements
the tale with hilarious illustrations in watercolors and marker that boldly
splash across the pages.
  Children are taken to a time long ago when Ostrich had a short neck that
made it difficult for him to gather food. One morning Crocodile wakes up with
a terrible toothache. He seeks help at the water's edge from a kudu, a baboon,
and the ostrich. Except for Ostrich, the animals heed Fish Eagle's warning not
to help Crocodile. Ostrich takes pity on Crocodile and puts his head in the
creature's mouth to check his teeth. Suddenly, in hunger, Crocodile clamps his
jaws down, trapping Ostrich's head. A tug of war ensues between Crocodile and
Ostrich, each pulling in opposite directions. Finally, Ostrich escapes, but now
he has a very long neck. Ostrich is thrilled. Finally, it's easy to find food. He
does, however, stay far from the river.

Bang, Molly. **The Paper Crane.** Illus. by author. New York: Greenwillow Books, 1985.
Molly Bang illustrates this short, gentle Japanese folktale with unique
three-dimensional paper cutouts.
  In a story full of feeling, Bang introduces children to a man whose
once-busy restaurant is now empty because a new highway was built and his
business is by-passed. One night a stranger comes to the restaurant. Although
the man has no money to pay for a meal, the restaurant owner cooks a fine
dinner for the stranger. As payment the man fashions a paper napkin into the
shape of a crane. He tells the man to clap his hands and the bird will come to
life and dance for him.
  People hear of the magic bird and come from everywhere to see it perform.
The restaurant is full again, and the owner once more enjoys cooking, serving,
and seeing people all day.
  After several months the stranger returns. He flies away on the back of
the crane, never to be seen again. People, however, still come to the restaurant
to hear the story of the crane.

Cartwright, Ann. **In Search of the Last Dodo.** Illus. by Reg Cartwright. Boston: Joy Street Books/Little, Brown, 1989.
Meet King Glut, a large, greedy king who loves to eat eggs. The king's
chef, Adrian, constantly invents new recipes that include eggs, but the king is
never satisfied. One day when the king reads that a dodo's egg rests on a distant
island, he orders Adrian to row them there in a small boat. One morning they
cross paths with a great ship. The captain reveals that he and his crew are on
a mission to protect the dodo's egg. King Glut is not deterred even when the
rowboat is capsized by rough seas and he and Adrian are rescued by the captain
and his crew. When they arrive on the island King Glut finds and grabs the dodo
egg. Just then the egg cracks, a baby dodo pops out and pecks King Glut on the
nose. The king is enchanted. He bans eating eggs in his kingdom. The captain
asserts that the dodo will live in peace and safety on the unknown island.

This is a satisfying story with striking illustrations executed in bold, dramatic colors.

Czernecki, Stefan, and Timothy Rhodes. **The Hummingbirds' Gift.** Illus. by Stefan Czernecki. Straw weavings by Juliana Reyes de Silva and Juan Hilario Silva. New York: Hyperion Books for Children, 1994.

Legend says that hummingbirds once performed a great service in the Mexican village Tzintzuntzan (a real place), where many hummingbirds come to drink nectar from the lovely flowers that bloom there.

The authors have written a beautiful tale based on the legend. A farmer, his wife, and their three small children work daily in the wheat fields and sell their crops at a nearby mill. One year no rain comes, everything withers, and the river is dry. Because the flowers shrivel, the hummingbirds have nothing to drink. Consuelo, the farmer's wife, devises a plan to help the birds. She follows the dry river to the lake, finds a bit of water, mixes clay with water, and molds tiny pots in the shape of flowers. She bakes and paints them with bright colors. Consuelo mixes sugar with the water and pours this "nectar" into the clay flowers. The hummingbirds come and drink from the "flowers." The family, however, has little to eat. The hummingbirds sense Consuelo's anxiety. The birds gather straw in their beaks, and then with Consuelo nearby they dart and weave the straw into beautiful tiny figures. Consuelo realizes the birds are showing her what to do to survive.

The family makes and sells their weavings at the marketplace during a festival and earn enough money to last the year. Weeks later the rain returns, but every year the family weaves and displays their straw figures.

The Hummingbirds' Gift is also a visual treat. Each page is framed with multicolored flowers that convey a bright and joyful feeling. Straw weavings are interspersed, and each one complements something in the text. The main illustrations are vivid with a primitive and tropical look.

Dixon, Ann, reteller. **How Raven Brought Light to People.** Illus. by James Watts. New York: Margaret K. McElderry Books/Macmillan, 1992.

Dixon has retold a story from the Tlingit Indians of Alaska in a sparse, straightforward way that holds the interest of youngsters. Watts uses a palette of yellows, browns, and black as well as pages of deep blues. He incorporates symbols and wood carvings of the region and paints faces in a realistic style.

Long ago when the earth was new, people had no light. Raven hears that a great chief keeps the sun, moon, and stars in three wooden boxes. Raven thinks this is wrong, and tired of the dark, he devises a plan to steal the sources of light from the chief.

He encounters the chief's daughter, turns himself into a spruce needle, and drops in her hands as she scoops and drinks water from the river. Once swallowed, Raven turns himself into a baby and is born to the chief's daughter.

The great chief loves the boy very much, and because of this, Raven can cry until he gets to hold each box in turn to quiet his wails. Even though he is supervised, Raven manages to release the sun, moon, and stars through the smoke-hole and into the sky.

As the boy turns himself into Raven to escape, the great chief realizes what has happened and casts a spell to shrink the smoke-hole. Raven rubs against the soot as he pushes to get through the opening. In this way he turns from blue to black.

Garland, Sherry. **Why Ducks Sleep on One Leg.** Illus. by Jean and
   Mou-sien Tseng. New York: Scholastic, 1993.

Youngsters are taken to Vietnam in a time when animals can talk and all are content except for three ducks who received only one leg each. The ducks can't paddle in the water, it's hard for them to find food, and they live in fear of foxes. They want to petition the Jade Emperor, ruler of heaven and earth, for three more duck legs. The ducks are advised by a goose to visit the village guardian spirit, who will relay their message to the emperor. When they arrive at the guardian spirit's abode they hear him yelling about an incense burner that has six legs instead of three. The guardian scoffs at their petition. The ducks become bold and ask if they can have the three extra legs on the burner. Their request is granted, but the spirit orders them to guard the legs so no one will steal them.

The golden legs fit perfectly and now the ducks can live normally. They remember the spirit's order and each night tuck their golden legs up under their wings out of sight.

Over time ducks from everywhere noticed this habit, adopted it, and found it a comfortable way to sleep. This is how the custom spread throughout the world.

Gates, Freida. **Owl Eyes.** Illus. by Yoshi Miyake. New York: Lothrop,
   Lee & Shepard, 1994.

In this retelling of a traditional Mohawk legend, youngsters are offered an explanation for why owls look the way they do. The beautiful paintings are rendered in greens and browns with touches of bright primary colors. Most are done as close-ups that cover the pages. You can see the ripple of muscles and the veins in the hands and feet of the main character, Raweno. His face and those of the animals are realistically painted. The landscape, too, looks lifelike. Author Gates's language and telling is sensitive and gentle. The tension between Raweno and Owl is captured well in the dialogue.

Raweno, "Master of All Spirits and Everything-Maker," creates the world and fills it first with woodlands. Because it is so quiet, Raweno decides to make birds and animals. After he fashions them out of clay, he doesn't finish them but instructs them to decide what they want for features and colors while he rests.

When Raweno returns, each animals knows what he wants. Each time an animal speaks, Owl says how he thinks the animal should look. Raweno ignores Owl, but, finally, irritated by Owl's interruptions, Raweno puts Owl in a tree and instructs him not to watch. When Owl still speaks up, Raweno stuffs Owl's head deep into his body, yanks his ears so they stand straight up, shakes him until his eyes grow huge in fright, and dunks Owl in the mud so his feathers are dull brown.

Raweno tells Owl that now, with a short neck, he'll only watch what is before him. With ears open, Owl will hear what he's told; with big eyes he'll be able to see in the dark. Raweno will work by day, and Owl will only be awake at night.

Haley, Gail E. **Birdsong.** Illus. by author. New York: Crown, 1984.

This is an incredible, moving, original tale with stunning, rich, deep, thickly outlined full-color illustrations.

A greedy woman named Jorinella hears the villagers grumble that she doesn't sell enough birds anymore for them to eat. Not long after, she sees a ragged young girl playing the pipes. Only Jorinella notices that the birds are drawn to the girl. Jorinella invites the girl, whom she names Birdsong, to live with her since the girl is an orphan. She gives Birdsong a magic feather that allows her to understand the language of the birds and to play their songs. The birds fly to her. One day Jorinella takes Birdsong to a hut and asks her to play the pipes. She locks Birdsong inside. When Birdsong is let out, she sees a multitude of birds trapped in cages.

Birdsong releases the birds at dawn. When Jorinella discovers what Birdsong has done she tries to hurt the girl, but the birds drive Jorinella away and carry Birdsong to a far-off kingdom where the girl plays her pipes for the people and builds a garden for the birds.

Maddern, Eric. **Rainbow Bird: An Aboriginal Folktale from Northern Australia.** Illus. by Adrienne Kennaway. Boston: Little, Brown, 1993.

This short, sophisticated tale illustrated in bold, dramatic watercolors creates a sense of action and will appeal to a wide age group.

When the world was fairly new there was a huge, mean, scary Crocodile Man who would not share fire with any of the other animals. Bird Woman lived in a nearby tree and was tired of raw fish, the darkness, and the cold. She watches and waits and one afternoon when Crocodile Man takes a long, wide yawn, Bird Woman flies down from her tree and snatches some firesticks before Crocodile Man can catch her.

Bird Woman shares the fire with the animals and people. She does a dance, puts the firesticks in her tail, and becomes the beautiful Rainbow Bird.

Polacco, Patricia. **Just Plain Fancy.** Illus. by author. New York: Bantam Books, 1990.

Author Polacco offers consistently fine books for youngsters, and **Just Plain Fancy** is no exception. The text is satisfying on several levels, and the illustrations are muted in understated colors that are in keeping with the lifestyle of the Amish characters.

Naomi is a young Amish girl who is responsible for tending the chickens on her family's farm. She complains to her sister Ruth that everything is plain around them and that it would "pleasure" her to have something fancy.

Naomi finds an unusual egg behind the henhouse next to the road (it flies out of a box of exotic eggs in a van seen in the illustration on the title page). Naomi puts the egg in Henny's nest to hatch, and when it does it's a fancy-looking bird, quite different from the other chicks.

One afternoon Naomi and Ruth overhear Aunt Sarai telling cousin Hannah about a person in a neighboring Amish community who was shunned for dressing too fancy. Hannah tells Naomi that according to Amish law they must be plain.

Naomi learns that to be shunned is to be shamed in front of the elders. Friends and neighbors can no longer talk to the person. Naomi worries that her bird, Fancy, is too fancy to be Amish. She and Ruth hide Fancy so the bird and they won't be shunned.

During the annual frolic, however, when Naomi is supposed to get her white cap for responsible behavior, Fancy darts out, flies around, and then spreads his full plummage. Naomi and Ruth are horrified. But, instead of being shunned, Martha, the oldest member of the gathering, tells Naomi that she didn't cause the bird's fanciness; only God could think up colors so beautiful. Naomi is presented with her cap and praised for taking good care of her flock of chickens and raising a fine peacock.

Rockwell, Anne, reteller. "Owl Feathers," pp. 20-22, in **The Acorn Tree and Other Folktales.** Illus. by author. New York: Greenwillow, 1995.

Rockwell's lighthearted, soft, childlike illustrations highlight this short, appealing tale.

Long ago when the animals gave parties the birds decide to hold a ball. Hawk delivers the invitations to birds worldwide. Owl responds that he can't attend because he has nothing to wear, he has no feathers. The other birds agree to lend Owl feathers to wear, but while at the ball owl decides that he won't return the feathers. Owl leaves the ball and hides from the other birds. Although they look for him, the birds can't find Owl.

San Souci, Robert D., reteller. **The Firebird.** Illus. by Kris Waldherr. New York: Dial Books for Young Readers, 1992.

This story has all the elements of a superior tale: strong female characters in the firebird and the princess who is willing to face adversity and help herself out of difficult circumstances, a determined hero, a battle between good and evil forces, conflict, tension, incredible action, an exotic and mysterious setting, and breathtaking illustrations.

Prince Ivan is lost in the woods when he sees a golden light through a gate in a high stone wall. It is the Firebird. Ivan enters the garden but cannot bring himself to kill the bird/woman. When he flings a net over her, she promises to give him one of her feathers, which will aid him in this dangerous place, if he releases her. When Ivan waves the feather three times, the Firebird will come to help him.

Ivan soon needs the Firebird's help. He meets Princess Elena and her handmaidens in the garden. They were kidnapped by the wizard Kastchei, who is called The Deathless One because no one knows where his death is hidden. The knights who have tried to save the women have been turned to stone.

When Kastchei returns, first as a dark storm cloud and then as a slender figure in black robes, Elena advises Ivan to wave the feather and summon the Firebird. The Firebird appears and stops time so she can tell Ivan and Elena of a copper key that lies at the root of a green-wooded oak beside a well. The key will unlock the secret of Kastchei's death. Elena and Ivan combine forces, find the key, and, with the help of magic water that will make any living creature go to sleep, they overcome three dragons to find a series of keys that ultimately lead to a golden casket. A hare leaps out of it, turns into a duck, and then turns into a crystal egg that holds Kastchei's life. The Firebird appears, as does Kastchei. Ivan throws the egg and it shatters. Kastchei is no more, the spells in the garden end, and the Firebird promises to help Ivan and Elena whenever they need her.

Illustrator Waldherr has created spectacular oil paintings to complement this incredible folktale from the Soviet Union. Follow Prince Ivan in the dark wood where the tree branches look like knurled limbs. Sense the menacing nature of Kastchei in his hooded robe, with skeletal hand sticking out. Marvel at the Firebird when she appears with feathery arms uplifted, looking like a cloak of flame.

Stevens, Kathleen. **Aunt Skilly and the Stranger.** Illus. by Robert Andrew Parker. New York: Ticknor & Fields Books for Young Readers, 1994.

A gray goose named Buckle, who lives with an old woman named Aunt Skilly in a cabin on the side of Which-Way Mountain, is the hero of this original and humorous tale.

A stranger in a slouch hat appears one day asking for water. He reveals that he saw Aunt Skilly's quilts hanging over her clothesline. Aunt Skilly says that a peddler is coming the next day to pay a high price for the quilts. The stranger, in his sneaky way, finds out that Aunt Skilly has no nearby neighbors, no dog, no bar on her door. He watches as Aunt Skilly puts the quilts in a gunnysack.

The stranger rides away as dark approaches. Later that night he sneaks in and steals what he thinks are the quilts. Buckle, who was under the cabin, bursts out, beats the air with his powerful wings, hisses, and nips at the stranger's heels.

When Aunt Skilly sees an old slouch hat on the ground she knows the stranger returned to steal her quilts. She rewards Buckle with seed corn and tells him the stranger was a fool. She knew all along what the stranger was up to and had put the quilts safely in a wooden chest.

Stevens's language has the rich flavor of an "Appalachian Mountain folktale," and the watercolor illustrations are in Parker's distinctive style of fluid, soft colors, sketchy with thin black outlines.

Booktalks

Bang, Molly. **Dawn.** Illus. by author. New York: William Morrow, 1983.

Molly Bang has illustrated her moving adaptation of **The Crane Wife,** a Japanese folktale, with paintings that are delicate and full of feeling, whether in muted color or in shades of gray and white.

Bang introduces children to a shipbuilder who is telling a story to his daughter, Dawn. He relates how he found a Canada goose that had a broken wing and nursed it back to health until it flew away. One day a young woman arrives and asks if he needs a sailmaker. She has scars on her arm and long neck.

Boats equipped with her sails almost fly. The woman marries the sailmaker and they have a child they name Dawn. The husband makes a sailboat for the family, and his wife makes the sails. Everyone calls these sails Wings of Steel.

One day a man asks the shipbuilder to make a racing schooner for him. He wants sails like the Wings of Steel. The wife says she cannot make sails like that again, but when her husband begs her to, she does, saying it may cause her death. She makes her husband promise never to come into the room when she's weaving the sails.

As she weaves, the wife gets weaker and her dress slowly turns scarlet. All night she works. In the morning, when he can wait no longer, the shipbuilder opens the door. He sees a great Canada goose plucking its last feathers and weaving them into the sailcloth.

A flock of geese suddenly rushes in. The great Canada goose spreads her wings for Dawn. The shipbuilder holds the goose. He doesn't want to lose either his daughter or his wife. But the goose goes off with the others and is never seen again.

When the shipbuilder finishes telling his daughter Dawn this story she says she'll go off in their boat and get her mother, and she sails away.

Isadora, Rachel, adapter. **Firebird.** Illus. by author. New York: G. P. Putnam's Sons, 1994.

Isadora's retelling is based on George Balanchine's version of the ballet with music by Igor Stravinsky. The illustrations make you feel like you're watching a ballet. Dancers glide across the pages and throughout there is a sense of motion. The full double-page illustrations are fluid and striking. Isadora's telling of this famous Russian tale is much simpler than most but equally satisfying.

Prince Ivan searches for a beautiful tree with magical, golden fruit, about which he's heard many stories. He knows that many have sought it but none have returned. Ivan does find the tree in a wondrous garden. He also sees the dazzling creature, the Firebird. He captures her but realizes she's meant to be free and releases her. Grateful, the Firebird gives Ivan a red feather from her tail, a magic charm. If he waves it in time of need, she will come.

Ten beautiful maidens appear, and the most lovely, a princess, reveals they were taken prisoner by the evil sorcerer Katschei. It is his garden and everything in it belongs to him. Ivan is determined to save them. Katschei suddenly appears with hideous creatures. When the monsters attack, Ivan waves the feather and the Firebird appears. She hands Ivan a golden sword with which he slays Katschei. The Firebird flies away. Ivan and the princess return to his kingdom and are married.

Keller, Holly. **Grandfather's Dream.** Illus. by author. New York: Greenwillow, 1994.

Children are transported to the wetlands of the Mekong delta at the end of the Vietnam War where young Nam's grandfather dreams of restoring the area to its original state. Canals were dug across the area during the war to drain the water and kill the vegetation so soldiers could not hide there. Birds and animals couldn't live there either, including the Sarus crane, the largest flying bird in the world. The Vietnamese treasure the crane as a symbol of long life and happy families, and Nam's grandfather is sure that if the land is restored to its natural state the cranes will return. Many villagers agree, but others feel that rice fields will be more useful. The village committee decides if the birds don't return before the next rainy season, the land in the reserve will be planted with rice. Nam's dogs are responsible for finding close to 200 cranes; when everyone sees them they agree they are beautiful and want them to stay.

Paterson, Katherine. **The Tale of the Mandarin Ducks.** Illus. by Leo and Diane Dillon. New York: Lodestar, 1990.

The stunning watercolor and pastel paintings, detailed yet uncluttered, are done in the style of eighteenth-century Japanese woodcuts. This is a beautiful story, wonderfully told, of a greedy lord who covets a mandarin duck for his beautiful plummage, takes the duck from its mate, and puts him in a cage to be admired. Alone, the duck looks droopy; the lord decides he no longer is pleased to look at it and orders the duck taken from his sight. Against the lord's orders Yasuko, the kitchen maid, releases the duck. The lord's chief steward, Shozo, is accused. He says nothing even when he is given a lowly job. Yasuko wants to confess but Shozo won't let her. When Yasuko and Shozo fall in love the lord decides that they both committed the crime and he sentences them to death.

Two messengers arrive to tell the lord the emperor has decreed that capital punishment is abolished and that the lord's guards are to take the couple to the capital. Soon, in the dark of the scary woods the guards leave the couple behind. The original imperial messengers lead the couple to a hut where they can bathe, eat, and sleep. In the morning when the couple awaken, food is cooking but there is no sign of the messengers. Outside on the path, however, the couple see a pair of mandarin ducks who seem to bow and then fly away.

Quackenbush, Robert. **Henry Goes West.** Illus. by author. Milwaukee, WI: Gareth Stevens, 1994.

Here is a humorous short story that first graders and up can read themselves and younger children will enjoy having read to them. The watercolor illustrations are not fine art, but they are amusing and break the solid blocks of text.

Henry the Duck misses his friend Clara, who is vacationing out West. When he decides to pay her a surprise visit, nothing goes right. After a series of mishaps in which Henry is kicked by a mule, taken for a wild ride on the back of a bucking bronco, and tossed over a fence, he learns from one of the cowboys that Clara went home the day before because she missed her friend Henry.

Children enjoy the constant action, cumulative events, and the ironic twist at the end.

Quackenbush, Robert. **Texas Trail to Calamity.** Illus. by author. New York: Prentice-Hall Books for Young Readers, 1986.

This book is one in a series of mysteries about Miss Mallard, the world famous ducktective. In this title Miss Mallard ends up at the home of Horace and Florence Butterball when she is thrown by her horse while vacationing at a dude ranch in Texas. The other characters include the Butterball's daughter Cindy, guests Phil and Tessie Scoter, the housekeeper Mrs. Scaup, and Clarence the cook.

During dinner Miss Mallard learns that many old documents and treasures from Texas's history were recently stolen from homes all over Texas. After dinner Horace shows the guests an historical document he keeps in a glass case that lists the first 300 duck families who settled in Texas. The document will be given to the state of Texas the next day.

In the morning Cindy discovers that the document has been stolen. The sheriff is called, but he can't solve the crime. Miss Mallard, however, pieces together a variety of clues to reveal the thief.

Demonstration/Participation Activities

Carlson, Laurie. **EcoArt! Earth-Friendly Art and Craft Experiences for 3- to 9-Year Olds.** Illus. by Loretta Trezzo. Charlotte, VT: Williamson, 1993.

The following crafts each come with a list of materials and extremely clear instructions: "Milk Carton Feeder" and "Jug Bird Feeder," p. 54; "Pine Cone Feeder and More," p. 55; and "Bird Cupcakes" and "Bird Bell," p. 64.

"Bird Bell" and "Bird Cupcakes" are a bit involved, and you would do best to demonstrate or show the completed craft. The other activities are easy, quick, and enjoyable for children to do themselves.

Drake, Jane, and Ann Love. "Call of the Wild," p. 74, and "Seed Feeder," p. 80, in **The Kids' Summer Handbook.** Illus. by Heather Collins. New York: Ticknor & Fields, 1994.

The text includes other crafts involving birds, including a purple martin apartment house and a watering hole, but they are difficult for the target age group to make.

The "Call of the Wild" is a wildlife caller, easy to make with popsicle sticks, a wide blade of grass, and a rubber band. The directions are clear and easy. You only need a few materials, primarily a milk carton, to make the simple "Seed Feeder" in this book.

Keeshan, Bob. "Birdseed Baubles," pp. 50-51, in **Family Fun Activity Book.** Illus. by Diane Palmisciano. Minneapolis, MN: Deaconess Press, 1994.

With glue, birdseed, string, and waxed paper you can follow these simple instructions and create original designs from birdseed to hang in a window.

Kohl, MaryAnn F. "Trim a Tree for Birds," p. 151, and "Plastic Bird Feeder," p. 166, in **Good Earth Art: Environmental Art for Kids.** Illus. by Cindy Gainer. Bellingham, MA: Bright Ring, 1991.

For the first craft you need a few materials, including stale bread, peanut butter, birdseed, cookie cutters, and a little time, and children will have a satisfying, completed gift to hang outside for the birds.

The feeder is not easy for most children to make, but if your schedule allows, it's worth making before the program and showing the children the completed craft. The children may then be inspired to make it at home with the help of an adult.

Zweifel, Frances. "Pinecone Bird Feeders," pp. 10-11, in **The Make Something Club: Fun with Crafts, Food and Gifts.** Illus. by Ann Schweninger. New York: Viking, 1994.

This is a simple craft that children love to make. You just need pinecones, peanut butter, and birdseed.

Chapter 3

Travel to Boston

Read Alouds

Adler, David A. **A Picture Book of Paul Revere.** Illus. by John and
  Alexandra Wallner. New York: Holiday House, 1995.

Unlike many nonfiction books and biographies, Adler's work is perfect to
read aloud to children. The biography is short but not slight. The text is
informative, but it's also a fine story with a clear beginning, middle, and end.
Adler has created an exciting read, full of tension, conflict, and a feel for the
historical period and the important events that shaped Paul Revere's life. The
author includes many anecdotes that will interest youngsters and makes Paul
Revere seem human, not just a one-dimensional figure.

The watercolor illustrations are sometimes stiff, but they do complement
the text well and convey an idea of the buildings, clothing, and styles that
existed in Paul Revere's time.

Carrick, Carol. **Left Behind.** Illus. by Donald Carrick. New York:
  Ticknor & Fields, 1988.

The Carricks, who live in the greater Boston area, have set this picture
book (one of many popular stories they have written about a young boy named
Christopher) in Boston.

Christopher and his classmates go on a class trip by bus and then subway to
the aquarium with their teacher Mrs. Snow. After enjoying the exhibits at the
aquarium, particularly the central tank, the class boards the subway for the return
trip. At the next train stop Christopher and several passengers must step down
onto the platform to let other people off the crowded train. Before Christopher can
get on again the doors close and the subway train moves down the tunnel. Lost,
Christopher panics at first, but then looks for a policeman. He gets mixed up going
from one level of the station to another because every subway platform looks the
same. Finally, Christopher enlists the aid of a subway worker who radios a
policeman. Christopher wonders if his teacher will find him and if she'll be angry,
but the story does have a happy and reassuring ending.

Although it isn't stated, Donald Carrick has captured the look of the
subway trains in Boston known as the "Green Line" and the excitement and
activity of the underground subway system known as the "T." Carrick also
accurately depicts the Boston harbor area and the central tank at the New
England Aquarium in Boston.

Lent, Blair. **Molasses Flood.** Illus. by author. Boston: Houghton Mifflin, 1992.

In 1919 a molasses tank exploded in the North End, the commercial district
near the Boston Harbor. Award-winning author and illustrator Blair Lent has
written a concise but rich and entertaining fictionalized account of this historical
event. The illustrations are classic Lent: They look like woodcuts and are painted
in hues of red brick, tan, white, gray, olive green, and yellow-brown.

Charley Owen Muldoon is watching the Boston waterfront with a spyglass
from his room. His house is right behind an old tank that stores molasses. On that
warm January day the tank expands and explodes. Charley runs to his roof and
rides his house like a boat on the sea of brown liquid. He sees the molasses ooze
through Quincy Market and up to the State House on Beacon Hill.

During the night it rains. The downpour mixes with the molasses, the temperature drops, it starts to snow, and in the morning the thick goo is frozen in place. Charley, who loves molasses, and his family gather quantities of molasses to store at home. People come from all around to collect the dark syrup until all that remains is the smell of the molasses.

After days of eating molasses cooked in baked beans, gingersnaps, gingerbread, cookies, and taffy, Charley gets sick of molasses.

McCloskey, Robert. **Make Way for Ducklings.** Illus. by author. New York: Puffin Books, 1969.

I have shared this modern children's classic with youngsters from five to 10 years old and they always enjoy listening to it. Maybe there's something comforting about a familiar, gentle story. Maybe it's Mr. and Mrs. Mallard's obvious love and concern for the safety of their ducklings that appeals to youngsters. McCloskey's writing style is solid, and the story contains lots of action. The large format illustrations in shades of brown and white are interesting; they give children a look at the famous sites in Boston as they appeared in the 1940s.

Mr. and Mrs. Mallard are seeking a good place to live and raise their family safely. The pond with an island in the Public Garden seems the ideal place to raise their ducklings until a boy riding a bike almost runs over Mr. Mallard.

The Mallards fly over Beacon Hill, the State House, Louisburg Square, and finally the Charles River, where they build a nest on an island. A police officer, Michael, feeds them peanuts every day when they paddle to the river bank.

Soon Mrs. Mallard lays eight eggs, and one day they hatch. Mr. Mallard decides to explore the rest of the river. Mrs. Mallard and the ducklings will meet him in one week at the Public Garden. Mrs. Mallard teaches the ducklings to swim, walk in line, come when called, and avoid things on wheels. The ducks quack loudly when they come to a highway and the speeding cars won't stop for them. Their quacking brings Michael, their police officer friend, who stops traffic. Michael also alerts police officers at the corner of Beacon Street to stop traffic for the ducks. In this way they arrive at the Public Garden, are reunited with Mr. Mallard and decide they like the island there and will make it their home.

Stover, Marjorie. **Patrick and the Great Molasses Explosion.** Illus. by Sharon Wooding. Minneapolis, MN: Dillon, 1985.

This version of the events of the molasses flood that occurred in Boston in 1919 adheres closely to the historical facts. It's a short text that seven-year-olds and up can read themselves. You, however, might like to share an excerpt from the book with youngsters. Soft pencil drawings add to the text.

Patrick loves molasses and is happy when his mother sends him to Mr. O'Conner's store for a pail of molasses. Since Mr. O'Conner has no molasses, Patrick decides to walk farther than he should to go to another store.

Suddenly the giant tank of the Purity Distilling Company explodes. Patrick tries to scoop the thick flowing syrup into his pail, but he falls. Coated with the sticky goo, Patrick returns home, but his mother doesn't believe his story. When Patrick's father arrives home covered in molasses Mama feels bad that she didn't believe Patrick.

Author Stover includes more facts about the molasses flood at the end of the book.

Booktalks

Banim, Lisa. **A Spy in the King's Colony.** Illus. by Tatyana Yuditskaya.
New York: Silver Moon Press, 1994.

While Banim's writing isn't outstanding, it is satisfactory, and she has penned an appealing story. Wide margins, large type, short chapters, and full-page pen and ink illustrations make this a good read for young children.

Eleven-year-old Emily Parker lives in Boston in 1775 when tensions are high between the Patriots and the British. Emily has a vivid imagination, and when she sees her life-long neighbor, 18-year-old Robert Babcock, standing near the British soldiers on the Boston Common, she begins to suspect that he is a spy. Emily later sees Robert talking to Mr. Andrews, a man with a scar she saw peering in her window the day before. She thought Robert believed in the Patriot's cause, even though the rest of his family sides with the British. Emily enlists her reluctant friend Maggie to help her snoop and pursue clues to find the truth about Robert.

Emily becomes frantic when her father holds a secret meeting to make plans against the British and Robert is chosen to deliver a message to George Washington. Emily wonders if he'll give it to the enemy instead. When the men at the meeting are warned that British soldiers are coming, the message for Washington is left behind in the commotion and Emily decides that she must risk crossing the Charles River to deliver it. When Robert catches up with her Emily must decide if she believes him when he says he's a Patriot and let him deliver the message.

Kulper, Eileen. **The Boston Marathon.** Mankato, MN: Creative Education, 1993.

The Boston Marathon is an event that has been held since 1897, and Kulper's book, consisting mainly of photographs and interesting facts about the marathon, will interest youngsters of all ages. Kulper highlights the determination of runners through the history of the marathon.

Ellison M. Brown, who won the race in 1936 and 1939, lived in a tarpaper shack with no running water or kitchen. He shared the two rooms with his wife and four children. Brown didn't train for the marathon, and he ran the race in a shirt made from an old quilt. In 1967, Katherine Switzer registered for the marathon as K. Switzer because, at that time, women were not allowed to compete in the race. When Jock Semple, the Boston Marathon organizer, tried to kick her out of the race, her boyfriend defended her and she became the first woman to run and finish the marathon.

Rappaport, Doreen. **The Boston Coffee Party.** Illus. by Emily Arnold McCully. New York: Harper & Row, 1988.

One of the titles in the I Can Read Book series, this book is an easy, lively read with a swift-moving plot, full of conflict and a sense of anticipation. Rappaport has included historical background about the true incident on which this story is based. During the Revolutionary War groups of women met to sew shirts for the rebel soldiers. They formed committees and asked local merchants to keep prices down on sugar and coffee. Most of the merchants obliged. Abigail Adams wrote a letter to her husband John Adams describing what happened to one wealthy merchant who hoarded coffee.

Sarah and Emma watch as Merchant Thomas sells Mrs. Arnold the sugar he was going to sell them because Mrs. Arnold will pay a higher price. The girls' mother is angry and predicts that one day the merchant will be sorry.

While at a sewing party Sarah and Emma's mom tells the other women not to buy from Merchant Thomas. Aunt Harriet rushes in and reveals that Merchant Thomas locked his barrels of coffee in his warehouse and will sell it at a high price when no one else has coffee to offer. The women and girls decide to teach him a lesson.

Combining forces, the women take Merchant Thomas's key by force, open his warehouse, and take all his coffee. The merchant threatens that the women will be sorry, and they respond that he'll be sorry when their husbands return.

White, E. B. **The Trumpet of the Swan.** Illus. by Edward Frascino. New York: Harper & Row, 1970.

In this modern classic tale E. B. White uses the swan boats in the Boston Public Garden as one of the settings for his story. You can present this story as a mystery to children. Make them curious to find out why a young trumpeter swan named Louis would be found at the Public Garden, swimming in front of a swan boat for a week. Describe how Louis blows a horn held in his right foot and swims with his left foot. Explain how he writes messages to people on the swan boats by using a slate he wears around his neck with a piece of chalk attached to it. Reveal that Louis also wears a medal and a money bag around his neck. Deepen children's curiosity by sharing that Louis sleeps at the Ritz Hotel in Boston. After these teasers children will want to learn who Louis is, where he came from, where he is going, and how and why he leads the incredible life he does.

Encourage young children to have an adult read this book to them. Children in grades three and up can read it themselves.

Poetry

Longfellow, Henry Wadsworth. "Paul Revere's Ride," pp. 56-61, in **From Sea to Shining Sea: A Treasury of American Folklore and Folk Songs.** Comp. by Amy L. Cohn. Illus. by 11 Caldecott Medal and four Caldecott Honor Book artists. New York: Scholastic, 1993.

Anita Lobel was a perfect choice to illustrate this famous poem about Paul Revere's ride to signal to the soldiers in Concord whether the British were coming by land or sea. Revere never reached Concord because he was captured just after leaving Lexington, but it's still an exciting episode in history. Lobel captures well the historical period, the look of the people, the tension, and the importance of the mission.

Demonstration/Participation Activities

Robinson, Jeri. **Activities for Anyone, Anytime, Anywhere.** (A Children's Museum Activity Book). Illus. by Barbara Bruno. Boston: Little, Brown, 1983.

One of a series of activity books produced by the Children's Museum of Boston, this work includes three crafts that you can do with youngsters.

Sitarz, Paula Gaj. "Guess the Famous Sites and Attractions in Boston."
   A matching game.

   When I was a children's librarian in Quincy, Massachusetts, I worked
close enough to Boston that I was able to travel into the city, take photographs
of famous buildings and locales there, and have the film developed into slides.
During this program I showed each slide to the children and let them guess
what they were seeing. Since most of the children were familiar with Boston I
didn't have to provide many clues before they guessed the answer.

   You, however, may live in Kansas; California; Virginia; London, England;
or Sydney, Australia; somewhere far from Boston. There is another way to enjoy
this game if you don't live in the Boston area. If you write to the Massachusetts
Office of Travel and Tourism, 100 Cambridge Street, Boston, MA 02202 or call
toll-free 1-800-632-8038 for a free kit of information, they will provide you with
brochures that include photographs of famous spots in Boston. Also, after I
explain how to play the game, I offer an annotated list of books about Boston
sites that include many color photographs you can use in this game.

   First, on a chalkboard, posterboard, or sheet of paper on an easel, write all
the locations you will be showing the children. Then, one at a time, show them a
photograph of each site taken from a book or brochure and offer clues about the
site until the children match the photo and description to one of the locations on
the list you've provided. The key is to select spots that are different enough from
each other that they'll be easy to guess. For example, your list might include a ship,
a park, a church, and a ballpark, all quite distinct from each other.

   In the following paragraphs I provide a sample of the matching game
"Guess the Famous Sites and Attractions in Boston."

   Sites and attractions to list on chalkboard, posterboard, or easel: Quincy
Market, Bunker Hill Monument, Park Street Church, Granary Burying
Ground, *USS Constitution*, Boston Celtics, Boston Public Garden, Museum of
Science, Fenway Park, and Paul Revere's House.

   Show each photograph. Read the clues for each location one at a time until
someone matches the photograph to the answer from the list.

1.   Built in 1680, this is the oldest building in Boston. Most of this man's
     16 children lived there. If you visit this building today you'll see cooking
     implements, cradles, a cannon, and bell. (Paul Revere's House)

2.   This attraction is also known as "Old Ironsides" and "America's great-
     est ship." It is the oldest ship in the United States Navy. It was
     launched in 1797 to protect American ships from British and French
     ships and from pirates. It never lost a battle. If you visit this attraction
     you can examine its three decks, masts, cannons, hammock beds, and
     kitchen. (*USS Constitution*)

3.   In this large building you can visit the Hall of Electricity and marvel
     at 15-foot-long lightening bolts, climb into an Apollo space capsule,
     play tic-tac-toe against a computer, and experience a tropical rain
     forest. Don't miss the spectacular astronomy show in the Hayden
     Planetarium. (Museum of Science)

4. In this dining and shopping area you'll see a central marketplace bordered by brick warehouses. Sample dishes from the dozens of food stalls in the main building. Enjoy the free entertainment outside. You might see a juggler or a magician. (Quincy Market)

5. Sit down and enjoy watching the Boston Red Sox, the Boston baseball team, play ball. Will anyone hit a home run over the "green monster," that high wall in the outfield? (Fenway Park)

6. When you want to relax, visit this large area filled with rare old trees, beautiful flower beds, and statues. Don't forget to see the "Make Way for Ducklings" statue in honor of Robert McCloskey's book. Also, bring food for the ducks and take a ride on the swan boats. The "captain of your boat" sits between the wings of the swan in the back and pedals you around the pond. (Boston Public Garden)

7. Wear a sturdy pair of shoes so you can climb to the top of this historical attraction. It's a tall granite obelisk 221 feet high. You'll have to climb 294 steps to get to the top. A famous battle of the Revolutionary War took place nearby at Breed's Hill, which you can see from the top of this spot. (Bunker Hill Monument)

8. When you visit this cemetery look carefully. You'll find markers and headstones for famous people in Boston's history, including Samuel Adams, Paul Revere, and John Hancock. It's also said that Mother Goose is buried here. (Granary Burying Ground)

9. You might like to get tickets to watch Boston's basketball team run up and down the court. (Boston Celtics)

10. During the War of 1812 gunpowder was stored in the crypt of this building. Members of the congregation worried that the gunpowder would blow them up. (Park Street Church)

The following books can be used for the guessing game, and you can also do booktalks on them. Children might like to read or scan them at home.

Booth, Robert; revised by Shirley Blotnick Moskow. **Boston's Freedom Trail: A Souvenir Guide.** Illus. by Jack Frost. Old Saybrook, CT: Globe Pequot Press, 1994.

A detailed map of the area in Boston where these sites are found is perfect to enlarge and have on display. The description of each site includes a photograph or a black-and-white illustration. Booth provides a history of each site and information on what is found there.

Byers, Helen. **Kidding Around Boston: A Young Person's Guide to the City.** Illus. by Sally Blakemore. Santa Fe, NM: John Muir Publications, 1990.

This book is useful for you, the programmer or teacher, to help you describe the sights of interest in Boston, including the Public Garden and Freedom Trail. You'll also get a concise overview of Boston's history, museums, sports and recreation, and entertainment.

Dunnahoo, Terry. **Boston's Freedom Trail.** Photos by U.S. Dept. of the Interior and the Bettman Archives. New York: Dillon/Macmillan, 1994.

Not only is this work a fine introduction to the Freedom Trail, the area in Boston where historically important events occurred, it's a solid introduction to Boston. Dunnahoo takes you site by site along the trail, provides a contemporary photograph for each spot, tells you what it's like to visit the place today, and provides information about the historical importance of the locale.

Dunnahoo includes many anecdotes that children would enjoy. For example, Boston's Freedom Trail is actually a continuous red line that is painted on sidewalks or marked by gray stones on red brick sidewalks. Another anecdote reports that in 1728 a law was passed that dogs in Boston couldn't be taller than ten inches. Before the law was passed dogs were constantly jumping up and biting off chunks of meat from the carcasses that hung from hooks outside butcher shops.

Goodman, Michael E. **Boston Celtics.** Mankato, MN: Creative Education, 1993.

Goodman's chronological history of the famous Boston basketball team is full of color and black-and-white photographs. It's written for the upper end of the target group, but one of the photos would be great for this guessing game.

Monke, Ingrid. **Boston.** (A Downtown America Book). Minneapolis, MN: Dillon, 1988.

The photographs in Monke's book are interesting and cover a wide cross-section of Boston's neighborhoods, attractions, and historical sites. Photos of the following places and things are perfect to use in this guessing game: the swan boats at the Boston Public Garden, Bunker Hill, the *USS Constitution*, and Paul Revere's House.

Rambeck, Richard. **Boston Red Sox.** Mankato, MN: Creative Education, 1992.

Like the other books in this series on sports teams in Boston, this text includes many interesting photographs on Boston's baseball team. The short, 32-page text is appropriate for second-grade readers and up.

Rambeck, Richard. **New England Patriots.** Mankato, MN: Creative Education, 1991.

This title is aimed at third graders and up but, again, you can use one of the photos of Boston's football team for the guessing game.

Rennie, Ross. **The Boston Bruins.** Mankato, MN: Creative Education, 1990.

You might like to use one of the action photos of Boston's hockey team in your guessing game.

Chapter 4

Cooks and Cookery

Read Alouds

Bang, Betsy, reteller. **The Old Woman and the Rice Thief: Adapted from a Bengali Folktale.** Illus. by Molly Bang. New York: Greenwillow, 1978.

In this colorfully, humorously, and richly illustrated tale, children meet an elderly woman who loves rice. Her life is fine until a thief steals some of her rice several nights in a row. The woman sets out to complain to the raja. On the way she meets a scorpion-fish, a wood-apple, a razor, a cowpat, and an alligator. They tell her she won't be sorry if she takes them home with her on the return trip. The raja is not available so the woman goes home with the creatures and items she met. That night each does its part to drive the thief (a mouse) away forever.

Barrett, Judi. **Cloudy with a Chance of Meatballs.** Illus. by Ron Barrett. New York: Atheneum, 1978.

Humorous cartoonlike pen-and-ink illustrations complement this wild tall tale about a tiny town called Chewandswallow, where all the food the people need rains down from the sky. It rains soup and juice. It snows mashed potatoes and green beans. Sometimes the wind blows in hamburgers. The menu is always varied, ranging from a shower of orange juice to low clouds of sunnyside-up eggs.

Everything is perfect until the violent storms come. There's a hurricane of bread and rolls, a downpour of maple syrup, a tomato tornado, and a hail of giant meatballs that damages houses.

Betz, Adrienne, and Lucia Monfried, comps. "The Magic Pot," pp. 48-53, in **Diane Goode's Book of Silly Stories and Songs.** Illus. by Diane Goode. New York: Dutton Children's Books, 1992.

Amusing illustrations are interspersed throughout this traditional tale. A poor girl who lives alone with her mother goes into the forest looking for food. There she meets an old woman who feels sorry for her and gives her a pot that will make porridge when she says the magic words and will stop when she utters another magic phrase.

One day the girl goes out and her mother says the magic words that make the pot full. The mother forgets the words to make the porridge stop, so the porridge fills the kitchen, the house, the entire street, and most of the houses in the village. The little girl comes home, says the magic words and stops the flow of porridge. Now, however, those who want to return to town have to eat their way back.

Blume, Judy. **Freckle Juice.** Illus. by Sonia O. Lisker. New York: Four Winds Press, 1971.

Andrew wants freckles more than anything. When Sharon, who loves to tease other students, hears this, she offers Andrew her secret freckle juice recipe for 50 cents. At home Andrew mixes the strange and horrible combination of ingredients that include grape juice, vinegar, mustard, and onion. Andrew manages to drink the concoction, but it gives him a violently upset stomach. When he doesn't get freckles, he realizes Sharon tricked him. Andrew doesn't want to let her have the satisfaction of tricking him so he draws freckles on his face with a blue marker. At school Andrew's sensitive teacher Miss Kelly helps him save face.

Share the part of the book in which Andrew prepares and drinks the freckle juice recipe. This excerpt is also adapted in "Can I Grow Freckles?," pp. 24-31, adapted from **Freckle Juice** by Judy Blume in **I Was Wondering** (A Supplement to Childcraft—The How and Why Library). Chicago: World Book, 1991.

Before the program I make the freckle juice recipe and place it in a clear container. During the program I show it to the children after reading the excerpt from the book. They groan, but they love it.

Blundell, Tony. **Beware of Boys.** Illus. by author. New York: Greenwillow, 1991.

The text is comical, and the cartoonlike illustrations, although not of the highest quality, are amusing and convey a sense of action.

When a boy is captured by a wolf, he convinces the wolf not to eat him raw but to cook him first. The quick-thinking boy lists the ingredients for and explains how to make Boy Soup. The wolf scurries to gather what he needs, but the boy tells him that he forgot the salt. The boy gives the wolf a better recipe for Boy Pie that includes six sacks of cement and a cowboy hat. Again the wolf runs around and the boy says he forgot the salt. The boy offers a recipe for Boy Cake. This dish requires a bathtub, a bicycle, and barn doors. When the wolf returns he's staggering under the pile of ingredients. He collapses, the ingredients land on him, and the boy is able to escape and return home to a hot supper. The bandaged wolf tries to pick his way out of the rubble.

Children enjoy hearing the recipes for Boy Soup, Boy Pie, and Boy Cake. They love watching the wolf run around for ingredients and the explanation of how each dish is cooked. In Boy Soup, the boy has to be washed well, especially behind the ears, and in Boy Pie, the boy has to be placed comfortably in the dish.

Brusca, María Cristina, and Tona Wilson. **The Cook and the King.** Illus. by María Cristina Brusca. New York: Henry Holt, 1993.

Inspired by a South American folktale this satisfying, well-told story features a strong female character and dialogue that holds children's interest. The watercolor illustrations are vivid and lively. They splash across the pages. The artist, María Cristina Brusca, incorporates realistic details of the food, music, and customs at carnival time. Wilson captures the celebration and dancing, dark of night, and a busy village market with equal skill.

Travel high in the mountains of South America to a tiny kingdom ruled by an unfair king. Florinda, a fine young cook whom everyone likes, is ordered to cook for the king. They strike a bargain. Florinda won't involve herself in the business of the kingdom. In return the king will grant her one wish, one time, whenever she asks.

Florinda soon learns that the king can't settle disputes between people. Each time the king makes an unfair decision, Florinda teaches him a lesson; soon he is so angry, he decides to burn Florinda at the stake. Florinda then exacts her wish and because of it gets the king to change his verdicts. The king even names Florinda the official judge of the kingdom.

dePaola, Tomie. **Jamie O'Rourke and the Big Potato: An Irish Folktale.** Illus. by author. New York: G. P. Putnam's, 1992.

Meet Jamie O'Rourke, the laziest man in Ireland, whose wife, Eileen, plants and harvests their meager potato crop until she wrenches her back.

Jamie, worrying about himself, decides to confess his laziness to the priest. On his way to the church at midnight he comes upon a leprechaun and demands his pot of gold. The clever leprechaun offers Jamie a wish instead. Jamie agrees when the leprechaun suggests he wish for the biggest potato in the world. When it's full grown the potato is so enormous the townspeople must help Jamie pry it out of the ground. The potato flies out of the hole, rolls down the hill, and gets wedged between stone walls on either side of the main road. Eileen suggests that everyone take home a piece of the potato. People get so sick of potato that in the spring when Jamie says he has potato seed to plant they tell him not to and say they'll **give** him and his wife enough food to eat.

dePaola, Tomie. **Strega Nona.** Illus. by author. Englewood Cliffs, NJ: Prentice-Hall, 1975.

Colleagues tease me because this is one of my favorite books and I'll look for any excuse to share it with a group of youngsters. No matter how many times they've heard it, children love the tale of the good witch Strega Nona and her not-so-bright helper Big Anthony. Strega Nona warns Anthony not to touch her magic pasta pot, but, when he sees her using it and then he gets his chance, Anthony can't resist saying the magic words that make pasta flow from the pot. Anthony, however, can't stop the pot because he didn't see Strega Nona blow the three kisses that must accompany the magic words. The townspeople have had enough: The pasta is pouring out of Strega Nona's house and down the street. Just in time, Strega Nona returns, stops the pasta, and gives Anthony a fitting punishment.

dePaola, Tomie. **Tony's Bread.** Illus. by author. New York: G. P. Putnam's Sons, 1989.

Meet Tony the baker, who lives in a small village but dreams of owning a bakery in Milano, Italy. Tony has a daughter, Serafina. He feels that no man is good enough for her. When Angelo, a wealthy nobleman, falls in love with Serafina and she with him, Angelo enlists the aid of three aunties to help him marry Serafina.

Angelo meets Tony and offers to get his bakery started in Milano. When Tony samples the fine pastries and breads in the city, he despairs of ever making such fine sweets. The three aunties help him experiment with his breads. People love them. He can set up in Milano. While Tony's being cheered, Serafina and Angelo quietly get married.

DeSpain, Pleasant. "Clever Gretel," pp. 57-58, in **Thirty-Three Multi-cultural Tales to Tell.** Illus. by Joe Shlichta. Little Rock, AK: August House, 1993.

This is a short, very funny story to learn and tell. Gretel gets into trouble when she prepares two hens for the mayor's guest and then, impatient while waiting, eats the hens. Gretel tricks the mayor into thinking the guest stole the hens. She tricks the guest into thinking the mayor wants to cut off his ear. Children laugh at the quick-thinking way in which Gretel gets herself out of trouble.

Gerson, Mary-Joan. **Why the Sky Is Far Away: A Nigerian Folktale.** Illus. by Carla Golembe. Boston: Little, Brown, 1992.

According to this wonderful, fresh folktale, there was a time long ago when the sky was so close to the earth that people did no farming, cooking, or gathering. They reached up, took a piece of sky, and ate it. The sky, however, got angry because the people always took more than they could eat and threw the rest on garbage heaps. A voice from the sky boomed to Oba, king of the land, that the people must stop their wastefulness or the sky would no longer be theirs. Oba's messengers warned everyone to take only what they can eat.

Unfortunately, one woman, Adese, loved to eat and was never satisfied. On the last night of a great festival the woman took so much food she could only eat a portion of it. Everyone else is too full to eat the rest so Adese threw the piece of sky on the rubbish heap. The sky struck lightning, decreed that it had not been treated with respect and would go far away. The people then had to plow, gather crops, and hunt for food.

Haviland, Virginia, reteller. "Johnny-Cake," pp. 29-35, in **Favorite Fairy Tales Told in England. Illus.** by Maxie Chambliss. New York: Beech Tree Books, 1994.

The language and rich flavor of this telling of "The Gingerbread Boy," or "The Pancake," isn't found in many versions of this old folktale. Here not only does the johnny-cake outrun an old man, an old woman, and a little boy, but he also outruns well diggers, ditch diggers, a bear, and a wolf. When he meets a fox lying by a fence, the fox lures the johnny-cake by saying he can't hear him. When the johnny-cake is close enough, the fox eats him.

This is a small-format book. It is, however, worth showing the illustrations that are colored in gray tones. The sly expression on the fox's face is cleverly drawn, as is the expressive johnny-cake, who looks like a lumpy potato with arms and legs.

Haviland, Virginia, reteller. "The Old Woman and the Tramp," pp. 23-33, in **Favorite Fairy Tales Told in Sweden. Illus.** by Iris Van Rynbach. New York: Beech Tree Books/William Morrow, 1994.

In this traditional tale, also known as "Stone Soup" and "Nail Soup," a hungry fellow outwits a stingy and complaining woman who says she has nothing to eat. The man offers to show her how to make nail broth. He tricks her into providing ingredients that result in a hearty soup. The woman is so appreciative she insists the fellow take her bed for the night while she sleeps on the floor. The next day she thanks him for teaching her how to live comfortably and gives him money.

This is a most satisfying and well-written version of this tale. Haviland underscores the way in which the fellow outsmarts the greedy woman.

Howe, James. **Hot Fudge. Illus.** by Leslie Morrill. New York: Morrow Junior Books, 1990.

Howe's lighthearted, funny story is told by Harold, the dog, who with his friends Chester, a cat; Howie, a dachshund puppy; and Bunnicula, an unusual rabbit; lives with the Monroe family.

Harold and the boy Toby Monroe love chocolate and share it all the time. One Saturday, however, Mr. Monroe makes his famous fudge and says it isn't for the animals. When the Monroes leave the house and the animals are left alone with the food they wonder if they're being tested. To get their minds off the chocolate they decide to guard the house. Soon strange things start happening. There's a bang and when they check, the fudge that was chocolate is now white. Another thud from the kitchen awhile later brings them back to check and they find the fudge gone. The animals see the thief and chase him until he falls. It's Toby. He explains what happened, and, because they didn't touch the fudge, he rewards the animals—with chocolate.

Kimmel, Eric A., adapter. **Three Sacks of Truth: A Story from France.** Illus. by Robert Rayevsky. New York: Holiday House, 1993.

From France comes this sophisticated, clever, and captivating folktale masterfully retold by Eric Kimmel and expressively illustrated by Robert Rayevsky.

A dishonest king with a craving for peaches proclaims he'll marry his daughter to the man who brings him the most perfect peach. He has no intention of keeping his word; he just wants free peaches.

In the king's domain there lives a widow with three sons. She owns a peach tree that blossoms once every ten years, each time producing only three perfect peaches.

In turn she sends her sons Pierre and Pascal to the king with the peaches. Both are rude to an old woman they meet and are rewarded accordingly. Finally, Petit Jean, the clever son, sets out. He is kind to the woman, and she in turn gives him a silver fife. The woman tells Petit Jean to use the fife if the king goes back on his word.

The king eats the peach, extols its perfection, but adds a twist to his proclamation. Petit Jean must take 10,000 rabbits to the meadow and bring them back in the evening, for four days.

On the first day, with the help of his fife, Petit Jean completes the task. The second day the king orders his daughter to trick Petit Jean and take one rabbit. Petit Jean uses his fife to get the rabbit. On the third day the king orders the queen to steal a rabbit, and on the fourth day the king gets a rabbit by disguising himself and kissing his donkey's mouth. Each time Petit Jean gets the missing rabbit by using the fife.

Undeterred, the king orders Petit Jean to reveal three sacks of truth in front of the entire court. This command is the king's undoing. In the first sack Petit Jean reveals that the princess gave seven kisses for one rabbit. In the second he tells how the queen stood on her head and showed her petticoats to secure a rabbit. Petit Jean doesn't get to reveal the third sack of truth because the king doesn't want everyone to know what **he** did to get a rabbit.

Kovalski, Maryann. **Pizza for Breakfast.** Illus. by author. New York: Morrow Junior Books, 1990.

Frank and Zelda own a small pizza shop and do excellent business until the factory nearby closes. The workers move away and no one comes to the restaurant.

One day a man comes in who says he cannot pay for a meal, but he can grant a wish. Frank and Zelda wish for a thousand paying customers every day. They're so busy that when the little man returns they ask if they can wish for help. The next morning there are hundreds of waiters bumping into each other. Frank and Zelda get another wish, for a larger restaurant. Now they are grumpy and tired, and Frank wishes they hadn't made the wishes. Frank and Zelda make a plan and are soon happy again. Children will laugh when they see the couple on a beach running a pizza truck stand.

Mahy, Margaret. **The Rattlebang Picnic.** Illus. by Steven Kellogg.
New York: Dial Books for Young Readers, 1994.

For a rollicking good time Mahy's fast-paced, funny text and Kellogg's trademark, colorful, detailed, zany illustrations can't be beat.

The McTavishes have seven children and an old "rattlebang car." They often picnic with Granny McTavish, and, although the picnics are enjoyable, Granny always makes tough pancakes, pizzas, and pies that can't be cut or eaten. One day when the McTavishes decide to picnic at the top of Mount Fogg, it erupts, being a volcano. The family hurries to the car and down the mountain, but a wheel falls off. Ironically, Granny's pizza saves the day.

McGovern, Ann. **Stone Soup.** Illus. by Winslow Pinney Pels. New York: Scholastic, 1986.

McGovern has penned an excellent version of this familiar tale in which a tired and hungry man comes to a big house where the lady says she has no food to offer. The man impresses the woman by saying he can make soup from a stone. Each time he mentions an ingredient that would make the soup better she fetches it from her garden. Soon the soup is so fine and rich with onions, carrots, beef bones, butter, and barley that the woman insists on setting a fine table to accompany the dish.

Once the man has eaten, he takes the stone with him, saying that it hasn't cooked enough and needs to cook more the next day. While walking away, he's thinking of tomorrow's meal when he'll try the same trick on someone else.

What a great story to read aloud to all ages. It's even better if you learn the story and tell it or act it out. Add ingredients to a pot or invite the children to add the food, either real or made of plastic or cardboard.

Illustrator Pels has created the perfect face for the lady, a somewhat piggish look, and the young man is drawn with an impish posture.

Mosel, Arlene, reteller. **The Funny Little Woman.** Illus. by Blair Lent.
New York: E. P. Dutton, 1972.

Share this modern classic, boldly illustrated, about a woman who lives in Japan and likes to make rice dumplings. When she chases a dumpling that rolls and falls through a crack in the earth, the woman tumbles underground where she is captured by the wicked oni and forced to cook rice for them. She uses the magic paddle that turns one grain of rice into a potful. When she gets her chance, the woman flees with the magic paddle and outsmarts the oni to return home. With the magic paddle the woman is able to make and sell rice cakes and become the richest woman in Japan.

Palatini, Margie. **Piggie Pie!** Illus. by Howard Fine. New York: Clarion
Books, 1995.

Children in kindergarten and up will catch the humor in this original, clever, and delightful book. The language is flavorful and presents unique imagery. The bright, bold illustrations are a bit surreal, fantastic, and fanciful. The witch's bed, for example, has sleepy eyes and a wide mouth with a tongue at the foot. The illustrations are very expressive. You'll see the witch looking angry with her warts red and huge. Scenes are shown from different angles, including aerial views, close-ups, and overviews, adding to the visual interest of this book.

Gritch the Witch wakes up grumpy and hungry. After much thought she decides the only thing that will please her is piggie pie. She has all the ingredients, including two shakes of a rattlesnake's rattle and three belly hairs of possum, except for the required eight plump, juicy piggies. After consulting the Yellow Pages in the telephone book Gritch heads to Old MacDonald's Farm.

When the pigs see Gritch approaching, they slip into the barn and don duck, cow, and chicken costumes. The pigs outsmart Gritch through their charade. On the way home, still wondering what to eat, Gritch meets a badly injured wolf who tells her that pigs are tricky. Gritch invites the wolf home with her. He agrees, and as they walk, each thinks of eating the other.

Patron, Susan. **Burgoo Stew.** Illus. by Mike Shenon. New York: Orchard, 1991.

Youngsters love this tall-tale version of **Stone Soup** with its catchy rhythms and colorful language. Author Patron quickly sketches the characters: a lanky, cranky big boy; a tough boy with grease on his knuckles; a boy with snarls in his hair. When the boys in the story run, they each have their own style; e.g., one runs fast like a wind blowing leaves, another runs faster than a stone sinks in a pond. The full-color illustrations are done in ink line and watercolor. They splash across the pages and are somewhat cartoonlike.

Old Billy Que is confronted by five rowdy bad boys who are hungry and looking to steal from him. Billy isn't afraid. He calmly says he'll make Burgoo Stew with his secret ingredient. Once he has the boys' attention he throws a stone in the pot, explaining it's what holds down his secret ingredient. Then he asks the boys if one might have a mama with an onion, a carrot, and several other food items. He tells them to ask kindly for the ingredients. Each does and they return with food stuff in their pockets, shirttails, and pant's cuff. Billy Que makes the stew. The boys eat it and kindly ask for more. They remain rough but are never quite so bad again.

Rockwell, Thomas. "How to Eat Fried Worms," pp. 301-304, in **The Random House Book of Humor for Children.** Selected by Pamela Pollack. Illus. by Paul O. Zelinsky. New York: Random House, 1988.

The dialogue rings true, and there's lots of humor and suspense in this excerpt from Rockwell's book. Billy bets that he can eat 15 worms in 15 days. If he does it, he wins a minibike. However, his opponents, Allan and Joe, are slippery.

In this selection Billy is preparing for his first bite of the first worm. He has everything he needs: ketchup, mustard, lemon, cheese, honey. . . . Allan and Joe enter carrying a covered silver platter. They pull off the lid to reveal a huge night crawler, brown and steaming. Billy has second thoughts, but he does want that minibike. He manages to chew fast.

If anyone is interested they can read the entire book (grade three and up) or have someone older read the book to them: Rockwell, Thomas. **How to Eat Fried Worms.** New York: Franklin Watts, 1973.

Rylant, Cynthia. **Mr. Putter and Tabby Pick the Pears.** Illus. by Arthur Howard. New York: Harcourt Brace, 1995.

Noted author Rylant has written a funny, touching story with rich language and a well-developed relationship between the main characters, Mr.

Putter and his cat. The vivid watercolors are full of interesting little details and expressive faces.

Mr. Putter has apples, tomatoes, and pears growing in his yard. What he dreams of most is eating pear jelly, but first he must pick the pears. His cranky legs, feet, and knees make it impossible for him to climb a ladder. Mr. Putter uses elastic from underwear, a piece of an old glove, and a stick to make a slingshot to knock the pears off the trees. First, he practices using apples from the ground. The apples zing out of sight. Mr. Putter continues firing apples until dark. The next day Mrs. Teaberry visits Mr. Putter with a basket full of an apple feast: turnovers, pies, jellies, cider. That morning she was amazed to find dozens of apples in her front yard. This gives Mr. Putter an idea for his pear tree. He'll wait for the pears to fall then use his slingshot to shoot them into Mrs. Teaberry's yard.

Schwartz, Howard, and Barbara Rush, selectors and retellers. "Chusham and the Wind," pp. 29-33, in **Jewish Tales from Around the World.** Illus. by Uri Shulevitz. New York: HarperCollins, 1991.

This story is an amusing version of "Lazy Jack" that comes from Iraq. It's fun to read but even more effective to learn and tell. Each time a little boy goes to market for his mother he can't remember how he's supposed to carry the item home. When his mother tells him what he should have done, the boy does that with the next item he purchases. The results are disastrous. The boy tells chickens to fly home and they don't. He ties eggs together and they break. He stuffs flour into a bag, the bag breaks, and the wind blows the flour all over him. The boy's mother loves him anyway and gives him a hug.

Wolff, Ferida. **Seven Loaves of Bread.** Illus. by Katie Keller. New York: Tambourine Books, 1993.

Grainy illustrations done in cross-hatch ink line and color perfectly complement this long but hilarious story. Hard-working Milly and lazy Rose live together on a farm. Every day Milly makes seven loaves of bread—for the dog, the goat, the hen, the peddler, the rooster, a neighbor, Mrs. Bandy, and Rose. Milly explains to Rose why she makes seven loaves. The animals and people who receive them are helpful. One day when Milly gets sick, she tells Rose to make the bread. Each day that Milly is ill, Rose makes one less loaf. Every day the animal or person who doesn't get bread doesn't do what they're supposed to until the farm is a mess, the garden is ruined, the goat is gone, the hen lays no eggs, and the rooster won't crow.

Rose must work very hard to right everything. Only then does she understand why Milly always says it's as easy to make seven loaves as it is to make one.

Zemach, Margot. **The Three Wishes: An Old Story.** Illus. by author. New York: Farrar, Straus & Giroux, 1986.

Humorously written and illustrated, this tale takes readers to a time long ago where they meet a man and woman who work as woodcutters and often go hungry. One day they rescue an imp caught under a fallen tree. The couple are rewarded with three wishes. Without thinking, the man wishes for a pan of sausages for dinner. His wife is so angry at this wasted request that she wishes the sausages were hanging from her husband's nose. The man and woman have one final wish. Anything can be theirs, but they realize that they must wish the sausages off the man's nose. There are the sausages in their cooking pan. The woodcutters decide they didn't do too badly—at least they have something to eat.

Booktalks

Aliki. **Milk: From Cow to Carton.** Illus. by author. New York: Harper-Collins, 1992.

Delightful watercolor, ink, and pencil crayon illustrations accompany this informative and entertaining book. Interested youngsters can read about the entire process of milk production, from where the cows graze and what they eat to how they digest their food, how and why they produce milk, and how cows are milked and the milk processed. Aliki includes information on types of milk and other products made from milk at the dairy. Directions are provided for making butter from heavy cream.

Conford, Ellen. **What's Cooking, Jenny Archer?** Illus. by Diane Palmisciano. Boston: Little, Brown, 1989.

Here's an easy read with full-page illustrations for youngsters in grade two and up. Younger children will enjoy having someone read this funny story to them.

Jenny goes into business making individualized lunches for her school friends. It isn't long before she realizes the drawbacks. Her friends don't like everything she makes, and they have specific requests. Jenny has to buy supplies out of her profits. Interruptions in the kitchen can lead to messes. Finally, Jenny's dog eats the chicken from the sandwiches she's making, Jenny has to improvise, and everyone wants their money back. Jenny is soon out of business, but she plans to be a famous cook someday.

Drew, Helen. **My First Baking Book.** Illus. by Brian Delf. New York: Alfred A. Knopf, 1991.

Although the recipes in this book would take longer to make than you probably have, author Drew does offer exciting ideas for snacks and desserts that children can bake at home with adult supervision. The recipes are simple and easy to follow. All the ingredients are shown life size, and the clear step-by-step instructions are accompanied by photographs. The pictures, including the life-size photos of the finished products, are eye appealing. Among the enticing recipes are those for pastry spiders, snakes, and worms; meringues in the shape of ghosts and snowmen; cupcakes with animal designs; lollipop cookies; and dinosaur cake.

Fison, Josie, and Felicity Dane, recipe compilers. **Roald Dahl's Revolting Recipes.** Illus. by Quentin Blake. Photogs by Jan Baldwin. New York: Viking, 1994.

Your stomach may churn, and most of these recipes are difficult and time-consuming for children to make, but youngsters find these recipes fun to peruse. The dishes are food items mentioned in Dahl's many books. The book includes a photograph of each "delicacy" and Quentin Blake's trademark zany watercolor illustrations.

The recipes range from "Wormy Spaghetti" and "Fresh Mudburgers," to "Bunce's Doughnuts" and "Lickable Wallpaper."

Hiser, Constance. **No Bean Sprouts, Please!** Illus. by Carolyn Ewing. New York: Holiday House, 1989.

Over and over James begs his mom not to pack him nutritious lunches, especially bean sprouts and wheat germ and soybean sandwiches. James's lunches change when he receives the Wonderful Lunch Box on his birthday from his Uncle Wesley, who often travels to far-off places. When James opens the lunchbox in the cafeteria he sees two hot dogs, cheese curls, and chocolate bars. The next day when he puts his friends' foods in, they change, too.

On the third day when James's lunch box is missing everyone assumes that Mean Mitchell took it. James and his friends follow a trail of clues to find the thief and the lunch box. They catch the thief, but it isn't Mean Mitchell. The crook is James's dog Tag.

Kimmel, Eric A. **The Three Princes: A Tale from the Middle East.** Illus. by Leonard Everett Fisher. New York: Holiday House, 1994.

In this love story, which is beautifully told and illustrated with rich colored paintings, a wise and beautiful princess likes three men who are cousins. Princes Fahad and Muhammed are rich and famous, but old, whereas Moshen is handsome and young, but poor. The princess is determined to marry Moshen but the chief minister scoffs because Moshen has nothing. The princess gives Moshen a chance to find something of value. She sends the three cousins into the world and decrees that she'll marry the cousin who finds the greatest wonder.

After a year the cousins meet. Muhammed has a crystal ball that shows what is happening anywhere in the world. Fahad secured a flying carpet, and Moshen discovered a healing orange that can cure any illness. The cousins wonder about the princess, look in the crystal ball and see that she is dying. Fahad's flying carpet takes them to the princess, and Moshen's orange cures her. Each cousin contributed to her recovery, but, the princess points out, only Moshen gave up his treasure to save her.

Kline, Suzy. **Orp and the Chop Suey Burgers.** New York: G. P. Putnam's Sons, 1990.

Children in grade two and up will enjoy reading this short, funny chapter book while younger children will enjoy having it read to them. Orp wants to travel, so when he sees an ad for a cooking contest in which the prize is a free trip to DisneyWorld, he gets to work. He must invent an original recipe incorporating Fu Chow Soy Sauce. Using the meager ingredients left in the kitchen Orp invents chop suey burgers. His sister thinks they look like worm patties.

Orp is chosen as a finalist in the New England Regionals. The other contestants are adults. Orp doesn't win, but he gets an Honorable Mention. His prize is five cases of Fu Chow chop suey vegetables.

Manes, Stephen. **Chocolate-Covered Ants.** New York: Scholastic, 1990.

Young readers and listeners love the wacky antics in this short chapter book. The shenanigans begin when Max's younger brother Adam receives an ant farm for his birthday. Max tells Adam that people eat chocolate-covered ants. Adam doesn't believe it, so Max bets that they can get someone to eat chocolate-covered ants. They can't find the candy in any store so Max makes the delicacy by taking ants from his yard, mixing them with chocolate, and microwaving them in a plastic bag. The bag explodes and the kitchen is a mess, but Max salvages some of the chocolate-covered ants. Other mishaps and sneaky tricks occur; for instance, Max slips pieces of the candy in Adam's chocolate-chip ice cream and Adam eats the mixture. When Adam finds out, he gets his revenge.

Nixon, Joan Lowery. **Beats Me, Claude.** Illus. by Tracey Campbell Pearson. New York: Viking Kestrel, 1986.

Nixon's humorous, action-packed, clever yarn zips along in three chapters full of lively, funny watercolors.

Shirley and Claude move to what they think is a quiet spot in Texas. Claude reveals that he's been craving a bubbly, oozing apple pie. Shirley has never been a good cook, but she tries to make an apple pie. Each time Shirley tries, she forgets an ingredient and some imposter or outlaw interrupts her cooking. The first man who intrudes is a fake preacher who, when he's found out, slams his fist and ends up with pie exploded all over him. That makes Shirley remember she forgot to cut slits in the crust for the steam to escape. The preacher leaves behind an orphan named Tom whose sister was left with someone else.

The next interloper is a bank robber who tastes the second pie Shirley makes, doesn't like it, and shoots at the skillet. The bullet bounces off the crust, hits the moose head on the wall, and the moose falls on the bank robber's head. Shirley remembers while she's waiting for the sheriff that she forgot to put sweetening in the pie.

Shirley tries again to make an apple pie. This time she's interrupted by three escapees from the army. After the escapees taste the pie, they think they've been poisoned. Shirley knows now she forgot the apples. The men are taken by a U.S. Army patrol.

Claude tries Shirley's pie and it's awful. But the orphan, Tom, made a pie and it's excellent. Finally, Claude, who was reluctant to let Tom stay, says he can. Shirley is also going to get Tom's sister.

Robbins, Ken. **Make Me a Peanut Butter Sandwich (And a Glass of Milk).** Photos by author. New York: Scholastic, 1992.

It's worth doing a talk on this book, which will appeal to that curious youngster or peanut butter lover in your group. Robbins's distinctive hand-tinted photographs make this a beautiful book. Robbins explains the process of making peanut butter from growing peanuts, removing peanuts from their shells, roasting them in ovens, crushing the peanuts, to putting them in jars. Robbins also explains the process of making bread from planting and harvesting wheat to slicing and wrapping the bread. The author also shows how milk is produced.

Siracusa, Catherine. **The Giant Zucchini.** Illus. by author. New York: Hyperion Books for Children, 1993.

Edgar Mouse and Robert Squirrel's adventure growing a zucchini for the county fair will appeal to children in kindergarten through second grade. The book has large type and lighthearted, childlike illustrations that will attract young readers.

Robert Squirrel buys one large zucchini seed, hoping he and Edgar can grow a giant zucchini and win first prize at the county fair. All that grows is a tiny zucchini, but the two friends drive to the fair anyway. To cheer up, Edgar and Robert sing a song about the zucchini growing bigger. They're surprised when the zucchini grows to a giant size. (It has magic powers.)

When Humphrey Hog, the zucchini champion, sees Roger and Edgar's zucchini, he hatches a plot to make sure they don't win the contest. The magic powers of the zucchini, however, don't fail Edgar and Roger.

Smith, Robert Kimmel. **Chocolate Fever.** New York: G. P. Putnam's Sons, 1972.

The older youngsters in your group will enjoy reading about Henry Green, whose love of chocolate leads him into adventure and trouble. Henry eats as much chocolate ice cream, candy, pie, cake, and cocoa-crispy cereal as he wants. Ultimately he breaks out in brown spots that are diagnosed as chocolate fever. People are intrigued by this disease, and they swarm Henry until he runs away. Henry confronts a group of tough kids. Then he accepts a ride from a nice truck driver named Mac. They're hijacked by thieves, but at the hideout dogs flock to Henry (they're attracted to the smell of chocolate) and in the hubbub the thieves are subdued. Henry accompanies Mac while he makes his delivery to Alfred Cane's warehouse. Mr. Cane has a cure for Henry—Vanilla Pills—and some advice: eat less chocolate.

Sobol, Donald J., with Glenn Andrews. **Encyclopedia Brown Takes the Cake! A Cook and Case Book.** Illus. by Ib Ohlsson. New York: Four Winds Press, 1983.

Invite the older readers in your group to join Encyclopedia Brown as he solves a variety of food-related mysteries. They might also like to make the recipes found throughout the text. In one case Encyclopedia and his partner Sally Kimball must find Josh's stolen garlic bread. Encyclopedia is sure that his nemesis Bugs Meany and his gang are responsible, but he needs proof. Readers can try to solve "The Case of the Oven Mitt," in which Encyclopedia must find the thief who stole mixers from Bella's dad's store. There are 14 cases, and the solutions to each are found in the back of the book. Menus included range from a Fourth of July party to an Italian dinner.

Poetry

Note: Sometimes, children don't respond enthusiastically to poetry, but these poems about food are hysterical and irresistible.

Adoff, Arnold. **Eats.** Illus. by Susan Russo. New York: Lothrop, Lee & Shepard, 1979.

Among my favorite poems in this collection are "Eats," about a character who is always hungry; "Not Me But," about a person who says food just finds its way into his mouth; and "Dinner Tonight," in which dinner is described as a jungle with oregano fogs and broccoli logs. Also worth sharing are "Love Song," "Chocolate," and "Burger."

Ciardi, John. **Mummy Took Cooking Lessons and Other Poems.**
Illus. by Merle Nacht. Boston: Houghton Mifflin, 1990.

I recommend sharing "Mummy Took Cooking Lessons and...," p. 1, in which a child's mother makes bread that's so hard it can't be cut, and "Lemonade for Sale," pp. 10-11, in which children are warned to watch out for lemon squirting in their eyes.

"Betty Bopper," pp. 6-7, is a fun tongue-twisting poem about a girl who pops too much corn with tragic results. Write the poem on poster board or a large sheet of paper and invite the children to read it with you.

Cole, William. **Poem Stew.** Illus. by Karen Ann Weinhaus. New York:
J. B. Lippincott, 1981.

There are some short gems in this collection that youngsters will want to recite with you: "A Thousand Hairy Savages," p. 2; "Song of the Pop-Bottlers," p. 3; "Rhinoceros Stew," p. 13; "When Father Carves the Duck," p. 21; "Speak Clearly," p. 32; "Table Manners," p. 59; and "O Sliver of Liver," p. 71.

Heide, Florence Parry. **Grim and Ghastly Goings-On.** Illus. by Victoria Chess. New York: Lothrop, Lee & Shepard, 1992.

There are three poems in this collection that would please your target group. "Hungry Jake" eats everything until he eats himself and gets an awful stomachache. Jake is depicted as a doughy and lumpy fellow with little teeth, tiny eyes, tufts of hair around his large ears, and a massive stomach. Be sure to share Chess's illustration of the girl in "Spinach." The girl has a mortified expression as the spinach on her plate takes on a fluid, lifelike form with eyes and hands that reach out at her. Children will love hearing the girl list why she hates spinach. The girl realizes, however, that although she doesn't like it, spinach likes her and if she doesn't eat it, the spinach will eat her. Your group will love the gruesome food "facts" in the poem "What You Don't Know about Food." They'll learn, for example, that jelly comes from jellyfish, spaghetti is really worms, and ice cream is made from dirty snow and grimy germs.

Lansky, Bruce, comp. **A Bad Case of the Giggles: Kid's Favorite Funny Poems.** Illus. by Stephen Carpenter. Deephaven, MN: Meadowbrook Press, 1994.

You'll want to share these poems by some of the finest poets: "Dinnertime," by Mary Ann Hoberman, pp. 48-49; "The Spaghetti Challenge," by Leslie D. Perkins, p. 50; and "If We Had Lunch at the White House," by Kalli Dakos, pp. 52-53, in which a child realizes that he and his classmates don't have the proper lunch manners for such a grand luncheon. They're still squishing milk cartons, sucking Jello up a straw, and blowing bubbles into milk. Children will also enjoy "Fast Food," by Robert Scotellaro, p. 56, which introduces some witches selling bizarre fast food snacks on the roadside; "Bleezer's Ice Cream," by Jack Prelutsky, pp. 58-59, which introduces some interesting ice cream flavors, from Tapioca Smoked Bologna to Broccoli Banana Bluster; "Recipe," by Joyce Armor, p. 60, in which a child prepares dinner by mixing such ingredients as mushroom soup, lemon juice, peanut butter, jam, and noodles; and "Doing a Good Deed," by John Ciardi, p. 72, which shows how children lighten the load of an ice-cream truck that gets stuck in a mudhole.

Prelutsky, Jack. **Something BIG Has Been Here.** Illus. by James Stevenson. New York: Greenwillow, 1990.

A noted poet and a renowned illustrator have teamed up to present this collection of poems that includes many verses about food. Children enjoy "Happy Birthday, Mother Dearest," p. 10, which shows youngsters making a breakfast of blackened toast, watermelon omelet, and popcorn for their mom; "Belinda Blue," pp. 16-17, about a girl who pulls a tantrum when her mother asks her to eat one green bean; "The Turkey Shot Out of the Oven," pp. 18-19, in which the turkey rockets into the air and splatters over the kitchen because the narrator stuffed the turkey with unpopped corn; "They Tell Me I'm Peculiar," p. 27, whose narrator likes to eat liver every day; "Grasshopper Gumbo," p. 52, with its description of lunch in the school cafeteria, including Pickled Pelican Parts, Boiled Bumblebee, and Cracked Crocodile Crunch; "The Rains in Little Dribbles," p. 53, about a town where it rains different drinks, from mocha malteds to lemon droplets; "My Mother Made a Meat Loaf," pp. 66-67, about a meat loaf that can't be cut with a chisel, ax, blowtorch, or power saw; "Nigel Gline," pp. 76-77, who gets bored with regular food, eats a leaf, and then a twig, branches, and the trunk until he turns into a tree; "My Younger Brother's Appetite," p. 92; and "A Goat Wandered into a Junkyard," pp. 98-99, about a goat who eats an assortment of rubber, steel, gears, bearings, glass, pedals, oil, and pistons, then digests them and coughs up a car.

Viorst, Judith. "Our Mom's a Real Nice Mom but She Can't Cook," pp. 58-59, in **Sad Underwear and Other Complications: More Poems for Children and Their Parents.** Illus. by Richard Hull. New York: Atheneum Books for Young Readers, 1995.

Children will love this poem in which Mom's mashed potatoes taste like dirty socks, her soup could substitute for glue, her salads are soggy, and she incinerates French fries. The poem does finish with a list of Mom's good qualities.

Westcott, Nadine Bernard, comp. **Never Take a Pig to Lunch: Poems about the Fun of Eating.** Illus. by author. New York: Orchard, 1994.

Westcott has selected a wonderful range of poems and rhymes about eating and food by noted authors and poets. Her illustrations are zany and comical and splash across the pages in their vivid colors. Included are poems about table manners and poems about eating silly things, eating too much, and eating foods people like. Be sure to share some of the following: "What You Don't Know about Food," p. 18; "Spaghetti! Spaghetti!" p. 22; "It's Hot!" p. 26; "Peanut Butter and Jelly," p. 27; "Yellow Butter," p. 28, a tongue twister; "Fudge!" p. 32; and "My Mother Says I'm Sickening," pp. 48-49.

Songs

Glazer, Tom. "On Top of Spaghetti," p. 38, in **Diane Goode's Book of Silly Stories and Songs.** Comp. by Adrienne Betz and Lucia Monfried. Illus. by Diane Goode. New York: Dutton Children's Books, 1992.

This is a classic song that many children know. You can put the verses on posterboard and invite the children to sing it with you.

Demonstration/Participation Activities

Baltuck, Naomi. "Grandma's Going to the Grocery Store," pp. 16-17, in **Crazy Gibberish and Other Story Hour Stretches: From a Storyteller's Bag of Tricks.** Illus. by Doug Cushman. Hamden, CT: Linnet Book/The Shoe String Press, 1993.

Youngsters will catch on quickly to this "call and response" activity that's great for a change of pace in your program.

Bernstein, Rebecca Sample. "Lemonade," p. 35, in **Addy's Cookbook: A Peek at Dining in the Past with Meals You Can Cook Today.** Middleton, WI: Pleasant, 1994.

This popular title in the American Girls Collection includes a straightforward recipe for lemonade that requires few ingredients and has extremely clear directions. To save time, cut the lemons before your program. Children enjoy squeezing the juice out of the lemon halves on a juicer, and they like to shake the jar vigorously with the lemon juice, sugar, water, and ice cubes. If time allows, let the children help you make several batches and sample the lemonade.

Bourgeois, Paulette. "Apple Printing," p. 42, in **The Amazing Apple Book.** Illus. by Linda Hendry. Reading, MA: Addison-Wesley, 1987.

Combine paint, apples you've cut in half ahead of time, large sheets of paper, and children, and you'll have a happy group stamping apple designs and making wrapping paper.

Brokaw, Meredith, and Annie Gilbar. "Annie's Peanut Butter Balls," p. 55, and "Peanut Rice Faces," p. 59, in **The Penny Whistle Lunch Box Book.** Illus. by Jill Weber. New York: Simon & Schuster, 1989.

These two recipes are fun and easy to make and don't require many ingredients. Just be sure none of the children are allergic to peanut butter.

Colen, Kimberly. **Peas and Honey: Recipes for Kids (With a Pinch of Poetry).** Illus. by Mandy Victor. Honesdale, PA: Wordsong/Boyds Mill Press, 1995.

Lighthearted, soft illustrations in colored pencil are interspersed throughout this delightful book of recipes, poems, and food facts. You'll find verses by Aileen Fisher, Jack Prelutsky, Steven Kroll, David McCord, and X. J. Kennedy. Each poet includes their memories of the particular food they wrote about in their poems.

On page 29 there's an easy recipe for peanut butter that children can help you make. You might like to demonstrate or have the children help make apple cream (recipe on page 55). Another recipe the children will enjoy making with you is "Banana Mouse," on page 57.

On page 37 there's a fascinating chart of different types of pasta. Try making a list of the pastas' names and invite the children to match the name to the right pasta in the illustration. Some are easy, like spaghetti, ziti, and bowties. Others like tagliatelle, fusilli, and rigatoni will be more challenging.

Share the riddle about potatoes on page 48 and let the children guess the answer.

Erickson, Donna. "Create a Smiling Snack," p. 47, in **More Prime Time Activities with Kids.** Illus. by David LaRochelle. Minneapolis, MN: Augsburg Fortress, 1992.

Each child will want to make their own smiling mouth using an apple, peanut butter, and miniature marshmallows. Save time and cut the apples into quarters ahead of time.

Evert, Jodi, and Jeanne Thieme, eds. "Homemade Butter," pp. 16-17, in **Kristen's Cook Book: A Peek at Dining in the Past with Meals You Can Cook Today.** Middleton, WI: Pleasant, 1994.

Children enjoy this simple activity, but I suggest you shake the cream in the glass jar for about 10 minutes before the program so it doesn't take as long to form butter during the program.

Gillis, Jennifer Storey. "Easy Blender Applesauce," p. 47, and "Scrambled Apple Words," p. 51, in **An Apple a Day! Over 20 Apple Projects for Kids.** Illus. by Patti Delmonte. Pownal, VT: Storey Communications, 1993.

Before your program, peel, core, and quarter the apples. The children will enjoy taking turns putting the apple pieces into the blender along with the other ingredients.

Write the "Scrabbled Apple Words" on a board and invite the children to unscramble the letters to make a list of words associated with apples.

Hausherr, Rosmarie. **What Food Is This?** Photos by author. New York: Scholastic, 1994.

Hausherr's book is a guessing game with large, clear photographs. Invite your group to look at the photograph of a food and ask them the accompanying question. Give them time to guess the answer then turn the page to reveal the solution.

Some of the foods are easy to guess (milk and cheese) while others (raspberries and rice) are more challenging.

Hetzer, Linda. "Chef's Hat," p. 59, in **50 Fabulous Parties for Kids.** Illus. by Meg Hartigan. New York: Crown, 1994.

You'll dazzle children if you demonstrate how to make this chef's hat using white crepe paper and white construction paper. It takes a bit of practice, so try it ahead of time. If you don't want to do every step in front of the children, show the hat in its various stages and have a sample of the finished product to show.

Hilton, Joni. "Squeeze Fresh Orange Juice," pp. 22-23, and "Make a Cookbook," p. 80, in **Five Minute Miracles: 373 Quick Daily Discoveries for You and Your Kids to Share.** Illus. by Matt Wawiorka. Philadelphia, PA: Running Press, 1992.

Often I forget that most children have never made orange juice, and it's so easy to do. Have several juicers and lots of oranges so everyone in the group can participate.

The cookbook is easy to make with paper and imagination. Encourage youngsters to draw their favorite things to eat and to write what they think the recipe is for each dish.

Kohl, MaryAnn F. "Dried Bean Pictures," p. 105, in **Good Earth Art: Environmental Art for Kids.** Illus. by Cindy Gainer. Bellingham, WA: Bright Ring, 1991.

You supply the cardboard, glue, crayons, and a variety of dried beans, and children will eagerly create pictures.

Kohl, MaryAnn F. "Marshmallow Sculpture," p. 113, in **Scribble Art: Independent Creative Art Experiences for Children.** Illus. by Judy McCoy. Bellingham, WA: Bright Ring, 1994.

One of the simplest activities, making designs out of stale marshmallows and toothpicks is a project youngsters of all ages enjoy. The first time I demonstrated this activity to a group of children, they couldn't wait to try it.

Mathews, Judith, and Fay Robinson. **Oh, How Waffle! Riddles You Can Eat.** Illus. by Carl Whiting. Morton Grove, IL: Whitman, 1993.

For a change of pace in your program, here's a book of riddles that you can ask children. Some of the riddles will make the children laugh, others will make them groan. Also included are visual riddles the author calls "Foodles." Show the children several of the illustrations and see if they can guess what they represent. For example, one foodle depicts a potato sweating, wiping its brow, and sipping a cool drink while lying in a beach chair. The answer is a hot potato.

Owen, Cheryl. "Fruit Pomanders," p. 24-25, in **My Nature Craft Book.** Boston: Little, Brown, 1993.

Oranges, lemons, cloves, and ribbon are all that's needed for children to complete this craft. They may need a little help securing the ribbon.

Pulleyn, Micah, and Sarah Bracken. **Kids in the Kitchen: 100 Delicious, Fun, and Healthy Recipes to Cook and Bake.** Photos by Evan Bracken. New York: Sterling, 1994.

All the recipes in this book are simple to make. Children will be eager to assist you in mixing the ingredients and sampling the results. Try: "The Ultimate Trail Mixes," pp. 30-31; "GORP," p. 35; "Sunshine Seen Between," p. 38; "Peanut Butter Balls," p. 86; and "PB Glop," p. 88. Check that none of the children are allergic to peanut butter.

Take beans, seeds, glue, and cardboard or posterboard and let each child make their own design in the craft "Bean and Seed Mosaic," p. 104.

Sitarz, Paula Gaj. "Food in the Title."

In this game children are invited to use food words to complete book titles. If you wish, make a word box that lists words from which the children can select to fill the blanks in the titles. If time allows, tell the children some information about each title.

The following titles work well in this game. (The word in parentheses is the word you would leave out during the game.)

1. Charlie and the (Chocolate) Factory
2. Stone (Soup)
3. (Blueberries) for Sal
4. Chicken Soup with (Rice)
5. Cloudy with a Chance of (Meatballs)
6. Each Peach Pear (Plum)
7. Sand (Cake)
8. The (Milk) Makers
9. Anna (Banana) and Me
10. The Sweetest (Fig)
11. The (Gingerbread) Boy
12. Green (Eggs) and Ham
13 James and the Giant (Peach)

Sitarz, Paula Gaj. "Scrambled Food Words."

Write the following scrambled words on large posterboard, a chalkboard, or on individual handouts. The solutions are in parentheses:

1. aaannb (banana)
2. zazip (pizza)
3. psuo (soup)
4. cei merac (ice cream)
5. sifh (fish)
6. nckechi (chicken)
7. ronc (corn)
8. hetspagti (spaghetti)
9. ehsece (cheese)
10. ufinmf (muffin)
11. lppae (apple)
12. burhamger (hamburger)
13. maoott (tomato)
14. ipe (pie)
15. tebrshe (sherbet)

Time-Life for Children. **What Makes Popcorn Pop? First Questions and Answers about Food.** Illus. by Andy Cooke. Alexandria, VA: Time-Life, 1994.

Use this fun book for a change of pace in your program. Ask children some of the interesting questions about food and give them time to offer answers. The questions ask, for example, why bananas have peels, how potato chips are made, why doughnuts have holes, where raisins come from, why soda has bubbles, and what makes popcorn pop.

Chapter 5

Fractured Fairy Tales

It has become popular in recent years for authors to write modern retellings of classic stories. Sometimes the retellings are very different from the original, have an unexpected twist, or combine more than one tale. Many writers are researching and offering versions of classic tales as told in different countries, too. Some children will be familiar with the original story, and you can share the retelling without explanation. If you're sharing a "fractured tale" and you don't think the children are familiar with the original, read or give a summary of the traditional story before you share the modern version.

Read Alouds

Ada, Alma Flor. **Dear Peter Rabbit.** Illus. by Leslie Tryon. New York: Atheneum, 1994.

This is an original and delightful collection of 12 imaginary letters sent between fairy-tale characters Goldilocks, Baby Bear, Peter Rabbit, and the Three Pigs. Author Ada cleverly weaves an interrelationship between the characters, lending a common thread to the letters. One of the funniest notes is from Wolf to his cousin. Wolf writes that he's sorry to hear about his cousin's tail and confides that one time he had his own encounter with the girl in red (alluding to Little Red Riding Hood). It's fun to read the entire book or you can share a few of the letters.

The illustrations are detailed, (colorful peacock feathers in a jug, the lovely lining on Peter Rabbit's jacket) engaging, light watercolors with a gentle feeling.

Presenting this book is even more fun and effective if you can have four different people read the letters written by the four main characters.

Berenzy, Alix. **A Frog Prince.** Illus. by author. New York: Henry Holt, 1989.

Deep, dark illustrations in rich colors complement the text in this tale with a twist. The story starts like the classic version by the Brothers Grimm, but the tale changes from there.

Frog watches the princess at play, admires her from afar, and loves her. One day she is crying because her golden ball fell in the water. She promises Frog if he gets it, she'll let him be her friend. When Frog retrieves her ball, the princess runs off with it instead, and Frog follows her.

When the princess mistreats Frog and tells him he's ugly, Frog sets out to search for a princess who can see the good in him. During his travels Frog confronts two trolls and a green-faced witch. During these encounters he helps and is befriended by a dove and a turtle who assist him until he reaches the End of the World. There, in a great castle, he finds his princess, a frog princess.

Calmenson, Stephanie. **The Principal's New Clothes.** Illus. by Denise Brunkus. New York: Scholastic, 1989.

Here's a hilarious version of Hans Christian Andersen's classic tale **The Emperor's New Clothes.** In this version a school principal, Mr. Bundy, is the sharp dresser duped by tricksters, here named Moe and Ivy. The men present themselves as tailors and convince Mr. Bundy to let them make him a suit with special powers. They say the special cloth will be invisible to anyone who is stupid or no good at his job. Of course, Moe and Ivy only pretend to make a suit, but who will tell the principal they have seen nothing? Not the vice principal Ms. Moore and not Roger, who has a reputation as a smart student. The inevitable happens. Mr. Bundy can't admit he sees nothing. He pretends to put on the clothing and enters the auditorium wearing his socks, shoes, and underwear. In this version a kindergarten child calls out the truth.

The richly colored illustrations convey a sense of movement and Moe and Ivy are great caricatures.

Campbell, Ann. **Once upon a Princess and a Pea.** Illus. by Kathy Osborn Young. New York: Stewart, Tabori & Chang, 1993.

The illustrations in this retelling of Hans Christian Andersen's fairy tale are contemporary, sophisticated, unique, and bold, with sharp angles and crisp colors.

Princess Esmerelda doesn't want to marry wealthy but almost toothless King Frobius so she runs away wearing her entire wardrobe.

In another kingdom Prince Hector's parents have insisted that he find a bride but that she must be a true princess. The test is whether the girl can feel a handful of peas under her mattress. Hector visits several castles, but none of the girls are real princesses and he doesn't like them anyway.

Driving in the rain Hector comes upon the bedraggled Esmerelda and offers her a ride. He likes her, she's pleasant, and he wishes she were a real princess. Esmerelda mentions she's a princess and that night the queen puts her to the test. Prince Hector is delighted when Esmerelda wakes up the next day (after sleeping on 20 mattresses, 50 quilts, and 100 blankets with a pea under all) and says she couldn't sleep all night.

DeLuise, Dom. **Goldilocks.** Illus. by Christopher Santoro. New York: Simon & Schuster, 1992.

The well-known comedian Dom DeLuise's hilarious, contemporary telling of **The Three Bears** is complemented by exaggerated, expressive, humorous, "over-the-top" illustrations. The author's writing is often tongue-in-cheek; at times he addresses the reader directly. The narrator admits at one point that a certain part of the story is cloudy: Mama made porridge or hot soup. Then the narrator says they'll go with the soup.

DeLuise fleshes out the characters and the action. Goldilocks's personality is more fully developed here—she is spoiled, headstrong, and full of attitude. The narrator tells readers that Goldilocks is a girl who never takes no for an answer.

After Goldilocks is caught, she apologizes and is invited to lunch with the bears. When she returns home, Goldilocks's parents tell her she can no longer go out until her homework is finished.

The book includes recipes for porridge, corn muffins, and Pasta E Fagioli, the soup Mama Bear makes.

Emberley, Rebecca. **Three Cool Kids.** Illus. by author. Boston: Little, Brown, 1995.

What a fabulously original take on **The Three Billy Goats Gruff!** The illustrations are made from colorful cut paper in a variety of textures, including fabric, twine, and cardboard. This version is set in the city, and the Three Cool Kids live on a lot with tall buildings on two sides. Grass and weeds are getting sparse, construction is going on so it's noisy and dusty, and the kids want to go to a vacant lot nearby where they can find food. What stops them are the tales they've heard about a huge rat that lives in the sewer under the street.

Finally, with nothing left to eat, they decide to move. Little goes first and hears the horrible voice of the rat coming from the sewer grate. Little Cool tells the rat to wait for his big sister. Middle Cool tells the rat to wait for her big brother. Big Cool asks the rat what his problem is, lets him know what he thinks of him, and sends him splashing into the sewer. The goats move into the new lot.

The language is flavorful and fun. Big Cool is "bossy and saucy." The bracelets on Middle Cool's legs make a "kachinga, chinga" sound.

This story is more fleshed out than the original and perfect for the times.

Ernst, Lisa Campbell. **Little Red Riding Hood: A Newfangled Prairie Tale.** Illus. by author. New York: Simon & Schuster Books for Young Readers, 1995.

Children of all ages will enjoy this original and funny telling. My eight-year-old daughter and I laughed while sharing this story. The text has "feisty" heroines and a pleasing rhythm and pacing. Pastel, ink, and pencil illustrations are uncomplicated, vibrant, and large. The characters' faces have expressive eyes and are cartoon- and childlike.

Meet a little girl who wears a red hooded sweat jacket when she rides her bike. She lives at the edge of a great prairie in the Midwest and loves wheat-berry muffins. The girl likes to visit her grandma and decides to bring her some muffins and lemonade.

Red takes a shortcut on her bike through a field. A hungry wolf is cutting through the same field and when he smells the muffins, he follows the scent. Soon he jumps in front of Red's bike.

Suspense builds as Wolf asks Red what's in her basket and where she is going while licking his lips. Wolf distracts Red into picking flowers for Grandma. He sets off thinking he'll get the feeble Grandma, steal her recipe, and when Red arrives take the muffins.

Wolf finds a note on Grandma's door saying she's out in the field. There Wolf sees a farmer riding a tractor and yells out for the "ancient" Grandma who lives in the house. The farmer seems not to hear, Wolf makes more disparaging remarks, and sneaks up behind the tractor. The farmer whirls, grabs him by his suspenders, and, while Wolf gasps and stammers, asks what he thinks he's doing. When Wolf says he's looking for the loony Grandma, the farmer reveals that Wolf is talking to her. That's when the original version and this modern telling really twist and tangle. It's the wolf who says what big eyes, ears, and hands Grandma has. She responds that the eyes are for seeing him skulking around; the ears, better to hear Wolf coming; and the hands, better to crush Wolf like a bug.

Just then Little Red Riding Hood arrives. The two females march Wolf into the kitchen and lecture him. Grandma thinks of a plan. She opens a muffin shop in town and makes Wolf chief baker, salesclerk, and dishwasher. He'll stay busy and out of trouble and can eat all the muffins he wants.

Goldberg, Whoopi. **Alice.** Illus. by John Rocco. New York: Bantam Books, 1992.

The exaggerated features, the caricatures, the curving and angular lines, and the surreal, fantastic quality of the illustrations perfectly match this wacky, wild, and outrageous retelling of **Alice in Wonderland** by actress and comedienne Goldberg. This modern, inner-city version of Alice with fascinating characters hooks youngsters and takes them on an adventure that never lets up. Alice lives in New Jersey with her best friend, an invisible rabbit, Salvador De Rabbit, and another pal, Robin, who looks like the Mad Hatter.

Alice wants to be rich, so she enters every contest and giveaway she can. Finally, one day, Alice receives a letter telling her she's the winner of a prize worth lots of money that she can get at an address on 44th Street in New York City. The friends scrape up enough money to take a bus. Once in the city, Alice and her friends take a subway, get lost, and ask help from Mrs. Tu Lowdown, a snobby and rich lady. When she hears that Alice is going to win money, Mrs. Tu Lowdown tries to get Alice's winning ticket. Alice escapes with Mrs. Tu Lowdown in pursuit. Alice visits a fortuneteller who gives her correct directions, but when Alice arrives she learns that they want to sell her swamp land in Florida.

Alice returns to the fortuneteller, who tells Alice that she is rich because she has friends who stick with her always. Alice agrees. Mrs. Tu Lowdown appears and Alice happily gives her the winning ticket. Alice and her friends return home and have a tea party. This tale is witty, sharp, touching, quick-moving, and wise.

Hooks, William H. **The Three Little Pigs and the Fox.** Illus. by S. D. Schindler. New York: Macmillan, 1989.

Hooks writes that this Appalachian version of **The Three Little Pigs** is based on several oral tellings he heard in the Great Smoky Mountains. The three pigs are Rooter, who loves to eat; Oinkey, a mama's boy; and Hamlet, the quick-witted female sibling. The children get so big they're squeezed tight in their stone house. Rooter, the oldest, is sent by Big Mama to build his own house. Mama tells him to watch for Fox, build a house of stone, and visit her on Sundays. Soon Rooter meets Fox, who puts him in his sack to save and eat. Oinkey is sent out when the house gets crowded again. He is also put in a sack by Fox. Finally, Hamlet sets out. When she meets Fox, she tricks him into the sack.

When Fox comes to her stone house, Hamlet knocks him about and gets him to reveal where her brothers are hidden. Then Hamlet gets rid of Fox for good—in a butter churn she throws into a creek. Hamlet frees her brothers, and, since it's Sunday, they visit Mama Pig.

The language has a great cadence and precise, evocative imagery, e.g., "tricky old drooly-mouth fox." Illustrator Schindler has individualized the animals with distinctive characteristics. Fox looks hungry with that bit of dripping saliva, and sly with his long nose, jaw, and tongue.

Jackson, Ellen. **Cinder Edna.** Illus. by Kevin O'Malley. New York: Lothrop, Lee & Shepard Books, 1994.

Cinderella and Cinder Edna both live with cruel stepmothers and stepsisters, but they approach life very differently in this tale. Cinderella needs a fairy godmother to help her, whereas Cinder Edna is practical and self-sufficient. Cinder Edna, instead of dwelling on her problems, realizes how much she's learning from housework and, once her work is done, teaches herself how to play an instrument and takes side jobs. Cinder Edna isn't beautiful, but she's strong, has a great personality, and knows good jokes.

When everyone goes to the ball, Cinderella needs a fairy godmother to help her attend. Cinder Edna had put a dress on layaway, and she wears practical loafers instead of glass slippers. Cinder Edna takes the bus to the ball. There she finds Prince Randolph boring, but his younger brother Rupert is fascinating. He's in charge of a recycling plant and a home for orphaned kittens. The two dance and learn that they share many interests.

At midnight Cinderella must leave because the magic will end. Cinder Edna must leave because the buses stop running at midnight.

Unlike Prince Randolph, who finds the glass slipper and has every woman try it, Rupert calls all the Edna's in the palace directory and asks how many recipes they know for tuna casserole, since Cinder Edna had told him she knew 16 ways to make it. Both princes find the women they seek, and they have a double wedding.

Cinderella and Randolph spend their time primping, and Cinderella gets bored fast. Rupert and Cinder Edna share activities like composting, caring for orphaned kittens, cooking, and playing music. The narrator asks the reader to guess who lived happily ever after.

Children and adults enjoy this witty tale with its large and exaggerated illustrations.

Johnston, Tony. **The Cowboy and the Black-Eyed Pea.** Illus. by
 Warren Ludwig. New York: G. P. Putnam's Sons, 1992.
 Johnston's version of **The Princess and the Pea** by Hans Christian Andersen is set in Texas and features a woman named Farethee Well, who must find the real cowboy who will love her for herself, not her money. Farethee Well sets up a test, keeping in mind that a real cowboy is sensitive. She'll have each suitor ride the range with a tiny black-eyed pea in his saddle blanket. Many swaggering cowboys come and are untroubled by the pea, until a real cowboy arrives. Fifty saddle blankets can't stop the pain of that pea for him.

Karlin, Barbara, reteller. **Cinderella.** Illus. by James Marshall. Boston:
 Little, Brown, 1989.
 Enjoy a fresh and funny version of this tale. The text is brief, expressive, modern, and moves along with contemporary language. The illustrations by Marshall are full-page, plain-fun watercolors. One of the most clever pictures depicts the prince lying in a hammock with his bare feet showing, one foot resting on his dog. The plump stepsisters are comical and ridiculous looking with their pig noses and huge lips. One of the best scenes occurs at midnight when the coach explodes—it's a pumpkin—the wheels fly and Cinderella is booted into the air.

Kellogg, Steven, reteller. **Jack and the Beanstalk.** Illus. by author.
 New York: Morrow Junior Books, 1991.
 Although Kellogg's version adheres closely to the original, I share this story with children just for Kellogg's extremely detailed, expressive, colorful, action-packed illustrations.

Marshall, James, reteller. **Goldilocks and the Three Bears.** Illus. by
 author. New York: Dial Books for Young Readers, 1988.
 Trust James Marshall to pen and illustrate an amusing, contemporary version of a folktale. Marshall underscores that Goldilocks is a girl who does as she pleases. The Bears are very dramatic. When Papa tries the porridge and

yells that he's burned his tongue, Baby Bear exclaims that Papa's dying. Baby Bear's room delights youngsters. It's a cyclone of toys, posters, open drawers, and books on the floor.

Marshall, James, reteller. **The Three Little Pigs.** Illus. by author. New York: Dial Books for Young Readers, 1989.

This retelling is written and illustrated the way you'd expect from James Marshall. It's full of laughs and contemporary language. The wolf looks like a punk or a bully.

Martin, Rafe. **Foolish Rabbit's Big Mistake.** Illus. by Ed Young. New York: G. P. Putnam's Sons, 1985.

Ed Young's impressionistic, subdued, but strong, full-color paintings fill each double-page spread. They complement this traditional Jataka tale that is, perhaps, the oldest version of "Henny Penny" or "Chicken-Little." The rhythmic quality of the text is entrancing.

Rabbit is the catalyst for panic among the animals of the jungle. He's lying under a tree and worrying about what would happen if the earth broke up. When he hears a crash, Rabbit decides that the earth has broken apart and spreads his message to all the rabbits, two bears, an elephant, and snakes, all of whom run in fear. Lion hears the hissing, trumpeting, moaning, and screaming and asks what is happening. When he hears the story he reassures the animals. Then he has Rabbit take him to the place where he heard the crash. Lion points to a tree. What Rabbit heard was an apple hitting the ground. The other animals want revenge, but Lion reminds them that they ran with Rabbit without checking his story.

Be sure to give the children ample time to enjoy the spectacular close-up painting of Lion in which his features, especially his majestic mane, fill the pages.

Palatini, Margie. **Piggie Pie!** Illus. by Howard Fine. New York: Clarion Books, 1995.

Take a familiar folktale setting, Old MacDonald's farm, and well-known folktale characters, including a witch, some pigs, and the wolf from **The Three Little Pigs,** and you have the basis for this original book. The language is pleasing; the illustrations surreal and fantastic.

Gritch the Witch is hungry, and only piggie pie will do. She needs some juicy piggies and sets off to Old MacDonald's farm. The pigs see the witch flying overhead and disguise themselves in duck, cow, and chicken costumes to outsmart her. Dejected, Gritch the Witch heads home. She meets a badly injured wolf and invites him to her house. The wolf accepts the invitation and as they walk, the witch and the wolf each think of eating the other.

Patron, Susan. **Burgoo Stew.** Illus. by Mike Shenon. New York: Orchard, 1991.

Who can resist this tall-tale rendition of **Stone Soup,** with its colorful language and characters. When Old Billy Que is confronted by five rowdy bad boys who are hungry and determined to steal from him, Billy isn't afraid. He holds them mesmerized as he explains how he'll make Burgoo Stew with a secret ingredient that is held in the pot by a stone. In this way, Billy gets the boys to do all the work, to ask their mothers kindly for some additional ingredients, and to enjoy the stew with him.

Scieszka, Jon. **The Book That Jack Wrote.** Illus. by Daniel Adel. New
  York: Viking, 1994.
   Scieszka's books are popular with youngsters and adults. Instead of the
nursery rhyme "The House That Jack Built," here we're taken into the book that
Jack wrote. Jack's story is full of characters from other nursery rhymes. Read the
tale, then go through slowly and ask the children to guess from what rhymes and
stories the characters are taken. Jack's text is short enough that you may want to
precede it by reading a version of **The House That Jack Built.**
   The illustrations are somewhat surreal, like the text. Paintings offer
unusual perspectives, exaggeration, and characters with oversized heads.
   Among the characters you'll meet are a cat who looks like the Cheshire
Cat from **Alice in Wonderland** and a baby, Baby Bunting, who gets hit in the
head by a pie launched by the Pieman from Simple Simon. Each character is
connected to the next by some action.

Scieszka, Jon. **The Frog Prince, Continued.** Illus. by Steve Johnson.
  New York: Viking, 1991.
   Children will appreciate the humor in this tale if they are familiar with
the original story by the Brothers Grimm. Author Scieszka reveals what
happened after the princess kissed the frog and he turned into a prince. Unlike
the classic version, they don't live happily ever after. When we meet them, they
are miserable. The princess can't tolerate the way the prince sticks out his long
frog tongue or hops on the furniture. The prince misses his pond.
   One day the prince and princess agree that it would be better if he were still
a frog. Off he hops into the forest to find a witch who can turn him back into a frog.
   The prince meets witches from **The Sleeping Beauty, Snow White,** and
Hansel and Gretel, but they scare him; he knows his fairy tales. Next, the
prince encounters the Fairy Godmother from Cinderella. She'll grant his wish.
She, however, turns him into a frog carriage. He's frightened, but at midnight
he turns back into a prince. He realizes the princess was the only one who
believed in him and loved him. He runs home, kisses her, and they both turn
into frogs. Now they live happily ever after. Clever.
   The deep, dark-colored paintings are expressionistic. Trees seem to bend
inward. The Prince has thin spindly legs, a green suit, bulgy eyes, and long, pointy
shoes. The Fairy Godmother is "dipsy" looking, and if you examine the close-up of
the poisoned apple, it looks like it has Gak (from Nickelodeon) on it.

Scieszka, Jon. **The Stinky Cheese Man and Other Fairly Stupid
  Tales.** Illus. by Lane Smith. New York: Viking, 1992.
   Some of these zany revisions of familiar fairy tales are best shared
one-on-one, but a few of these are perfect to share with a group. Read each one
suggested, then ask the children to guess what story it's based on.
   "The Princess and the Bowling Ball," pp. 10-11. The prince will never
marry because none of the young women can feel a pea under 100 mattresses.
Finally the prince slips a bowling ball under the mattresses, and that is
definitely felt.
   "The Other Frog Prince," pp. 16-17. This frog convinces a princess to kiss
him by saying he's really a prince upon whom a spell was cast. After the princess
kisses him, he remains a frog, says he was kidding, and leaves the princess to
wipe the frog slime off her lips.

"The Stinky Cheese Man," pp. 34-42. Meet the lonely old man and woman who decide to make a man out of stinky cheese. He runs away (like the gingerbread boy in the original), but the man smells him and decides he isn't hungry and the old woman decides she isn't lonely. The cow doesn't chase him because he fears the odor would give him a stomachache. A boy and girl don't chase him because they fear their teacher might make them eat him. A skunk faints. Then the stinky cheese man meets the sly fox, who offers him a ride on his back across the river. Halfway across, the fox smells the odor, coughs and gags, and the Stinky Cheese man flies into the river and falls apart.

Scieszka, Jon (as told to him by A. Wolf). **The True Story of the Three Little Pigs.** Illus. by Lane Smith. New York: Viking Kestrel, 1989.
    Like the other "fractured fairy tales" by Scieszka, this story is unique, clever, and amusing. The illustrations are full of action, humor, and small details.
    Alexander T. Wolf, known as Al, gives his version of what really happened between him and the three pigs. Al feels he's been misunderstood.
    Al says he was making a birthday cake for his dear granny even though he had a horrible, sneezing cold. Al needed sugar for the recipe, so he went to ask his neighbor, a pig, for a cup of sugar. Al says when he knocked, the door fell in. He didn't want to step inside so he called to the pig. He swears he was going to leave, but he had a sneezing fit and the house fell down and the pig was dead. It seemed a waste to leave a good ham dinner, so he ate the pig.
    A. Wolf still needed sugar, so he went to the next neighbor's house, the first pig's brother. Al couldn't help it if he had another sneezing fit, this house fell down, the second pig died, and he ate him so the pig wouldn't spoil.
    When Al went to the third pig's house, the pig was rude to him. A. Wolf remained calm until the pig insulted his granny and that made him crazy. Al says he was trying to break the door down and was sneezing when the police came. The news reporters arrived, thought the real story was boring, so they made him the Big Bad Wolf and fabricated a more exciting version of what had happened.

Trivizas, Eugene. **The Three Little Wolves and the Big Bad Pig.** Illus. by Helen Oxenbury. New York: Macmillan, 1993.
    Mother wolf sends her three little wolves out into the world and warns them of the big bad pig. The wolves build a house of bricks. The pig uses a sledgehammer to knock down the house. The wolves escape and build a house of concrete. The pig uses a pneumatic drill to smash the house. Again the wolves flee and build a house with armor plates, barbed wire, and iron bars. The tenacious pig blows up the house with dynamite. Finally, the wolves meet a flamingo from whom they purchase flowers to build a fragile house. The pig prepares to huff and puff, smells the flowers, and becomes pleasant and good. He sings, dances, plays games with, and ultimately lives with the wolves.
    Children find this a funny and clever story. They love the expressive, appealing watercolors.

Vozar, David. **Yo, Hungry Wolf! A Nursery Rap.** Illus. by Betsy Lewin. New York: A Doubleday Book for Young Readers/Delacorte Press, 1993.

Author Vozar cleverly retells **Little Red Riding Hood, The Three Little Pigs,** and **The Boy Who Cried Wolf** by creating a story line that follows the same hungry wolf as he looks for something to eat. Vozar uses rap language that lends a modern and rhythmic flavor to this tale. You'll want to practice the story before you share it with children to do justice to the rap style. The illustrations are large, splashy watercolors with thick black outlines. They are funny, express character well, and have a cartoonlike flavor.

Meet a hungry wolf with a "hollow and spongy" stomach who wants pig to eat. The first two pigs hide in their brother's house of brick with aluminum siding. When the wolf goes down the chimney, the soup that's boiling in the pot is so hot it sends him up the chimney.

The wolf decides to go to Granny's to see what's for dinner. Granny hits the wolf over the head and tangles with him until she tires and the wolf locks her in a closet. When Little Red Rappinghood comes, she's not fooled by the wolf dressed in Granny's clothes. She insults the way he looks and tells the wolf he better think of something else to eat. If he comes back, he'll get a beating. Wolf appeals to all wolves. He says he's changing his diet and now eating junk food.

The story takes us to the bakery owned by the boy who cried wolf. Since business is slow, the boy is constantly pulling stunts to get people into his shop. When the wolf visits and the boy threatens to scream, the wolf ignores him because he knows no one will come. The wolf eats all the doughnuts and pastries he wants, then goes home happy. He wonders how he'll get his meals the next day.

Young, Ed, trans. and reteller. **Lon Po Po: A Red Riding Hood Story from China.** Illus. by author. New York: Philomel Books, 1989.

Mother reminds her three daughters to keep the door latched when she leaves to visit grandmother overnight. An old wolf sees the mother leave, disguises himself as an old woman, insinuates his way into the house by saying he's their grandmother Po Po, and blows out the candle so the room is in darkness.

Sisters Paotze, Shang, and Tao are in bed with the wolf when Shang stretches and touches the wolf's tail. Shang remarks that Po Po's foot has a bush on it, but he explains it away as hemp strings he brought to weave them a basket. When Shang touches the wolf's claws he explains it's an awl to make shoes. Shang is the eldest and most clever. She manages to see the wolf's hairy face before he blows out a light she lit. Shang thinks quickly and tells the wolf about ginko nuts that grow on the top of a tree. The girls will gather them. This gives Shang the chance to tell her sisters about the wolf and to devise a plan to get rid of him. Shang convinces the wolf he must climb the tree and get the nuts himself for their magic to work. The sisters will hoist him up in a basket. In this way they are able to lift him halfway then let the basket drop.

Booktalks

Wilson, Barbara Ker. **Wishbones: A Folktale from China.** Illus. by Meilo So. New York: Bradbury Press, 1993.

The author asserts that this story is the oldest version of **Cinderella.** The writing is solid, and the text much shorter than the original. The illustrations in deep colors are expressionistic and offer a fresh style.

Youngsters are taken to a cave among the hills of China thousands of years ago. There Chieftain Wu lives with his daughter, Yeh Hsien (whose mother died), and his second wife and her daughter. The stepmother and stepsister force Yeh Hsien to do difficult and dangerous tasks. One day Yeh Hsien finds a small fish with red fins and golden eyes, takes it home, cares for it, and moves it to a pond near the cave when it grows big. Yeh Hsien's stepmother tricks the fish into appearing to her. She catches the fish, cooks it for supper, and buries the fish bones. Yeh Hsien returns and is sad to find her fish gone.

An old man appears to Yeh Hsien, tells her where the bones are buried, and reveals that the bones are magic. With the bones, she can wish for anything she wants.

When Cave Festival time comes the family goes, but Yeh Hsien is left behind. She dresses herself beautifully in one of her hidden robes, goes to the festival, and enjoys herself until she sees her stepmother and stepsister staring at her. Frightened that they recognize her, Yeh Hsien goes home and changes her clothes. In her rush, one of Yeh Hsien's silken slippers falls from her foot.

In the nearby kingdom of T'o Huan the cave people present the king with the slipper they found. When the slipper doesn't fit any of the women in his household, messengers are set to search the countryside. In Wu's cave the slipper fits Yeh Hsien. As in other traditional versions, Yeh Hsien becomes queen.

Poetry

Lansky, Bruce, comp. **A Bad Case of the Giggles: Kid's Favorite Funny Poems.** Illus. by Stephen Carpenter. Deephaven, MN: Meadowbrook Press, 1994.

Included in this collection are some hysterical "fractured" nursery rhymes. Use them for a change of pace in your program.

"Mary Had a Little Ham," by Bruce Lansky, p. 92. Eat this mixture and you'll get a bellyache.

"Mary Had Some Bubble Gum," by Anonymous, p. 93. Find out what happens when Mary chews her gum at school.

"Mary Had a Little Lamb," by Anonymous, p. 94. Find out what happens when Mary eats lamb, lobster, prunes, pie. . . .

"There Was an Old Woman," by Bill Dodds, p. 95. The old woman has bigger problems than living in a shoe.

"Hickory, Dickory, Dock!" by Robert Scotellaro, p. 97. Here's what happens when a goat eats a child's sock and shirt.

Lansky, Bruce, creator. **The New Adventures of Mother Goose: Gentle Rhymes for Happy Times.** Illus. by Stephen Carpenter. Deephaven, MN: Meadowbrook Press/Simon & Schuster, 1993.

Lansky's collection of modern versions of Mother Goose rhymes is clever and extremely funny. His verses are new, but he has retained the rhythm and rhyme patterns of the original Mother Goose rhymes. Children will probably know the originals, but if not, share the original and then the updated version.

You'll find Little Bo Peep, Old King Cole, Jack and Jill, Humpty Dumpty, and the other characters from Mother Goose, but they're doing very different things. In "Mary Had a Little Jam," p. 5, Mary eats 10 jam sandwiches and then feels awful. "The girl with the curl in the middle of her forehead," p. 7, tries to stick it back in place with glue. "Little Miss Muffet," p. 8, was licking an ice cream cone when the spider came along. Miss Muffet told him to get his own. "Jack Was Nimble," p. 10, but when he jumped over the candlestick, he got too close to the flame and now his pants smell like burnt toast. (Note the accompanying illustration. Jack is seen with burnt pants, and a cat nearby is holding its nose.) In "Humpty Dumpty Sat on a Wall," p. 15, the poet laments that they didn't have super glue back then.

The rest of the verses are equally original and humorous.

Viorst, Judith. **Sad Underwear and Other Complications: More Poems for Children and Their Parents.** Illus. by Richard Hull. New York: Atheneum Books for Young Readers, 1995.

Try these poems for a change of pace. They're funny and thoughtful.

". . . And Beauty and the Beast, Once the Spell Had Been Broken, Lived Happily (Sort of Happily) Ever After," p. 28. Beauty is pouting because once the spell was broken, everyone thought the Beast better looking than her.

". . . And When the Queen Spoke Rumpelstiltskin's Name, He Became So Enraged That He Tore Himself in Two," p. 29. The poem is told from Rapunzel's point of view.

". . . And After a Hundred Years Had Passed, Sleeping Beauty Awoke (at Last!) from Her Slumber," p.30. Beauty describes what shape the castle is in when she awakens.

". . . And the Fisherman Asked for No Reward for Sparing the Life of the Fish, but the Fisherman's Greedy Wife Was Not Content," pp. 31-33.

". . . And While Poor Hansel Was Locked in the Witch's Cage, Awaiting His Doom, Clever Gretel Came to Her Brother's Rescue," p. 34. Gretel is upset. Why isn't the story called "Gretel and Hansel" since she pushed the witch into the oven and she saved her brother?

Demonstration/Participation Activities

Baltuck, Naomi. "Little Rap Riding Hood," pp. 42-44, in **Crazy Gibberish and Other Story Hour Stretches: From a Storyteller's Bag of Tricks.** Illus. by Doug Cushman. Hamden, CT: Linnet Book/The Shoe String Press, 1993.

Children will want to do this participation story more than once. Baltuck's clever rapping rhythm in this short rendition of the classic tale is catchy. Youngsters love to join in, clapping, pointing, and snapping their fingers. Be sure to practice before the program so you can do this smoothly.

Eaton, Deb, and others, eds. "Twisted Tales," p. 58, in **Games and Giggles Just for Girls.** Illus. by Paul Meisel. Middleton, WI: Pleasant Company, 1995.

Eight fairy tales have been renamed with words that mean the same as the original. Ask the children to guess the original titles. An example is "Two Plus One Tiny Oinkers." The original title is **The Three Little Pigs.**

Hetzer, Linda. "Clue" and "Simple Simon Says," p. 42, in **50 Fabulous Parties for Kids.** Illus. by Meg Hartigan. New York: Crown, 1994.

"Clue" is a delightful game in which children are invited to look at an item and guess what fairy tale it represents. The author offers wonderful suggestions for this enjoyable game.

"Simple Simon Says" is a traditional game that people of all ages enjoy.

Marzollo, Jean, comp. **The Rebus Treasury.** Illus. by Carol Devine Carson. New York: Dial Books for Young Readers, 1986.

You'll find 41 nursery rhymes and traditional songs in rebus form. Children in your group will, hopefully, know many of these rhymes and songs and will easily figure out the rebuses. Some are easy, others a bit more challenging. Do these puzzles for as long as children are enthusiastic.

Introduce the activity by explaining what a rebus is. Each rebus is in very large print and symbols, making them easy to share with a group. The ditties range from "Little Bo-Peep" and "The Old Woman Who Lived in a Shoe," to "Home on the Range" and "Oh, Susanna."

The Rebus Treasury is an eye-appealing book. The artwork comprises colored pencil drawings and rubber stamp images.

Chapter 6

Games and Sports

Read Alouds

Abbott, Bud, and Lou Costello. "Who's on First?" pp. 312-13, in **From Sea to Shining Sea: A Treasury of American Folklore and Folk Songs.** Comp. by Amy L. Cohn. Illus. by 11 Caldecott Medal and four Caldecott Honor Book artists. New York: Scholastic, 1993.

Children find this classic comedy routine hilarious. In it Lou Costello is very confused when Bud Abbott tells him the name of the men on the St. Louis baseball team they're going to play. "Who" is on first base, "What" is on second base, and "I Don't Care" is the shortstop.

The key to making this successful is to do it with another adult and to practice several times before your presentation. The skit is fast paced, and timing is everything.

Allard, Harry. **Miss Nelson Has a Field Day.** Illus. by James Marshall. Boston: Houghton Mifflin, 1985.

The twists, the sophisticated humor, and the classic Marshall illustrations ("color cartoons") blend seamlessly in this story. The illustrations splash over the pages in a variety of colors.

Everyone at school is dejected by the Smedley Tornados' abysmal football record. The players goof around, and Coach Armstrong is ineffective. When the janitor mentions to Miss Nelson the team needs an expert and when Miss Nelson overhears the students saying they need Miss Viola Swamp, she devises a plan.

Miss Nelson makes a cryptic phone call and takes out an ugly black sweatsuit. Soon, Coach Swamp appears and puts the team to work. She's tough, but the team improves. On Thanksgiving Day they beat the Werewolves. Miss Nelson, at home, is thanking her twin sister for substituting for her (while she was The Swamp).

Bruchac, Joseph, reteller. **The Great Ball Game: A Muskogee Story.** Illus. by Susan L. Roth. New York: Dial Books for Young Readers, 1994.

In this short but entertaining, witty, sophisticated, action-packed tale, an argument ensues between Birds and Animals as to which group is better. They decide to play a game to settle the dispute. The first side to score a goal wins the argument.

Bat doesn't know which side he should play on: he has wings, but he also has teeth. Bat goes back and forth, but neither side wants him because he's small and doesn't seem useful. When the birds laugh at Bat, Bear feels bad for him and lets him join the Animals.

The creatures play stickball with two rackets, one held in each hand. The contest goes back and forth until dark, when it seems Crane will score. Then Bat comes onto the field, gets the ball, and darts around. He doesn't need light to see, and no bird can catch him. Bat wins for the Animals.

The illustrations, which consist of collages in brilliant colors, are visually appealing and fresh. Children get a sense of texture because several kinds of paper, many handmade, are used.

Carrick, Donald. **Harald and the Great Stag.** Illus. by author. New
York: Clarion Books, 1988.

This is a beautifully written story about a boy's courage. Carrick's illustrations capture the setting, clothing, and details of the Middle Ages. He also
conveys a strong sense of character through his paintings.

Young Harald has always known the king's hunters, and he's heard since
he was little about the Great Stag. One day he sees the stag and is awed by its
majesty. When he hears that the Baron has declared a hunt for the Great Stag,
Harald is disheartened. An old hunter tells Harald that the animals of the
forest are for the Baron's sport and Harald must accept this. Harald, however,
is determined to help the stag. Harald succeeds in confusing the hunting dogs
and getting them off the stag's trail. When the hunt ends, the old hunter who
had spoken to Harald tells him he did a very brave thing. Harald realizes the
old hunter is really a friend of the stag.

DeSpain, Pleasant. "Rabbit's Last Race," pp. 21-23, in **Thirty-Three
Multicultural Tales to Tell.** Illus. by Joe Shlichta. Little Rock, AK:
August House, 1993.

Frog challenges Rabbit to a race, and Rabbit is sure he'll win. Frog,
however, calls to all the frogs his size, about 400 of them, and asks them to line
up one leap apart. In leapfrog fashion Frog wins, and Rabbit doesn't figure out
that more than one frog was involved.

This story is even more effective if you learn it and tell it.

Hausman, Gerald, comp. and reteller. "How Bat Learned to Fly," pp.
6-10, in **How Chipmunk Got Tiny Feet: Native American
Animal Origin Stories.** Illus. by Ashley Wolff. New York: Harper-
Collins, 1995.

Storyteller Hausman includes an introduction that allows you to read this
tale with some understanding of how and why such stories were first told to
children. This tale is retold from a traditional Koasati Creek folktale. Illustrator Wolff's linoleum block prints painted with rich watercolors and thick black
outlines are stunning.

Youngsters are taken to a time long ago when Mouse was playing football
with his friends. The animals start wondering why Mouse constantly drops the
ball and they offer suggestions on how he can hold the football with his small
hands. Mouse is ready to give up playing when he hears the gentle voice of
Mother Earth tell him he'll be a fine player some day. She tells him to jump as
high as he can when the ball is coming and wrap himself around it. Soon no one
can catch Mouse—he's the best and fastest football player.

Luenn, Nancy. **Nessa's Fish.** Illus. by Neil Waldman. New York:
Atheneum, 1990.

Introduce children to Nessa and her grandmother, Eskimos who live on
the Arctic tundra. The cool watercolors in shades of blue and white are perfect.
The illustrations of life on the tundra are authentic.

Nessa and her grandmother catch enough fish in a frozen lake to feed
everyone in camp. Grandmother doesn't feel well, so young Nessa guards the
fish and bravely protects it from foxes, wolves, and a bear.

Schwartz, David M. **Supergrandpa.** Illus. by Bert Dodson. New York: Lothrop, Lee & Shepard Books, 1991.

The story tells of a determined 66-year-old grandfather who wants to enter the 1,000-mile tour of Sweden but is barred from doing so because of his age. Gustaf decides to enter the race unofficially. While the young riders sleep at night, Gustaf pedals over the Swedish countryside. During the day the young riders pass Gustaf, but during the night he overtakes them again. Crowds gather in town after town to cheer for Gustaf and the children think of him as a hero. On the sixth morning of the race, Gustaf crosses the finish line first. Schwartz' story is based on a real character. Illustrator Bert Dodson uses rich watercolors to convey the Swedish countryside and to capture the expressive faces of the Swedish people.

Seibert, Patricia. **Mush! Across Alaska in the World's Longest Sled-Dog Race.** Illus. by author. Brookfield, CT: Millbrook Press, 1992.

Although this is a nonfiction title about the annual Iditarod dog sled race in Alaska, it is well written and flows nicely as a read aloud. The lovely border art and illustrations add to the text.

Shannon, David. **How Georgie Radbourn Saved Baseball.** Illus. by author. New York: The Blue Sky Press/Scholastic, 1994.

At times this is a dark story, but children do get caught in the tension and conflict. The narrative is fascinating, and it does have an upbeat ending. The paintings are done in acrylics with deep, dark colors.

Young listeners hear that Georgie Radbourn is born in winter because it has remained winter since baseball was declared illegal. Then they are taken back in time to learn how this happened.

A young ballplayer named Boss Swaggert, who was in a slump, was jeered and booed until he vowed never to play baseball again and to someday prevent everyone from playing. Over time Swaggert attains great power until he becomes head of America, convinces people that baseball is bad, outlaws baseball, and replaces the ballfields with factories so everyone can have jobs. Anything that suggests baseball is outlawed, including baseball jargon.

Like everyone else, the Radbourns are happy at first to have money and jobs. When it remains winter always and only Swaggert gets rich, people get tired and sad. The Radbourns have a son, Georgie. They should be happy, but they worry because he has the odd habit of saying forbidden baseball sayings when he means other things. His parents fear that the Factory Police will find out and, ultimately, they do. Georgie is arrested and tried by Swaggert. Georgie proposes they have a contest to settle things. If Georgie can strike Swaggert out on three pitches, he'll be freed and baseball will return. Georgie does win, Swaggert falls in a heap, the sun comes out, and baseball returns.

Van Allsburg, Chris. **Jumanji.** Illus. by author. Boston: Houghton Mifflin, 1981.

Now that there is a movie version of **Jumanji,** I've had the opportunity to talk to children about it and to learn that many of them have never heard or read the book. As is often the case, the screenplay is different from the original story. Don't miss the chance to share the book.

Jumanji is illustrated in Van Allsburg's trademark style. The pencil drawings are rendered in shades of black and white. They are striking and offer a variety of unusual perspectives.

Judy and Peter are quickly bored when their parents leave for the afternoon. They go outside to play and find a board game called Jumanji. A postscript advises to read the directions carefully and a note warns that once the game is started it can't end until one player reaches The Golden City. Peter thinks the game will be boring, but it is far from that. On his first roll Peter lands on "Lion attacks" and a real lion chases Peter. Judy rolls to "Monkeys steal food..." and two mischievous monkeys appear. The game continues with monsoons, a tsetse fly that bites Peter, a herd of rhinoceros that crushes furniture, a menacing python, and a volcanic eruption with lava and steam, until Judy gets out of the jungle to the end of the game. The steam clears, everything is as before, the children quickly put the game where they found it.

When their parents return with guests, the Budwings, Mrs. Budwing talks to Judy and Peter about her two sons, who never read directions or finish what they start. From the window Peter and Judy see the two boys with the Jumanji game in hand. Children can imagine what will happen when the two boys play the game.

Williams, Vera B. **Three Days on a River in a Red Canoe.** Illus. by author. New York: Greenwillow Books, 1981.

Children will gain a good idea of camping and canoeing when you share this story of a young girl who goes on an outdoor adventure with her mother, her Aunt Rosie, and her cousin Sam. The four relatives map the trip and shop for supplies. During the trek they lower the canoe over a waterfall and shower under it; use a pool of water as a sink; learn to tie knots, pitch a tent, tell stories by the fire, fish, paddle through strong currents, sit out a rainstorm, and camp on an island; and almost lose their tent in a wild wind.

The soft full-color illustrations are detailed, fun to look at, and informative, too. There are sidebars with diagrams of knots and instructions on how to put up a tent. Children will also find a recipe for the dumplings and fruit stew the characters eat.

Wisniewski, David. **Rain Player.** Illus. by author. New York: Clarion Books, 1991.

Everyone, including young Pik, hears the prophecy from Ah Kin Mai that there will be a drought for the coming year. Pik speaks badly of Chac, the rain god, is confronted by him, and ultimately challenges Chac in a game of pok-a-tok. The author's note at the end of the book is important. It gives a background of Mayan history and legend, which were the inspiration for this book. Word definitions and pronunciations are provided. You'll learn and can tell your listeners that pok-a-tok was a favorite game of the Maya. It was a fast-paced combination of soccer and basketball played with a solid rubber ball on a walled court. The object was to send the ball through stone rings above the players' heads. Only padded hips, shoulders, and forearms were used. The ball couldn't be touched with hands or feet.

The best two out of three games wins the contest. If Pik wins he'll get Chac's forgiveness and rain. If he loses, he'll become a frog. Pik's father gives him objects entitled to him in a ceremony held early in Pik's life. Pik's father also urges him to seek the advice of Jaguar and the colorful blue bird, Quetzel.

During the contest Chac sends a whirlwind and lightning to help himself, but Pik, with help from Jaguar and Quetzel, wins. Eventually Pik gains renown as the Rain Player.

This exciting and original story is perfectly complemented by the incredible, striking, cut-paper illustrations in brilliant, bright colors. The artwork was inspired by Mayan art and architecture.

Booktalks

Christopher, Matt. **Zero's Slider.** Illus. by Molly Delaney. Boston: Little, Brown, 1994.

Matt Christopher is a reliable author of sports fiction for young readers. He writes about sports from baseball and basketball, to soccer and football and, more recently, has added female characters in main roles. **Zero's Slider,** like many of his shorter, more recent books, can be read to children in grades one and two and read alone by third graders and up.

Zero Ford's pitching isn't going well because, bored with throwing just fastballs and slowballs, he's trying to get fancy and be impressive. When Zero slams his finger in the car door and the finger has to be bandaged, Zero can suddenly throw sliders. Could it be because of the bandage?

Climo, Shirley, reteller. **Atalanta's Race: A Greek Myth.** Illus. by Alexander Koshkin. New York: Clarion Books, 1995.

This is a brilliant and sophisticated telling of one of my favorite Greek myths. The watercolor paintings are striking and fluid and, although the setting has a classical look, the people seem real; you know it's a tale of long ago, but it is approachable.

The Greek King Iasus wants a grandson to inherit the throne. When he orders his daughter, Atalanta, to marry, she gets his permission to marry whom she wants and to choose him however she determines. Atalanta decides that she'll marry whomever can outrun her in a race. Those who lose face beheading. Atalanta is surprised that numerous men want to try anyway. Many men come and fail.

The Greek warrior Melanion, one of the judges of the contest, is the hero and athlete who wants to marry Atalanta. She tries to dissuade him from competing, but he insists. With the assistance of three apples of gold given by Aphrodite, the goddess of love, Melanion manages to win the race. The couple marry, Atalanta loves Melanion, and some time later they have a son.

The couple live a carefree life riding in the hunt and competing in sports. They are too busy to honor the gods or to offer thanks to Aphrodite for her gift of the golden apples. Aphrodite complains to the mother goddess that all the couple care about are the hunt, games, and races. The mother goddess decides that if that is what they want, that is what they'll have. They can race and hunt forever. She turns Atalanta into a lioness and Melanion into a lion.

Fraser, Mary Ann. **On Top of the World: The Conquest of Mount Everest.** Illus. by author. New York: Henry Holt, 1991.

This well-researched, fairly detailed, factual account of the final stages of the conquest of Mount Everest by Sir Edmund Hillary and Tenzing Norkey in 1953 is well worth the read. It will appeal to the upper end of the target age group. The text has all the qualities of good fiction. The language is rich, and there is a constant tension and feel for the challenges and dangers the men faced. Acrylic paintings in shades of blue and white give a sense of the extreme cold. The illustrations capture the drama, the teamwork, and the sheer determination of the men. The author's note provides two pages of historical information.

Hiser, Constance. **Dog on Third Base.** Illus. by Carolyn Ewing. New York: Holiday House, 1991.

Children will enjoy reading this lighthearted, fun, short chapter book with full-page black-and-white ink drawings.

It's spring break and James's friends only want to play baseball. James doesn't want to play because he can't catch or hit. His friends have a meeting, and then T.J. (a female friend) offers James her lucky bat. He uses it, and immediately his hitting improves.

During the vacation the friends have a variety of mishaps. Mrs. Abernathy yells when they hit a ball into her garden, and Mean Mitchell and his scary dog Tiger taunt them. When third base gets lost, James's dog Tag serves as a base until he gets hit by a ball and runs away. The children search for Tag and can't find him, and Mean Mitchell hits a baseball through Mrs. Abernathy's window and tries to blame James. Happily, Tag is found at Mrs. Abernathy's eating chocolate chip cookies, Mrs. Abernathy punishes Mean Mitchell, and the kids find out she's really nice.

The friends also reveal to James that the bat wasn't lucky. They said it was to give James confidence. He really did the batting himself. Now that James can hit, maybe he can learn to catch.

Kherdian, David. **The Great Fishing Contest.** Illus. by Nonny Hogrogian. New York: Philomel, 1991.

The soft, muted, full-page paintings by award-winning illustrator Hogrogian are interspersed throughout this chapter book that second graders and up can read themselves.

The excitement builds when Jason and Sammy, great friends and fishing partners, decide to enter The Great Fishing Contest. The boys check the pond to select the best spot to catch the largest fish. They choose their equipment, practice, review the rules, and decide on a strategy. The boys and girls who enter the contest have two hours in which to catch fish.

Jason catches some small fish. With time running out he takes a risky gamble, gets his hook stuck, and, after a struggle, catches the biggest fish ever.

Kuklin, Susan. **Going to My Ballet Class.** Photos by author. New York: Bradbury Press, 1989.

In a first-person narrative, a young girl named Jami shows and tells in short, concise, interesting text and in full-color photographs what she does in her ballet class that includes boys. This book will particularly appeal to children at the younger end of your target group. Included are information and photos of the students stretching and doing other warm-up exercises, demonstrating the five ballet positions, and practicing cartwheels, pliés, and leaps.

Kuklin, Susan. **Going to My Gymnastics Class.** Photos by author. New York: Bradbury Press, 1991.

One of many of Kuklin's interesting books for young readers, this work includes her sharp, full-color photographs.

In this first-person narrative young Gaspar explains what he does in his beginning gymnastics class. Readers will learn in an entertaining way that the children do a variety of warm-ups, tumbles, tucks, and forward rolls. They do things properly to protect their bodies. The gymnasts do backward rolls, cartwheels, and use a springboard, rings, balance beam, and trampoline.

Levine, Caroline. **The Detective Stars and the Case of the Super Soccer Team.** Illus. by Betsy Lewin. New York: Cobblehill Books/Dutton, 1994.

In this short chapter book with line drawings, readers will meet Veronica and Ernest, owners of the Detective Stars Agency. Mr. Jackson, who coaches the Eagles soccer team, gives them a mystery to solve. He wants to know how the Foxes soccer team is suddenly winning. Mr. Jackson is sure the team is cheating.

Veronica and Ernest watch the Foxes play soccer. The players stumble, kick, bump, and trip each other, yet they score goals. Something is wrong and it's up to the sleuths to collect clues, take pictures, and set a trap for the Foxes.

McMullan, Kate. **The Biggest Mouth in Baseball.** Illus. by Anna DiVito. New York: Grosset & Dunlap, 1993.

This sports story has many endearing qualities. William tries out for The Drills baseball team, sponsored and coached by Dr. Payne, the town dentist—a clever use of names. William's older sister Anna was an outstanding player for the Drills, but the present team isn't playing well. William is constantly telling corny jokes. His jokes help his teammates, but they don't help William when he's at bat or fielding. William loses his concentration. At the end of the season William figures it out: jokes for his teammates, serious playing for him. William doesn't get a home run or win the game for the team at the end of the big game. He's out at home plate but happy that after sliding, his uniform is finally filthy.

The humor continues when the team needs a new sponsor and Ms. Cornblatt, owner of Cornblatt's Canned Corn, offers. She has faith in the players and wants the corny jokes to continue.

Pfeffer, Susan Beth. **Sara Kate, Superkid.** Illus. by Suzanne Hankins. New York: Henry Holt, 1994.

There still aren't enough good sports stories with females as the main characters, but this is one, a short book that children in grades one and up will enjoy. Full-page black-and-white line drawings break up the solid blocks of text.

Sara Kate is leading a normal, ordinary life until one Saturday when her brother, Stevie, grabs her by the arm to make her accompany him while he registers for the basketball-throwing contest being held that night at the high school. The person who throws the ball farthest and makes a basket wins $1,000.

Sara Kate's arm feels tingly and weird. Soon, Sara Kate is amazed at her ability to throw. She can make a basket from across the street. Sara Kate learns from Gran that it's a special power she's inherited, a family trait. She'll have no control over it and it can go at any time.

Gran decides to sign Sara Kate up for the basketball contest. That night while Sara Kate is waiting her turn (she's number 212), her arm feels tingly again. Gran knows the power may go at any time so she has Stevie switch numbers with Sara Kate. Sara Kate throws the ball in from the far door of the gym, but the man in charge disqualifies her. She can't win because in the rules it stated that no one could trade numbers. She had to wait her turn.

Sara Kate knows she broke the rules. Yet, the crowd wants her to win. She's given a gift certificate to the department store, where she buys a teddy bear for herself and a video game for her brother.

Ross, Pat. **M and M and the Haunted House Game.** Illus. by Marilyn Hafner. New York: Puffin Books, 1990.

Children will enjoy meeting Mandy and Mimi, also known as M and M, great friends who on this day decide to play the Haunted House Game. To play, the girls need scary decorations, costumes, frightening noises, a dark house, and someone to scare. M and M do all that, and, then, they hear scary noises that they aren't making. The girls are scared. Readers are quickly reassured when they find out Fred, the handyman, is making the banging noises. He's fixing leaks in the old brick wall.

Ross, Pat. **M and M and the Super Child Afternoon.** Illus. by Marilyn Hafner. New York: Viking Kestrel, 1987.

Children in kindergarten and up will enjoy having this book read to them, while good first and second grade readers can enjoy this book themselves.

M and M (Mimi and Mandy) want to take after-school classes together. After some thought, Mandy decides she'd like to try ballet and Mimi decides to take gymnastics. The girls will sign up for ballet and then gymnastics. After that they'll make a mutual decision on what to take. Ironically, Mimi is a natural at ballet and Mandy has no talent for it. Then Mandy excels at gymnastics and Mimi flops at it. So now, each wants to do what the other originally wanted to do. They still need a solution as to how they can be together at the program.

Stevenson, James. **The Mud Flat Olympics.** Illus. by author. New York: Greenwillow, 1994.

Kindergartners will enjoy listening to this story, whereas first and second grade readers will enjoy this on their own. The book is classic Stevenson, amusing in text and watercolor illustrations.

The animals are holding an Olympics. The Deepest Hole Contest is held first. Moles dig as deep as they can. It seems, however, that the mole who wins is the one who tells the best story. Kevin says he dug to the middle of the earth, but Kimberly says she dug to China.

It's a slow and difficult race in the All-Snail High Hurdles. Finally, Burbank, the judge, goes off; he's so tired of watching. The snails devise a plan to show Burbank how smart they are. When Burbank returns, all the snails are at the finish line, and they declare all of themselves the winners.

The judges don't like the Smelliest Skunk Contest. They have to judge the odor of the skunks. Elderly Mr. Tokay wins again. (The judges' expressions are great: hair on end, eyes bulging.)

In the river-cross freestyle Waldorf the hippo, Hugh the turtle, and Ardsley and Hastings, the elephants, are going to compete when, suddenly, Crocker the crocodile joins the race. Crocker knocks Hugh in the air and tries to disqualify Waldorf. However, Ardsley and Hastings know Waldorf has never won a race, and they blast Crocker down river so Waldorf can win.

Poetry

Prelutsky, Jack. "My Brother Is a Quarterback," pp. 118-19, in **Something BIG Has Been Here.** Illus. by James Stevenson. New York: Greenwillow, 1990.

An amusing poem about an athletic youngster, it is told from the point of view of his nonathlete brother.

Song

Norworth, Jack, lyricist; Albert Von Tilzer, composer; and Randa Kirshbaum, arranger. "Take Me Out to the Ball Game," pp. 296-97, in **From Sea to Shining Sea: A Treasury of American Folklore and Folk Songs.** Comp. by Amy L. Cohn. Illus. by 11 Caldecott Medal and four Caldecott Honor Book artists. New York: Scholastic, 1993.

Many children are familiar with this song and will sing it with enthusiasm. Show the double-page, soft watercolor painting by Marc Simont in which he depicts the spectators, vendors, and ball players.

Demonstration/Participation Activities

Ardley, Neil. "Ramp Racer," pp. 12-13, in **The Science Book of Gravity.** Photos by Pete Gardner. New York: Gulliver Books/Harcourt Brace Jovanovich, 1992.

Children would be interested in watching you demonstrate how to make the ramp. Have one or two other ramps prepared ahead of time and then have the children try the ramp with toy cars you supply.

Cash, Terry, Steve Parker, and Barbara Taylor. "Make a Fishing Game," p. 75, in **175 More Science Experiments to Amuse and Amaze Your Friends.** Illus. by Kuo Kang Chen and Peter Bull. New York: Random House, 1990.

Make the fishing game ahead of time. The materials are few, the directions concise. You may want to make several fishing game "tanks" because only two people can play at a time. During the program the children will enjoy trying to catch the cardboard fish with their fishing poles made of thin sticks with string and small magnets attached. They try to catch the fish that have paper clips attached to their backs.

Day, Alexandra. "A Baseball Lexicon," pp. 304-305, in **From Sea to Shining Sea: A Treasury of American Folklore and Folk**

Songs. Comp. by Amy L. Cohn. Illus. by 11 Caldecott Medal and four Caldecott Honor Book artists. New York: Scholastic, 1993.

Take the list of terms used in baseball and turn it into a guessing game. List the terms on one half of a sheet of posterboard or a chalkboard and on the other half write the definitions for the words. Invite the children to match the words to their definitions. If you prefer, say the terms and have the children guess their meanings. "A Baseball Lexicon" also includes sentences using baseball terms. You can invite the children to translate the sentence using the terms and their definitions.

Fiarotta, Phyllis, and Noel Fiarotta. "Game of Skill," p. 76, and "Bottle Cap Toss Game," p. 152, in **Cups and Cans and Paper Plate Fans: Craft Projects from Recycled Materials.** Photos by Ray Solowinski. New York: Sterling, 1992.

Each youngster needs a paper cup, cord, and rubber washer to make the "Game of Skill." Once they put them together, they can try getting the washer that is attached to the cord into the cup.

You'll need different size bottle caps, cardboard, glue, and dried beans to prepare the easy "Bottle Cap Toss Game." The bottle caps are numbered, and youngsters try to toss the beans into them to score points.

Hilton, Joni. "Play 'Button Billiards'," pp. 112-13, in **Five Minute Miracles: 373 Quick Daily Discoveries for You and Your Kids to Share.** Illus. by Matt Wawiorka. Philadelphia: Running Press, 1992.

Here's another game you'll want to have set up before the program. All you need are eight paper cups taped to the sides of a table so they hang down like pockets on a pool table. During the program invite children to take turns trying to flick buttons across the table and into the cups.

The author offers alternative ways to play the game and a list of other items besides buttons you can use.

Keeshan, Bob, "Captain Kangaroo" and "Sticky Stuff," pp. 150-52, and "Jug Hands," pp. 175-76, in **Family Fun Activity Book.** Illus. by Diane Palmisciano. Minneapolis, MN: Deaconess Press, 1994.

"Sticky Stuff" takes a bit of time to make, but it's worth it. Prepare it beforehand and during the program describe how you made the "Sticky Stuff Dartboard" and the ping-pong ball darts. Then invite the youngsters to throw the "darts" (that have Velcro on them) at the felt dartboard.

Demonstrate how to make "Jug Hands." Have several sets made ahead of time. Show the children how to catch different objects, from rubber balls to stuffed socks.

Milord, Susan. "Puzzle Pieces," pp. 90-91, in **Adventures in Art: Art and Craft Experiences for 7- to 14-Year Olds.** Illus. by author. Charlotte, VT: Williamson, 1990.

You can purchase a traditional Tangram square with its seven pieces, or you can make one or several Tangrams out of cardboard. It's easy to do if you follow Milord's straightforward instructions. During the program, scramble the seven puzzle pieces and invite the children to work in teams to create different figures. The author shows how to make a whale, a sailboat, and a dog out of the puzzle pieces.

Oakley, Ruth. "Ring Taw," pp. 26-27, in **The Marshall Cavendish Illustrated Guide to Games Children Play Around the World: Games with Sticks, Stones, and Shells.** Illus. by Steve Lucas. New York: Marshall Cavendish, 1989.

Many children today have never played with marbles. Recently a colleague offered an after-school program in which she taught children a variety of games using marbles. The response was enthusiastic.

"Ring Taw" is best played outdoors, but you can adapt it to use indoors. Instead of a ring drawn on the ground, you can make a ring out of colored tape or chalk (both can be removed easily afterwards).

Richards, Roy. "A Clothespin Shooter," p. 18, and "A Touch Tester," p. 45, in **101 Science Surprises: Exciting Experiments with Everyday Materials.** Illus. by Alex Pang. New York: Sterling , 1993.

It's easy for young children to make the clothespin shooter. Once they have, set up some cups and let the children shoot pieces of paper into the cups.

Make the touch tester before the program; the directions are easy. During the program put objects in the touch tester and let the children take turns guessing what is inside.

Robson, Denny. "Frisbee," pp. 14-15, in **Kites and Flying Objects.** Rainy Day series. Photos by Roger Vlitos. New York: Gloucester Press, 1992.

Children will enjoy making and flying their frisbees. All you need are paper plates, stickers, paint, and paintbrushes.

Smolen, Wendy. "Freeze Dance," p. 29, in **Playing Together: 101 Terrific Games and Activities That Children Ages 3-9 Can Do Together.** Illus. by Jill Weber. New York: Fireside Book/Simon & Schuster, 1995.

A wide age range will enjoy this game in which the children dance until the music stops. At that point they must freeze in position.

Warner, Penny. **Kids' Party Games and Activities: Hundreds of Exciting Things to Do at Parties for Kids 2-12.** Illus. by Kathy Rogers. Deephaven, MN: Meadowbrook Press, 1993.

In "Sense-Sational," pp. 28-29, children identify items by touch and smell. The preparation time is minimal; the game is easy to play. Warner offers many suggestions of items to include.

"Charades," pp. 148-49, is a traditional game. Here, the author explains how to play this game with a group of children.

"Puzzle Bags," pp. 166-67, is an extremely clever game. You'll prepare one or several bags by gathering items relating to a theme. During the program, give the children time to guess what the items have in common. Again, Warner offers other ways to play the game.

Chapter 7

How-and-Why Stories

A few of the how-and-why stories described in this chapter are also found in the chapters "Birds," "Cooks and Cookery," and "Games and Sports." Unlike the annotations found in those chapters, the citations for these books in this chapter emphasize what makes each title a how-and-why story.

Many Native American tales are how-and-why stories. I have only included a few here to avoid excessive duplication. Check for how-and-why stories that come to us from Native American folklore in the chapter "Native American Tales."

Read Alouds

Aardema, Verna. **How the Ostrich Got Its Long Neck.** Illus. by Marcia Brown. New York: Scholastic, 1995.

Children are taken to a time long ago when Ostrich had a short neck that made it difficult for him to gather food. He takes pity on Crocodile and puts his head in the creature's mouth to check for his sore tooth. In hunger, Crocodile clamps his jaws on Ostrich's head and a tug of war starts between the two. Ostrich finally escapes, but now he senses something wrong. The ground seems further away, but he can reach it easily. He realizes his neck is now long, and he is delighted. Ostrich does, however, stay in the bush, far from the river. Since then, no ostrich has trusted a crocodile.

Aardema, Verna, reteller. "Leelee Goro," a Temne Tale from Sierra Leone, pp. 1-6, in **Misoso: Once upon a Time Tales from Africa.** Illus. by Reynold Ruffins. New York: An Apple Soup Book/Alfred A. Knopf, 1994.

You can't help but want to tell this tale aloud. A glossary with a pronunciation key is included to assist you.

In this story children will hear the origin of eight phenomena in nature. Long ago at the beginning of earth rain falls on the first night and puts out the fires. The animals are tired and cold, and when they see smoke rising from a hut on a hillside Lion sends Antelope to get the fire.

The woman of the house tells Antelope he'll have to fight her daughter Leelee Goro for the fire. Leelee Goro swings Antelope into the air. He falls with mouth open into sand that makes him cough. Antelope has coughed ever since. Leopard is sent and tossed, and when he falls blood splatters; to this day he has a spotted coat. Elephant is sent, but he too is thrown. When he falls he hits his two front teeth; they swell and forevermore elephants have two long tusks. The fourth to visit the hut is Spider, who has two hands and two feet. When spider is flung, he falls and has eight feet. Conk offers to try, the animals laugh, and Lion whacks Conk for his foolishness. To this day all conks have the mark of that hit on their backs. Conk, however, puts spit on his fighting spot to make it slippery and travels to the hut. During the fight Leelee Goro slips on the spit, falls, and Conk throws her. Leelee Goro's mother can't see her and cries, bringing crying into the world. Leelee Goro cries, and her mother hugs her, bringing hugging into the world to stop crying. Conk brings fire to the animals, who can now cook and eat.

Aardema, Verna, reteller. **Princess Gorilla and a New Kind of Water.** Illus. by Victoria Chess. New York: Dial Books for Young Readers, 1988.

In this clever tale, complemented with playful, light illustrations in which each animal has its own personality, readers find out why talapoin monkeys now live in treetops.

In a jungle in Africa a gorilla king decides it's time for him to select a strong and brave husband for his daughter. She wants to marry someone who loves her, like the gorilla with whom she plays tag.

King Gorilla stumbles upon a barrel full of vinegar. When he tastes it and it burns his throat, he thinks he's found a new type of water. He devises a test: whoever can drink this barrel of "water" will marry his daughter.

Many animals try and fail. Then the talapoin monkey says he can do it. He cheats and enlists the aid of 100 monkeys who each take a sip. When all 100 monkeys appear and demand to marry the princess, Leopard calls them cheaters and bats them until they scatter into nearby trees. Since then that's where they have lived. And ever since, the monkeys travel in large groups because they remember what they accomplished together.

Bowden, Joan Chase. **Why the Tides Ebb and Flow.** Illus. by Marc Brown. Boston: Houghton Mifflin, 1979.

A stubborn woman wants a hut to live in, but Sky Spirit is always too busy to give her a home. One day when the woman asks for a rock for her abode, Sky Spirit answers "yes" without thought. The woman quickly sails on the ocean in her stewpot and, despite Sky Spirit's pleas, takes the rock in the hole at the bottom of the sea. The water immediately swirls and pours into the bottomless pit. Neither dog's nose, young maiden's knees, nor young man's backside can block the hole. Sky Spirit says that if the woman returns the rock, she can borrow it twice each day forever. She agrees and that is why there is low tide and high tide every day.

The rich text is complemented by Brown's artwork done in black and white on yellow.

Bruchac, Joseph. "Chipmunk and Bear," pp. 53-56, in **The Boy Who Lived with the Bears: And Other Iroquois Stories.** Illus. by Murv Jacob. New York: HarperCollins, 1995.

Long ago when animals could talk, Bear boasts that he is the biggest and strongest animal. Bear feels he can do anything he wants or bid anyone to do what he tells them. Chipmunk says Bear should be able to tell the sun not to come up in the morning. Bear is sure he can do that.

All night Bear chants for the sun not to come up, and Chipmunk sings that the sun will rise. The sun, of course, rises. Chipmunk laughs and calls Bear a fool. Bear snatches Chipmunk in his paw, but Chipmunk thinks quickly, praises bear, and, when Bear releases his hold a bit, Chipmunk dives for his hole. Before Chipmunk reaches safety, Bear scrapes his claws down Chipmunk's back.

Chipmunk remains in his hole for the winter to allow his back to heal. When he emerges in the spring, Chipmunk has stripes on his back. To this day Chipmunk has a striped back.

Bruchac, Joseph, reteller. **The Great Ball Game: A Muskogee Story.**
Illus. by Susan L. Roth. New York: Dial Books for Young Readers,
1994.

The Birds and Animals decide to settle an argument by playing a game.
The first side to score a goal wins. Bat, however, doesn't know which side he
should play on, and neither side wants him. Finally, Bear feels bad for Bat and
lets him join the Animals. This proves to be a wise decision because Bat wins
the game.

As a result, Bat is accepted as an Animal, and he is chosen to set the
penalty for the Birds. Bat decides the Birds must leave the land for half of each
year. According to this tale, that's why birds fly south each winter. Because Bat
won the game due to his ability to see in the dark, that's also why every day at
dusk Bat still comes flying to see if the Animals need him to play ball.

This fast-paced "pourquoi" tale is complemented by visually appealing
and refreshing illustrations that consist of brilliantly colored collages.

Bruchac, Joseph. "How the Birds Got Their Feathers," pp. 34-39, in **The
Boy Who Lived with the Bears: And Other Iroquois Stories.**
Illus. by Murv Jacob. New York: HarperCollins, 1995.

This story takes children to a time long ago when the birds had no feathers
and were hot in the summer, cold in the winter. In a dream the Creator tells
the birds they can send one bird to the Skyland to bring back clothing for the
birds. Buzzard is chosen as messenger and after traveling far, he is hungry and
eats some rotten fish. He continues so high the sun burns the top of his head.
When he arrives at Skyland, Buzzard is given first choice of clothing for his
bravery and determination.

Buzzard looks at the suits of clothing made of beautiful feathers. The
Creator tells him that any suit will fit him. If Buzzard doesn't like the outfit,
he can take it off and another bird will receive it. The Creator warns that once
buzzard tries and takes off a suit, it can't be his. Buzzard is very choosy. He
tries on suit after suit and finds something wrong with each until only one suit
remains. It fits tightly, it doesn't cover his legs, its feathers are brown and dirty,
and it doesn't cover his bald, red, sunburned head. Buzzard doesn't like the suit
but it's the last one, so he must wear it and has ever since.

Bryan, Ashley. **The Story of Lightning and Thunder.** Illus. by
author. New York: Atheneum, 1993.

Striking, colorful, thickly outlined illustrations that have a primitive look
and feel mesh with this solid retelling of a West African tale.

Long ago Thunder was a mother sheep and her son Lightning a ram. They
lived on the west coast of Africa, and there they helped call for rain when it was
needed. Mother and son were honored because it was their calling of rain that
often saved the crops.

Their status changed when, at a celebration, Ram Lightning couldn't see
over the crowd and he used his head to butt people and send them flying. The
king scolded them, and they were sent to live at the edge of town. Soon, at the
village market, Ram got in trouble when he started eating the straw maker's
hats and baskets and then fought with the straw maker. The king moved Ram
and his mother to the center of the forest. Once again Ram got into trouble. He
tried to stop an Ox from eating the farmer's crop. Ox, however, threatened to

fight back and Ram ran. Ram raced so quickly he created sparks that caught the dry leaves on fire. The flames destroyed the farmer's crop. Ma Sheep called the rain, but it was not enough. The king declared that the people no longer feel safe with Ma Sheep and Ram living on earth so their home will be in the sky.

Every now and then Ram Lightning gets away from home, causes trouble, and strikes things on earth. Ma Sheep Thunder runs after him and we hear her rumbling voice calling Ram to return.

DeSpain, Pleasant. "How the Mosquitoes Left Kambara," pp. 53-55, in **Thirty-Three Multicultural Tales to Tell.** Illus. by Joe Shlichta. Little Rock, AK: August House, 1993.

Share this short, satisfying tale from Fiji. In it a prince visits the island of Kambara and finds the buzz of mosquitoes soothing. The prince decides to take them back home to Oneata with him. The island people trap the mosquitoes and exchange them with the prince for a magic shell that makes fish swim to shore and allow themselves to be caught.

Dixon, Ann, reteller. **How Raven Brought Light to People.** Illus. by James Watts. New York: Margaret K. McElderry Books/Macmillan, 1992.

In this tale from the Tlingit Indians of Alaska, children hear how Raven used magic to gain entrance to the house of the great chief who held the light of the world in three wooden boxes. Raven turns himself into a child, is born to the chief's daughter, and is able to release the sun, moon, and stars through the smoke-hole in the chief's home. When he turns himself from a child into Raven and flies up to the smoke-hole to escape, the chief realizes how he's been tricked. The chief casts a spell to shrink the smoke-hole shut. Raven rubs against the sooty smoke-hole, pushes, and ekes through. The soot turns him from blue to totally black. Since then, all ravens are black. Also, since then, the sun, moon, and stars shine on the people who live on earth.

Forest, Heather, reteller. "The Magic Mill," pp. 21-24, in **Wonder Tales from Around the World.** Illus. by David Boston. Little Rock, AK: August House, 1995.

This is one of the many variants of the Norwegian folktale also known as "Why the Sea Is Salt." It's written in the finest oral tradition and is most effective when you memorize it and tell it to your audience.

As in other versions, an old man rewards a younger brother for sharing his meager meal with him by telling him how to get a Magic Mill. The man teaches the younger brother how to use the mill, and it isn't long before the fellow's greedy older brother offers to buy the mill. The younger brother sells it to him, but only tells him how to start it. Later, when the older brother can't get the mill to stop making porridge and he and his wife are almost drowning in it, the younger brother tells him how to stop the mill for another 300 gold pieces and the return of the mill.

Time passes and now the younger brother lives in a huge house on the harbor. A sea captain visits and wants to know if the mill can make salt. He needs salt to preserve the fish he catches until he gets them to market. The brother refuses to sell the mill, but during the night the sea captain steals the mill and sets sail.

When his nets are full of codfish, he puts the mill to work. Because the captain doesn't know how to stop the mill, the salt flows and makes the boat heavy until it sinks. It is said that to this day the Magic Mill is still grinding salt.

French, Vivian. **Why the Sea Is Salt.** Illus. by Patrice Aggs. Cambridge, MA: Candlewick Press, 1993.

Youngsters enjoy author French's clever, fresh retelling of this classic Norwegian folktale. The story is long, but it moves swiftly. Delicate, expressive, crisp watercolor and pen line illustrations that capture the swift action are interspersed throughout the text.

Young Matilda lives with her mother and 16 siblings. They are poor, so Christmas will be bleak. Their wealthy uncle gives young Matilda only a bottle of water and some dried bacon. On the way home when Matilda shares her meager food with a dusty old man he tells her to go to the darkest wood and ask for the churn behind the door. Matilda has a strange, scary encounter with a voice and a shadow, but she secures the churn. Soon she learns how to use it carefully and what to say to make it start and stop. The churn provides whatever Matilda and her family want and they have a happy holiday.

The wealthy, greedy uncle visits and declares that since he gave Matilda the food she shared, the churn belongs to him, and he takes it. At his home he asks for porridge and fish, but he doesn't know how to make the churn stop and the porridge takes over his house.

The uncle asks Matilda for help. She assists him in return for the churn. All Matilda's family can smell is fish, so they move and live by the sea. There, one day a tall man appears, crying because he has nothing. Kind Matilda gives him the churn. The man is really Matilda's uncle.

Matilda's uncle is traveling on a ship and gloating about the riches that can be his. Hungry, he begins to eat his meal, decides it needs more salt, and demands the churn produce salt. He still doesn't know how to stop the churn. The boat gets heavier until it, the crew, and the uncle sink to the bottom of the sea, where the churn cranks out salt to this day.

Gerson, Mary-Joan. **Why the Sky Is Far Away: A Nigerian Folktale.** Illus. by Carla Golembe. Boston: Little, Brown, 1992.

Original, bold illustrations rendered in collage and oil pastels blend well in this fresh folktale. It is said that long ago the sky was so close to the earth that when people were hungry, they reached up, took a piece of sky, and ate it. Eventually, after giving the people several chances not to be greedy, the sky decides that the people are wasteful and do not treat the sky with respect. It decides to go far away. The sky tells the people that they will have to plow the land, gather crops, and hunt. Maybe if they have to work for their food they'll learn not to waste the gifts that nature gives them. From then on people have grown their own food and the sky has stayed distant.

Hausman, Gerald, compiler and reteller. "How Bat Learned to Fly," pp. 6-10, in **How Chipmunk Got Tiny Feet: Native American Animal Origin Stories.** Illus. by Ashley Wolff. New York: HarperCollins, 1995.

Retold from a Koasati Creek folktale, this story is stunningly illustrated with linoleum block prints painted with rich watercolors.

Long ago Mouse's friends offered suggestions on how he could hold the football with his small hands when he played with them. The animals felt bad that he constantly dropped the ball. Mother Earth encouraged Mouse, told him he'll be a fine player, and offered some suggestions.

The next time Mouse played football he leapt high in the air, the ball went into his belly, he wrapped his body around it, and he went flying through the air. No one could catch him. In this way Mouse became the best football player.

One day Mouse jumped up and flew over the ball. He went so high in the sky, he never came down. Mouse soared through the air and laughed at his ability to fly. Mother Earth then told Mouse that he can fly because he is not a Mouse. He will be called Bat, and he has been called Bat ever since.

Hayes, Joe. "One Day, One Night," pp. 104-106, in **Best Loved Stories Told at the National Storytelling Festival.** Selected by the National Association for the Preservation and Perpetuation of Storytelling. Jonesborough, TN: National Storytelling Press, 1991.

Learn and tell this funny, clever, and fast-paced story in which children learn how we came to have regular days and nights. At the beginning of time it was sometimes dark for ten years and light for one day, or dark for eight years and light for one day. Many of the animals complained to the sun. Others were happy with the arrangement. Sun asked for one speaker from each group and whichever animal could say what he wanted the longest, that's the way things would be. Bear and Frog were selected to speak. Whereas Bear's voice eventually got hoarse, Frog endlessly repeated his request for one day, one night.

Johnston, Tony. **The Tale of Rabbit and Coyote.** Illus. by Tomie dePaola. New York: G. P. Putnam's Sons, 1994.

When Tony Johnston and Tomie dePaola create a book together, you know it will be a hit. DePaola's illustrations in vibrant watercolors (golds, blues, and reds of the Southwest) suggest the Mexican countryside where this legend from the Zapotec Indians originated. Johnston's telling is rich with sly humor and mischief. The author includes a glossary of Spanish expressions and a pronunciation key.

Rabbit angers the farmer when he starts eating his field of chiles. The farmer catches Rabbit and decides to cook him. Poor Coyote comes along and Rabbit tricks Coyote into taking his place. Soon Coyote finds himself in a pot of hot water. He jumps out and chases Rabbit, but Rabbit outwits him again. Several times Rabbit outwits Coyote, mistreats him, and puts him in awful situations, including one where Coyote is stung by wasps. Rabbit's final trick is to point to the moon's reflection in the water and tell Coyote he can share this cheese with him. Rabbit tells Coyote he'll have to drink all the water to get the cheese. Coyote drinks so much that when Rabbit runs away, he's too heavy to chase him. Rabbit climbs a ladder to the moon, then hides the ladder.

Even today Coyote gazes at the moon. Now and then he howls at it because he's still very angry with Rabbit.

Maddern, Eric. **Rainbow Bird: An Aboriginal Folktale from Northern Australia.** Illus. by Adrienne Kennaway. Boston: Little, Brown, 1993.

This short folktale has wide appeal and a certain sophistication. Large-scale, dramatic, brilliant watercolors add to the text.

This book takes readers to a time when the world is almost new, and mean, scary Crocodile Man is the only one who had Fire. When the other animals beg for it, Crocodile Man laughs and frightens them. Time passes, and Bird Woman, who lives in a nearby tree, pleads with Crocodile Man for fire. She's tired of living in darkness, being cold at night, and eating raw food. Crocodile Man refuses to share. Bird Woman watches and waits, and one afternoon when Crocodile Man has a long yawn, Bird Woman flies down, snatches the firesticks, and gives Fire to the people by putting some into the heart of every tree.

From that day people have been able to make fire using dry sticks and logs from trees. Since then people cook food, stay warm at night, and light up the darkness.

Bird Woman was pleased that she could help people. She danced and put the firesticks into her tail, so becoming the beautiful Rainbow Bird.

Moore, Robin. "How the Turtle Cracked His Shell," A Cherokee Story, pp. 142-45, in **Ready-to-Tell Tales: Sure-Fire Stories from America's Favorite Storytellers.** Ed. by David Holt and Bill Mooney. Little Rock, AK: August House, 1994.

Long ago Turtle and Possum spent their days working and playing together. One day while Possum is throwing persimmons down to Turtle to eat, Wolf comes along and takes the fruit. Turtle tells Possum to throw the biggest persimmon to Wolf, who chokes. Turtle and Possum leave, and the other wolves rescue Wolf. Humiliated, Wolf, with the help of the other wolves, catches Turtle. Turtle keeps his wits about him and tricks the wolves into throwing him into the river. Since the wolves don't know turtles are good swimmers, they throw him in. Turtle does get away, but he hits a big rock in the center of the river first. His beautiful shell was and remains cracked in 13 tiny pieces.

Hints for telling this short, funny, clever tale are included.

Olson, Arielle North. **Noah's Cat and the Devil's Fire.** Illus. by Barry Moser. New York: Orchard Books, 1992.

When Noah refuses to let the devil on the ark right before the flood, the devil turns himself into a mouse and sneaks onto the ark under the lion's mane. Once the flood starts, the devil-mouse tries to cause trouble on the ark by awakening the animals, swimming in Noah's washbowl, and scattering grain. Nothing bothers Noah, so the devil decides to chew a hole in the ark so it and everything on it will sink. The devil causes his own undoing when he enlists the help of the two mice who are watching him. Since Noah let the animals on the ark two by two, he realizes the problem when he sees three mice, and he goes after the devil-mouse. The cats go after the creature, too. One cat gobbles him, but the heat of the mouse makes the cat spit him out. The devil turns himself into a viper fish and swims away.

Noah's cats saved the ark and the animals, but the cat who pounced on the devil-mouse is changed. The cat's fur makes sparks when Noah pets her and her eyes gleam in the dark. Since then all cats act that way. Maybe the devil left a little fire inside the cat.

The tale builds well and the author's language is meaty, the words descriptive. Barry Moser's paintings are captivating and powerful. He uses deep, dark colors and reveals many things in shadow.

Pellowski, Ann. "Why Some Reeds Are Hollow," pp. 45-46, in **Hidden Stories in Plants: Unusual and Easy-to-Tell Stories from Around the World, Together with Creative Things to Do While Telling Them.** Illus. by Lynn Sweat. New York: Macmillan, 1990.

You might like to memorize and tell (rather than read) this short, unusual, and unique Thai (Buddhist) myth.

When the Monkey King realizes that an ogre lives in the pool of water he and his followers rely on, and that anyone who goes near the pool for a drink disappears, the king thinks of a plan so the monkeys can get the fresh water they need to live.

The Monkey King takes tall reeds from near the pond, recites a prayer, and blows into the reed stalk. The reed becomes hollow. Now he and the other monkeys can extend the reed while they are far from the water, have it reach the water, and drink without the ogre being able to catch them.

Since then, many reeds have been hollow and can be used as drinking straws.

Ross, Gayle, reteller. **How Turtle's Back Was Cracked: A Traditional Cherokee Tale.** Illus. by Murv Jacob. New York: Dial Books for Young Readers/Penguin Books, 1995.

Gayle Ross, a Cherokee storyteller, draws children into this popular tale immediately. Award-winning artist Murv Jacob captivates youngsters with his brightly colored, richly patterned artwork in acrylics on watercolor paper. His illustrations are stylized yet expressive. He captures the animals' personalities well—Turtle so full of himself but appealing, the wolves threatening. Jacob lends a feel for the ancient world, for its beauty and sense of wonder.

Possum and Turtle are best friends who play and work well together. One day when Possum is high in a tree picking persimmons and dropping them down into Turtle's mouth, Wolf comes, leaps, and snatches the persimmons. Turtle doesn't see this because he closes his eyes when he opens his mouth. Turtle does know that he isn't getting persimmons and he's angry. Possum sees what Wolf is doing and throws a huge persimmon down that sticks in Wolf's throat and chokes him.

Turtle opens his eyes, sees dead Wolf, and within minutes convinces himself that he felled the wolf. He feels entitled to take a "tribute" from the animal. It's a custom that allows him to capture a piece of the animal's spirit. Turtle takes Wolf's ears and makes wolf-ear spoons with them.

Turtle knows it's the custom for people to offer visitors food, so he visits everyone he knows and even strangers to have an excuse to show off his wolf-ear spoons. In this way, the other wolves find out. Angry, they capture Turtle, but they can't decide what to do with him. Turtle keeps his wits and finally convinces the wolves to throw him in the river. That should be fine because Turtle can swim, but Turtle is thrown so hard he hits his back on a rock in the middle of the river, and his beautiful shell cracks into 12 pieces. Turtle uses healing plants to repair his shell, but today, if you look closely, you'll see the lines where Turtle's back cracked.

Tan, Amy. **The Chinese Siamese Cat.** Illus. by Gretchen Schields. New York: Macmillan, 1994.

This appealing, original, clever tale is eye-catching with its detailed, colorful paintings that sprawl over the pages and include stunning borders.

Long ago Sagwa was one of three white kittens born to Mama Miao and Baba Miao. They lived in the house of the Foolish Magistrate, who issued absurd and hurtful rules. Sagwa, who always gets into trouble, is watching his parents write the rules for the magistrate. They have black tails because the magistrate makes them write the rules with their tails in black ink that doesn't wash off. Sagwa is watching from a high shelf. The rule of the day is that the people cannot sing while they work. Sagwa's parents also have to write the names of everyone who broke the rule—even though the people don't know what the rule is yet.

Sagwa leaps and lands in the ink-pot. The ink coats her face and ears, making them brown-black. Sagwa wipes her nose against a piece of paper below her paws. It's the scroll of rules and Sagwa has blotted the word "not" so the rule reads that people must sing during the day. Sagwa dips her tail in the ink to add an exclamation point to the rule, and she dips her paws in the ink and dances over the names of the people who were to be fined.

Sagwa is pleased, but seeing her changed appearance in a mirror, she is scared that the magistrate will find out what she did. She'll be punished along with her family.

The Reader of Rules proclaims the rule aloud in the town square. The rule makes everyone happy. Immediately everyone starts to sing. The Magistrate is furious until he hears many of the songs are in praise of him, and he is happy.

When the Magistrate lifts Sagwa she is frightened, as is Sagwa's family. The Magistrate surprises them by issuing new and fair rules. He declares that all Chinese cats will have dark faces, paws, tails, and ears to honor Sagwa of China.

Wolkstein, Diane, collector. "Bye-Bye," illus. by Donald Crews, p. 367, in **From Sea to Shining Sea: A Treasury of American Folklore and Folk Songs.** Comp. by Amy L. Cohn. Illus. by 11 Caldecott Medal and four Caldecott Honor Book artists. New York: Scholastic, 1993.

Diane Wolkstein first heard this short but amusing tale in Haiti from a girl named Michelle.

The birds are flying from Haiti to New York, but Turtle can't go because he has no wings. Pigeon feels sorry for turtle and offers to hold a piece of wood in his mouth while Turtle holds the other end in his mouth so he can come, too.

Flying near an ocean, Turtle sees animals on shore waving good-bye to the birds. The animals see Turtle, and he is so happy to hear everyone talking about him that he says the one English word he knows, "Bye-bye!" When Turtle opens his mouth he falls into the sea. That's why there are many pigeons in New York, but Turtle still remains in Haiti.

Donald Crews's sprightly watercolors offer four views of turtle as he falls. The illustrations look like time-lapse views.

Xiong, Blia. **Nine-in-One, Grr! Grr! A Folktale from the Hmong People of Laos.** Adapted by Cathy Spagnoli. Illus. by Nancy Hom. San Francisco: Children's Book Press, 1989.

Long ago, the first female tiger wanted to know how many cubs she would have. When she visits the god Shao, who lives in the sky, he tells her she'll have nine cubs each year if she remembers what he has told her. Tiger composes a song, the title of this tale, so she won't forget how many cubs she'll have. The Eu bird, a blackbird, hears the song and asks Shao what it means. When Shao explains, the bird says this will be terrible because there will be too many tigers and they'll eat the other animals. Shao, however, can't take back his word. As long as Tiger remembers the number that's how many cubs she'll have. Bird decides to distract Tiger, make her forget her song, and then tell her the tune is "One-in-Nine." Tiger then believes she'll have one cub every nine years. That is how the Hmong people of Laos explain why there aren't too many tigers on earth today.

Not only will this lovely story appeal to children, but they'll be fascinated by the full-page, clean, clear, bold illustrations in solid blocks of color that were created with silkscreen, watercolor, and colored pencil.

Demonstration/Participation Activities

Breckenridge, Judy. "I Think I'll Eat Worms," pp. 50-51, in **Simple Physics Experiments with Everyday Materials.** Illus. by Frances Zweifel. New York: Sterling, 1993.

Children will find it fascinating when you use some cooked spaghetti, water, vinegar, and baking soda to make spaghetti dance. After you dazzle the group, tell them why the spaghetti rose and fell. A clear explanation is included in the book.

Cobb, Vicki, and Kathy Darling. **Wanna Bet? Science Challenges to Fool You.** Illus. by Meredith Johnson. New York: Lothrop, Lee & Shepard, 1993.

These three quick demonstrations require few materials and little time to do: "A Light Snack," p. 38; "Raw Power," p. 43; and "Egg Beater," p. 78. Clear explanations are included for why each phenomena happens. If time allows, invite the children to try the activities.

Lewis, James. "Stick Together," pp. 38-39, in **Measure, Pour and Mix Kitchen Science Tricks.** Illus. by Steve McInturff. Deephaven, MN: Meadowbrook Press, 1990.

The author challenges children to pick up one ice cube with another ice cube. Few materials are needed, clear instructions with accompanying illustrations are provided, and a short, clear explanation is given for why this trick works. Set up several stations with the materials for this activity and let the children try it.

Chapter 8

Japanese Tales

Read Alouds

Baker, Keith. **The Magic Fan.** Illus. by author. New York: Harcourt
   Brace Jovanovich, 1989.

   Children are awed by this beautiful, sensitive tale of magic set in Japan.
A young boy named Yoshi lives in a village by the sea. He enjoys building things
the people need, but the day comes when Yoshi desires to build what he has
never made, things that reach beyond his village. He sees a fan floating toward
him in the water and takes it. When he opens it he sees a boat with a golden
sail. Yoshi decides the fan is magic, that it has shown him what to build, and
so he creates such a boat. Yoshi wonders what he could build that would be as
high as the clouds. Again, the answer is in the fan—a huge kite. Later when he
wonders what he could build that would stretch across the sky like a rainbow,
he looks at the fan and sees a bridge arching over the village. Yoshi builds the
bridge.

   The villagers, however, are angry. They didn't need the boat or the kite,
and the bridge blocks the sun. Yoshi wonders why the fan showed him the
bridge. He is about to destroy it when he feels the bridge shaking. Yoshi opens
the fan and sees Namazu, the earthquake fish. Then, a tsunami, a huge wave,
rises and rushes to the village. Yoshi warns the people and hurries them onto
the high bridge. Everything is destroyed in the village. The fan is gone, too, but
Yoshi still sees clearly. They can rebuild everything. Yoshi realizes, too, that
the magic is his own.

   This special story is appropriately accompanied by illustrations painted
within a fan shape. The artwork is breathtaking, with true, rich colors, and the
artist effectively mixes a sense of reality and fantasy.

Compton, Patricia A., reteller. **The Terrible EEK.** Illus. by Sheila
   Hamanaka. New York: Simon & Schuster Books for Young Readers, 1991.

   Expressive, bold, and dynamic oil paintings complement this amusing
tale of mishaps and misunderstandings.

   Long ago it rained on a small house in Japan. Inside, a boy and his father
talk of their fears. The father says that among people, he's most afraid of a
robber. A thief, who is on the roof, hears this and is glad. The father reveals
that among animals he fears wolves. A wolf is sneaking around intent on
stealing a chicken, hears the father's comment, and is happy. Then the father
says the most frightening thing of all is a terrible leak. When the wolf hears
this, he thinks a leak must be an awful creature. Because the wind is howling
the thief mistakenly hears "eek" for leak and wonders what this eek is. The
robber slips, falls on the back of the wolf, and thinks he landed on the eek. The
wolf, thinking the terrible leak has landed on him, runs toward the woods
hoping the leak will fall. That's when things get interesting.

Hamanaka, Sheila, reteller. **Screen of Frogs: An Old Tale.** Illus. by
   author. New York: Orchard Books, 1993.

   This subtle and wise tale is complemented by bold, visually appealing
illustrations.

Long ago in Japan a wealthy and lazy boy named Koji grew into a lazy man. When his parents die he doesn't work. He sells the property and possessions he inherited to get money. Koji is finally left with only one house, mountain, and lake.

A giant frog beseeches Koji not to sell the mountain for if he does it will set off a disastrous chain of events that will affect many animals.

Koji is troubled by the picture of doom painted by the frog. He pays his debts by selling his few possessions and is left with a futon to sleep on and a blank folding screen. Koji, however, sleeps happily because he spared the frogs and other creatures.

In the middle of the night Koji hears frogs. He sees hundreds of wet frog prints on the floor, follows them, and sees his once blank screen covered with pictures of frogs.

Word of this sight spreads and although many want to buy the screen, Koji refuses. He starts working hard and learns much from the peasants. Koji marries, has a family, and with them works the fields. Years later when Koji dies the screen of frogs fades and becomes blank. Koji's family keeps the land for generations and the frogs remain.

Johnston, Tony. **The Badger and the Magic Fan.** Illus. by Tomie dePaola. New York: G. P. Putnam's Sons, 1990.

Here's another satisfying and entertaining book by this perfect author-illustrator combination. It's a sprightly tale of mischief and magic with sparkling, colorful, playful paintings.

Three little tengu or goblin children are playing with a magic fan that can make noses larger and smaller. Badger tricks the tengu and steals the fan. Then Badger sees a beautiful girl with a rich father, sneaks up, and fans her nose. No one in Japan can make her nose smaller—not doctors or witches. The rich father promises his daughter in marriage and half his riches to anyone who can make her nose short.

Badger comes, uses the fan and marries the daughter. After the wedding feast, while Badger is sleeping, the tengu find him and use the magic fan on Badger. His nose grows to heaven where the heavenly workers are building a bridge across the sky. They think Badger's nose is a pole and yank it and him into the sky. Badger is never seen again, and the tengu children keep the magic fan.

Kalman, Maira. **Sayonara, Mrs. Kackleman.** Illus. by author. New York: Viking Kestrel, 1989.

Wacky, almost surrealistic, illustrations accompany this unusual, fast-paced, amusing story that imparts a sense of life in contemporary Japan.

Alexander and his sister Lulu travel to Japan after seeing the opera, "The Mikado." Once the pair arrive there, young listeners and readers are drawn into the mood and flavor of Japan. They'll learn some of the language and what the Japanese alphabet looks like. With Alexander and Lulu they'll see narrow streets and people on bicycles. Other images include futons on the floor; school children in uniforms; hot wet white towels used to wipe hands in a restaurant; rock gardens; a fish market with sushi on display; a temple where people put wishes on paper and tie them to a tree; an outdoor bath in steamy water at the top of a mountain; a ride on the Bullet Train; and a night at a Nóh play.

Kroll, Virginia. **Pink Paper Swans.** Illus. by Nancy L. Clouse. Grand
Rapids, MI: William B. Eerdmans, 1994.

The artwork in this book, full-color cut-paper collages, is striking and
clean, simple looking but full of feeling. The illustrations perfectly complement
this contemporary tale of friendship in which a Japanese woman hands down
the traditional art of origami to a young girl.

Janetta spends almost her entire summer outside watching her neighbor
Mrs. Tsujimoto make things out of squares of colored paper. The day before
school begins, Janetta approaches Mrs. Tsujimoto and finds out that the art is
origami. Mrs. Tsujimoto sells it in stores.

During the school year Janetta treasures the pink paper swan Mrs.
Tsujimoto gave her. When summer returns Mrs. Tsujimoto doesn't come outside, so Janetta goes to her apartment. She learns that Mrs. Tsujimoto has
arthritis and it is too painful for her to do origami. That is how Janetta becomes
Mrs. Tsujimoto's fingers. Mrs. Tsujimoto shares her knowledge, and Janetta
slowly learns how to make the origami figures that they then sell together.

The book includes two pages of detailed, clear instructions to make a pink
paper swan like the one in the story.

Levine, Arthur A., reteller. **The Boy Who Drew Cats: A Japanese
Folktale.** Illus. by Frédéric Clément. New York: Dial Books for
Young Readers, 1993.

As in many Japanese folktales, the story is set in a time long ago. In this
story a mother worries about her frail younger son, Kenji, who will never be
able to work the farm but who can draw beautiful pictures in the earth that is
always dry.

Kenji's mother takes him to a monastery where the kindly young priest
Takada likes him and loves his drawings, especially those of cats. The older
priest Yoshida wants Kenji to work only, and when he draws once too often
Yoshida tells him to leave. Before Kenji goes, Takada gives him a gift of brushes
and ink and warns him to avoid large places at night.

Ashamed, Kenji does not return home. He walks in the opposite direction
and comes to a village where the people are strange and scared. Kenji sees a
temple at the top of a mountain and climbs to it, not knowing the stories of the
Goblin Rat with his magical sword who has taken over the temple.

In an open room Kenji sees tall white screens. While he waits for the
priests to return he paints cats in honor of Takada, who enjoyed his drawings
of cats. His cats have watchful eyes and sharp claws. When he finishes, Kenji
hears a scratching noise and hides in a cabinet. Kenji is terrified when he hears
growling and screaming and the floor rumbles.

In the morning the temple is quiet. Kenji comes out of hiding, surveys the
room, and sees shattered screens and wood and paper strewn over the floor.
The broken screens are empty, the cats gone except for the King of Cats, who
has the sword of the Goblin Rat at his feet.

The villagers are grateful and invite Kenji to live there. He does and
becomes a famous artist.

This is an excellent, sensitive retelling of a traditional Japanese folktale
that captures children's interest and holds it. I particularly like this version of
the tale over many others I read because the author leaves the violence to the
reader's imagination. The illustrations are breathtaking and otherworldly. The

Japanese garden depicted is tranquil, the cranes exquisite, and the Goblin huge and looming. Each page of text has a Japanese character rendered in calligraphy with brush and black ink on rice paper. At the end of the book, Levine provides a list of the Japanese characters used and their pronunciation and meaning.

McDermott, Gerald, reteller. **The Stonecutter: A Japanese Folktale.** Illus. by author. New York: Viking, 1975.

McDermott tells this ancient Japanese fable with an economy of words and in abstract images that consist of dramatic, striking blocks of color. The combination makes for a powerful book.

Tasaku is a stonecutter. He chips at the mountain with his hammer and chisel and forms the blocks of stone that are used to create temples and palaces. Tasaku asks for nothing, and this pleases the spirit of the mountains.

One day, however, Tasaku sees a prince carried by servants. Envious, Tasaku wishes that he could be rich. The spirit hears and transforms the stonecutter into a prince with riches. Soon Tasaku is not satisfied when he sees how powerful the sun is. The spirit makes Tasaku that powerful, and he burns the fields and dries the land. When a cloud covers him, Tasaku decides the cloud is more powerful. Again the spirit grants his wish and turns him into a cloud. Tasaku sees that though he can now make storms and floods and wash palaces away, the mountain remains. Tasaku wants to be the more powerful mountain. The spirit grants this wish then leaves. As a mountain Tasaku is stronger than sun, prince, and cloud, but he feels the sting of a chisel and shakes when he realizes it's a stonecutter cutting into him.

Mosel, Arlene, reteller. **The Funny Little Woman.** Illus. by Blair Lent. New York: E. P. Dutton, 1972.

Children of all ages never tire of hearing this classic tale set in Japan about a woman who likes to make rice dumplings. One day she chases a dumpling that falls through a crack in the earth, tumbles with it, and is captured by wicked oni who make her cook rice for them. The woman uses their magic paddle, which turns one grain of rice into a potful. She ultimately escapes with the magic paddle, returns home, and uses the paddle to make and sell rice cakes. She becomes the richest woman in Japan.

O'Callahan, Jay. "The Magic Mortar: A Story from Japan," pp. 147-50, in **Ready-to-Tell Tales: Sure-Fire Stories from America's Favorite Storytellers.** Ed. by David Holt and Bill Mooney. Little Rock, AK: August House, 1994.

This is a variant of "The Magic Mill," also known as "Why the Sea Is Salt," that is fun to learn and tell. In this version from Japan the good brother has no rice for the New Year's celebration and his mean older brother won't share any. When the poor brother tells his woes to an elderly man, the man gives him a rice cake with honey. He instructs the poor brother to go to the small statue of the Buddha, where he will see some little men. He is to give them the rice cake only when they give him a mortar and pestle.

The brother uses the mortar and pestle to get all he needs. His greedy brother discovers his secret, takes the mortar and pestle at night, and flees in a boat. He is hungry and decides that his rice cakes need salt so he starts the mortar and turns the pestle, but he doesn't know how to stop it. The boat sinks to the bottom of the sea with the magic mortar, and since the pestle is still turned to the right, salt continues to pour from it.

San Souci, Robert D. **The Samurai's Daughter.** Illus. by Stephen T. Johnson. New York: Dial Books for Young Readers, 1992.

One of my particular favorites, this book is a beautiful telling by a master storyteller enhanced by evocative paintings in pastels. It's a wonderful adventure story with a strong, active female character.

Meet a noble samurai, a widower, with a beautiful daughter named Tokoyo. Tokoyo's father teaches her samurai virtues and a warrior's duty to protect others. By age five she can shoot a bow and arrow and ride a horse. When Tokoyo is older her father wants her to learn the lessons of a lady, but Tokoyo still wants to prove herself strong and brave. She joins the women who dive for oysters. Tokoyo can withstand the icy water better and hold more air in her lungs than men.

Tokoyo's life changes when her father is exiled to the Oki Islands for displeasing the ruler. Tokoyo decides she must be with her father and undertakes the treacherous journey. When she reaches the Oki Islands she encounters a man about to push a girl into the water. Tokoyo rescues the girl and the man explains that there is a curse on them, placed by a white serpent. Every year the serpent demands the sacrifice of a young person and, if he is refused, the serpent raises horrible storms.

Tokoyo offers to plunge into the water. With her dagger in her teeth, she dives in, finds the sea-demon, battles with it, and ultimately triumphs. She sees and brings to shore a wooden statue of the Japanese ruler. In the village Tokoyo is reunited with her father and learns that the wooden statue was carved and cursed by a man the ruler had banished. When the statue was thrown into the sea, the statue summoned the sea serpent and caused the ruler's madness. Now the ruler's mind is sound, and he orders Tokoyo and her father to return home.

Snyder, Dianne. **The Boy of the Three-Year Nap.** Illus. by Allen Say. Boston: Houghton Mifflin, 1988.

Meet Taro, the laziest boy in town, whose mother, a widow, works hard sewing day and night. When Taro is almost an adult, a rich merchant, his wife, and daughter move into town. Taro's mother suggests that Taro try to get a job working for the merchant. Instead, Taro dresses like the patron god of the town and tells the merchant his daughter must marry Taro or she'll be turned into a clay pot.

When the merchant visits the widow she immediately knows what Taro has been up to and implements her own plan to trick the merchant and her son.

The writing is tight and clever. There are many twists and turns and children wonder what will happen next. The text consists mostly of fine, colorful dialogue. The illustrations offer touches that set the scene in Japan, and the illustrator paints very expressive faces.

Stamm, Claus. **Three Strong Women: A Tall Tale from Japan.** Illus. by Jean and Mou-sien Tseng. New York: Viking, 1990.

This long tale is funny, with pleasing and expressive watercolors.

A famous wrestler named Forever-Mountain sets out to wrestle before the emperor. He sees a round little girl with a bucket on her head and decides he must tickle her. The girl blocks his hand and makes him return home with her.

There the wrestler learns what real strength is. The girl's mother carries the cow to and from the field because the stones hurt its feet. When Grandmother trips over the roots of an oak tree, Mother pulls the tree by the roots and heaves it up the mountainside. Forever-Mountain agrees to stay with them for the three months before the wrestling contest to increase his strength. Every day the wrestler does the work of five and every evening he wrestles Grandmother, who always wins. Without realizing it, though, Forever-Mountain does get stronger. Finally, when he stamps his foot, people think they're hearing thunder, and he can pull up a tree and throw it. Now, he's ready to wrestle before the emperor. If he wins, the girl, Maru-me, can marry him when he returns.

At the competition, Forever-Mountain merely stamps his foot and the first wrestler bounces into the air and out of the ring. Several wrestlers decide not to compete, and Forever-Mountain picks up the others and places them before the emperor. The emperor makes Forever-Mountain promise to never wrestle again. Forever-Mountain decides to become a farmer, and he returns to Maru-me with the prize money.

Tompert, Ann. **Bamboo Hats and a Rice Cake.** Illus. by Demi. New York: Crown, 1993.

An elderly man and his wife feel they need rice cakes for good fortune in the new year, but they have nothing to eat. The elderly woman insists that her husband sell her wedding kimono. On the way to the village the man passes six statues of Jizo, protector of children. The man has nothing to leave them, but he brushes them clean. On the road to the village he meets people less fortunate than him, and in this way he trades the kimono for fans, the fans for a gold bell, and finally the bell for bamboo hats.

On the way home he apologizes to the Jizo because he has nothing to offer. He brushes the snow off them and then realizes he can give them the five bamboo hats from the trade and the hat from his head to protect them from the snow. The man explains to his wife what he did, and she feels that making an offering to Jizo was more important than buying rice cakes. That night the couple is awakened by a loud thud. They look outside and see a giant rice cake. They also see the six Jizo statues walking off.

The story is beautifully illustrated. The paintings are simple yet evocative, colorful, delicate, and detailed. Some of the words in the story are in Japanese characters. A key in the borders on each page is included. On the last page of the book the author explains the Japanese traditions of New Years and the importance of rice and rice cakes to the holiday.

Uchida, Yoshiko. **The Two Foolish Cats (Suggested by a Japanese Folktale).** Illus. by Margot Zemach. New York: Margaret K. McElderry Books/Macmillan, 1987.

This story will appeal to a wide age group. The book combines the talents of award-winning author Uchida and illustrator Zemach.

Big Daizo, a huge and fierce black-and-white cat with seven toes on each paw gets along well with Suki, a small and skinny, greenish-gray cat. The field mice and birds in the forest are afraid of them until one spring morning.

Daizo and Suki are trying to catch a fish at the stream. They fail and head home, wet, hungry, and angry at each other. The cats see two rice cakes, but one is large and one small, and they fight over who should get which cake. An old badger tells them to seek the advice of wise Monkey, who'll be sure they get equal shares.

Monkey agrees to solve their problem. He places the rice cakes on a tiny pair of scales. He takes a bite from the big one, then realizes he ate too much and eats a bite from the smaller one, and continues until the rice cakes are gone. Monkey looks slyly at the two cats and tells them there's nothing to fight over now. The cats feel foolish. Everyone in the forest hears and laughs. Since then the two cats have lived peacefully.

The text moves along well, the plot is humorous, and the language is precise and vivid. The watercolor paintings have the quality of Japanese (written) characters in the brushstrokes. Everything has a delicacy yet a strength. When the cats fight you can almost feel their fur standing on end. Mr. Monkey is precious. He is depicted sipping tea from a small cup and wearing a traditional robe, a tall black hat, and small spectacles perched on the bridge of his nose.

Uchida, Yoshiko. **The Wise Old Woman.** Illus. by Martin Springett. New York: Margaret K. McElderry Books/Macmillan, 1994.

In this graceful tale readers are taken to a village in the hills of Japan long ago. The land is ruled by a cruel young lord who decreed that anyone older than 70 is not useful and must be taken to the mountains and left to die. One young man realizes he can't fulfill the decree and hides his mother in a secret room he builds for her.

One day three fierce warriors come from mighty Lord Hilga with the warning that in three days Lord Hilga will conquer the village. The young lord of the village, who is cruel but not brave, begs to be spared. Since Lord Hilga respects a clever mind, if three impossible tasks can be solved, the village will be spared. The tasks are to make a coil of rope out of ashes, to run a single thread through a length of crooked log, and to make a drum that sounds without being beaten.

The young lord orders the six wisest people to solve the riddles. He asks the gods and the clever badger for assistance. None can offer answers. When it is posted that a bag of gold will go to anyone who can help, the young farmer tells his mother. She has her son get three things, and with them she solves the tasks.

The young farmer presents the solutions to the young lord, who demands to know who really solved the riddles. When the farmer reveals it was his mother, whom he had hidden, the young lord realizes he's been wrong. He decides that instead of being sent to die, the elderly will be treated with respect and honor and the younger generations will learn from their wisdom.

Author Uchida uses an economy of words, yet the telling is full and rich. The relationship between mother and son is finely drawn. Tension and conflict almost from the first moment hook children and make them want to know what will happen next.

The paintings are done in solid blocks of color, all outlined in thick black. They are striking and bold, very classic. Faces are stylized, yet they convey emotion well.

Wisniewski, David. **The Warrior and the Wise Man.** Illus. by author. New York: Lothrop, Lee & Shepard, 1989.

In this exciting and dynamic tale readers are taken to Japan long ago, where they meet an emperor who has twin sons. Tozaemon is brave and fierce, whereas Toemon is thoughtful and gentle. The emperor creates a trial to decide which son will someday be emperor. The first son to bring him the five eternal elements will win. The elements are Earth, Water, Fire, Wind, and Cloud, and each is guarded by a hideous demon and its army.

Tozaemon takes the elements by force, each time causing damage to the demon's domain. Toemon arrives second each time and repairs the destruction with the help of the elements the demons give him. Tozaemon brings the elements home first, but he also incurs the wrath of the five demons and their armies. It is Toemon who, with the help of the elements and his wisdom, saves his people from destruction. The emperor decides that Toemon will be the next emperor.

The book includes an important author's note that explains the importance of warriors and wise people in twelfth-century Japan.

The illustrations are the result of research into Japanese arts. Many of the designs and clothing are copied from twelfth-century originals. The illustrations are unique, made from cut paper. The figures are silhouettes on black paper. This artwork is very striking and dramatic. The cut-paper figures convey much emotion, expression, and action. The demons are truly frightening, especially the Fire Demon, with his massive brown arm extended amidst the flames while Toemon stands nearby, small but brave.

Booktalks

French, Fiona. **Little Inchkin.** Illus. by author. New York: Dial Books for Young Readers, 1994.

Set in Japan long ago, this folktale is compact, with each page an inclusive scene. Children are drawn to the appealing main character. Little Inchkin is tiny but dreams big and never gives up. He's proud and determined, kind and forgiving, and children want him to succeed.

The paintings are done in the style of eighteenth-century Japanese prints, in vivid colors that splash across the pages. The milky white faces of the stylized people are reminiscent of the performers in traditional Kabuki, a form of Japanese theater.

Hana and her husband Tanjo pray to the great Buddha for a child. Their wish is granted, but their baby is no bigger than a thumb. As he gets older, the child, Inchkin, doesn't grow much bigger. He's kind and wishes to be a tall, brave swordsman. His parents are ashamed of him, and the children ignore him. Inchkin leaves to seek his fortune.

When his nutshell boat flips during a storm, Inchkin is rescued by Prince Sanjo and becomes an officer in the prince's guard, getting rid of pesky rats and cockroaches in the royal kitchen. Impressed, the prince sends Inchkin as guard for his daughter on a journey to the temple far away.

When two demons block their way, Inchkin climbs to one demon's nose and stabs it. The demons flee. At that moment the bells in the temple ring, and Inchkin grows into a tall, handsome warrior. He's been rewarded by Lord Buddha for his bravery. The princess marries Inchkin, who forgives his parents and invites them to the wedding.

Hamilton, Virginia. "The One-Inch Boy," pp. 23-26, in **The Dark Way: Stories from the Spirit World.** Illus. by Lambert Davis. New York: Harcourt Brace Jovanovich, 1990.

Virginia Hamilton's version of this classic Japanese folktale is beautifully written. As in the version by Fiona French, the One-Inch Boy, named Issun-boshi, sets out to seek his fortune. He becomes a companion to the nobleman's daughter. One day while returning from the temple, a demon threatens to eat the princess. The demon, an oni, is huge, green, and has three eyes and a horn on his head. (There is an appropriately scary illustration of the oni.) Issun-boshi pricks the oni's nose and tongue with his tiny needle sword. Here the oni drops his club, runs in circles, and vanishes. The princess picks up the club. She's heard that some demons carry magic clubs on which you can make wishes. She asks that Issun-boshi grow tall. He does, they are both grateful, and after a few years they marry.

Hodges, Margaret. **The Wave.** Illus. by Blair Lent. Boston: Houghton Mifflin, 1964.

Noted storyteller Hodges's fascinating tale is complemented by Blair Lent's striking illustrations in shades of gold, brown, and black.

Readers are taken to a village by the sea long ago, where the people tend rice fields on the mountain nearby. The harvest is their wealth. High up on the mountain lives Ojiisan, a wise man, and his grandson, Tada.

One day when the harvest is ripe and the people are ready to celebrate, Ojiisan feels an earthquake coming. He senses the slow shaking. Ojiisan sees the ocean receding. He also sees the 400 villagers on the stretch of beach. Ojiisan knows, but the people don't, that the ocean will return with great force.

The only way Ojiisan can warn them quickly from high on the mountain is to set his stacks of dry, precious rice on fire so the people will see the flames and come running. The people do come. Some are angry; Tada thinks his grandfather is mad. Then the tidal wave comes, tearing the land and destroying the homes. The villagers realize that Ojiisan saved them.

Merrill, Jean, reteller. **The Girl Who Loved Caterpillars: A Twelfth-Century Tale from Japan.** Illus. by Floyd Cooper. New York: Philomel, 1992.

Exquisite, muted oil paintings, noted particularly for their depiction of individualized and expressive faces, perfectly match this character study of an independent girl living in a structured society.

Izumi is the daughter of the provincial inspector. She comes from wealth and position and her parents hope she'll marry a nobleman or be a lady-in-waiting in the emperor's court. Izumi, however, is not like other girls of her time. She doesn't pluck her eyebrows or blacken her teeth like they do. Izumi loves to observe caterpillars, worms, toads, and insects. She plays with boys from families of "low standing" who bring her bugs. Izumi's friends, ladies-in-waiting, and neighbors gossip about her.

The captain of the stabler ultimately hears about her and, curious, spies on her. They correspond through notes, and he realizes just how independent she is.

San Souci, Robert D. **The Snow Wife.** Illus. by Stephen T. Johnson. New York: Dial Books for Young Readers, 1993.

When an apprentice woodcutter takes shelter in a hut during a snowstorm, a young woman appears to him. She promises not to harm the young man, but he must vow never to speak of her.

Later, on the road, the young woodcutter meets a lovely woman, Yuki, whom he marries. One night he tells her the story of the lovely woman who appeared to him during the storm. The woman was Yuki. Because he broke the promise, Yuki changes into the Woman of the Snow and disappears.

The woodcutter's search for Yuki takes him to the shrine of the Wind God, who lives on the peak of Bitter Mountain. On the way he is challenged by Mountain Man and the horrible Mountain Woman. Eventually the woodcutter reaches the Wind God and pleads for Yuki's return.

Say, Allen. **Tree of Cranes.** Illus. by author. Boston: Houghton Mifflin, 1991.

Say's book will appeal to that special child who likes a story that is more a mood piece, a poem, or a memory.

The illustrations are soft and warm, simple yet full of feeling. A young boy, who lives in Japan, remembers his first Christmas.

His mother is busy making cranes out of origami. She digs up the boy's tree from outdoors and places it in a pot indoors. Then she decorates it with the cranes. The boy's mother explains that she came from California, where, right now, they are celebrating Christmas. She explains the customs to her son. He thinks the tree is beautiful. In the morning the boy finds a gift, the kite he always wanted.

Schroeder, Alan. **Lily and the Wooden Bowl.** Illus. by Yoriko Ito. New York: Delacorte Press, 1994.

Beautiful illustrations painted with deep, rich colors enhance this love story. The book will appeal particularly to girls in the upper age range of the target group.

An elderly woman named Aya lives with her beautiful granddaughter Lily. Before she dies, Aya gives Lily a paper crane and a small wooden rice paddle. She also makes Lily promise to wear a wooden bowl upside down on her head to cover the upper part of her face. Aya says it will protect Lily from men.

Left poor and alone Lily works in the rice fields. The other workers tease her until one day her paper crane beats its wings and chases them away. Yamoto, a wealthy farmer, asks Lily if she'd nurse his sick wife Matsu. Yamoto promises Lily will be treated like a daughter. Matsu, however, is cruel and jealous of her. Yamoto's eldest son, Kumaso, returns home. Despite his mother's lies about Lily, Kumaso courts her, and they fall in love and want to marry. Yamoto agrees but Matsu is angry and gives a condition. Lily must prepare rice for the wedding feast the next day—for 100 people. Matsu gives Lily one grain of rice and locks her in the kitchen. Matsu spies on Lily and sees her making the rice with the paddle from her grandmother. Matsu summons rats from everywhere, tells them to eat the rice, then storms in and blames Lily for the mess. Just as she's about to hit Lily, Yamoto and Kumaso enter. Lily and Matsu tell their versions. Matsu declares that Lily must go or she goes. Yamoto knows Lily speaks the truth, and he banishes Matsu.

Kumaso and Lily marry. When Lily drinks the traditional cup of wine, the wooden bowl splits in half and jewels fall from it. The bride is beautiful.

Uchida, Yoshiko, reteller. **The Magic Purse.** Illus. by Keiko Narahashi. New York: Macmillan, 1993.

A touching tale with an air of mystery, this story will appeal to that special reader who can stick with a slower paced story that focuses on mood, feelings, and character.

A poor young farmer finds himself on a strange road when he belatedly decides to join his friends at the Iseh shrine. The road takes him to the Black Swamp, where a young girl approaches and explains she is a prisoner of the ruler of the Black Swamp. She asks the farmer to take a letter to her parents who live in the Red Swamp. The farmer hesitates because no one has ever come out of the Red Swamp alive, but he agrees. She gives the farmer a red purse with gold coins and tells him as long as he leaves one coin he will always have a full purse.

The farmer finds the girl's parents and hands them the letter. He goes to their home and is given food and gold coins that allow him to live well. Each spring the farmer sends a tray of rice cakes and wine floating on the water in the Black Swamp. Each time the tray drifts back the next day with a token on it. The farmer never sees the girl, but he hears her telling him not to forget her.

Demonstration/Participation Activities

Aytüre-Scheele, Zülal. **The Great Origami Book.** New York: Sterling, 1987.

This is one of the few books on origami that features figures easy enough for beginners, both youngsters and adults. The author shows a basic form in paper folding and then shows figures that can be made from that form. The instructions are easier to follow than those in most books. This book includes photographs of the actual paper, often with hands seen folding the paper. Written instructions are also included.

Try demonstrating "Sailboat," p. 16; "Salt-and-Pepper Dish," pp. 22-23; and "Cup," p. 63.

Brudenell, Iain MacLeod. "Flying Fish," pp. 14-15, and "Origami Cygnets," pp. 20-21, in **Animal Crafts.** Photos by Zul Mukhida. Milwaukee, WI: Gareth Stevens, 1994.

An enjoyable craft for all ages, "Flying Fish" uses easy-to-find materials and isn't too time consuming if made out of paper. The author explains that May 5 is Children's Day in Japan. On that day many Japanese children hang kites outside their homes.

If you're ambitious and time allows, practice making the "Origami Cygnet" and demonstrate how it is done for the children.

Carlson, Laurie, and Judith Dammel. "Paper Folding: Floating Boat," p. 114, and "Paper Folding: Swimming Duck," p. 115, in **Kids Camp! Activities for the Backyard or Wilderness.** Illus. by Sean O'Neill. Chicago: Chicago Review Press, 1995.

Here are two easy origami figures for children to make. Clear diagrams and instructions are included.

Drake, Jane, and Ann Love. "Fan-Tastic," pp. 162-63, and "Paper-Folding," pp. 166-67, in **The Kids Summer Handbook.** Illus. by Heather Collins. New York: Ticknor & Fields, 1994.

Children love to make fans for themselves or someone else. Although this craft doesn't require a lot of materials and they're all readily available, you'd be wise to do the first step in this activity before the program (putting holes in the end of each popsicle stick.) Then, during the program, all the children can decorate the curved strips of construction paper that will form the top of the fan.

Origami is not easy, but using "Paper-Folding" you can teach children the basic folds used in origami. Then you can demonstrate how to make the frog, swan, or boat, for which directions and diagrams are included.

Kneissler, Irmgard. **Origami: A Children's Book.** Illus. by Dieter Jonas. Photos by Max Schwendt. Chicago: Children's Press, 1992.

Complete instructions and diagrams are included for each step of every figure in this book. Practical items that children can make and then use are: "Sailboat Race," pp. 16-17; "Snapper," p. 17; "Useful Things," pp. 22-24; and "Hat Parade," pp. 25-26. Inspire the children before they attempt these figures by showing them the color photographs of children using their origami toys.

In the section "Useful Things" you'll find origami forms that are particularly easy for you to demonstrate and for children to then make. Step-by-step instructions take you from the basic triangle shape to make a cup, a coin holder, and a small basket. These are the three objects I can make reasonably well.

Milord, Susan. "Fold-and-Dye Wrapping Paper," p. 48, in **Adventures in Art: Art and Craft Experiences for 7- to 14-Year Olds.** Illus. by author. Charlotte, VT: Williamson, 1990.

Explain to the children, as the author does, that this is a popular way to decorate paper in Japan. You need absorbent paper and food colors. You may also want to experiment with rice paper and colored inks. Although this craft can be completed quickly, you may need to help some of the children fold their paper. They'll want to try this several times.

Milord, Susan. "Launch a Floating Toy," p. 38, and "Make a Windsock for Tango No Sekku," p. 60, in **Hands Around the World: 365 Creative Ways to Build Cultural Awareness and Global Respect.** Illus. by author. Charlotte, VT: Williamson, 1992.

The author explains that Japanese children know how to make a boat out of paper. Simple directions and diagrams are included in "Launch a Floating Toy." Most children will be able to do this craft after you demonstrate it.

With glue, markers, tissue paper, the easy-to-follow directions, and a little help, children can successfully "Make a Windsock for Tango No Sekku."

Temko, Florence. **Origami for Beginners: The Creative World of Paperfolding.** Rutland, VT: Charles E. Tuttle, 1991.

You might like to read this clear and concise book that explains the history of origami and the basic techniques involved. You'll find some forms that are easy to learn and demonstrate and some that the children could do. Check "Blintz Base," pp. 8-9, for simple card forms; and "Kite Base," p. 12, for a trick mouse and a pine tree figure. The color photographs of the finished products may inspire you and the youngsters.

Toney, Sara D. "Byobu: Japanese Folding Screens," pp. 82-84, in **Smith-sonian Surprises: An Educational Activity Book.** Illus. by Stephen Kraft. Washington, DC: Smithsonian Institution Press, 1985.

Although the materials are simple enough, this activity is best done when most of the children in your group are older. It does require adult assistance and takes some time, but the results are worth it.

Chapter 9

Lazies, Sillies, and Fools

Read Alouds

Aardema, Verna. **Anansi Finds a Fool.** Illus. by Bryna Waldman. New York: Dial Books for Young Readers, 1992.

Humor abounds in this satisfying tale about the well-known character Anansi, the spider. In this Ashanti story from West Africa, lazy Anansi tells his wife, Aso, that he's going into the fishing business, but he's going to find someone else to do all the work. Aso tells her friend Laluah, who tells her husband Bonsu. Bonsu decides he'll offer to fish with Anansi and trick Anansi into doing all the work. Bonsu confuses Anansi by saying he'll cut the branches and Anansi can get tired for Bonsu. Anansi replies that he'll do the cutting and Bonsu can get tired for him. Bonsu continues to confuse and trick Anansi this way until Anansi has done all the work. Bonsu tells Anansi that he was looking for a fool to fish with and he was the fool himself.

The rich watercolor illustrations are expressive and capture well the essence of the characters.

Betz, Adrienne, and Lucia Monfried, comps. **Diane Goode's Book of Silly Stories and Songs.** Illus. by Diane Goode. New York: Dutton Children's Books, 1992.

This collection contains three stories about lazies, sillies, and fools that you'll want to share.

"Get Up and Bar the Door," pp. 16-19, is a funny, short tale about a silly couple. Be sure to show the children the accompanying illustration. The couple is depicted with sharp features, and the thief, who wears a half mask, looks like a harlequin.

A husband and wife are in bed one night when a strong wind blows their door open. Each wants the other to shut the door, but neither will. The couple argues so intensely that they don't see a thief listening. Then, the husband says, the first one to speak must shut the door. The thief uses this wager to his advantage. He walks in boldly, steals what he wants, smears soot on the couples' faces, and leaves. They say nothing.

In the morning, the couple see each others' faces. The wife cries out, and the husband says she spoke first and must shut the door.

Children will laugh at "The Husband Who Was to Mind the House," pp. 6-13. Youngsters and adults love this classic Norwegian folktale in which a husband complains about his work and says that his wife does nothing around the house. The wife offers to go in the fields and mow while her husband does the housekeeping.

The husband has one absurd mishap after another. He leaves the butter churn to get ale from the cellar and when he returns finds a pig licking cream that spilled from the overturned churn. He forgets the ale barrel, out of which he'd taken the tap, and when he does return to the cellar, the ale has run out.

The husband half finishes each task he begins, which leads to disaster. He leaves the cow on the roof to eat grass and spills cream in the well. While he's preparing dinner, the man worries the cow might fall off the roof, so he takes a rope, ties one end to the cow's neck, slips the other down the chimney, and ties it around his leg. The cow does fall, the man is pulled up the chimney. Mercifully, his wife returns home and fixes everything.

Don't forget to share the illustration that accompanies this short tale. It's expressive, humorous, and has a European flavor.

In "Sweet Giongio," pp. 40-47, a sensible young man falls in love and marries a pretty young woman in this version of "The Three Sillies" from southern Italy. During the wedding feast the bride goes to the wine cellar, notices a piece of broken glass on the floor, and cries thinking someday she'll have a son who will find the glass and hurt himself on it. Her father, brothers, sisters, and cousins hear her cries, listen to her tale, and weep with her.

When the groom hears the tale, he thinks they're foolish and he won't return until he finds three people sillier than them. In this version he finds a man who feeds oxen with a spoon, a man who is trying to retrieve the moon from a lake with a fishnet, and an innkeeper who tries to jump into his pants. The groom suggests alternative methods to these three sillies and then returns to his wife.

Birch, David. **The King's Chessboard.** Illus. by Devis Grebu. New York: Dial Books for Young Readers, 1988.

What a clever, satisfying, and original tale this is about a proud and foolish king. Trouble comes when a wise man performs a service for the king of Deccan and the king demands the wise man choose a reward, even though the wise man wants nothing. Pressed to request something, the wise man sees the king's wooden chessboard and asks for: One grain of rice for the first square on the chessboard. On the second day, he wants two grains for the second square. On the third day he'll have four grains and so on. The king can't figure how much rice that will be in all and he doesn't want to ask the wise man because he doesn't want to admit there's something he doesn't know. So, the king foolishly grants the request.

At first the granary workers count the grains. Then the Weigher of the King's Grain must weigh the rice. The Grand Superintendent is notified and gets concerned when the wise man receives four sacks of rice and soon eight tons of rice. The king learns what is happening and the Royal Mathematician computes that the king promised the wise man almost 600 billion tons in all. Realizing he was silly and foolish the king asks the queen for advise, and she tells the king he must ask the wise man to release him from the promise. The wise man points out that he was satisfied all along.

The watercolor and colored pencil illustrations are not overly cluttered and suggest life in ancient India. People are drawn in a stylized fashion.

DeSpain, Pleasant. "The Silly Farmer: An African Tale," pp. 35-37, in **Twenty-Two Splendid Tales to Tell from Around the World: Volume One.** Illus. by Kirk Lyttle. Little Rock, AK: August House, 1994.

A funny, fast-paced folktale, this is most effective when you memorize and tell it.

A silly farmer named Zaheed lives in Ethiopia with his wife, who is pregnant. Zaheed visits a wise old woman, gives her a gold coin, and asks what gender the baby will be. The woman tosses ancient bones and says Zaheed's wife will have either a boy or a girl. Zaheed thinks this is wonderful and when his wife has a girl, marvels that the old woman was right.

When it's time for the baby to be baptized, the parents can't decide on a name. Zaheed returns to the old woman, gives her another gold coin, and she whispers the name of the child (so she says) in his hands. The old woman tells Zaheed to keep his hands closed so he won't lose the name, but he slips in loose hay. Zaheed asks the farmhands to help him find the lost name in the haystack. A woman from the village walks by, hears what's happening and says "It is nonsense!" Zaheed thinks the woman has found his daughter's name and she is called "Nonsense."

DeSpain, Pleasant. "The Three Wishes: A Swedish Tale," pp. 55-56, in **Twenty-Two Splendid Tales to Tell from Around the World: Volume One.** Illus. by Kirk Lyttle. Little Rock, AK: August House, 1994.

Memorize and tell this short, pleasing version of a classic tale, and you'll have children laughing. A woodcutter is about to cut down an old pine tree when a wood nymph who lives in it begs him not to. The woodcutter complies, and the wood nymph grants him three wishes.

The woodcutter doesn't believe in magic so he forgets about the wishes. At home, while eating his meager dinner, he wishes he had a juicy sausage. It appears. That's when the woodcutter remembers the three wishes and tells his wife. She's angry because he wasted a wish. The woodcutter is so upset with his wife's tirade that he wishes the sausage on her nose. When they can't pull the sausage off, they must use the third wish to remove it.

French, Vivian, reteller. **Lazy Jack.** Illus. by Russell Ayto. Cambridge, MA: Candlewick Press, 1995.

A young man called Lazy (who usually gets out of bed in the afternoon, eats, drinks, and returns to bed), is sent to find work by his mother. In this version Lazy works for a builder, a farmer, a dairyman, a baker, a fishmonger, and a grocer. Each time he handles his earnings wrong, his mother tells him how he should have carried each payment, and Lazy carries the next thing that way. As always, the results are disastrous. Milk sloshes in his pocket, cheese melts on his head, a puppy tears his coat, a fish is ruined.

This is a modern, wonderful retelling of a classic tale in which Jack's mother thinks he's silly, but the people for whom he worked disagree. They argue that he isn't stupid, that he did a good job. Each of them hire Lazy for one day a week and give him the same payment. Now Jack knows what to do with his pay.

Give the children ample time to look at the humorous illustrations, which resemble Maurice Sendak's artwork with a French twist. Jack is depicted with a sleepy look, his eyes always closed.

Galdone, Paul, reteller. **The Three Sillies.** Illus. by author. New York: Clarion Books, 1981.

Galdone's books are always great to share with a group. His illustrations are colorful, uncluttered, and large. His telling of this traditional English folktale appeals to all ages.

A young gentleman's sweetheart, mother, and father are so silly. They all end up in the cellar crying over an ax that's stuck in the roof of the cellar. They're worried the ax might someday fall on the head of the daughter's (maybe) future child. The young man wonders if he can meet three people as silly as them—and he does.

After the young man meets a woman who puts her cow on the roof to feed it grass, a man who runs and jumps into his pants to get them on, and people who are trying to get the moon out of a pond, he realizes his sillies aren't the silliest.

Ginsburg, Mirra, reteller. **The Chinese Mirror: Adapted from a Korean Folktale.** Illus. by Margot Zemach. San Diego: Gulliver Books/Harcourt Brace Jovanovich, 1988.

In this short, silly tale that will have children shaking their heads in disbelief and delight, a man travels to China from his village in Korea, where no one has ever seen a mirror. In China the man sees what he thinks is a strange, round shiny object. He looks in the mirror, thinks what he's seeing is another man, is fascinated, and buys the mirror.

When the man returns home, misunderstanding abounds. For example, the man's wife looks in the mirror and thinks her husband has another woman in the house. No one can convince anyone else of what they've seen, because each sees himself and thinks it's someone else. The couple has a child and several years later the boy wonders why everyone's arguing. A neighbor sees the boy staring into the mirror, takes a look, thinks he's seeing a big bully, and smashes his fist into the bully's face. The mirror crashes into shiny splinters, and that's the end of all those people everyone thought they saw.

The delicate watercolors in shades of brown, tan, white, and blue suggest the Korean countryside.

Ginsburg, Mirra. **The King Who Tried to Fry an Egg on His Head: Based on a Russian Tale.** Illus. by Will Hillenbrand. New York: Macmillan, 1994.

For pure fun and foolishness share this short, satisfying book with children. A poor and silly king makes an unwise promise and must then allow the Sun, the Moon, and Raven to marry his daughters. The king visits each daughter, learns a trick from Sun, Moon, and Raven, and after each visit tries to show his wife the trick. None of the tricks, however, work for the king. He can't fry an egg on his head like Sun, light the bathhouse with his finger like Moon, or sleep in a tree like Raven.

Ginsburg, Mirra, trans. and editor. "Who Will Wash the Pot? A Russian Tale," pp. 8-11, in **The Lazies: Tales of the Peoples of Russia.** Illus. by Marian Parry. New York: Macmillan, 1973.

I love telling this short, funny tale of a stubborn and lazy elderly couple who argue because neither wants to wash the pot. They decide that whoever speaks first in the morning will wash it. The next day they don't speak or get out of bed. Worried, the neighbors come, but the couple won't answer their questions. The mayor decides that someone must stay with them. One woman offers, but she wonders who will pay her. The mayor says there's a new coat hanging in the couple's house and that will be her payment. That's when the wife yells that no one will take her coat, and her husband simply says that she must wash the pot.

González, Lucía M., reteller. "Juan Bobo and the Buñuelos," pp. 240-41, in **From Sea to Shining Sea: A Treasury of American Folklore and Folk Songs.** Comp. by Amy L. Cohn. Illus. by 11 Caldecott

Medal and four Caldecott Honor Book artists. New York: Scholastic, 1993.

Share this short, witty story about Juan Bobo (Juan the Fool), a poor farmer who is foolish, easy to cheat, and always getting into trouble. One day Juan finds three bags of gold. He shows the riches to his wife, who knows they must belong to robbers. The gold must be kept a secret, but Juan can't keep a secret. The wife devises a plan to keep the gold and to keep her and Juan safe.

The wife scatters fritters on the ground so her husband thinks it rained fritters. She turns the donkey so his tail is facing the hay and tells her husband the donkey is eating with its tail. In this way, when Juan tells everyone about the gold, and three mean-looking men come looking for it, Juan honestly says he found the gold the day before, when it rained fritters and the donkey ate with its tail. The three men think Juan is crazy and leave.

Lighthearted watercolors by Donald Crews lend a sense of whimsy to this funny story.

Hewitt, Kathryn, reteller. **The Three Sillies.** Illus. by author. New York: Harcourt Brace Jovanovich, 1986.

Author Hewitt offers a clever version of this classic English folktale. Her illustrations are muted, deep-hued, detailed, and give a flavor of old Europe. Here, the characters are pigs, which works well and makes the tale even more amusing.

As in other tellings, a young man goes into the cellar and finds his girlfriend, her father, and mother crying over an ax stuck in the ceiling beam. The farmer and his family fear that some day if the daughter has a son he'll go to the cellar to get cider and the ax will fall on his head. The young man hears this, laughs, and promises that if he can find three bigger sillies, he'll return and marry the daughter. The fellow does find three wildly foolish people.

Kimmel, Eric A. **Anansi Goes Fishing.** Illus. by Janet Stevens. New York: Holiday House, 1992.

Illustrator Stevens's large, bright, expressive watercolors capture the humor of this tale and the character of Anansi the lazy spider. Anansi decides to trick Turtle into catching fish for him. Turtle, however, is not stupid. He will teach Anansi how to catch fish without Anansi realizing he's actually doing the work. Turtle explains that first they must make a net, but it will be tiring work. Since Anansi doesn't want to get tired, he decides that he'll let Turtle get tired while he, Anansi, makes the net. And so it continues for each task. Turtle will get tired and Anansi will set the net in the river, catch the fish, and cook the fish. Then Turtle tells Anansi that when he eats he gets full, so one of them should eat and one get full. Naturally, Anansi would rather be full, so Turtle eats the fish.

Anansi finally realizes he's been tricked and goes to the Justice Tree. The judge knows how lazy Anansi is and doesn't believe his story.

Mantinband, Gerda. **The Blabbermouths: Adapted from a German Folktale.** Illus. by Paul Borovsky. New York: Greenwillow Books, 1992.

You'll find similarities between this folktale and the one by Gonsález about Juan Bobo. Here a poor farmer is given an iron chest full of gold by an old woman. She says he can set her free from the spell she's under by keeping the chest and telling no one about it.

As soon as he gets home, the farmer tells his wife and later a neighbor who blabs to her brother. In this way the news travels until everyone in the village knows, including the magistrate. When the official sends for the farmer, the wife goes in his place. The magistrate insists the farmer stole the gold, and the wife responds that no one should listen to her husband because he's crazy. The magistrate wants them both in court in two weeks. That's enough time for the clever wife to implement a plan that plays on her husband's gullibility and that will convince everyone her husband is crazy and that there is no gold.

I particularly like the clever wife, who does love her foolish but honest husband.

The language has a pleasing rhythm in the best oral tradition. The illustrations in watercolors, colored pencils, and black ink are delicate and charming. The people's faces with their long noses and fat lips remind me of the artwork of Peter Max.

Mayo, Margaret. "The King Who Wanted to Touch the Moon," pp. 54-58, in **Magical Tales from Many Lands.** Illus. by Jane Ray. New York: E. P. Dutton, 1993.

In this short and silly tale, children meet a king who wants to touch the moon. He orders the royal carpenter to make it possible. Everyone in the kingdom is told to bring their wooden chests to the king. When they don't stack to the moon, all the trees in the kingdom are cut and the wood made into chests. The king climbs them, but he needs one more to reach the moon. So, the king orders the carpenter to take one chest out from the bottom of the pile and put it on top. When the carpenter does, everything tumbles, including the king.

Morris, Winifred. **The Magic Leaf.** Illus. by Ju-Hong Chen. New York: Atheneum, 1987.

Meet Lee Foo, swordsman and scholar, smart-looking but not very bright, who lives in northeast China. When he drops his sword in the water and it sinks to the bottom of the lake, Lee Foo marks the side of his boat where the sword entered the water. He figures he can return later and he'll know where to find the sword. The reader quickly realizes Lee Foo is foolish, although he thinks he's smart because he reads large, heavy books.

One day Lee Foo reads a book of magic. He reads and follows the instructions for finding a magic leaf. Lee Foo finds the leaf but drops it in a large pile of leaves. Lee Foo takes the leaves to his wife and as he holds them up one by one he asks her if she can see him. Finally, tired of saying yes, she says no. Lee Foo decides he has the magic leaf since his wife said that he had made himself invisible.

Lee Foo peeks into the mayor's garden, which he's wanted to see since he was a boy. He's caught, taken to jail, and then brought before the judge. Fortunately the judge believes in magic and heavy books. While holding the "magic leaf" the judge asks Lee Foo if he can see the judge. When Lee Foo says no, the judge releases him, but Lee Foo must leave the magic leaf with the judge.

Children can decide who is more foolish, Lee Foo or the judge.

Philip, Neil, selector and reteller. "The Wishes," pp. 38-42, in **Fairy Tales of Eastern Europe.** Illus. by Larry Wilkes. New York: Clarion Books, 1991.

Children enjoy this clever Hungarian version of "The Three Wishes" with a twist. When a man helps a woman whose carriage is stuck, the woman grants him three wishes of his wife's choosing. The man's wife wishes for sausages. When the husband knocks the pan and the sausages fall, the wife, in fright, wishes the sausages on her husband's nose. He convinces his wife to use the third wish to get the sausages off his nose. In this telling, however, the couple's dreams come true with hard work.

Pitre, Felíx, reteller. **Juan Bobo and the Pig: A Puerto Rican Folktale.** Illus. by Christy Hale. New York: Lodestar, 1993.

Bold linoleum-block prints in warm, vivid colors outlined in thick blue capture the spirit and Caribbean flavor of this humorous story.

Juan Bobo (folk hero of Puerto Rico) watches his mother prepare for church. She curls her hair; cinches herself into a girdle; dons a fancy dress, earrings, necklaces, and bracelets; and applies makeup. Then she sashays to church. Juan must stay behind and watch the pig. The pig squeals even after Juan feeds it and gives it something to drink. Juan decides the pig wants to go to church. He takes the pig to his mother's room and dresses the pig in girdle, dress, and jewelry. When he opens the door, the pig runs into a mudhole. Juan's mother returns, Juan tells his story, and his mother is horrified.

The narrator reveals that's why even now in Puerto Rico when a person dresses fancy and tries to be a show-off, people say the person looks like "Simple John's pig."

Spanish words are interspersed in a natural way. This is a clever, modern version of a classic tale.

Rockwell, Anne. "Mr. Vinegar," pp. 60-65, in **Puss in Boots and Other Stories.** Illus. by author. New York: Macmillan, 1988.

A poor man and woman live in a vinegar bottle until, one day, Mrs. Vinegar accidentally thumps too hard with her broom and the house crashes. Mr. Vinegar puts the house's door on his back, and the couple go to seek their fortune. That night they place the door in the branches of a tree and sleep on it. During the night, Mr. Vinegar awakens and hears thieves dividing their spoils. Terrified, Mr. Vinegar trembles, the door shakes and falls on the thieves, who flee without their gold coins.

In the morning Mrs. Vinegar tells her husband to go to the fair in a nearby town and buy a cow with the golden coins. Mr. Vinegar buys the cow, but before he returns to his wife, he's enthralled by a variety of items—bagpipes, gloves, and a walking stick—and trades each item for the next. Finally, a parrot sees Mr. Vinegar, recounts how Mr. Vinegar traded foolishly, and calls him a simpleton. In his anger, Mr. Vinegar throws the stick at the bird and returns to his wife with nothing.

Schwartz, Amy, reteller. **The Lady Who Put Salt in Her Coffee: From the Peterkin Papers by Lucretia Hale.** Illus. by Amy Schwartz. New York: Harcourt Brace Jovanovich, 1989.

Amy Schwartz combines an appealing retelling with humorous paintings full of many details. The illustrations are a visual delight and suggest the Victorian period, in which the story is set. The characters' bodies are fluid, and their faces stylized. Although the story was first published in 1867, it's not dated. The tale is full of hilarious and silly people.

The zaniness begins when Mrs. Peterkin puts salt in her coffee instead of sugar. It tastes awful and she doesn't know what to do, so she asks her family. Agamemnon suggests they ask the chemist for help. He puts chemicals in the coffee, but it doesn't help. The herb woman puts hop, spruce gum, catnip, and other herbs in the coffee, which make it taste horrible. It's getting late, Mrs. Peterkin wants her coffee, so Elizabeth Eliza suggests they ask the wise lady who's visiting from Philadelphia. The lady suggests Mrs. Peterkin make a fresh cup of coffee. Mrs. Peterkin's five children wonder why they didn't think of that.

Schwartz, Howard, and Barbara Rush, selectors and retellers. "Chusham and the Wind," pp. 29-33, in **Jewish Tales from Around the World.** Illus. by Uri Shulevitz. New York: Harper-Collins, 1991.

This amusing tale from Iraq is related to the "Lazy Jack" tales. Here, the family doesn't get angry with the young boy, they just love him. Children enjoy this story best when you memorize and tell it, rather than read it.

Chusham is always eager to go to market for his mother, but he never can remember how he's supposed to carry the food home. When his mother tells him what he should have done, Chusham does that with the next item he purchases. The results are disastrous. Chusham tells the chickens to fly home, but they don't. He ties eggs together, drags them along, and they break. Chusham stuffs flour into a bag, the bag breaks, and the wind blows the flour over him. Grandmother laughs, but she and Chusham's mother, father, sister, and brother hug him because they love him unconditionally.

Schwartz, Howard, and Barbara Rush. "Moving a Mountain," pp. 85-92, in **The Diamond Tree: Jewish Tales from Around the World.** Illus. by Uri Shulevitz. New York: HarperCollins, 1991.

The foolish people who live in Chelm, Poland, consider Beryl, Shmerel, Moishe, and Oysher the wise men of the city and go to them for advice. Their advice, however, is ridiculous. One summer it's extremely hot. The wise men suggest bringing snow from the mountain tops, but the snow melts. The wise men suggest fooling the sun into thinking it's winter by wearing heavy clothing, but the people get hotter. Finally, they decide the mountain outside of Chelm is blocking the breeze. Two strong men, Mendel and Lemel, are told to move the mountain. They push the mountain for hours, getting hotter until they remove their shirts. Unseen, a thief takes the shirts and flees. When Mendel and Lemel realize they've been robbed, they go to the wise men, who exclaim that Lemel and Mendel have done a great deed. If they can't see their shirts, they must have moved the mountain far.

Singer, Isaac Bashevis. "The Fools of Chelm and the Stupid Carp," pp. 205-11, in **The Random House Book of Humor for Children.** Selected by Pamela Pollack. Illus. by Paul O. Zelinsky. New York: Random House, 1988.

A funny tale by a master storyteller, this story is most effective if memorized and told.

Chelm is a city of fools. The "wise men" of Chelm, including Treitel Fool and Schmendrick Numskull, give Gronam Ox, the community leader of Chelm, a trough of water with a large, live carp in it in appreciation of Gronam Ox's wisdom. When Gronam leans close to examine the carp, the fish lifts its tail and smacks Gronam across the face. Gronam can't believe the carp did this. He declares the carp a fool and says the carp must be punished. While Gronam thinks of a suitable punishment, the carp is catered to and kept healthy. Finally, Gronam decrees that the carp will be drowned. The executioner throws the carp in the lake. Gronam proclaims further that if the carp didn't drown, and if it's ever caught again, they'll punish the carp by building a large pool for it and making it prisoner for life. This book is very funny, and the humor is not lost on children.

Uchida, Yoshiko. **The Two Foolish Cats (Suggested by a Japanese Folktale).** Illus. by Margot Zemach. New York: Margaret K. McElderry Books/Macmillan, 1987.

Uchida's tale will appeal to a wide age group. The plot moves swiftly, the story is humorous, and the language is vivid. Zemach's watercolor paintings have a delicacy yet a strength. They have the quality of Japanese art in the brushstrokes.

Two cats, Big Daizo and Suki, play and catch fish together. One day they catch nothing and head home wet, hungry, and angry at each other. When the cats see two rice cakes, one larger than the other, they fight over the cakes. Badger suggests they ask wise Monkey for advise. Monkey puts the cakes on a tiny pair of scales and nibbles a bite from each until they are gone. The cats feel foolish.

Demonstration/Participation Activities

Burr, Daniella. "Freeze Frame Game," p. 35, in **Don't Just Sit There! 50 Ways to Have a Nickelodeon Day.** Illus. by Steve Henry. New York: Grossett & Dunlap, 1992.

All you need is a group of children who are willing to make funny faces. The game is a take-off on the traditional game "Gossip."

Murphy, Jim. **Guess Again: More Weird and Wacky Inventions.** New York: Bradbury Press, 1986.

Murphy's book includes 45 strange but real inventions, some that worked, others that didn't. The author adapted original drawings that were submitted to the United States Patent Office by the inventors and illustrations from nineteenth-century issues of **Scientific American.**

Most of these inventions are silly looking, and their intended uses are often funny. The inventions range from a life preserver for horses and a mechanical dance partner to a scalp massager and a machine for patting a baby to sleep.

You can turn this book into a game. Read the description of an invention to the children. Show them the accompanying illustration. Read the three possible names for the item and give the children time to guess which of the answers is correct. Then turn the page and show the children the illustration of the invention as it was intended to be used. Continue doing this with various inventions as long as the children are interested.

If you'd like to extend this activity further, give the children time to invent their own time-saving devices. They can draw their inventions, invite the other children to guess what they've invented, and then describe their creations.

Sitarz, Paula Gaj. "Lazy-Day Activities Pantomime."

Invite the children to act out these and any other lazy-day activities you and they can think of. Continue as long as children are interested.

Lazy-Day Activities:

1. Read a book.

2. Play a board game.

3. Put on headphones, listen to, and move to different types of music.

4. Lie on a grassy hill, look at the clouds, and pick out patterns in them.

5. Get a pillow and take a nap in your favorite sleeping position.

6. Make a puzzle.

7. Collect appropriate materials and draw a picture.

8. Your mom asks you to stir the sauce she's cooking for dinner. Stand at the stove and stir the tomato sauce slowly and without enthusiasm.

9. Dad tells you to take out the garbage. It's hot and you're drooping. Leisurely drag the trash cans to the curb.

10. You're in a pool on a hot day. Lie on an inflatable raft, trail your hand in the water, and float around.

Sitarz, Paula Gaj. "Silly Face."

Before the program make several odd-shaped heads out of different-colored pieces of felt. Design and cut out colorful and zany eyes, ears, noses, and mouths.

During the program put one of the heads on a felt board. Invite each child in turn to add a feature to the face until the group has created a "silly face." Continue as long as the children are having fun.

Chapter 10

Magic and Magicians

Read Alouds

Anderson, Joy. **Juma and the Magic Jinn.** Illus. by Charles Mikolaycak. New York: Lothrop, Lee & Shepard, 1986.

Juma, a young boy who lives on the island of Lama off the coast of Kenya in the Indian Ocean, is banished from school for daydreaming. Alone at home he decides to release the jinn from the family's jinn jar, although his mother has warned him against doing so. You never know if your jinn is good or bad. Juma thinks his wishes are perfect until they come true. His experiences make him realize that where he began is where he wants to be.

Ayres, Becky Hickox. **Matreshka.** Illus. by Alexi Natchev. New York: A Doubleday Book for Young Readers/Delacorte, 1992.

A young girl named Kata lives with her grandfather in a Russian forest. One day Kata is returning home from town when she shares her bread and cheese with a hungry woman. Grateful, the woman gives Kata a little wooden doll named Matreshka that she carved and painted.

Matreshka saves Kata's life when Kata comes to a house on giant chicken legs, knocks on the door, and is pulled in by Baba Yaga, a witch. Baba Yaga locks Kata in a small room and declares that she'll cook Kata for dinner on Sunday. Matreshka actually consists of five dolls, one inside the next. As Matreshka helps Kata escape and the situation requires a slightly smaller doll, the next one pops out. When Kata is finally free, the Matreshkas hop back together. A satisfying tale of magic and adventure, this story holds children's interest. The author builds tension well. Youngsters wonder if Baba Yaga will see the dolls and if she'll succeed in cooking Kata.

The rich, deep, vivid watercolors sprawl over the pages. They are more tableaux, capturing specific moments in the story. The artwork is sometimes expressionistic; you see only pieces of an entire setting but feel the whole. For example, you see a door with a key, yet you picture the entire house. Illustrator Natchev also conveys Baba Yaga's horrible appearance well. Here she has a bulbous, downward pointing nose with warts, small beady eyes, a wide wrinkled chin, and a mouth that reveals her gums and her few remaining teeth.

Betz, Adrienne, and Lucia Monfried, comps. "The Magic Pot," (Traditional), pp. 48-53, in **Diane Goode's Book of Silly Stories and Songs.** Illus. by Diane Goode. New York: Dutton Children's Books, 1992.

Amusing illustrations are interspersed in this tale of a poor girl who lives alone with her mother and who, while looking for food in the forest, meets an old woman who gives her a magic pot. When the girl wants porridge she must say "Cook, little pot, cook." The girl and her mother are no longer hungry. One day the little girl goes out, the mother says the magic phrase, eats until she's full, and then forgets the words to make the pot stop. By the time the little girl returns home, porridge fills the house, the street, and the neighboring homes. The girl makes the pot stop, but those who want to return to town must eat their way back.

Cole, Joanna. **Doctor Change.** Illus. by Donald Carrick. New York: William Morrow, 1986.

Donald Carrick's illustrations are beautiful period paintings, expressive and absorbing.

Tom, a poor boy and a stranger in town, is happy to become the house servant of Doctor Change until, despite the doctor's warning, he looks through the keyhole of Doctor Change's attic room and sees the doctor alter his shape. Tom is frightened, but Doctor Change won't let Tom leave. One day, when the doctor is away, Tom sneaks into the attic room, reads the Doctor's book of magic and learns some spells and how to change his form. By changing into a puddle of water Tom drips onto the front step, transforms into himself, and escapes. Tom meets Kate, whom he helps retrieve a lost coin, and when Doctor Change comes looking for Tom to bring him back, Kate helps Tom escape and outwit Doctor Change for good.

Cooper, Susan. **The Silver Cow: A Welsh Tale.** Illus. by Warwick Hutton. New York: Atheneum, 1983.

This is both a story of magic and a magically told story by a master storyteller. Young Huw's father is mean and greedy. Huw must work the land and take the cows to pasture instead of going to school. Often Huw sneaks his harp out and plays it in the fields. The magic people of Wales, the Tylwyth Teg, hear Huw and give him a silver cow as a gift. Huw's father becomes rich once the silver cow gives birth to many calves, but he locks up his gold and gives nothing to his wife and son.

When the silver cow is old, Huw's father decides to have it butchered. The Tylwyth Teg take revenge by calling all the cows into the lake and taking all the gold. White water lilies appear in the lake in place of the cows.

Day, David. **The Sleeper.** Illus. by Mark Entwisle. Nashville, TN: Ideals Children's Books, 1990.

Mark Entwisle's beautiful, muted, impressionistic watercolors perfectly complement this tale of magic and enchantment.

Wu Wing Wong of Wulung lives high in the Tong Mountains of China in the oldest and finest monastery, which also houses the greatest library in China. One day Wu's peaceful existence ceases when the emperor, Chin the Merciless, commands that the books from every library be given to him.

The emperor gives the librarians 100 days to empty their libraries. On the 99th day Wu must deliver the last three bundles of books to the emperor's officers. Wu's journey is interrupted by a storm, an attack by a tiger, and a plunge in the river. Eventually he retrieves the horses and the books and finds shelter in a cave, where a man dressed in white and one dressed in black are playing chess. The man in white wins and gives the winning white pawn to Wu. The pawn is a miniature of Wu. Looking into the man's eyes Wu falls asleep. When Wu awakens he doesn't realize that he has slept for 200 years. People are fleeing to the mountains. A war is in progress between an army in black and one in white. Chin the Emperor had burned all the books, and without them, it is impossible to prove which side should rule. Wu restores peace and becomes a hero because he has the sacred Book of Ancestors, which reveals who should be emperor.

Dennis, Christopher. **The Fool of the World and the Flying Ship: A Russian Folktale from the Skazki of Polevoi.** Illus. by author. New York: Philomel Books, 1994.

Dennis offers an exciting retelling of a classic Russian folktale and illustrates it with beautiful paintings of lush landscapes and charming animal characters. Members of a poor peasant family of mice hear a proclamation from the czar that he will marry his daughter to whomever can build a flying ship. The third mouse son, the Fool, meets The Old One, who likes the trusting Fool and tells him how to make a flying ship appear. The Fool must take everyone he meets while on his journey.

When he finally arrives at the czar's castle the Fool is accompanied by Listening One, Swift-of-Foot, Marksman, Gobbler, Thirstyman, Woodman, and Strawmonger. The czar is unwilling to marry his daughter to a peasant, so he challenges the Fool to complete a series of impossible tasks. The Fool, with the assistance of his companions, easily outwits the czar and scares him, too.

dePaola, Tomie. **Strega Nona.** Illus. by author. Englewood Cliffs, NJ: Prentice-Hall, 1975.

This wonderful story by author-illustrator dePaola is perfect to read aloud or to tell. Big Anthony, who is not very bright, is hired by Strega Nona. She works magic for the people of the village but is getting older and needs help with her chores. Strega Nona warns Anthony not to touch her pasta pot, but when Anthony overhears Strega Nona saying magic words to the pot and pasta appears, he decides that someday he will use the magic pot. In his excitement he doesn't hear or see the magic needed to stop the flow of pasta. Anthony's experiment with the magic pot leads to disaster.

dePaola, Tomie. **Strega Nona Meets Her Match.** Illus. by author. New York: G. P. Putnam's Sons, 1993.

When Strega Amelia visits her friend, the good witch Strega Nona, she's amazed at how many people see Strega Nona to get husbands and cures for warts and headaches. Some time later Strega Amelia returns with modern equipment to cure the same ailments. Soon the townspeople visit her instead, Strega Nona has no customers, and she must let go her helpers Big Anthony and Bambolona. Big Anthony gets a job with Strega Amelia and soon, with business booming, Strega Amelia leaves Big Anthony to run everything for a few days. Big Anthony, who is sweet but not bright, runs the husband and wife machine backwards, mixes the wart cream and hair restorer, and ruins everything. Everyone rushes back to Strega Nona. They'll stick with the old ways—the magic of Strega Nona.

dePaola, Tomie. **Strega Nona's Magic Lessons.** Illus. by author. New York: Harcourt Brace Jovanovich, 1982.

Bambolona, the baker's daughter, is tired of working in the bakery day and night so she visits Strega Nona, the good witch, and begins learning magic from her. Big Anthony, Strega's assistant, is angry when Strega Nona says she can't teach him magic. Anthony learns that only females can be Stregas, so he disguises himself as a young lady and returns to Strega Nona. Anthony can't get the magic right. Bambolona and Strega, who know it's Anthony in disguise, decide to play a trick on Anthony so he won't want to fool with magic again.

Haviland, Virginia, reteller. **The Talking Pot: A Danish Folktale.** Illus. by Melissa Sweet. Boston: Little, Brown, 1990.

This delightful story is complemented by soft watercolors that convey humor, liveliness, and a sense of action. The talking pot is a precious character, personified with eyes, nose, and mouth. The artwork gives a flavor of Danish architecture, clothing, and housewares.

When a poor Danish family is reduced to selling the family cow, the father trades the cow for a talking pot. Three days in a row the pot runs to the rich man's house on its three legs and is filled on each successive day with ingredients for pudding, enough wheat to feed them for years, and gold coins. When the pot returns to the rich man's house on the fourth day, the rich man is there. He knows what the pot has done, demands the pot return his gold and flings himself on the pot. The rich man sticks to the pot, which skips far away.

Howe, James. **Rabbit-Cadabra!** Illus. by Alan Daniel. New York: Morrow Junior Books, 1993.

Visually appealing illustrations accompany this madcap story written in the style of Howe's other titles about Harold the dog and Chester the cat.

Toby loves magic, and he's excited that The Amazing Karlovsky is coming to town. His animals, however, have a different reaction. Chester tells Harold and Howie, Toby's other dog, that Bunnicula, Toby's rabbit, is the real magician and a vampire rabbit, too. Chester's imagination runs away with him until he decides that the magician Karlovsky is from Transylvania and that he pulls vampire rabbits out of his hat.

Once Toby and his family leave for the magic show, Chester galvanizes the animals into action. They must keep the vampire rabbits from doing their dastardly deeds. He needs garlic to ward the vampires off, but old pizza they find in the trash will do. The animals run to the magic show, and Chester sends Harold running onstage with pizza in his teeth. Bedlam occurs. Later Chester and the animals learn the real story.

The author includes instructions for "The Rabbit-Cadabra! Magic Trick," which children can do with a paper hat and sock rabbit.

Johnston, Tony. **The Badger and the Magic Fan.** Illus. by Tomie dePaola. New York: G. P. Putnam's Sons, 1990.

Here's a lighthearted tale of mischief and magic with sparkling, playful paintings by a tremendous author-illustrator team.

When Badger sees three goblin children playing with a magic fan that can make noses larger and smaller, he tricks the goblin children and steals the fan. Badger then sees a beautiful girl with a rich father, sneaks up, and fans her nose.

The rich father promises his daughter in marriage and half his wealth to anyone who can make her nose short again. Badger appears, uses the magic fan, and marries the daughter.

After the wedding feast, while Badger is sleeping, the goblins find him and use the fan on Badger. His nose grows to heaven, where the heavenly workers think the nose is a pole they can use. They yank the nose and Badger into the sky. The goblin children keep the magic fan.

Kimmel, Eric A. **Baba Yaga: A Russian Folktale.** Illus. by Megan Lloyd. New York: Holiday House, 1991.

Megan Lloyd's illustrations are sharp, deep, full of rich colors, and have a distinctive European flavor.

Marina is the kind-hearted daughter of a wealthy merchant. She would be beautiful except for a big ugly horn that grows out of the middle of her forehead. When Marina's mother dies, her father eventually marries a proud, haughty woman whose daughter, Marusia, is spiteful and lazy. When the merchant journeys to a foreign land and doesn't return after several years, Marina's stepmother assumes he's dead and is cruel to Marina. When Marusia says that Marina's horn distresses her, the stepmother tricks Marina into running an errand to Baba Yaga the witch. On the way Marina meets a tiny green frog who tells her what she must do to remain safe. At Baba Yaga's house Marina does what the frog told her and saves herself. The story is particularly exciting when Baba Yaga chases Marina in her giant mortar with pestle.

Marina gets rid of her horn, her father returns from his journey, and the stepmother and daughter are banished and get their just rewards at the hands of Baba Yaga. Kimmel's telling moves swiftly and is spellbinding throughout.

MacDonald, Margaret Read. "The Little Rooster and the Turkish Sultan," pp. 57-65, in **Twenty Tellable Tales: Audience Participation Folktales for the Beginning Storyteller.** Illus. by Roxane Murphy. Chicago: H. W. Wilson, 1986.

You'll find this story easy to learn and tell because it has lots of repetition. It's a tale of magic that's very funny.

A Little Old Lady lives with her Little Pet Rooster. One day the rooster finds a diamond button while pecking for something to eat. The rooster is carrying the diamond in his beak to give to the woman, when the Turkish Sultan happens along. The Sultan sees the diamond and demands that his servants catch the rooster and take the diamond.

Several times the rooster demands his diamond button. Each time, the sultan gets angry and punishes Rooster. With his magic stomach, Rooster is able to free himself. He's thrown in a well and able to drink all the water. Then rooster is thrown into a fire, but he spits out the water and puts out the fire. Rooster is next thrown into a bee hive, but he eats all the bees and they can't sting his magic stomach.

Infuriated, the Sultan commands that the rooster be dropped into the seat of his baggy pants so he can sit on Rooster. Inside the Sultan's pants Rooster tells his stomach to let out the bees and they sting the Sultan's bottom. Finally, the Sultan releases Rooster and returns the diamond button.

Mahy, Margaret. "The Boy Who Bounced," pp. 75-80, in **Tick Tock Tales: Twelve Stories to Read Around the Clock.** Illus. by Wendy Smith. New York: Macmillan, 1993.

When a young boy, who has the bad habit of bouncing like a ball, bounds into a sleeping magician and refuses to apologize, the magician turns the boy into a big, red, rubber, bouncing ball. The magician will meet the boy in a year to decide if he will return him to human form. During that year the boy, now a ball, is swept by waves and wind across many countries. He also rescues a magician from 12 evil men. His good deed results in the original magician turning him back into a boy, for the magician he saved is the other magician's brother.

Meyers, Odette, reteller. **The Enchanted Umbrella.** (Based on a French Folktale). Illus. by Margot Zemach. San Diego: Harcourt Brace Jovanovich, 1988.

Meyers tells this short, whimsical story with an economy of words that captures the character's emotions and move the tale smoothly from one incident to another. Meyers builds tremendous sympathy for the good character Patou. Margot Zemach's colorful yet soft and fluid watercolors capture the many moods of this tale, from somber and sad to threatening and fanciful. Zemach is such a fine illustrator that her pictures help propel the plot.

Patou is an umbrella maker's assistant, but the two men are more like family to each other. Patou cares for the man and does all his work when he is ill. The umbrella maker's greedy nephew does nothing. When the man dies, however, the nephew throws Patou out in the rain and gives him a ragged umbrella he says his uncle left for Patou.

Patou soon learns that the umbrella is magical when he's attacked by thieves and the umbrella sweeps Patou in the air. When Patou uses his umbrella to rescue a rich couple who are threatened by a tiger, the rich man steals Patou's umbrella. The magic umbrella flies the rich man into the air and drops him in the river. When Patou realizes he's been robbed, he yells "thief," but the rich man has Patou thrown in the river. About to drown, Patou sees his umbrella floating upside down, gets in it, and floats to a land where the people have never seen an umbrella. These people know that long ago kings had umbrellas, so they crown Patou king and give him a house. Patou wants everyone to have an umbrella and sets up shop.

The delightful book includes a brief history of umbrellas.

Moore, Inga. **The Sorcerer's Apprentice.** Illus. by author. New York: Macmillan, 1989.

Franz, a wild boy who always gets into trouble, is thrown out by his father. He becomes an apprentice to the sorcerer Ludvig Hexenmeister. When he sees the sorcerer's vast laboratory, Franz thinks his job will be exciting. His task, however, is to go up and down a steep flight of steps three times to get enough water from the river to fill the big, black cauldron. Franz gets up at dawn every day to do this difficult work that leaves him with his legs feeling like jelly.

Once his chores are done, Franz watches the sorcerer do his spells. The charm he likes best is the one that makes an old broom able to do work. Franz thinks he could do that spell, but the sorcerer's rule is to watch and learn, and not to touch.

One morning the sorcerer is away, and Franz tries to create the magic potion and recite the chant that will make the broom work. The broom grows arms and stands on its bristles. It fetches water and fills the cauldron, but Franz forgets the words to make it stop. In desperation he chops the broom in two with an ax. Now there are two brooms with four buckets. Franz panics and smashes the broom. Each splinter becomes a broom. An army of brooms go back and forth to the river and the water gets deep in the lab.

The sorcerer returns and rights everything. Franz prepares for a scolding, but, while the sorcerer says there must be a penalty, he does think Franz will someday make a good magician.

This tale will hold the interest of a wide age range. The writing has a pleasing rhythm, and the language holds you from the first page. The full-color illustrations are magical and fantastic looking. The painting of the brooms marching with metal buckets and Franz standing on his spindly legs and staring at the brooms with his hair sticking straight up is incredible. Moore depicts scenes from different perspectives. Linger over the paintings of the views from above of the magician's laboratory and the steps that lead down to the river.

Rhee, Nami. **Magic Spring: A Korean Folktale.** Illus. by author. New York: G. P. Putnam's Sons, 1993.

Author Rhee introduces children to an elderly couple who have no children, do their own work, and never complain. Their neighbor is rich, greedy, and has a staff of servants.

One spring day the old man sees and hears the beautiful voice of a tiny bluebird. He follows the bird through woods, over a stream, and up one side of a mountain and down the other into a valley where he finds a small spring of water between the rocks. Thirsty, the man drinks the cold water. When he returns home his wife is amazed because now he is a young man. The wife drinks from the spring, and she, too, becomes young. The greedy neighbor visits and learns their secret.

When he doesn't return from the spring the newly young couple search for him. They find, wrapped in the cloak of the greedy neighbor, a tiny baby—the child they've always wanted.

Schwartz, Howard, and Barbara Rush, selectors and retellers. "The Magic Sandals of Abu Kassim," pp. 45-52, in **The Diamond Tree: Jewish Tales from Around the World.** Illus. by Uri Shulevitz. New York: HarperCollins, 1991.

This story is accompanied by beautiful and vivid watercolors.

Abu Kassim is a poor rag seller who lives in Turkey. One day an elderly, tired man approaches as Abu is about to eat his lunch, a piece of crusty bread. When Abu gives the bread to the man, the man grants Abu a special wish.

Abu wishes for a pair of shoes. His wish is granted and his fortunes change. Eventually he is wealthy and tries to get rid of his now ragged sandals. No matter what he does they are returned to him. Ultimately he realizes the sandals are magic and never tries to get rid of them again.

Snyder, Zilpha Keatley. **The Changing Maze.** Illus. by Charles Mikolaycak. New York: Macmillan, 1985.

Snyder's tale is sophisticated, fascinating, and attention-grabbing. Youngsters will listen eagerly to learn what will happen next. Hugh, a shepherd boy, lives with his elderly granny and an orphan lamb. Hugh's granny often tells him the tale of a wizard king who commanded his gardeners to create a maze that grew and changed its configuration constantly. The king invited nobles to solve the mystery of the maze and promised them the gold hidden in the maze as a reward. None could unlock the secret, but all were changed by it, even the king. Hugh believes in this story of long ago.

One winter day when his lamb disappears into the maze beside the now crumbling castle, Hugh follows, finds the lamb, and then is drawn by both the cry of the lamb and the golden hum from the chest of gold. When he responds to the moan of the lamb rather than the hum from the gold, Hugh secures his freedom and breaks the spell of the maze.

The illustrations are realistic, vivid, and sprawling. They are rendered in shades of white, brown, gray, and green.

Steig, William. **The Amazing Bone.** Illus. by author. New York: Farrar, Straus & Giroux, 1976.

A young pig named Pearl finds a talking bone that can speak several languages, make sounds, and create music. The bone belongs to a witch, but it would prefer to go home with Pearl. On the way home the bone's magic scares three robbers intent on harming Pearl and rescues Pearl from a fox intent on cooking her.

Steig, William. **Solomon the Rusty Nail.** Illus. by author. New York: Farrar, Straus & Giroux, 1985.

One day a seemingly ordinary rabbit named Solomon happens to scratch his nose and wiggle his toes at exactly the same time and he turns into a rusty nail. Solomon discovers that when he thinks, "I'm a rabbit!" he turns back into himself. Solomon keeps his magic power a secret and plays tricks on his family. One day he makes the mistake of turning into a nail and then back into a rabbit in front of a nasty cat named Ambrose. When Solomon turns back into a nail to escape Ambrose, the cat takes Solomon home. Ambrose and his wife plan to eat Solomon when he turns back into a rabbit. But Solomon remains a nail. In his anger Ambrose hammers Solomon the nail to the outside of his house. Ultimately a fire leads to Solomon's freedom and he returns home.

Steig, William. **Sylvester and the Magic Pebble.** Illus. by author. New York: Windmill Books, 1969.

Sylvester Duncan, a young donkey, loves to collect pebbles of unusual shape and color. His hobby gets him into trouble one rainy day when he finds a shiny, round pebble that grants wishes. On his way home a lion confronts Sylvester, and in his panic he wishes to be a rock. Now the pebble is nearby but unless it touches him and he wishes to turn back into himself, Sylvester will remain a rock.

Seasons pass and one day in the spring Sylvester's parents go on a picnic, find the magic pebble, place it on the rock that is Sylvester, and comment on how Sylvester would like the pebble. This action finally lets Sylvester become himself again.

Van Allsburg, Chris. **The Garden of Abdul Gasazi.** Illus. by author. Boston: Houghton Mifflin, 1979.

Young Alan is taking care of Miss Hester's mean-tempered dog, Fritz. While out walking, Alan and Fritz come to the garden of Abdul Gasazi, a retired magician. Fritz breaks out of his collar and runs ahead. Alan follows and meets Gasazi the Great, who leads him to Fritz, whom he has turned into a duck. Fritz takes Alan's hat and flies away. When Alan explains to Miss Hester that Fritz is lost, she says that Alan was fooled by Gasazi because Fritz is there and he's clearly a dog. After Alan leaves Miss Hester's, there's an illustration of Fritz with Alan's cap.

Van Allsburg complements his mysterious text with fascinating illustrations done with carbon pencil in dark and light shades. His drawings have a mixed air of reality and illusion.

Van Allsburg, Chris. **The Sweetest Fig.** Illus. by author. Boston: Houghton Mifflin, 1993.

Allsburg's part-realistic, part-fantastic illustrations in muted shades of brown, white, and flesh tones blend seamlessly with his mysterious story.

Monsieur Bibot is a cold-hearted, greedy dentist who is even mean to his dog. A woman with a toothache comes to his office begging for help. Thinking of the money he'll make, Bibot extracts her tooth. When the woman admits she has no money to pay and instead gives Bibot two figs that she says will make his dreams come true, Bibot is angry and refuses to give her the painkillers she needs.

That evening Bibot eats one of the delicious figs. In the morning while walking his dog he sees his reflection and realizes he's dressed in his underwear. He also sees the Eiffel Tower drooping. This is what he dreamed the previous evening.

Now he believes the figs are magic and does everything to be sure he'll dream he's the richest man on earth. He also decides that his dog, Marcel, won't be in his new life. Marcel, however, eats the second fig. The next morning Bibot realizes he's become a dog and Marcel is now a man. Marcel's dream came true.

Van Allsburg, Chris. **The Widow's Broom.** Illus. by author. Boston: Houghton Mifflin, 1992.

A witch lands on her broom near the farmhouse of Minna Shaw, a lonely widow, when the broom loses its strength in the air. The witch leaves her old broom with Minna, but it still has some magic left. It can chop wood, fetch water, play the piano, and sweep the floor. Minna's neighbors, the Spivey's, are sure the broom is the devil, and they burn it.

Soon, night after night, what appears to be the ghost of the broom holding an ax circles the Spivey home until they decide to leave town. Minna stays with her friend, the broom. It was not a ghost; Minna had coated it with white paint. (It never really burned.)

Van Allsburg's illustrations are rendered in incredible shades of brown, white, gray, and black. They enhance the text and add to its magic and mystery.

Willard, Nancy. **The Sorcerer's Apprentice.** Illus. by Leo and Diane Dillon. New York: The Blue Sky Press/Scholastic, 1993.

Author Willard has updated and created her own unique version of this classic tale. The text is in rhyme, and Willard's imagery is vivid. The illustrations by the award-winning Dillons are detailed and executed with a sense of movement and liveliness. Their watercolors are full of surprises, with scenes shown from different perspectives on each page. Their creatures are original.

Sylvia, the apprentice, arrives on a bicycle. Tottibo, the magician, wants Sylvia to make new clothes for his dragons, gryphons, and other creatures. Sylvia, however, wants to learn magic. Tottibo warns that spells must be practiced. Finding her work as a seamstress frustrating, Sylvia ignores Tottibo's warning and attempts to work some magic. Everything goes haywire; the sewing machine stitches the dishes to the table and appliqués dirty socks across the sky. Sylvia cannot undo the spell, but Tottibo awakens, rights matters, and lets Sylvia stay and learn magic properly.

Wright, Jill. **The Old Woman and the Jar of Uums.** Illus. by Glen
Rounds. New York: G. P. Putnam's Sons, 1990.

Jill Wright's story zips along and never slows down. Glen Rounds's
interpretation of the characters are wonderful.

A little old woman's troubles begin when she finds a funny-looking jar
and it says, "Pick me up." It's empty so the woman fills it with sugar. Soon
young Jackie McPhee arrives. The woman gives him a talking-to for throwing
rotten eggs at her house. As they talk and eat and add sugar from the jar to
their tea, Jackie and the woman start saying nothing but "uum." When the old
woman realizes it's a haunted uum jar that makes you say "uum" if you drink
or eat out of it, she goes to visit the scary Willy Nilly Man. He knows magic,
and she's sure he can stop the "uums."

When the old woman realizes the jar belongs to the Willy Nilly Man and
he thinks she stole it, she can't defend herself because she can only say "uum."
The Willy Nilly Man threatens to turn her into a crawdaddy, but Jackie, who's
been hiding in a wheelbarrow, saves the day and scares the Willy Nilly Man
into thinking that the old woman has magic of her own. The Willy Nilly Man
is only too happy to tell the old woman how to undo the magic of the uum jar.

Yolen, Jane. **Greyling.** Illus. by William Stobbs. New York: World, 1991.

This updated edition of **Greyling** (first published in 1968) has new
illustrations. Author Yolen has retold this story from the Islands of Shetland
of a fisherman and his wife who desperately want a child. The fisherman finds
a small gray seal stranded on shore, and when he brings the bundle home it
contains a child with gray eyes and silvery gray hair—a selchie. As the child
grows, the couple are careful to keep him away from the sea. One day when
Greyling is a young man his father is caught in a raging storm while fishing.
Greyling jumps into the sea and attempts to rescue him. He saves the fisherman
but turns back into a seal.

Zemach, Margot. **The Three Wishes: An Old Story.** Illus. by author.
New York: Farrar, Straus & Giroux, 1986.

A man and woman who work as woodcutters and often go hungry learn
that magic must be used carefully. One day a grateful imp whom the couple
rescues from beneath a fallen tree grants them three wishes. Without thought,
the man wishes for a pan of sausages. His wife is so angry that she wishes the
sausages were hanging from her husband's nose. Unfortunately, the couple
must use the last wish to get the sausages off the man's nose.

Booktalks

Carey, Valerie Scho. **Tsugele's Broom.** Illus. by Dirk Zimmer. New
York: A Laura Geringer Book/HarperCollins, 1993.

Carey's story is humorous and clever, and Zimmer's illustrations are
detailed etched paintings, bold and amusing.

Tsugele is a young girl who lives with her parents in the village of Potsk
in Poland. One day when Tsugele's parents say it's time for her to marry,
Tsugele declares that she doesn't need to marry and will do so only if her
parents find a man as reliable as her broom.

Her parents present two men; both are lazy and self-absorbed. Tsugele goes to a neighboring town and becomes a housekeeper for the Mendel's. One night Tsugele dreams that her broom changed into a man and they married. The next day Tsugele can't find her broom but outside she sees a stranger with straw hair sticking up. His name is Broom.

Cecil, Laura, reteller. **The Frog Princess.** Illus. by Emma Chichester Clark. New York: Greenwillow Books, 1994.

The queen tells her sons Bruno, who loves to eat, Lucca, who adores clothing, and Marco, a dreamer, that they must marry. She orders them to each shoot an arrow and where the arrows land is where they'll find their brides. Bruno's arrow leads to the baker's daughter and Lucca's arrow to the tailor's daughter. Marco's arrow lands in a ditch near a green frog.

The queen declares that, since her sons are fools, the son with the most clever woman will rule. She gives the women three tasks: bake a perfect loaf of bread, weave a perfect length of cloth, and train a dog. Marco's frog completes the tasks best. The queen says the wedding will be the next day (no one has seen the frog). When Marco says he'll marry the frog, the spell she was under is broken and she turns into a princess. They marry and rule wisely.

Cole, Joanna. **The Magic School Bus at the Waterworks.** Illus. by Bruce Degen. New York: Scholastic, 1986.

This work is one of several clever, informative, and entertaining books by author Cole in which she blends factual material with her story. The books in this series are an interesting blend of text, labeled illustrations, word bubbles for the characters, and splashy illustrations.

Ms. Frizzle has a unique way to teach her class subject matter. They hop in the school bus and magically enter whatever they're studying. In this book the students enter a water purification system. Any interested youngster can learn water facts and material about reservoirs, filters, pipes—the entire waterworks.

You might also like to recommend other titles in this series, including **The Magic School Bus Inside the Earth, The Magic School Bus and the Solar System, The Magic School Bus in the Human Body,** and **The Magic School Bus Inside the Hurricane.**

Demi. **The Firebird.** Illus. by author. New York: Henry Holt, 1994.

"Horse of Power," a magical horse, is the hero of this famous Russian folktale, beautifully told and illustrated. Demi's artwork consists of spectacular, detailed paintings in brilliant watercolors and fine black ink lines on gold backgrounds.

Trouble begins for Dimitri, a young archer, when, in spite of his wise and magical horse's warning, he picks up a feather from the legendary Firebird and presents it to Czar Ivan. The mean and greedy czar commands Dimitri to bring him the Firebird. Unsatisfied, the czar demands Dimitri bring the princess Vassilissa from the Land of Never to be the czar's bride. Dimitri succeeds because of the wisdom of his horse.

Dimitri falls in love with the princess but must present her to the old czar. Vassilissa doesn't want to marry the czar, and to delay the wedding she says she must have her wedding dress. Dimitri is sent to retrieve the dress from under the sea. Again, he succeeds because of his magical horse.

Vassilissa has another plan to outwit the czar. She demands that Dimitri be thrown into a pot of boiling water. Unseen, Vassilissa sprinkles magic dust in the water so the archer comes out alive and a handsome prince. The czar wants to be young and handsome so he, too, jumps in the cauldron, but he disappears forever. Dimitri and Vassilissa marry and rule the kingdom well. The magical horse, "Horse of Power," is given appropriate thanks and credit.

Grimm, Jakob and Wilhelm Grimm. **The Wishing Table.** Trans. by Anthea Bell. Illus. by Eve Tharlet. Saxonville, MA: Picture Book Studio, 1988.

The tailor's three sons are sent away by their father when the family goat lies and says that the sons don't feed him. The eldest son is given a magic table from the joiner to whom he is apprenticed. On the way home he stops at an inn where the landlord switches tables on him. When he returns home to show off his magic table he is embarrassed instead. The same misfortune befalls the second son, who is tricked out of his magic donkey by the same landlord. The third son gets a cudgel from his master, but when he stays at the inn he tricks the keeper into trying to steal the thick stick. When the cudgel starts to hit the landlord, the third son is able to demand his brothers' magic table and donkey, reveal the thieving innkeeper, and reunite his family.

Haugaard, Erik Christian. **Princess Horrid.** Illus. by Diane Dawson Hearn. New York: Macmillan, 1990.

This book is too lengthy to share as a read aloud and probably has more appeal for girls. The illustrations are detailed, lighthearted, and amusing, especially in the facial expressions of the characters. Illustrator Hearn captures well the atmosphere of a French court.

A nasty princess pulls one prank too many on the members of the royal family when she short-sheets the duchess's bed. The duchess, who knows how to cast spells, turns the princess into a kitten. The kitten is taken care of by the maid Pots-and-Pans, who soon realizes that she's caring for the princess. Pots-and-Pans is resourceful and finds the spell and the ingredients that will restore the princess to human form.

Helldorfer, M. C. **Cabbage Rose.** Illus. by Julie Downing. New York: Bradbury Press, 1993.

Illustrator Downing uses a full range of watercolors in her eye-appealing pictures. She captures well the Elizabethan period, from the marketplace to the clothing and the landscape.

A plain girl called Cabbage lives and works at her brother's inn. One night while her lazy brothers are asleep and Cabbage is painting, a magician enters her room. In the morning he is gone, but he has left Cabbage a new paintbrush. When she paints with it everything she paints becomes real. Cabbage enjoys painting toys and small gifts to give to people, but her greedy brothers force Cabbage to paint riches for them.

Finally Cabbage escapes to the marketplace of the king's city. There she paints for room and board. Soon she is summoned by the king, who commands her to paint. The prince watches and calls her Rose. One day Cabbage paints the portrait of a beautiful woman and becomes her. The prince is sad. He wishes for and asks her to paint Cabbage Rose. Cabbage breaks the paintbrush in half and becomes herself again.

Hutchins, Hazel. **The Three and Many Wishes of Jason Reid.** Illus.
by Julie Tennent. New York: Viking Kestrel, 1988.

Eleven-year-old Jason Reid is a smart boy, so when he meets Quicksilver,
Elster of the Third Order, and is granted three wishes, Jason thinks carefully
before he wishes. Finally, he uses two wishes and makes his third wish a wish
for three more wishes. In this way he has many wishes. Finally, Jason wants
to wish for something that will be good for the entire community. While
Quicksilver is trying to fulfill Jason's huge wish he starts to fade. So Jason gives
up everything he wished for to this point so the wish that will benefit everyone
can come true.

This is a delightful and clever chapter book.

Kimmel, Eric A. **I-Know-Not-What, I-Know-Not-Where: A Russian
Tale.** Illus. by Robert Sauber. New York: Holiday House, 1994.

In this extremely long but well-written folktale, Frol, a young soldier and
archer for the czar, clips the wing of a dove but does not kill it when the dove
begs him not to. The dove, whom Frol names Frolya, rewards him for his
kindness but inadvertently leads him into dangerous and seemingly impossible
tasks. The czar wants the talking dove, Frol refuses to give up the dove, and
the czar's minister, operating on the advise of his wife, attempts to get rid of
Frol. Frol is sent to find the late czar in the other world. He succeeds with the
help of Froyla's golden egg. The minister then sends Frol to the Land of Nine
Times Nine to bring back Kot Buyan, the Talking Cat. Again, with Frolya's
help, Frol accomplishes the deed.

Then the minister's wife advises him to command Frol to bring back
I-Know-Not-What from I-Know-Not-Where. Frol meets the old witch Baba Yaga
on his journey, who helps him because she realizes that the dove Frolya is her
granddaughter, who was turned into a dove to escape an evil wizard. Frol
travels to a mountain of glass where nasty giants guard the Water of Life. This
and I-Know-Not-What are essential to return Frolya to life, whom the minister
shot in Frol's absence. Reunited, Frol and Frolya defeat the czar and his court
and reign justly in their place.

Kimmel, Eric A. **Iron John: Adapted from the Brothers Grimm.**
Illus. by Trina Schart Hyman. New York: Holiday House, 1994.

Author Kimmel is an outstanding, consistently fine contemporary storyteller. The oil paintings by illustrator Hyman are more muted and dreamlike
than her usual style, perfect for this long story.

A wild man named Iron John, with matted gray hair from head to toe, is
kept in a cage by a powerful king. One day, when young prince Walter's golden
ball is swept into Iron John's cage, Iron John offers to return it in exchange for
his freedom. Walter wants to go with Iron John into the forest where Iron John
is king. Iron John instructs Walter to guard the hidden spring and be sure
nothing falls into it or its powers will be lost. Three times, Walter unthinkingly
lets something drop into the water. He and Iron John must part, but Iron John
gives Walter a horn and tells him that if he ever needs anything to go to the
spring and blow the horn three times.

Walter returns to the king's court but is so filthy that he is sent to help
the garden girl, Elsa, with whom he gets along fine. Walter first uses the horn
to be transformed for the king's ball. When Walter hears there's to be a

tournament of the bravest knights, he again calls upon Iron John's magic. Walter wins the contest and, as at the ball, leaves flowers for Elsa. Walter later learns from Elsa that robber knights attacked the king, killed the knights, and took the princesses. Again Iron John uses his magic to allow Walter to catch the traitors and free the princesses. During the battle Walter is wounded. Iron John returns to the king's kingdom dressed regally. He had a curse on him, but the spell has been broken and he is free. However, he grieves for Walter, who can only live if the tears of a maid who truly loves him touch him. The princesses are repulsed by him, but Elsa holds him and sheds tears. Walter arises dressed as a prince with golden hair. Elsa becomes his wife, and in Iron John's kingdom Elsa is Walter's queen.

Mayer, Marianna. **The Spirit of the Blue Light.** Illus. by Laszlo Gal. New York: Macmillan, 1990.

A poor soldier named Michael, returning from war with nowhere to go, is walking through the woods when he meets a mysterious old man named Lawrence. The soldier offers to carry Lawrence's bundle of sticks, and in reward Lawrence tells the soldier of a magic mountain where, if he is innocent and good, he can find the greatest secret, a blue light. The soldier also finds rooms filled with copper, silver, and gold, but he only takes the light. Outside the mountain Lawrence is gone, and the soldier loses his way and falls into a ditch. The Spirit of the Blue Light appears and asks what the soldier wishes for—he is there to serve Michael when summoned. Once out of the ditch Michael also wishes for a horse and some money. From his room at the inn where he stays, Michael sees the king's daughter in a tower. Long ago a wizard decreed that the princess would marry a common soldier. In a rage the king banished the wizard and locked his daughter in the tower. Michael summons the Spirit of the Blue Light and asks it to bring the princess to him. Later, thinking it was a dream, the princess tells her father. He doubles the guards and has a maidservant watch the princess. Again the Spirit brings the princess to the soldier. The servant tries to mark the soldier's door so he can be found, but the Spirit marks all the doors. The third time Michael is not so lucky. He is captured and condemned to death by the king. Once again the Spirit comes to Michael's rescue. Once the king promises to allow Michael to marry the princess, the Spirit reveals himself as the wizard who was banished for his prophecy and the same man, Lawrence, that Michael helped.

Petersen, P. J. **The Amazing Magic Show.** Illus. by Renée Williams-Andriani. New York: Simon & Schuster Books for Young Readers, 1994.

This book is ideal for a second- or third-grade reader or for an adult to read to a younger child. The chapters are short, the type is large, the margins are wide, and the text is interspersed with full-page, lighthearted black-and-white illustrations.

Hal and his older brother Chuck want to see the one-day-only performance of The Amazing Victor, the magician, with their friends Sally and Rick. Chuck wants to find an easy way to earn the money for tickets, but ultimately they pull weeds for their dad. At the magic show they are amazed by the magician.

Hal is inspired to learn magic tricks and perform them for his family and friends, but Chuck, who has read many magic books, spoils everything by telling everyone how the tricks are done. How can Hal prove he's a good magician and fool his brother? Hal, with his friends Sally and Mrs. Brown, devises the perfect trick, and Chuck can't unravel it.

San Souci, Robert D. **Young Merlin.** Illus. by Daniel Horne. New York: Doubleday, 1990.

San Souci, a consistently fine storyteller, recounts the story of the childhood of Merlin, the legendary magician. Merlin's father leaves before he is born, and the villagers whisper that his father was an elf or a demon. When his mother dies Merlin is raised by nuns. Because Merlin can see into the future of other people and look into the past, the villagers taunt him.

One day Merlin is taken by knights before King Vortigern, who says the stars decree that Merlin's blood must be sacrificed to secure the fortress tower. Merlin's fortunes change when he correctly tells the king that two dragons live beneath the tower and that's why it crashes down constantly. Merlin is named chief counselor.

Soon Princes Aurelius and Uther, sons of the true king, charge with their armies to defeat Vortigern. The princes succeed, and Merlin flees to the woods. Ultimately Merlin becomes like a brother to King Aurelius. When Aurelius dies in battle Merlin serves King Uther and then King Uther's son, King Arthur.

The story is long but full of adventure, excitement, and rich emotion.

Yolen, Jane. **The Girl in the Golden Bower.** Illus. by Jane Dyer. Boston: Little, Brown, 1994.

Author Yolen, a remarkable teller of tales, has penned another well-written, sophisticated, poetic, strong, and original folktale. Jane Dyer's illustrations are breathtaking. Executed on golden pages, many of the soft paintings spill out onto the exquisite borders.

A woodsman lives near an overgrown castle. The queen has died, the king disappeared, and people say that a lone beast roams the castle. One day the woodsman finds a young woman, whom he eventually marries. Soon they have a yellow-haired daughter, Aurea. When Aurea is five a woman comes to the woodsman's house asking for work. She's offered a job as cook. The woman is actually a sorceress who has come to the woods to find a great treasure. She is sure that the charm that will lead her to the treasure is in the woodsman's domain.

Aurea's mother dies but gives Aurea a russet comb that she says belonged to her mother. She says the comb will protect Aurea.

The sorceress decides that Aurea has the charm she needs and plots to snatch it from Aurea. She banishes Aurea to the forest and casts a spell that puts her to sleep. The animals of the forest, however, protect Aurea. When the sorceress returns to take the comb she finds something quite surprising and meets a fitting fate. Aurea, now awake, meets the beast and, unafraid, combs his tangled mane, takes a strand of her hair, braids it into the beast's forelock, and then leads him through a golden gate. Once through the gate the beast turns into a tall man. All is revealed, and Aurea learns that her mother was the king's daughter and this man is the king, her grandfather.

Demonstration/Participation Activities

Do a magic show for the children. You can invite the youngsters to check out the books from which the tricks were taken to find out how to do them and to learn others. If you prefer, you can do several tricks and show the children how they are done. Another alternative is to demonstrate several magic tricks and then invite the children to do them.

The following books have magic tricks that I've found easy enough to do myself, and they contain magic tricks simple enough for children to learn. They do not require a lot of preparation, coordination, or materials, and they can be done by one person.

Baillie, Marilyn. **Magic Fun.** Boston: Little, Brown, 1992.

Baillie's book is visually appealing; it contains splashy photographs that show young people doing the magic tricks. Simple, step-by-step diagrams are included for each trick, as are a list of materials you'll need, an explanation of the setup, and instructions on how to do the trick.

Specific magic tricks I recommend are: "Body Shrinker," p. 6; "Loopy Loop," p. 7; "Mystery Box," pp. 8-9; "Mysterious Mixtures," p. 10; and "Fast Fortune Flicker," pp. 20-21.

Cobb, Vicki, and Kathy Darling. "One-Sided Contest," pp. 118-19, in **Wanna Bet? Science Challenges to Fool You.** Illus. by Meredith Johnson. New York: Lothrop, Lee & Shepard, 1993.

Tell the children that, using magic, they can cut a figure eight in half so that it forms a single loop.

Day, Jon. **Let's Make Magic.** Illus. by Chris Fisher. New York: Kingfisher Books, 1991.

Most of the tricks in Day's book can be done by the target age group with practice, especially those found in the section, "Easy Magic," pp. 2-24. Try "Flyaway Money," pp. 4-5; "The Magic Bottle," pp. 10-11; "The Vanishing Key," pp. 12-13; and "The Drop Flip," p. 52.

Hendry, Linda. **Foodworks: Over 100 Science Activities and Fascinating Facts That Explore the Magic of Food**. Reading, MA: Addison-Wesley, 1987.

There are three easy tricks to demonstrate from this book: "Magic Potion," p. 88; "Rainbow Brew," p. 88; and "Magic Egg Predictor," pp. 88-89.

Hetzer, Linda. "Amazing Clips," p. 70, and "Walk Through Paper," p. 70, in **50 Fabulous Parties for Kids.** Illus. by Meg Hartigan. New York: Crown, 1994.

Children (and you) will find these tricks easy to do.

Johnson, Stephanie. **My First Cup, Ball, and Paper Magic Tricks.** Illus. by Kerry Manwaring. New York: SMITHMARK, 1992.

Dazzle children with "Unpoppable!" in which you stick pins in a balloon and it doesn't pop. "True Colors" looks complex, but is easy. It will look like you changed a red ball into a blue ball. When you do "The Great Balloon Blow-Up," it will look like you blew up a balloon without touching it.

The step-by-step instructions are clear and accompanied by appealing line drawings.

Keeshan, Bob, "Captain Kangaroo" and "The Magic Beanstalk," pp. 39-41, in **Family Fun Activity Book.** Illus. by Diane Palmisciano. Minneapolis, MN: Deaconess Press, 1994.

Here's an easy activity for children ages six and up to do. Just provide them with time, old newspapers, tape, and scissors.

Knoles, David. **Spooky Magic Tricks.** New York: Sterling, 1993.

The easiest magic tricks I've done from this book are "A Spooky Knot," pp. 10-11; "The Vanishing and Re-Appearing Wand," pp. 22-23; and "The Key Through the Wand," pp. 32-33.

Mandell, Muriel. **Simple Science Experiments with Everyday Materials.** Illus. by Frances Zweifel. New York: Sterling, 1989.

"Paper Magic: The Moebius Strip," p. 36, and "Through the Index Card," p. 37, are two of my favorite magic tricks. The first is easy for children to do if you prepare the materials ahead of time. I did this trick with a group of cub scouts, and they were still puzzling over the magic trick even after they did it several times. "Through the Index Card" requires good fine motor skills, so you may want only to demonstrate it.

Marks, Burton, and Rita Marks. **Give a Magic Show!** Illus. by Don Madden. New York: Lothrop, Lee & Shepard, 1977.

This is an older title, but I include it because it has some of my favorite magic tricks: "Rabbit in a Hat," pp. 33-34; "The Funny Paper Loops," pp. 48-49; "Impossible Trick," pp. 50-52; and "The Magic Cone," pp. 53-55. The last trick is the most dazzling.

Wyler, Rose, and Gerald Ames. **Magic Secrets.** Illus. by Arthur Dorros. New York: HarperTrophy, 1990.

Children will find this book easy to read and the tricks simple to do. Included are straightforward tips on how to practice and do the tricks. Try the following: "Make a Pencil Disappear," pp. 14-15; "Tame an Egg," pp. 19-21; "Good-bye, Penny," pp. 24-25; "Cut a Lady in Half," pp. 50-51; "Milk in a Hat," pp. 60-62; and "Bag of Surprises," pp. 63-64.

Wyler, Rose, and Gerald Ames. **Spooky Tricks.** Illus. by S. D. Schindler. New York: HarperCollins, 1994.

This is an I Can Read Book full of tricks that children can learn with little practice. Among the easiest magic tricks are "Your Phantom Finger," pp. 7-8; "Spooky Hand," pp. 9-10; "Willie Writes a Message," pp. 24-25; "Candy for Willie," pp. 39-40; "Ghost on the Wall," pp. 44-45; and "Mixed-Up Mummies," pp. 55-58. "The Spooky Handkerchief," pp. 14-17, requires a bit more practice to learn.

Chapter 11

Music and Musicians

Read Alouds

Aardema, Verna. **Bimwili and the Zimwi.** Illus. by Susan Meddaugh. New York: Dial Books for Young Readers, 1985.

When Tasha and Tete disobey their mother and don't watch their younger sister, Bimwili, carefully at the beach, Bimwili wanders off and is captured by an ugly, old Zimwi.

The Zimwi puts Bimwili in his big drum and travels from town to town, where he insists Bimwili sing the song about a shell he'd heard her sing on the beach. In return for listening to the singing drum, the people in each village give the Zimwi a free meal.

One day Zimwi arrives at Bimwili's village. Bimwili hears her mother's voice and changes the words of her song to reveal herself. Her sisters hear Bimwili, distract Zimwi, rescue their sister, hide her, and replace her with sand in the drum. When Zimwi leaves the village he realizes he's been tricked and turns himself into an "All-Devouring Drum," who chases the sisters. Thwarted, the Zimwi turns into a seagull and flies away.

Anderson, Lonzo. **Arion and the Dolphins: Based on an Ancient Greek Legend.** Illus. by Adrienne Adams. New York: Charles Scribner's Sons, 1978.

Illustrator Adam's trademark artwork in soft, muted watercolors accompany this gentle tale of music and justice.

Arion enjoys playing the lute and singing. He makes friends with the dolphins, who dive and dance to his music. The king tells Arion of a musical contest in far-off Sicily where the prize is all the gold the winner can carry. When Arion sails to Sicily, the crew listen to his music and the dolphins follow the boat. Arion wins the gold, and on the way home the crew thinks only of Arion's gold. They decide to kill him, but Arion begs to sing one last song. Hearing the music the dolphins swim to the ship, Arion leaps overboard, and the dolphins carry him swiftly home ahead of the ship.

Arion tells the king what happened. When the seamen return and say Arion didn't come back with them, Arion steps out of hiding and the sailors beg for their lives. The king demands they return Arion's gold. They do and then flee. Arion leaves to play and sing for the dolphins.

Bartos-Höppner, Barbara. **The Pied Piper of Hamelin.** Trans. by Anthea Bell. Illus. by Annegert Fuchshuber. New York: J. B. Lippincott, 1985.

This classic tale is based on the legend that in 1284 in the town of Hamelin all the children were lured away by a stranger who played his pipe. The story is about music, but it's also a mystery and rather scary. It's best told to children in the upper end of the target age group.

The mayor and the people in Hamelin are frustrated, overwhelmed by, and disgusted with an infestation of rats and mice. One day a stranger appears and says that he's called the Pied Piper, that music is his trade, and that he can get rid of the rodents. The men promise him riches and agree to pay the piper 100 gold pieces when the job is done.

Early the next morning the Pied Piper plays his music and the thousands of rats and mice follow him into the river. Everyone in Hamelin is elated, but the mayor refuses to pay the Piper.

The Piper leaves only to return several weeks later, playing his pipe. He looks different, and his music is strange. The children of Hamelin flock around him and go for a walk with him. They don't hear their parents' cries for them to stop. Their parents assume the children will return when they're tired and hungry, but they don't. Years pass and no one knows where they are.

The author captures well the eeriness and scariness of this legend. The illustrations are beautiful full-color paintings with a European flavor. They are particularly deep and dark when the Piper leads the rats and mice out of town. The two-page spread that depicts the mice and rats in pots, sacks of grain, and baskets offers a relieving touch of humor.

Brett, Jan. **Berlioz the Bear.** Illus. by author. New York: G. P. Putnam's Sons, 1991.

Exquisite illustrations rich in color and detail and Brett's trademark intricate borders beautifully complement her original story, which will appeal particularly to the younger children in your group.

Berlioz the bear and his fellow musicians are supposed to play in the village square, but Berlioz is so distracted by the strange buzz coming from his double bass that he doesn't see a hole in the road and the front wheel of their wagon gets stuck in it. The mule who was pulling the wagon sits. While a rooster, a cat, a schnauzer, a goat, a plow horse, and an ox try to pull the wagon out and can't, the musicians put on their concert tailcoats and tune their instruments. Finally, in frustration, Berlioz pulls his bow across the strings of his bass. Out of his instrument shoots an angry bee who was finally disturbed once too often to stay. The bee stings the mule, and the mule jumps to his feet and pulls the bandwagon of musicians out of the hole and to the square in time for the performance. Everyone plays well, and, appropriately, the encore tune is "Flight of the Bumblebee."

Downing, Julie. **Mozart Tonight.** Illus. by Julie Downing. New York: Bradbury Press, 1991.

Sprightly, bright, and lavish watercolors complement this fascinating story about the famous musician Wolfgang Amadeus Mozart.

As Mozart and his wife, Constanze, approach the Prague opera house where he is going to conduct his new opera, **Don Giovanni,** Mozart talks about his hopes and reminisces about his life. Mozart's life is full of interesting tidbits that will interest children. Mozart wrote musical notes when very young, and at age six he played a violin before he had lessons. At a young age, he and his sister, Nannerl, gave concerts in many European cities to huge crowds, who gave them gifts. At age 16 Mozart was ordered to serve the new archbishop. He was treated like a servant and ordered to play only when the archbishop demanded it. Often, Mozart would sneak out at night to play what he wanted.

Mozart reminisces further about living in four tiny rooms in Vienna, having little money, and being badgered by creditors. The story comes full circle when it returns to the present and explains how Mozart didn't finish the opera **Don Giovanni** until five o'clock in the morning on the day of the performance. It was a big hit.

This is a satisfying story with a sense of beginning, middle, and end and a feeling of triumph over hardship.

Gershator, Phillis, reteller. **Tukama Tootles the Flute: A Tale from the Antilles.** Illus. by Synthia Saint James. New York: Orchard, 1994.

Tukama, a wild and lazy boy, lives with his grandmother on a rocky island in the Caribbean Sea. All day until dark he climbs the dangerous rocky cliffs and plays his flute. Tukama never heeds his grandmother's warning to beware the two-headed giant who likes to eat wild children.

The two-headed giant grabs Tukama one day and demands he play his flute. Each time Tukama plays, the giant tells Tukama to climb a little higher on him and play, until Tukama is on the giant's nose. The giant smells the boy and takes him home in a sack to fatten him up and eat him.

The giant's wife feeds Tukama. The next day when the giant goes out, Tukama plays his flute. The giant's wife wants to hear more and more, and each time he plays, Tukama gets the woman to open the bag a bit more until he's able to run away.

Tukama returns home, stays away from the rocks, helps his grandmother, and plays his flute for her.

The story is satisfying, the dialogue lively, and Tukama's song has catchy nonsense words. There's a pleasing symmetry between the giant having Tukama climb him step-by-step to play his flute and the giant's wife releasing him from the sack bit-by-bit when Tukama promises it will improve his playing. One sequence results in Tukama's capture, and the other sequence results in Tukama's release.

The striking oil paintings consist of solid blocks of color and shapes. They're lively, add atmosphere, and convey touches of the scenery and the food of the Virgin Islands.

Kennedy, William, and Brendan Kennedy. **Charlie Malarkey and the Singing Moose.** Illus. by S. D. Schindler. New York: Viking, 1994.

What a delightful, action-packed original story this is, with colorful, expressive, sprawling, and humorous illustrations.

A young boy, Charlie Malarkey, and his friend Iggy go to the circus, where Charlie is eager to see Barnaby the singing moose. Barnaby is a fantastic singer, but he looks so sad. Charlie learns that Barnaby wears a magic tie that makes him sing. Barnaby also reveals that his trainer, Ralph T. Bungaroo, is really a moosenapper who keeps Barnaby chained and only wants to make money from Barnaby's singing. Charlie and Iggy promise Barnaby they'll guard the necktie and keep it from Bungaroo.

Tension builds when Charlie's monkey gets the necktie, sings on Charlie's front porch, Charlie's neighbor sees the monkey and calls the television station, and Bungaroo views the segment. Bungaroo goes to Charlie's house and holds Charlie's monkey hostage until they return the tie.

Charlie and Iggy return to the circus, release Barnaby, and with his help expose Bungaroo.

Nygren, Tord. **Fiddler and His Brothers.** Illus. by author. New York: William Morrow, 1987.

Teddy and Neddy are jealous of their younger brother, Fiddler, because he plays the violin "like an angel" and is popular. Fiddler always plays a tune when people ask, and they sing, dance, and forget their worries. When the brothers set out to seek their fortunes, Teddy and Neddy say Fiddler can join them if he doesn't play his fiddle. The brothers ask for work at many farms, but no one needs help. The people will, however, give the brothers a meal if Fiddler plays for them. This just makes Fiddler's brothers more jealous.

One evening the brothers come to a cottage where a mother and daughter witch have a lantern, a billy goat with long golden horns, and a vest of roses. The woman won't let them stay.

Finally, the brothers get jobs at the mansion of the king of the land, who has a beautiful daughter, Princess Ingrid. Teddy and Neddy are still jealous of Fiddler and would like to get rid of him. When they learn that the witch has stolen the lantern and the goat they saw, they make sure that Fiddler is sent to retrieve the items. Each time, Fiddler succeeds and is given fields, meadows, a house, and, finally, the princess' hand in marriage.

Nygren's story, originally published in Swedish, is well-written with satisfying dialogue and a captivating story line. It has witches, conflict, danger, tension, and slyness. The illustrations, done in earth tones, have a European flavor and enhance the story.

Ober, Hal, reteller. **How Music Came to the World.** Illus. by Carol Ober. Boston: Houghton Mifflin, 1994.

This ancient Mexican myth tells of the time when Sky God and Wind God met and brought music to the world. Sky God declares that it's too quiet on Earth because there's no music. Sun has all the singers and music makers, and he won't share. Sky God wants Wind God to get the music. With the help of Sky God's servants, Wind God arrives at the House of the Sun. There he sees the golden yellow flute players, the blue wandering minstrels, the white lullaby singers, and the red singers of love songs. Sun tells the musicians not to speak to Wind God, but Wind God whips up thunder and lightning. In fear, the musicians go to Wind God, who brings them to Earth. Eventually, they play and sing and soon the people sing and play.

The text flows swiftly, the dialogue is rich, the tale is told with an economy of words, and tension builds well. The bold, vibrant full-color artwork is done in large designs in shades of red, orange, yellow, green, and blue. The illustrations are cutout oil pastel drawings.

Seeger, Pete. **Abiyoyo: Based on a South African Lullaby and Folk Story.** Illus. by Michael Hays. New York: Macmillan, 1986.

A boy and his father are forced to move to the edge of town when the grown-ups tire of the boy clinking on his ukulele and his father performing irritating magic tricks. The townspeople don't believe the stories they've heard of a giant named Abiyoyo who likes to eat people until Abiyoyo appears shaking the ground and eating livestock. The banished father tells his son if the boy can get the giant to lie down, he can get rid of him. Father and son run from the edge of the forest toward the giant, who has long fingernails, slobbery teeth, matted hair, and stinking feet.

The boy plays his ukulele and sings "Abiyoyo," a song about the giant. Because the song is about him, the giant grins and dances. Faster and faster the boy plays and faster and faster the giant dances until, out of breath, the giant falls flat. The father uses his magic wand to make Abiyoyo disappear. Father and son are welcomed back to town.

Notes are included for this well-known song. Dramatic oil paintings accompany this short, fun story.

Sherman, Josepha, reteller. **Vassilisa the Wise: A Tale of Medieval Russia.** Illus. by Daniel San Souci. San Diego: Harcourt Brace Jovanovich, 1988.

Beautiful, rich, detailed illustrations with a Russian look enhance this well-written tale that features a musician and his wise and clever wife.

Staver is a handsome, young merchant-prince who plays the gusla, a stringed instrument that looks somewhat like a zither. One evening at the feast held at the court of Prince Vladimir, everyone is laughing and partying except for Staver. When the Prince calls attention to his silence, Staver says he doesn't feel like playing. The prince takes his silence as an insult, although Staver is just thinking about his new bride, with whom he'd rather be. The prince taunts Staver until Staver shouts that he isn't jealous of the prince's riches because he has the greatest treasure, his wife Vassilisa, who is wiser than the prince. The prince has Staver thrown in the dungeon.

Staver's serving man speeds ahead of the princes' soldiers to warn Vassilisa of their intent to seize her. Vassilisa quickly devises a plan. She cuts her hair, dons a Tartan outfit, and mounts her fastest horse. The soldiers approach cautiously, fearing she is a Tartan horseman. In disguise, she declares that Vassilisa is gone and she is Vassili, an ambassador from the Tartans who expects the prince to pay 12 years of golden tribute to the Tartans.

The prince is worried when Vassili appears and makes her demands, which include marriage to the prince's niece, Princess Zabava. The princess is sure that Vassilisa is a woman, and the prince tests Vassili three times to find out. Each time Vassili outsmarts the prince.

That night at a feast, Vassili looks sad and says he wants to hear music to cheer him. Vassili isn't pleased by the musicians and singers the prince presents. Vassili says he's heard of a man who plays the gusla sweetly. The prince has Staver brought to them. Staver recognizes his wife, but she signals him to say nothing. Staver plays and sings of his wife. Angry at first, the prince realizes there's love in the music and he's no longer angry. Vassili says instead of marrying the princess, he'd rather have Staver as his musician. The prince agrees. Vassili leaves the room and returns as herself, Vassilisa. The prince laughs and agrees with Staver that Vassilisa is wiser than he.

Steig, William. **Zeke Pippin.** Illus. by author. New York: HarperCollins, 1994.

Zeke Pippin finds a harmonica, but every time he plays it his family falls asleep. Finally, Zeke can't stand it and he leaves home, traveling downriver on a raft he made. Soon, when everyone he plays the harmonica for falls asleep, Zeke realizes it wasn't his parents' fault; they weren't being insulting. The harmonica has magic powers. Zeke wants to go home.

Zeke can't float upstream so he starts walking home. He meets several unsavory characters, but each time he makes them fall asleep by playing his harmonica.

Once Zeke returns home he uses his special harmonica to serenade children and patients at the hospital to sleep.

Stevens, Janet, reteller. **The Bremen Town Musicians.** Illus. by
author. New York: Holiday House, 1992.

Stevens's retelling of this beloved tale is ideal to share with a large group
because of its oversized illustrations in pastels and ink. The animal characters'
faces are individualized, humorous, and expressive.

An old donkey who is sure his master will get rid of him decides to go to
Bremen, where he can be the town musician and play the lute. On the way he
meets an old hound, a cat, and a rooster who all fear their masters will get rid
of them. The donkey invites the animals to join him. The hound can play the
kettle drum, the cat can sing, and the rooster can add high notes.

Night descends and the animals are drawn to a light in a farmhouse. The
donkey sees robbers inside eating a feast. The animals scare the thieves away
with their singing and then eat and sleep in the farmhouse.

One robber is sent back to check the situation. Because of his clumsiness,
the robber gets scratched by the cat, bit by the dog, kicked by the donkey, and
swooped upon by the screeching rooster. The thief runs in fear to the forest,
where he tells the other robbers a witch clawed him, a ghost stabbed him in the
leg, a monster hit him with a club, and a judge on the roof screamed at him.
The robbers decide not to return, and the animals live peacefully and safely in
the house.

Wilhelm, Hans, reteller. **The Bremen Town Musicians.** Illus. by
author. New York: Scholastic, 1992.

In this wonderfully told and illustrated version of the classic tale by the
Brothers Grimm, four animal friends leave their masters, intent on becoming
musicians in Bremen. At night the animals happen upon a house inhabited by
thieves, but they scare the robbers by "performing" their music. While standing
on top of each other, the donkey brays, the dog barks, the cat meows, and the
rooster crows. They burst into the room and the robbers flee in terror, thinking
it's a goblin. While the animals feast, the robbers wonder why they were so
frightened and send one robber back to check the house. Inadvertently, the
animals scare the robber once again and are left to live peacefully.

The animals' names are amusing—the cat is Whiskerwiper and the
rooster is Redhead. The telling, which follows the original German text closely,
is straightforward, strong, and exciting. Wilhelm has drawn the robbers to look
similar to the ex-owners of the "musicians." The animals look childlike, whereas
the adults are greedy and mean looking. The donkey's master is priceless with
his wild red hair and mustache, receding hairline, and bushy eyebrows.

Wolkstein, Diane. **The Banza: A Haitian Story.** Illus. by Marc Brown.
New York: Dial Press, 1981.

Diane Wolkstein, a noted storyteller, and Marc Brown, a popular author-
illustrator, combined talents to create this delightful, moving story. Brown's
artwork incorporate symbols from Haitian art. His illustrations are colorful,
oversized, and expressive.

A little tiger, Teegra, and a little goat, Cabree, find shelter in the same
cave during a storm. Although normally enemies, they become friends. When
Teegra's parents find him, he leaves. The next day Teegra brings lonely Cabree
a banza, an instrument similar to a banjo, that Teegra promises will keep
Cabree warm and safe because the banza belongs to the heart.

Cabree soon discovers how the banza can keep her safe when 10 hungry tigers threaten her. To Cabree's surprise she sings a song about eating tigers raw and convinces the tigers she really does this. The head tiger manages to tell a few tigers at a time to leave until only he remains.

Cabree realizes that all she had to do was play the banza and sing what's in her heart. She tells the head tiger to find Teegra and tell him that Cabree's heart and the banza are one.

Booktalks

Aiken, Joan. **The Moon's Revenge.** Illus. by Alan Lee. New York: Alfred A. Knopf, 1987.

In this richly textured, many-layered story, readers meet Seppy, the seventh son of a seventh son who wants to play the fiddle as well as his grandfather had, but whose father, a coach maker, tells him he must learn the trade.

One midnight Seppy goes to a ruined house where people say they've heard the voices of devils. Seppy whispers through a crack in the wall and asks how he can learn to be the best fiddler in the country. A voice whispers that each night for seven nights, Seppy must throw his shoe at the moon. Seppy finds his old pairs of shoes that his mother kept in the inside of the grandfather clock and throws one of each pair at the moon for seven nights.

Seppy's wish to be a fiddler must be granted, but the moon, angry at having its face marked by Seppy's dirty shoes, exacts revenge. Seppy must go barefoot for seven years, and until he puts the seven pairs of shoes back in the clock, his sister won't speak and his family will be in great danger.

Seppy does fiddle well, and a beautiful violin is revealed to him by the ghost of a king who likes his fiddling. Also, Seppy's fiddling saves the family many times. Finally, however, he must confront a huge monster who threatens the village. It has teeth as long as doorposts, seven legs, and a damp, rotting smell. Once again Seppy's fiddling saves them.

Aiken's language is rich and the narration moves swiftly. The full-color illustrations are dramatic and evocative. Alan Lee captures the swelling water, the shadows, the warm countryside, and the cold and gray monster equally well.

Haseley, Dennis. **The Old Banjo.** Illus. by Stephen Gammell. New York: Macmillan, 1983.

This book will appeal to that special, sophisticated young reader. The text is a poem. The language is descriptive and precise. Gammell's artwork consists of his classic black-and-white drawings in which he does so much with shading. Gammell creates a mood of mystery and captures the harsh landscape on a farm during the Depression era. His characters are finely drawn, particularly the close-up of the father's worn yet gentle face.

A boy and his father work on a farm surrounded by instruments. Although the boy would love to hear music, his father says there's too much work to do. So the old banjo in the attic wails, the trombone lies under a bed, the old piano sits in the barn, and the violin waits in a shed with a trumpet and clarinet.

One day near dusk the old banjo remembers a woman and her children sitting on the porch and playing the instrument. The banjo gives a "pluck." The violin hears the banjo and responds by stretching its bow along its strings. The banjo answers. The piano pushes on a chipped key, the trombone blows, the trumpet hears the others and replies, until all the instruments are playing.

Father and son hear the sound. When they find the instruments, the rusty sounds become melodic. In the attic the banjo is listening to the beautiful sound.

Kovacs, Deborah. **Brewster's Courage.** Illus. by Joe Mathieu. New York: Simon & Schuster Books for Young Readers, 1992.

Kovacs's book is a delightful, humorous, sensitive, and exciting story with appealing, well-developed characters. Brewster, the hero of the story, is a rare, shy, black-footed ferret from South Dakota. He is pure, sensitive, trusting, and just wants to be accepted. Brewster is determined and always maintains a positive attitude.

Brewster loves to ride his bike more than anything. One day he hears the incredible music of Wild Turkey and the Loblollies. Brewster had never really heard music before, and he is enthralled by the group: a raccoon with a fiddle, a beaver with a guitar, an alligator with a washboard, and a turkey with an accordian. When Brewster compliments the musicians, they tell him that if he has the chance, to come hear them at the Jolie Blonde Café in the Moustafaya Swamp in Louisiana's bayou country.

Riding his bike Brewster sets off to hear the group. He has many adventures, meets an incredible array of animals, and faces many dangers. Brewster handles every situation, from being teased and lying on a fire ant colony to confronting the dangerous Bayou Bloodhounds. It's worth it to Brewster when he fulfills his dream and plays the triangle with Wild Turkey and the Loblollies.

Joe Mathieu's black-and-white artwork captures the characters' personalities and their range of emotions well. Note particularly Sally the crocodile with her pearls, bracelets, and long eyelashes; the wild boar with his lumpy body poured into his overalls; and the mangy-looking bloodhounds with their hanging tongues.

Kroll, Steven. **By the Dawn's Early Light: The Story of the Star-Spangled Banner.** Illus. by Dan Andreasen. New York: Scholastic, 1994.

Many children will enjoy this concise, lively, and tension-filled account of how Frances Scott Key wrote "The Star-Spangled Banner." The exquisite oil paintings in dark, deep colors look like classic "old-time" American artwork. Historical background on the War of 1812 is included along with a photograph of Frances Scott Key's original manuscript. You'll also find an etching of Francis Scott Key, a copy of the music and lyrics for the entire four verses of "The Star-Spangled Banner," a bibliography, and an index.

Youngsters are drawn in immediately to Frances Scott Key's adventure on a British ship, where he's seeking the release of his captured friend, Dr. William Beanes. Ultimately the British major general agrees to release Beanes but only after the British attack Baltimore. So the Americans are forced to watch the bombardment. All his life Key had written poetry, so during the heavy shelling he keeps checking to see if the American flag is flying, and he writes his poem. It's first printed with the title "The Defense of Fort McHenry."

Nichol, Barbara. **Beethoven Lives Upstairs.** Illus. by Scott Cameron. New York: Orchard, 1993.

Although this book won't appeal to every child, it is worth mentioning for that sophisticated reader in your group. Youngsters learn interesting, personal information about the composer Ludwig Van Beethoven through letters that 10-year-old Christoph exchanges with his Uncle Karl. Christoph's feelings about his mother's boarder, Beethoven, change as he learns more about the musician. Christoph learns of Beethoven's many peculiarities. The musician has a piano with no legs so he can feel the beat of the music. He writes music on the walls and sometimes pours water over his head in the middle of the room.

Pillar, Marjorie. **Join the Band!** Photos by author. New York: Harper-Collins, 1992.

In this photo-essay, a brief text and fine, sharp, interesting photographs capture the camaraderie of students who are in a school band. The book is a good introduction to what playing in a band involves and what instruments are used. Youngsters will enjoy seeing other children getting instruments ready, practicing, and rehearsing for and performing in a spring concert.

Sharmat, Marjorie Weinman, and Craig Sharmat. **Nate the Great and the Musical Note.** Illus. by Marc Simont. New York: Coward-McCann, 1990.

One of many books in the popular beginning reader series about the detective, Nate the Great, this is light, humorous, and fun. Nate and his dog Sludge agree to help Pip figure out where his mother wants him to go at four o'clock. Pip's mom left a message for him, but Rosamund turned the telephone message into a music lesson with a secret meaning and she won't reveal what it signifies. There are false clues and leads and wrong solutions before Nate solves the musical mystery.

Poetry

Prelutsky, Jack. "I Am Growing a Glorious Garden," pp. 12-13, in **Something BIG Has Been Here.** Illus. by James Stevenson. New York: Greenwillow Books, 1990.

Children will enjoy hearing about this garden of music with its gongs and guitars, its arbor of harps, its blooming zithers, and its many other "garden" instruments that play music.

Songs

Baltuck, Naomi. "On Top of Spaghetti," pp. 72-73, in **Crazy Gibberish and Other Story Hour Stretches: From a Storyteller's Bag of Tricks.** Illus. by Doug Cushman. Hamden, CT: Linnet Book/The Shoe String Press, 1993.

Author Baltuck has created a wonderful echo song to the tune of "On Top of Old Smokey." She includes storyteller's tips and tells you how to sing this song in a melodramatic way that will have the children laughing.

Bates, Katharine Lee. **America the Beautiful.** Illus. by Neil Waldman. New York: Atheneum, 1993.

Adults and children will be awed by the beautiful, impressionistic acrylic
paintings that accompany this classic song. It was originally a nineteenth-century
poem that was later set to music. Children will see lavish illustrations of Niagara
Falls, the Great Smoky Mountains, the Grand Canyon, Mount Rushmore, and
the Statue of Liberty. The song is followed by three pages of small versions of
the paintings with captions that describe each site.

Say it as a poem, sing it, and then invite the children to join you.

Betz, Adrienne, and Lucia Monfried, comps. **Diane Goode's Book of
Silly Stories and Songs.** Illus. by Diane Goode. New York:
Dutton Children's Books, 1992.

There are several songs children will enjoy from this collection. I particularly like "On Top of Spaghetti," p. 38. Most children know the tune to this
funny, classic song by Tom Glazer. The youngsters may not know all the words,
so you might want to copy the verses on posterboard or a chalkboard. "Michael
Finnegan," p. 59, is a comical old song that can be repeated over and over, faster
and faster, as long as the children are interested.

Cohn, Amy L., comp. **From Sea to Shining Sea: A Treasury of
American Folklore and Folk Songs.** Illus. by 11 Caldecott
Medal and four Caldecott Honor Book artists. New York: Scholas-
tic, 1993.

The following songs, found in the above collection, will probably be
familiar to many of the children. If they aren't, the youngsters will catch on
quickly. The tunes are enjoyable and fun to sing.

"Yankee Doodle," pp. 62-63. Be sure to show the illustration by Anita
Lobel of George Washington astride his horse, looking majestic.

"Jennie Jenkins," pp. 74-75. Children love this nonsense song. Invite
youngsters to suggest what color Jennie will wear next and think of a word to
rhyme with the color.

"Hush, Little Baby," pp. 98-99. This traditional song is complemented by
Molly Bang's striking artwork in solid blocks of bold colors.

"Oh, Susannah," pp. 180-81. Most children know the tune, but if you don't
think they know the words, make copies or write the words on a chalkboard or
on posterboard. Show Barbara Cooney's simple yet expressive watercolor of a
bearded man panning for gold. In a few brilliant strokes Cooney captures the
times and the mood of the Gold Rush.

"Michael Finnegan," pp. 244-45. Four verses are included for this hilarious song. Share Donald Crews's interpretation of Finnegan, with his crinkling
eyes, hair blowing behind him, and whiskers straggling over his chin.

"Take Me Out to the Ball Game," pp. 296-97. Most children know this song
and sing it with enthusiasm.

"The Ghost of Tom," p. 330. If children don't know this song, they'll learn
it quickly, because it's so short, and will want to sing it over and over.

"This Land Is Your Land," pp. 370-71. This classic song is complimented
with soft watercolors.

Karas, G. Brian. **I Know an Old Lady.** Illus. by author. New York: Scholastic, 1994.

Quirky illustrations accompany this retelling of the "Little Old Lady Who Swallowed a Fly," in which the lady eats a fly, a spider, a bird, a cat, a dog, a goat, a cow, and a horse. The artwork is hilarious. Rooms have walls that tilt and doors at odd angles. The old woman's nose is rectangular, her fingers are squared-off, and her eyes are often crossed lines. People are made of angles.

Karas hasn't changed the words, but he's definitely added a dimension of cleverness and humor in the illustrations. The pictures tell a second story. A boy sees the lady eating the fly from his apartment and watches her eat the spider through his binoculars. The boy peeks in her apartment and sees her with a feather hanging out of her mouth. He follows her outside, hides behind trash cans, and takes notes as he watches. The boy follows the woman as she eats larger and larger animals and gets bigger and bigger. He reacts to her peculiar eating habits by gasping, covering his eyes, and photographing the woman once she's eaten the horse. The woman's behavior and appearance is hysterical, too. She stands on a chair and stretches her greedy fingers to get the spider. As she gets fatter, the woman's face gets greener and she has red swirling circles around her eyes. When she nabs a dog to eat, the woman is seen with outstretched hands and a grin like a jack-o'-lantern.

Share the book first as a story, allowing time for the children to savor the incredible, clever illustrations. Then invite the children to sing the song; music and lyrics are included.

Krull, Kathleen, collector and arranger. **Gonna Sing My Head Off! American Folk Songs for Children.** Illus. by Allen Garns. New York: Alfred A. Knopf, 1992.

This is a wonderful collection of songs that includes piano and guitar accompaniments. You'll find children's favorites, including "Home on the Range," "If I Had a Hammer," "I've Been Working on the Railroad," "Michael, Row the Boat Ashore," "The Mockingbird Song," "Oh, Susanna!" "On Top of Old Smoky," "She'll Be Coming 'Round the Mountain," "Take Me Out to the Ball Game," "This Land Is Your Land," and "Yankee Doodle."

Demonstration/Participation Activities

Ardley, Neil. **101 Great Science Experiments.** New York: Dorling Kindersley, 1993.

"Beat Some Drums," pp. 80-81, features a tin drum that is easy for children to make with a round cookie tin (that has been cut out ahead of time), tape, cord, and a balloon. The tom-tom in this section is not difficult to make, but time consuming. You might like to make one before the program and show it to the children. You might also like to demonstrate the set of pipes, "Play a Pipe," pages 82-83.

Cash, Terry, Steve Parker, and Barbara Taylor. "Rubber Band Guitar," p. 35, and "Make a Scraper," p. 43, in **175 More Science Experiments to Amuse and Amaze Your Friends.** Illus. by Kuo Kang Chen and Peter Bull. New York: Random House, 1990.

Children will need only a little adult supervision to make these musical crafts. Few materials are required, and the instructions are clear and concise.

Deshapande, Chris. "Try Making Your Own Rainmaker," pp. 20-21, in **Food Crafts.** Photos by Zul Mukhida. Milwaukee, WI: Gareth Stevens, 1994.

What a wonderful craft for children to make. Provide a cardboard tube for each youngster, a box of craft sticks, and chickpeas. You will have to make the slits in the cardboard tubes, but the rest of the craft is easy. Children are always delighted with their rainmakers, which create music by being turned upside down. Directions are easy to follow.

Drew, Helen. **My First Music Book: A Life-Size Guide to Making and Playing Simple Musical Instruments.** Photos by Dave King. Illus. by Brian Delf. New York: Dorling Kindersley, 1993.

Here's a stunning book with oversize, full-color photographs of the finished instruments that will inspire children. The musical instruments are made with common materials and are easy to create. Youngsters enjoy "Star Shaker," "Metal Maraca," and "Gravel Slide," p. 8; and "Sunshine Shaker" and "Button Box," p. 9. You might like to demonstrate how to make the more involved "Box Harp," p. 41.

Hart, Avery, and Paul Mantell. **Kids Make Music! Clapping and Tapping from Bach to Rock.** Illus. by Loretta Trezzo Braren. Charlotte, VT: Williamson, 1993.

"Tissue Box Lute and Shoe Box Guitar," p. 64, and "Pie Plate Tambourines," p. 70, are extremely easy to make even for the youngest child in your group.

Hausherr, Rosmarie. **What Instrument Is This?** Photos by author. New York: Scholastic, 1992.

Invite youngsters to guess the instrument hinted at by the one sentence clue offered. If no one guesses, show the color photograph above the clue. Then, turn the page and children will see the instrument being used by children and adults in a variety of situations. Some of the instruments are fairly easy to guess, including recorder, flute, bagpipe, violin, piano, and drums.

Hetzer, Linda. **50 Fabulous Parties for Kids.** Illus. by Meg Hartigan. New York: Crown, 1994.

"Maracas" and "Kazoo" on p. 22 are easy to make, require easily obtained materials, and take little time. The kazoos can be played immediately. You might also like to try the games on p. 23, including "Musical Squares" and "Musical Circles."

Hewitt, Sally. **Pluck and Scrape**. (Get Set—Go!). Photos by Peter Millard. Chicago: Children's Press, 1994.

Hewitt's book has an appealing format. There's a clear list of materials for each musical instrument, easy instructions for how to make the craft, and hints on how to play it. Each right-hand page has a photograph of a child or children playing the instrument. On each left-hand page watercolor drawings show each instrument in some stage of being made.

All the instruments require common materials, and most are simple to make. Only a few require adult supervision. Children will enjoy making "Sound Boxes" with cups, jars, boxes, and rubber bands. The "Tissue Box Guitar" requires a tissue box, rubber bands, and cardboard. Youngsters can create different notes with the "Double Bass." You'll need a long stick, large cardboard box, string, and a button for each child. The "Rubber Band Harp" is also popular, as is the "Bottle Bass," which requires some adult supervision.

Hilton, Joni. "Make a Kazoo," p. 61, and "Play Musical Straws," pp. 83-84, in **Five Minute Miracles: 373 Quick Daily Discoveries for You and Your Kids to Share.** Illus. by Matt Wawiorka. Philadelphia: Running Press, 1992.

Hilton offers instructions for two quick and satisfying musical instruments that can be made by the youngest child in your group. The first requires a cardboard tube, waxed paper, and a rubber band. For the second each child needs a plastic straw.

Milord, Susan. "Make a Drum," p. 40, in **Hands Around the World: 365 Creative Ways to Build Cultural Awareness and Global Respect.** Illus. by author. Charlotte, VT: Williamson, 1992.

Here's an enjoyable craft that most youngsters can do with little assistance. Each child needs an oatmeal box, a grocery bag, and paper tape. The instructions are short and clear.

Morris, Ting, and Neil Morris. **Music.** (Sticky Fingers). Illus. by Ruth Levy. Photos by John Butcher. New York: Franklin Watts, 1993.

In the section "Shake, Rattle and Roll," pp. 8-9, you'll find clear line drawings and simple directions for six musical instruments that are easy to make with simple materials, including yogurt containers and liquid soap bottles. The youngest child in your group can do these. Each child can make the same instrument or you can supply the materials and let everyone select one of the six to make.

Also included in this book are directions for "Kazoo Band," pp. 16-17. In four easy steps youngsters can make their own kazoos. They can make them in different sizes, decorate them, and play them.

Oates, Eddie Herschel. **Making Music: Six Instruments You Can Create.** Illus. by Michael Koelsch. New York: HarperCollins, 1995.

You'll find this a beautifully packaged book. The text and watercolor illustrations are clear, clean, sharp, and inviting. The book is well organized. A large illustration of the completed instrument is followed by a list of materials needed with an illustration of each item. Step-by-step instructions follow, again with illustrations, and, finally, there's a full-page illustration of a child playing the instrument. Often children are inspired by a picture of the completed craft.

The instruments include "Balloon Tom-Tom," "Wrench Xylophone," "Xylo-Drum," "Garden-Hose Trumpet," "Spoon Roarer," and "Singing Sitar." The "Balloon Tom-Tom" is fairly easy to do during a program. Each child will need an oatmeal box, a balloon, and a rubber band.

Robins, Deri, Meg Sanders, and Kate Crocker. "X Is for Xylophone," p. 75, in **The Kids Can Do It Book.** Illus. by Charlotte Stowell. New York: Kingfisher Books, 1993.

Dazzle children by filling glass tumblers to the levels shown in the line drawing and then playing a tune as directed. Children will want to try this, too.

Warner, Penny. "Noisemakers," p. 3, in **Kids' Holiday Fun: Great Family Activities Every Month of the Year.** Deephaven, MN: Meadowbrook Press, 1994.

You'll find easy directions and a clear list of materials for making kazoos. The author also offers ideas for making other types of noisemakers.

Wiseman, Ann. **Making Musical Things: Improvised Instruments.** Illus. by author. New York: Charles Scribner's Sons, 1979.

An older title, this book is still a fine one, with easily understood directions, clear lists of materials, and instructions. Children are invited to use items found at home to create instruments. The following are among the easiest and most fun: "Drum Improvisations," p. 18; "Drum Sticks," p. 19; and "Sand Blocks," p. 29. If you have time in your program, the following are more involved but satisfying crafts: "Bugles and Horns," pp. 36-37; "Castanets and Clappers," pp. 42-43; and "Thumb Pianos," pp. 50-51.

Chapter 12

Mysteries and Detectives

Read Alouds

Bartos-Höppner, Barbara. **The Pied Piper of Hamelin.** Trans. by
Anthea Bell. Illus. by Annegert Fuchshuber. New York: J. B.
Lippincott, 1985.

According to legend, in 1284 in the town of Hamelin all the children were
lured away by a stranger. The story remains a fascinating mystery to people
today who wonder if the tale is true and, if so, what happened to the children.
The author captures well the mystery of this tale that is best told to children
in the upper end of the target age group.

The mayor and the people in Hamelin are frustrated and disgusted with
an infestation of rats and mice. One day a stranger who calls himself the Pied
Piper appears and says he can get rid of the vermin. The leaders of the town
agree to pay him 100 gold pieces.

Early the next morning the stranger plays his pipe and the hordes of rats
and mice follow him to the river. When the Piper tries to exact payment, the
mayor refuses. The Pied Piper leaves but returns several weeks later looking
different and playing strange music. The children of Hamelin flock around him
and walk out of town with him, never to return.

The illustrations are beautiful, full-color paintings with a European
flavor. They are particularly deep and dark when the Piper leads the rats and
mice out of town.

McCully, Emily Arnold. **Crossing the New Bridge.** Illus. by author.
New York: G. P. Putnam's Sons, 1994.

The mayor of a town by a river decrees that a new bridge must be built
when the old bridge crashes into the river. The mayor takes credit for the idea,
which was offered by his scribe, an intelligent and efficient-looking young lady.
When an elderly woman says they should ask the Jubilattis to build the bridge,
the mayor acts as if this were his idea, too.

When the happy Jubilattis family arrives and agrees to build a new
bridge, the mayor is delighted until the elderly woman reminds him of the
town's tradition: The first person to cross the new bridge must be the happiest
person in town. Cackling, the woman says if anyone else crosses first, a curse
will fall on all of them.

Tension builds as the Jubilattis work quickly on the new bridge and the
mayor, advised by the scribe, searches to solve the mystery of who the happiest
person in town is. The mayor is frantic as he learns that none of the following people
are the happiest: the Banker, the Grocer, the Female Poet, a mother with 12
healthy children, the Pie Seller, the Apothecary, the Barber, or the Miller.

The solution to the mystery is delightful and clever. The Jubilatti cross
the bridge first and when they say how happy they are because they built the
best bridge of their lives, the mayor and the scribe realize they've found the
happiest person in town.

This is a lovely and fun book, an original folktale.

Van Allsburg, Chris. **The Stranger.** Illus. by author. Boston: Houghton
Mifflin, 1986.

Farmer Bailey accidentally hits and then nurses to health a mysterious
stranger. The whole family wonders who he could be, but the stranger cannot

remember. When the doctor takes the stranger's temperature, the mercury sticks at the bottom of the thermometer. The stranger is confused by button-holes and buttons. Steam rising from soup fascinates him and when he blows on it, Mrs. Bailey feels a draft. The animals on the farm aren't afraid of the stranger, and, even though he helps with chores in the field, the stranger never gets tired.

After two weeks the stranger still doesn't remember who he is. Farmer Bailey notices the weather is odd. It seemed like autumn was approaching, but now it still feels like summer and the leaves on the trees stay green.

One day while standing on a hill the stranger sees that trees in the distance have changed color and he thinks it would be better if the leaves on the trees around the Bailey farm were colorful. The next day he takes a green leaf from a tree and, without thinking, blows on it and it turns orange.

That evening, the stranger hugs the Baileys and disappears. The air turns cold, and the leaves on the trees suddenly are full of color. Every fall since the stranger's visit the trees near the farm stay green for a week after the trees to the north turn colors. Then overnight they change to the brightest colors around. Etched in the frost on the windows of the farmhouse are the words, "See you next fall."

Van Allsburg's full-color illustrations are evocative and surrealistic, with interesting perspectives.

Van Allsburg, Chris. **The Sweetest Fig.** Illus. by author. Boston: Houghton Mifflin, 1993.

Monsieur Bibot is a cold-hearted, greedy dentist who is mean even to his dog. A woman with a toothache comes to his office begging for help. Thinking of the money he'll make, Bibot extracts her tooth. The woman then admits she has no money to pay and instead gives Bibot two figs that she says will make his dreams come true. Bibot is angry and refuses to give her the painkillers she needs.

That evening Bibot eats one of the delicious figs. In the morning while walking his dog he sees his reflection and realizes he's dressed in his under-wear. He also sees the Eiffel Tower drooping. This is what he dreamed the previous evening.

Now Bibot believes the figs are magic and does everything to be sure he'll dream he's the richest man on earth. He also decides that his dog, Marcel, won't be in his new life. Marcel, however, eats the second fig. The next morning Bibot realizes he's become a dog and Marcel is now a man. Marcel's dream came true.

Allsburg's part-realistic, part-fantastic illustrations in muted shades of brown, white, and flesh tones blend seamlessly with his mysterious story.

Van Allsburg, Chris. **The Wretched Stone.** Illus. by author. Boston: Houghton Mifflin, 1991.

On a sea voyage a crew stops at an island not recorded on any map. There they find a large, strange, glowing stone that they bring aboard. To the captain's dismay the normally cheerful, singing, dancing, and reading crew only wants to stare at the stone. They ignore their duties, eventually walk stooped over, and then look like hairy apes. During a storm the captain must sail the ship alone and it is ravaged. The captain discovers that reading and playing music has a positive effect on the crew. The stone becomes dull. When they are rescued, the captain sets fire to the vessel, and the stone sinks with the ship.

Yolen, Jane. **Picnic with Piggins.** Illus. by Jane Dyer. New York: Harcourt Brace Jovanovich, 1988.

The Reynard household is busy with preparations for a picnic that includes a surprise for Piggins, the family butler. Accompanied by friends, the Reynard family drives to a lovely picnic spot. They play games, eat the delicious foods, and tell stories, and then, most of the group fall asleep. A crash and a splash awakens them. Piggins hears that Rexy, one of the Reynard children, is missing. There are clues and everyone declares Rexy's disappearance a mystery, but Piggins says it's a hoax. Find out what's really happening.

This satisfying tale is accompanied by amusing, detailed, full-color illustrations rendered in watercolor and colored pencil.

Yolen, Jane. **Piggins.** Illus. by Jane Dyer. New York: Harcourt Brace Jovanovich, 1987.

During a dinner party hosted by the Reynards and attended by the butler, Piggins, Mr. Reynard shows his guests Mrs. Reynard's diamond necklace and explains that it has a curse on it. Mr. Reynard asks if any of the company would like to buy the necklace. Suddenly, the lights go out, there's a strange tinkling, a scramble of feet, and the sound of objects thudding to the floor. When the chandelier is turned back on, Mrs. Reynard's necklace is gone.

Inspector Bayswater can't find the necklace, but, with the few clues available, Piggins solves the crime.

Booktalks

Adler, David A. **Cam Jansen and the Mystery of the Stolen Diamonds.** Illus. by Susanna Natti. New York: Dell, 1980.

Jennifer Jansen is known as Camera, Cam for short, because she has a photographic memory. When she wants to remember something, Cam says "click" when she looks at it. Cam's incredible ability helps her solve crimes. In this short book Cam sees a robbery at the jewelry store in the mall. Everyone sees and remembers a man running out of the store, but Cam sees and follows a couple with a baby who walked out of the store and to the exit. She trails the couple with her friend Eric, finds out what really happened, gets caught by the thieves, but keeps her wits until the police arrive.

There are many stories in this series about Cam Jansen, the young detective. They are short and satisfying books with pen-and-ink illustrations.

Adler, David A. **Onion Sundaes: A Houdini Club Magic Mystery.** Illus. by Heather Harms Maione. New York: Random House, 1994.

Meet Herman "Houdini" Foster, an aspiring young magician, and his cousin Janet. "Houdini" has demonstrated his "Onion Sundae Trick" for Janet, in which he turns an onion into a jar of chocolate syrup. He will explain the trick to Janet and members of the Houdini Club at their friend Dana's house, but first they need to go to the supermarket to get the ingredients for the trick. While at the market "Houdini" and Janet learn that someone is stealing money from women's handbags. The thief is switching shopping carts. "Houdini" and Janet figure out who the thief is and are rewarded with a bag of free groceries. Pen-and-ink illustrations complement this short, easy read.

Anderson, Scoular. **A Puzzling Day at Castle MacPelican.** Illus. by author. Cambridge, MA: Candlewick Press, 1995.

When Thomas and Esmerelda visit their Uncle Hector MacPelican at his castle, he has a treasure hunt for each of them. Uncle Hector is sure there's a thief in the castle that he'd also like them to track.

Thomas and Esmerelda are taken to different spots in the castle, from the great staircase, game room, kitchen, and dining room to the garden, cellars, bathhouse, and bedrooms. In each location, seen in a full, detailed, double-page pen-and-watercolor illustration, Thomas and Esmerelda find many puzzles and are challenged to find specific things.

This is the type of book children love. The puzzles and mysteries are very challenging, but children can do as many puzzles on a page as they want. I confess, I was hooked.

Clifford, Eth. **Flatfoot Fox and the Case of the Missing Whoooo.** Illus. by Brian Lies. Boston: Houghton Mifflin, 1993.

Black-and-white illustrations enhance the text and make this short read more appealing to second graders and up. Children in kindergarten and first grade will enjoy having this book read to them.

Detective Flatfoot Fox is hired by Silly Goose to find Mournful Owl's "whoooo." The first chapter is reminiscent of the famous "Who's on First" routine by Abbott and Costello. In spite of Silly Goose's interruptions, the nonsense of Early Bird Robin and Cranky Worm, and the preening and boasting of Pushy Peacock, Detective Fox is able to solve the mystery.

Conford, Ellen. **A Case for Jenny Archer.** Illus. by Diane Palmisciano. Boston: Little, Brown, 1988.

This amusing, entertaining short book is well written and zips along.

When Jenny starts reading mystery books during the summer, the stories stimulate her imagination. Jenny decides that the new neighbors are crooks. She interprets innocent activity as nefarious deeds. As Jenny continues to read mysteries, she decides the new neighbors are gangsters and the girl with them isn't their daughter but someone they kidnapped. Jenny sees the movers with a collection of valuable-looking paintings and now decides the neighbors, the Moores, are art thieves.

One night when Jenny sees a moving van and a man carrying a painting out of the Moore's she decides they're making a getaway and dials 911. The police come, the robbers are caught, but they aren't the Moores. The neighbors are art collectors and someone was trying to rob **them.**

Levy, Elizabeth. **Rude Rowdy Rumors: A Brian and Pea Brain Mystery.** Illus. by George Ulrich. New York: HarperCollins, 1994.

Well-written with dialogue that rings true, this book is a good read for children in second and third grade.

Seven-year-old Brian signs up for the peewee soccer league's spring minicamp, and his younger sister Penny helps with the equipment. Soon Penny hears that Brian is getting private soccer lessons, and Mookie, Brian's friend, hears that Brian is adopted. Then Penny hears another rumor, very nasty, that Brian is taking drugs to make himself stronger. Penny decides to find out which teammate is spreading these outrageous lies. Her plan backfires, but it does lead to the culprit.

Quackenbush, Robert. **Lost in the Amazon: A Miss Mallard Mystery.** Illus. by author. New York: Pippin Press, 1990.

This short, enjoyable mystery has a contemporary issue at its center. Bright, fun, light watercolor illustrations outlined in black ink make this book even more appealing for second and third grade readers. Children in kindergarten and first grade will enjoy having this book read to them. This title is one of several in the series about Miss Mallard, world-famous ducktective.

Miss Mallard is in Rio de Janeiro, Brazil, at the invitation of her friend Dr. Albert Eiderstein. Miss Mallard is listening to Dr. Eiderstein explain his latest discovery, Jungle-Nu, which can reverse damage to the jungles and rainforests. Several businessmen, who are also listening at the press luncheon and who profit from the destruction of the rainforest, are against Dr. Eiderstein's discovery.

Suddenly, a parade of samba dancers comes into the room, dances through, and leaves. Dr. Eiderstein is gone, too. Inspector Alfonso Buffle-head, who's in charge of the investigation, needs Miss Mallard's help.

Miss Mallard's inquiries take her down a raft on the Rio de Shivers, where she faces river rapids, water snakes, and piranhas before she finds Dr. Eiderstein with his adoptive son, who had rescued him because of threats against him. Dr. Eiderstein's laboratory papers were stolen, and he was hoping to escape with his vial of Jungle-Nu so he could analyze it and restore the formula. Miss Mallard knows where the vial is and manages to retrieve it and reveal who was involved in the plot against the doctor.

Sharmat, Marjorie Weinman. **Nate the Great and the Boring Beach Bag.** Illus. by Marc Simont. New York: Dell, 1987.

Sharmat has written a series of easy-reader mysteries about Nate the Great, the boy detective that young children enjoy.

Nate doesn't have many clues to help Oliver find his missing blue beach bag, which has his clothes, shoes, and a special seashell in it. Oliver says his beach ball is still in the original spot, but the bag is gone. The solution is simple and funny once children read it.

Sobol, Donald J. **Encyclopedia Brown and the Case of the Disgusting Sneakers.** Illus. by Gail Owens. New York: Morrow Junior Books, 1990.

The titles in Sobol's popular series about the boy detective Encyclopedia Brown are best read by children in grades three and up. Each book presents at least 10 short cases. Youngsters are encouraged to solve each case with Encyclopedia. The solutions are provided at the end of the book.

Encyclopedia Brown, actually Leroy, whose father is chief of police in Idaville, is renowned for his ability to solve mysteries. When Mr. Brown can't solve a case, he presents the facts to his son.

In "The Case of the Teacup," Becky is sure Bugs Meany, prime suspect in many Encyclopedia cases, has stolen her cup, and Encyclopedia is able to prove it. In "The Case of the Rented Canoes," Encyclopedia figures out who stole three fishing rods from the ranger's station.

Yolen, Jane. **Piggins and the Royal Wedding.** Illus. by Jane Dyer. San Diego, CA: Harcourt Brace Jovanovich, 1988.

Piggins, butler to the Reynard family, has made sure the Reynards are ready for the royal wedding. Trixy Reynard is the flower girl, and her brother Rexy is ring bearer. All runs smoothly until the king enters the room where Rexy and the men are. They bow to the king, and when they stand, the ring that was attached to the pillow Rexy was holding is gone. Rexy is a suspect.

Piggins is called in to investigate when Inspector Bayswater can find nothing. On the basis of a smudge on the pillow, a thread, a crumpled silver paper, and an examination of everyone's white gloves, Piggins is able to name the thief.

Demonstration/Participation Activities

Ardley, Neil. "Write in Invisible Ink," p. 55, in **101 Great Science Experiments.** New York: Dorling Kindersley, 1993.

Easy instructions are included for writing secret messages with a mixture of lemon juice, iodine, and water.

Cobb, Vicki, and Kathy Darling. "A Bright Idea," p. 111, in **Wanna Bet? Science Challenges to Fool You.** Illus. by Meredith Johnson. New York: Lothrop, Lee & Shepard, 1993.

Children will be dazzled when you demonstrate and then let them write secret messages with laundry detergent. An alternate method for writing secret messages that uses sunscreen lotion is provided, too.

Hetzer, Linda. "Detective," p. 118, in **50 Fabulous Parties for Kids.** Illus. by Meg Hartigan. New York: Crown, 1994.

In this enjoyable game of recall, children are invited to guess what object has been removed from the room.

Hindley, Judy, and Donald Rumbelow. **The KnowHow Book of Detection.** Illus. by Colin King. London: Usborne, 1990.

Hindley offers a mystery story, puzzles to solve, and projects to teach children detecting skills. There are several activities that children will enjoy doing. Try one or more of the following:

"How to Make a Warrant Card," p. 4. Each child will need cardboard, plastic, and a photograph of herself.

"Box File," pp. 4-5. Provide a cereal box for each child, and they'll easily make this item.

"Detective Language," p. 5. The author lists detective lingo with the meaning of the terms. Mix the lingo and meanings and invite the children to match them correctly.

"Searching for Fingerprints" and "Fingerprint Kit," pp. 14-17. This is a great activity to share with the children. They'll learn how to lift and develop fingerprints. It's not too time consuming and definitely interesting.

"Collecting Evidence," p. 27. Youngsters will have fun practicing the proper way to collect evidence without touching it.

Kohl, MaryAnn F. "Mystery Picture," p. 45, in **Scribble Art: Independent Creative Art Experiences for Children.** Illus. by Judy McCoy. Bellingham, WA: Bright Ring, 1994.
Children enjoy this fun activity, which requires few materials and is easy to do.

Mandell, Muriel. "Invisible Ink," p. 44, in **Simple Science Experiments with Everyday Materials.** Illus. by Frances Zweifel. New York: Sterling, 1989.
This is an easy activity in which children use lemon juice to write a secret message.

Warner, Penny. "Twenty Questions," pp. 76-77, in **Kids' Party Games and Activities: Hundreds of Exciting Things to Do at Parties for Kids 2-12.** Illus. by Kathy Rogers. Deephaven, MN: Meadowbrook Press, 1993.
Warner offers clear instructions for this mystery game and some creative alternative ways to play it.

Zeleny, Robert O., ed. "Observation," p. 308, in **Childcraft: The How and Why Library: Make and Do,** Volume 11. Chicago: World Book, 1987.
In this fun game, you place a variety of items on a table, give children a minute to observe them, then cover the objects and see how many things the children can recall.

Chapter 13

Native American Tales

"Native American" refers to native peoples of the United States, Canada, and Mexico. I have also included some folktales, legends, and myths of the Inuit (Eskimo) peoples. They comprise cultures that are distinct from the Native American Indians on this continent.

Before you do a program on Native American tales you might like to read: Slapin, Beverly, and Doris Seale. **Through Indian Eyes: The Native Experience in Books for Children.** Philadelphia: New Society Publishers, 1992. This title helped me gain sensitivity and provided guidelines for selecting books to share with children in a program of Native American stories. The authors include book reviews, checklists, and a bibliography.

Read Alouds

Begay, Shonto. **Ma'ii and Cousin Horned Toad: A Traditional Navajo Story.** Illus. by author. New York: Scholastic, 1992.

Ma'ii, a coyote, is hungry and decides to visit his cousin Horned Toad, who owns a farm. Despite his rudeness, Toad brings coyote corn and squash stew. When Ma'ii asks for more and more, Toad says Ma'ii must work the cornfield. When Ma'ii goes to fetch water, he drinks it all. Ma'ii decides to get rid of cousin Toad and have the farm for himself. He fakes a toothache and convinces Toad to climb in his mouth and fix it. Then Ma'ii swallows Toad. Alive in coyote's belly, Toad drives him crazy by talking to him and poking him in the ribs. Coyote wants Toad out.

What a wonderful read in the best oral tradition. The story moves along smoothly and the dialogue is captivating. The double-page paintings rendered in earth tones are expressive and convey a sense of action. Note particularly the probing eyes of the coyote.

Bruchac, Joseph, reteller. **Gluskabe and the Four Wishes.** Illus. by Christine Nyburg Shrader. New York: Cobblehill Books/Dutton, 1995.

Bruchac, an award-winning storyteller of Abenaki Indian origin, writes in a straightforward yet rich, lyrical, and pleasing style that holds children's interest. Shrader's artwork is fluid and executed in soft colors, yet there is a strength in her paintings.

Four Abenaki men decide to journey to a far island where Gluskabe, helper of the Great Spirit, lives. Gluskabe let it be known that anyone who came to him would be granted one wish. The men travel by canoe, and the trek is a dangerous one. Gluskabe says they worked hard to get to him and have earned the right to each make one wish.

The first man has almost no possessions and wishes to own many fine things. The vain man is second and he wishes to be taller than any man. Third is the man who is afraid of dying and wants to live longer than any man. Last is a man who tries hard to be a good hunter but isn't. He wishes to become a good enough hunter to provide enough food for his family and the people of his village.

Gluskabe only smiles at the fourth man, but he gives each a pouch. He says they'll find what they want, but they must not open the pouches before they return to their homes. The first three men don't wait. The first man opens the pouch in his canoe, riches pour out and are so heavy they sink him and his canoe. The second man opens the pouch before he reaches home and turns into a pine, the tallest of trees. When the third man opens his pouch he turns into a great boulder that can stand unchanged for much longer than the life of any man.

The fourth man has the longest journey, but he doesn't open his pouch until he returns to his own lodge. When he opens it, great understanding pours into his mind. He is filled with the knowledge of how to hunt and how to show respect for the animals so they'll allow him to hunt them.

Bruchac, Joseph, and Gayle Ross. **The Story of the Milky Way: A Cherokee Tale.** Illus. by Virginia A. Stroud. New York: Dial Books for Young Readers, 1995.

This lovely tale that explains how the Milky Way came to be isn't long, but has a sophistication and universal quality.

Long ago when the world was new, there weren't many stars in the sky, and people depended on corn for food. One morning an elderly man and woman go to the bin of cornmeal kept behind their home and discover that someone stole some of it. That night their grandson hides and watches near the bin. He sees an eerie light in the shape of a great dog that eats the cornmeal.

The next day the villagers go to Beloved Woman, leader among the people, old and wise, who explains to the puzzled people that they have seen the powerful spirit dog. She tells them what they must do to frighten the dog.

That night, when the dog is at the bin, Beloved Woman gives a signal and everyone makes noise with their drums and turtleshell rattles. Frightened, the dog runs and the people chase it to the top of a hill where the dog leaps into the sky and runs across until it can't be seen. The cornmeal that spilled from the dog's mouth becomes a band of light across the night sky. Each grain of cornmeal that falls becomes a star.

The telling is lyrical and beautiful in its straightforward, poetic style. Much is said with an economy of words. The acrylic paintings are rendered in a full range of bold, bright, solid blocks of color. The people are drawn in a stylized way; the Spirit Dog is ethereal.

Caduto, Michael J., and Joseph Bruchac. **Keepers of the Animals: Native American Stories and Wildlife Activities for Children.** Illus. by John Kahionhes Fadden. Golden, CO: Fulcrum, 1991.

There are two stories in particular from this collection that I recommend you memorize and tell. The first could also be included in the program "Games and Sports," and the second could also be used in the program "How and Why."

In "Turtle Races with Beaver" (Seneca-Eastern Woodland origin), pp. 61-62, Turtle outsmarts Beaver when Beaver builds a dam in Turtle's pond while Turtle is hibernating. Turtle says whoever can win a contest will live in the pond, and they decide on a swimming race. Turtle clamps onto Beaver's tail and finally bites so hard Beaver flips his tail and Turtle goes up and over and lands on the bank ahead of Beaver.

"Why Possum Has a Naked Tail" (Cherokee-Southeast origin), pp. 173-75, is a clever and witty story. The animals, especially Rabbit, are tired of listening to Possum brag about his beautiful tail, which is covered with long silky hair. Rabbit has an idea. He tells Possum about the council meeting presided over by Bear. He says that Bear wants Possum to sit near him and speak first because of his grand tail. Rabbit says Possum's tail is a little dirty so he'll clean it with a special medicine. The liquid is actually a tonic that will loosen the hair on Possum's tail. Rabbit then wraps Possum's tail in old snakeskin.

At the council Possum speaks and then reveals his tail. All the hair falls off and the tail is naked and ugly. Ashamed, Possum falls to the ground and pretends to be dead. Even today, whenever he feels threatened, Possum plays dead.

Caduto, Michael J., and Joseph Bruchac. **Keepers of the Earth: Native American Stories and Environmental Activities for Children.** Illus. by John Kahionhes Fadden and Carol Wood. Golden, CO: Fulcrum, 1989.

Each story in this collection comes from a different Native American tribe. Following are stories that read well or can be memorized and told.

"How Grandmother Spider Stole the Sun," pp. 49-50, comes from the Muskogee (Creek) of Oklahoma. When the Earth was first made and there was no light the animals decided that someone must steal the sun and put it in the sky. Fox sneaks to where sun is, grabs a piece in his mouth, and runs. The sun is so hot Fox drops it. The sun burned Fox's mouth and turned it black forevermore. Possum tries next by hiding a piece of sun in her bushy tail. The hot sun burns off all the hair on her tail, and she loses hold of the sun. To this day possums have bare tails. Grandmother Spider succeeds by weaving a bag and placing a piece of the sun in it. Buzzard can fly the highest so he is chosen to put the sun in the sky. Buzzard places Sun in a bag on top of his head, where it gets hot. Buzzard does fly to the top of the Sky and places Sun there, but the sun burned the feathers off the top of his head, and that's why Buzzard has a naked and ugly head.

"Gluscabi and the Wind Eagle," p. 67, is an Abenaki tale from the Northeast Woodlands. Gluscabi can't paddle as strong as the wind can blow so he decides to stop the wind. Gluscabi succeeds, but once the wind stops, Gluscabi learns that the wind also brings some good with it that he had not realized. He decides to free Wind Eagle.

"How Turtle Flew South for the Winter," pp. 157-58, comes from the Dakota (Sioux) of the Midwest. Turtle sees the birds gathering in the trees to fly south for the winter where it's warm and there's much food. Turtle strikes a deal so he can go with them. Two birds will each grab one corner of a stick and Turtle will clamp on with his teeth. During the flight, Turtle wants to ask questions, finally starts to talk, and falls. Turtle pulls his legs in but hits the ground so hard his shell cracks.

Caduto, Michael J., and Joseph Bruchac. **Keepers of the Night: Native American Stories and Nocturnal Activities for Children.** Illus. by David Kanietakeron Fadden. Golden, CO: Fulcrum, 1994.

The authors provide useful information to sensitize the presenter so he or she can tell these stories in the proper context with understanding and sensitivity. These tales are most effective when memorized and told.

"How the Bat Came to Be," pp. 21-22, is an Anishinabe tale from the Eastern Woodland. It tells of a time long ago when the sun came too close to Earth, became tangled in the top branches of a tall tree, and couldn't escape, so it remained dark. A small brown squirrel finds the sun and works to free it. As Squirrel chews the branches, the sun grows brighter. Squirrel continues even though the heat of the sun turns his fur black, burns his tail, and blinds him. Sun has pity on Squirrel and grants him a wish. Squirrel has always wanted to fly so Sun turns him into a bat.

"The Great La Crosse Game," pp. 97-99, is a Menominee story from the Eastern Woodland. The birds and animals decide to settle a dispute with a game of lacrosse. Whoever scores the first goal will win. The creatures align on both sides, but then a small creature appears. It has fur but doesn't look like an animal. It has wings, but they aren't like a bird's. No one wants him on their side, but Otter says no one should be left out, so the creature is allowed to join the animals. The birds appear to be winning until the little brown creature leaps into the air, spreads out its legs, unfolds its leathery wings, grabs the ball from the birds, darts and dodges easily in the growing darkness, and scores a goal for the animals. When the animals ask the creature its name he tells them it is Bat. They reward Bat by letting him sleep during the day so at night he'll have lots of insects to eat.

Carey, Valerie Scho, reteller. **Quail Song: A Pueblo Indian Tale.** Illus. by Ivan Barnett. New York: G. P. Putnam's Sons, 1990.

Bold, clean illustrations with a southwestern flavor complement this humorous and clever story.

While gathering grass seed, Quail cuts herself on the sharp grass and cries "Ki-ruu, Ki-ruu." Coyote hears Quail, thinks it's a beautiful song, locates Quail, and demands Quail teach him the song. When Quail explains that it isn't singing, but a cry of pain, Coyote threatens to swallow Quail unless she teaches him the tune. Once he learns the song, Coyote heads home, but he trips into a prairie dog hole and drops the song. He returns two more times for the song. Quail is tired of this so she paints a rock to look like her and leaves. Once again Coyote loses the song. He speaks to the rock he thinks is Quail, and when he gets no response, Coyote swallows the rock and breaks his teeth. Coyote cries "AIEEE." Lizard hears the cry, thinks it's a song, and wants Coyote to teach it to him. Coyote is angry that Lizard can't distinguish a cry of pain from a song, and he wants to eat Lizard, but Coyote can't bite without his teeth.

Cohen, Caron Lee, reteller. **The Mud Pony: Traditional Skidi-Pawnee Tale.** Illus. by Shonto Begay. New York: Scholastic, 1988.

Here's an exciting and touching tale with active, fluid, and expressive illustrations.

A poor, young boy wishes he could have a pony of his own like the other boys in his Indian camp. He shapes a pony out of mud. When his people break camp to follow the buffalo, the boy is accidentally left behind. Mother Earth brings the mud pony to life and tells the boy he must do what the pony says. The boy travels until he arrives in the camp on the third night. The chief feels the boy has great power since he found them. He must join them in battle against the enemy. The pony tells the boy how to protect himself, and he leads his people to victory.

dePaola, Tomie. **The Legend of the Bluebonnet: An Old Tale of Texas.** Illus. by author. New York: G. P. Putnam's Sons, 1983.

This is a lovely story, well told and illustrated in Tomie dePaola's child-like, colorful style.

The famine has been long and dreadful for the Comanche. They dance to the Great Spirits, but no healing rains come. All this is witnessed by She-Who-Is-Alone, a young girl, whose family perished in the famine. In her lap is a warrior doll made of buckskin with brilliant blue feathers on its head. It is all she has left from her family. When the shaman returns and announces the Great Spirits said the people must sacrifice and make a burnt offering of the most precious possession among the people, the girl knows the Spirits mean her doll.

That night she offers her doll and scatters its ashes. In the morning wherever the ashes fell the ground is covered with flowers as blue as the feathers in her doll's hair. The flowers are a sign of forgiveness from the Great Spirits. The rain falls and the people prosper. Every spring in Texas the bluebonnets bloom.

dePaola, Tomie. **The Legend of the Indian Paintbrush.** Illus. by author. New York: G. P. Putnam's Sons, 1988.

In this beautiful telling with childlike, colorful illustrations, youngsters hear an explanation for how sunsets were brought to the earth.

Little Gopher is not like the other boys, who will grow to be warriors. He is artistically inclined. When he is older a dream vision comes to Little Gopher in which a maiden tells him to find a pure white buckskin. She tells Little Gopher that one day he'll paint a picture as pure as the colors in the evening sky.

Little Gopher makes paints out of berries, flowers, and rocks, and he paints on animal skins, but the paintings never satisfy him. A voice tells him to go to the place where he watches the sun set in the evening. Little Gopher goes and finds brushes filled with paint sticking out of the ground, each bearing one color of the sunset. Little Gopher paints the sky with them. The colors of the sunset leave the brushes on the hillside, and the next day the hill is ablaze with color. The brushes took root in the ground and multiplied into plants. Every spring the hills and meadows burst into bloom. Every evening the sunset Little Gopher painted dazzles the people. His new name is He-Who-Brought-the-Sunset-to-the-Earth.

Dixon, Ann, reteller. **How Raven Brought Light to People.** Illus. by James Watts. New York: Margaret K. McElderry Books/Macmillan, 1992.

In this tale from the Tlingit Indians of Alaska, children hear how Raven used magic to gain entrance to the house of the great chief who held the light of the world in three wooden boxes. Raven turns himself into a child, is born to the chief's daughter, and releases the sun, moon, and stars through the smoke-hole in the chief's home. Raven then turns himself from a child into a Raven and flies through the smoke-hole to escape.

The text is straightforward and sparse but also appealing and captivating. The full-page illustrations include symbols, totem poles, and wood carvings of the Tlingit Indians.

Durell, Ann, comp. "The Coyote and the Bear," pp. 25-31, in **The Diane Goode Book of American Folk Tales and Songs.** Illus. by Diane Goode. New York: E. P. Dutton, 1989.

Bear suggests and Coyote agrees to farm land together and share the crop. They plant potatoes, and Bear says he'll take what grows below the ground and

Coyote will take what grows above. Coyote gets the inedible potato tops. The next spring Bear offers to let Coyote take what grows below the ground and Bear will take what sprouts above. They plant corn so Bear gets the stalks and ears; Coyote gets the roots. During the winter Coyote sees Bear eating fish. Bear tells Coyote to put his tail in a hole in the ice to catch fish and not to move until Bear tells him. The hole freezes around Coyote's tail and Bear laughs. Coyote must stay that way until the ice thaws. He never forgives Bear or speaks to him again.

Garner, Alan, reteller. "Glooskap and Wasis," pp. 210-11, in **From Sea to Shining Sea: A Treasury of American Folklore and Folk Songs.** Comp. by Amy L. Cohn. Illus. by 11 Caldecott Medal and four Caldecott Honor Book artists. New York: Scholastic, 1993.
Mighty Glooskap, who with his brother Malsum the Wolf made the world, boasts that he can command anything. A Mohican woman laughs and says she has in her wigwam someone Glooskap hasn't conquered and can't. Glooskap confronts this creature, Wasis, a baby, who is sucking on a piece of maple sugar. He demands that Wasis come to him. Shouts, roars, spells—nothing moves the child. The baby simply says, "Goo."

Goble, Paul. **Dream Wolf.** Illus. by author. New York: Bradbury Press, 1990.
Goble's richly colored, dynamic illustrations complement his beautiful writing.
Two Plains Indian children, Tiblo and Tanksi, are separated from their mothers when they climb high into the hills while picking berries. When it gets dark, the children can't find their way home. Lost, tired, and hungry they crawl into a cave for shelter. Tiblo dreams that a wolf lies next to them to provide warmth. In the morning, Tiblo sees the wolf, and the wolf tells him that he protected Tiblo and Tanksi the night before. The wolf also helps them return home. When Tiblo and Tanksi's people hear this, they leave gifts to give thanks to the wolf.

Goble, Paul. **The Gift of the Sacred Dog.** Illus. by author. New York: Macmillan, 1980.
The Great Plains Indians are hungry because no buffalo herds can be found. One boy in the camp, in particular, can't bear to see everyone suffering and to hear his people crying with hunger. He goes to the hills to ask the Great Spirit for help. The boy sees another youngster on the back of a beautiful animal. The rider tells the boy that the Great Spirit is giving them the gift of the Sacred Dogs, who can carry them far and run faster than the buffalo. The boy sleeps and when he awakens to return home, he sees Sacred Dogs running out of a cave toward him. They follow the boy, and he explains to his people what they are and how to use them to hunt buffalo. The people live as relatives with the Sacred Dogs (horses) and all living things.

Goble, Paul, reteller. **Iktomi and the Boulder: A Plains Indian Story.** Illus. by author. New York: Orchard, 1988.
Goble has carefully researched this traditional tale and ably captures the personality of Iktomi the trickster, who is amusing, insincere, and lazy. Goble's

striking illustrations consist of bright, bold colors outlined in black. This particular tale explains why bats have flattened faces and why there are rocks scattered over the Great Plains.

Iktomi is walking to visit his relatives when the sun gets so hot he decides he doesn't need to carry his blanket anymore. He tells the large boulder that provided him with shade that he'll give it his blanket to keep the sun off it. When Iktomi notices thunder clouds he decides he wouldn't want his clothes to get wet, so he takes back his blanket and sits under it while it rains. The boulder comes after Iktomi and pins him to the ground. Iktomi asks the animals for help, but none can free him. When darkness comes the bats appear and Iktomi tells them that Boulder has been insulting them. Iktomi makes the bats so furious they hit the boulder until pieces break off and only little chips are left.

Goble, Paul. **Iktomi and the Buzzard: A Plains Indian Story.** Illus. by author. New York: Orchard, 1994.

Paul Goble captures well the character of Iktomi the trickster, his vanity and laziness. Here Iktomi is full of himself as he walks to the powwow wearing his feathers for the Eagle Dance. Iktomi comes to the river, doesn't want to get his feathers wet, and tricks Buzzard into carrying him across. As they fly over the river, Iktomi makes fun of Buzzard behind his back, but Buzzard knows because he can see Iktomi's shadow. Buzzard gets his revenge when he drops Iktomi into a hollow tree. Iktomi tricks two girls with axes into chopping down the tree and gets out of trouble again.

Kronberg, Ruthhilde, and Patricia C. McKissack. "The Legend of Tutokanula," pp. 37-39, in **A Piece of the Wind: And Other Stories to Tell.** San Francisco: Harper, 1990.

This delightful tale is best when memorized and told and offers opportunities for audience participation.

Kodo and Kabato, two brothers, are so cold from swimming in the river that they lie in the sun atop a large boulder. While they are in a deep sleep the boulder grows until it reaches the sky. The boys' parents can't find them, but the animals know where they are because they saw the boulder grow.

Coincidentally, the boys' parents find a wounded raccoon and nurse it to health. The raccoon realizes they are Kodo and Kabato's parents, and he asks the other animals to help get the boys down from the boulder. Many animals try to jump and reach the top of the boulder but can't. When Tutokanula the inchworm offers to try, the other animals don't see how he can help. Step-by-step, however, Tutokanula crawls up the boulder, awakens the boys, and teaches them how to climb down.

Once again, as in so many Native American tales, it is the smallest and most often overlooked creature that succeeds where others fail.

London, Jonathan, reteller, with Lanny Pinola. **Fire Race: A Karuk Coyote Tale.** Illus. by Sylvia Long. San Francisco: Chronicle Books, 1993.

Illustrator Long did much research to capture the settings and traditions of the Karuk Indians of California. Her artwork is detailed and richly colored. The animals' faces are lifelike and expressive, and the outdoor scenes are breathtaking.

In a time long ago the animal people have no fire, so they eat their food raw, freeze in the winter, and live in the dark. Wise Old Coyote gathers the animals and says that fire is at the end of the world guarded by the mean Yellow Jacket sisters, who won't share the fire. Trickster Coyote has a plan to get fire.

Coyote goes to the end of the world, meets the Yellow Jacket sisters, and offers to make them pretty. He uses blackened coal to mark their faces and bodies with stripes. Coyote says if they close their eyes he'll make them prettier. While their eyes are shut, Coyote takes some fire at the end of a piece of charred oak in his teeth and races away. Angry, the Yellow Jacket sisters fly after Coyote, who relays the fire to Eagle. As the Yellow Jackets reach him, Eagle hands off the fire to Mountain Lion. So it goes, the Yellow Jacket sisters give chase, the fire is passed off in turn to Fox, Bear, Measuring Worm, Turtle, and Frog, who swallows the fire and stays under water with it until the Yellow Jackets give up and leave. Frog comes up and spits the coal into the roots of a willow. The tree swallows the fire. Coyote shows the animal people how to get fire by rubbing two willow sticks together over dry moss.

Martin, Rafe. **The Boy Who Lived with the Seals.** Illus. by David Shannon. New York: G. P. Putnam's Sons, 1993.

From the Chinook Indians comes this legend, beautifully told by author Martin. A young boy tries to find his way from the river to his camp but can't, and no one finds him. One night long after, an old woman of the tribe speaks of an island with seals and a boy who lives with them. The boy's parents go to the island and bring their son home. The boy behaves like a seal, but with time he acts like a human. The boy makes canoes and paddles for his people as well as excellent bows and arrows. When the boy speaks of the seals, his people feel the sea moving in his words and they are uneasy. They avoid the boy. Each time the boy paddles across the river or into the sea, he hears the seals, who want him to swim with them. The boys' parents put a deer hide over him so he won't see the seals. One day, however, the boy struggles to free himself, jumps in the water, and returns to the seals. His parents throw his box of carving tools into the water and let it sink. Each year when the tribe returns to this spring camp, there is a new, beautifully carved canoe on shore that the boy has made for them.

McDermott, Gerald. **Coyote: A Trickster Tale from the American Southwest.** Illus. by author. New York: Harcourt Brace, 1994.

McDermott's rhythmic telling of this Zuni tale is accompanied by his strong, expressive artwork in brilliant colors, which was inspired by Zuni folklore and southwestern design.

Blue Coyote constantly gets into trouble. There's humor in his mishaps; for example, he pokes his nose in Badger's hole and gets bitten. Coyote sees a flock of crows chanting and dancing as they fly through the air, and he decides he wants to fly. Then he'll be the greatest coyote in the world.

When Old Man Crow hears Coyote's desire to fly, he tells the other crows they can have fun with Coyote. They each take a feather from their left wings and stick them in Coyote. He flies off balance and falls to the ground. Each crow gives him a feather from their right wings. Soon the crows tire of teasing Coyote because he is rude, boastful, and sings off key. The crows take back their feathers, Coyote falls, his tail catches fire, and he lands in a pool in the mesa.

Coyote hears the crows laughing, runs after them, and trips in the dirt. He returns home wet and dusty, and that's the color he's remained.

McDermott, Gerald. **Raven: A Trickster Tale from the Pacific Northwest.** Illus. by author. New York: Harcourt Brace Jovanovich, 1993.

McDermott combines a smooth, pleasing telling with his bold, graphic-style illustrations in this traditional tale.

Raven, sad for the humans who must live in the dark and cold, decides to search for light. He flies far until he sees light coming from the house of the Sky Chief. Raven sees the Sky Chief's daughter drinking water from a basket. He changes himself into a pine needle that floats into the water that the girl drinks. Months later the girl gives birth to a child, Raven reborn as a boy. In this guise Raven searches for the source of the light. Finally, Raven sees a large, glowing box in the corner of the lodge. Sky Chief gives him what's inside, a ball blazing with light. Raven takes it, turns back into a bird, flies through the smoke-hole of the lodge, disappears, and puts the sun high in the sky.

Moore, Robin. "How the Turtle Cracked His Shell," A Cherokee Story, pp. 142-45, in **Ready-to-Tell Tales: Sure-Fire Stories from America's Favorite Storytellers.** Ed. by David Holt and Bill Mooney. Little Rock, AK: August House, 1994.

Long ago Turtle and Possum spent their days working and playing together. One day while Possum is throwing persimmons down to Turtle to eat, Wolf comes along and takes the fruit. Turtle tells Possum to throw the biggest persimmon to Wolf, who chokes. Turtle and Possum leave, and the other wolves rescue Wolf. Humiliated, Wolf, with the aid of the other wolves, catches Turtle. By keeping his wits about him, Turtle tricks the wolves into throwing him into the river. Turtle swims away but hits a big rock in the center of the river first. His beautiful shell is and remains cracked in 13 tiny pieces.

This story is most effective when memorized and told.

Munsch, Robert, and Michael Kusugak. **A Promise Is a Promise.** Illus. by Vladyana Krykorka. Toronto: Annick Press, 1988.

On the first nice day of spring Allashua, an Inuit girl who lives in the Arctic, tells her mother she's going fishing in a crack in the ice of the ocean. Mother warns Allashua not to fish on the sea ice because the creature Qallupilluit grabs children when they come too near the cracks in the ice. Mother advises that she fish in a lake. Allashua says a promise is a promise, but instead she heads for the sea ice.

To be sure there are no Qallupilluit nearby, Allashua yells insults about the creatures. Hearing nothing she fishes. Then she hears the voice of Qallupilluit. Allashua denies being the child who insulted the creature, but they drag her under the sea anyway.

The Qallupilluit release her when Allashua promises to return with her brothers and sisters. Her family agrees that a promise is a promise, but her mother devises a plan to fulfill the promise and outwit the Qallupilluit at the same time.

This amusing tale is complemented by expressive illustrations that convey the cold and feel of ice and offer characters with individualized faces.

Rodanas, Kristina. **Dragonfly's Tale.** Illus. by author. New York: Clarion Books, 1991.

Based on a traditional Zuni tale, this story reads aloud well and is matched by full-page illustrations in deep and rich colors.

In a time long ago the tribe of Ashiwi in the village Hawikuh is watched over by two powerful spirits, the Maidens of the White and Yellow Corn. Year after year the people have bountiful harvests. One year the head chief of the tribe decides to show off their wealth by having a mock battle with weapons made of bread and dough. The corn maidens disguise themselves as beggars to see what is happening. A boy and his little sister offer the women food, but an elder says not to waste the food on the beggars. People from neighboring tribes watch the mock battle. The corn maidens are so upset they vow to teach the people a lesson so they won't waste food again.

A great famine comes and the people must leave their village and seek help. The boy and his little sister are left behind. To comfort his sister, the boy carves a butterfly's body from the core of a dry cornstalk, legs from straw, and wings from brittle corn leaf. When the little girl asks the butterfly to search for food it goes to the land of the corn maidens and tells them about the children. The corn maidens remember the kindness of the children and have food delivered to them. The butterfly toy (or cornstalk creature) hovers nearby.

The children plant corn, and it grows in four days. The people return to the village, humbled, and intend to replant the fields. They decide to honor the Corn Maidens and learn from the children. As for the cornstalk creature, to this day in early summer it appears and is known as Dragonfly.

Sage, James. **Coyote Makes Man.** Illus. by Britta Teckentrup. New York: Simon & Schuster Books for Young Readers, 1994.

Sage has written a short, interesting, thought-provoking, and cleanly told version of this Native American creation tale. It is illustrated with sophisticated, original, striking collage artwork in earthtones.

Coyote finishes making the earth and then asks all the animals what his final creation, Man, should be like. Each animal mentions a feature they have. Coyote gives each animal a lump of clay with which he wants them to show him their idea of Man. When the animals are asleep, Coyote looks at the models and sees that each animal made Man in his own image. Coyote pours water over the models until they are lumps of clay. He shapes his own image of Man, and then gives Man the gift of Life.

Sloat, Teri, reteller. **The Eye of the Needle: Based on a Yupik Tale As Told by Betty Huffman.** Illus. by author. New York: Dutton Children's Books, 1990.

The author's poetic text brings to life this legend from the Yupik Eskimos of Alaska. It is illustrated in lively watercolors in soft shades of brown, gray, and blue that convey the beauty of the ocean and shore.

When Amik is sent by his grandmother to find food, he consumes a series of animals, each bigger than the next, thinking he'll get something better to bring home. When Amik is full he realizes he saved nothing for his grandmother. He is huge, yet when he returns to his hut, grandmother tells him to come down through the smoke-hole, through the eye of her needle and, miraculously, he does. When he slides through the needle, there's a loud pop and a rush of water swirls around Amik. Out of him come all the sea animals.

Sloat, Teri, reteller. **The Hungry Giant of the Tundra.** Illus. by Robert and Teri Sloat. New York: Dutton Children's Books, 1993.

The Sloats learned this version of this Yupik (Eskimo) folktale from a storyteller in a remote village in Alaska where they taught for many years. The short and swiftly paced text is complemented by illustrations that capture the landscape, the giant, and the children well.

The children in an Alaskan village are warned to come home before the hungry giant comes looking for its evening meal. One day, as they often do, the children pretend not to hear their parents. Soon they smell the giant, who snatches them, takes off his trousers, puts the children inside, and ties them to a tree with his suspenders. While the giant goes to get a knife, the children ask a chickadee to free them. It does and the children fill the giant's pants with rocks. The children run until they come to a river. A crane on the other side stretches her legs so they can walk across. When the giant finds out he's been tricked, he chases the children and stomps to the river. The crane stretches her legs, but when the giant gets to the deepest part of the river, she pulls back her long legs. The giant, who can't swim, is carried to the bottom of the sea, and the crane flies the children back to their parents.

Steptoe, John. **The Story of Jumping Mouse.** Illus. by author. New York: Lothrop, Lee & Shepard, 1984.

Strong and moving artwork in black and white complement this special, poetic, concisely told interpretation of a moral tale from the American Indians of the northern Plains.

A young mouse, who has grown up listening to the stories of the old ones, dreams of journeying to the far-off land he heard so much about. The way is long and difficult, but the mouse is bolstered by a magic frog who names him Jumping Mouse, gives him powerful legs to cross the river, and tells him he will realize his dream. Jumping Mouse travels from the bush, across the desert to a grassy plain, and then through the mountains. Along the way he gives his eyesight to a blind bison and his sense of smell to a wolf. Both animals protect Jumping Mouse and get him to the far-off land. Once there, Jumping Mouse doesn't know what to do, but Magic Frog appears and rewards him for his unselfishness and compassion. He tells Jumping Mouse to jump high, and, when Jumping Mouse does, the air lifts him higher and higher into the sky. Once again he can see and hear. Magic Frog gives him a new name, Eagle, for that's what Jumping Mouse has become.

Stevens, Janet, reteller. **Coyote Steals the Blanket: A Ute Tale.** Illus. by author. New York: Holiday House, 1993.

Stevens's trademark oversize, richly colored, expressive illustrations complement her telling of this tale about Coyote the trickster.

Coyote ignores Hummingbird's warning that there's danger ahead and he mustn't touch the beautiful blankets he'll see because they don't belong to him. Coyote takes one of the blankets and soon hears a rumble behind him. The rock from which Coyote stole the blanket is chasing him. Various animals try to stop the rock, but the rock is undeterred. Hummingbird insists that Coyote return the blanket. Only when coyote's tail is pinned by the rock does he agree. Hummingbird whirs its wings, kicking up dust and wind until with a crack the rock falls apart. Coyote rushes off. The final view is of Coyote with all the blankets on and all the rocks they were draped over chasing him.

Van Laan, Nancy, reteller. **Rainbow Crow: A Lenape Tale.** Illus. by Beatriz Vidal. New York: Alfred A. Knopf, 1989.

Colorful illustrations that convey a sense of action and are noted for the expressive eyes of the animal characters complement this fine tale.

Long ago the world was warm and the animals happy, but suddenly the Earth grew cold and snow fell. The animals decide that one of them must travel to the Great Sky Spirit and ask him to stop the snow. Rainbow Crow, the most beautiful bird on Earth, offers to go.

Great Spirit says he can't stop the snow or cold, but he can give the animals the gift of Fire. Crow flies home with a bit of fire on the end of a stick. As Crow flies, sparks of Fire darken his tail feathers and then cover them with soot. Smoke and ash blow into Crow's mouth and his voice becomes crackled.

Crow returns to Earth and brings Fire to the animals. The animals sing Crow's praises, but Crow is sad because his rainbow feathers are gone and he can't sing his sweet song. Great Spirit tells Crow that Man will soon come, take Fire, and be master of all creatures, but Crow will be free. Man won't hurt or capture crow because Crow won't taste good. Crow's black feathers will shine and reflect all the colors of Earth. Now Crow is proud; he's Black Crow.

Yolen, Jane. **Sky Dogs.** Illus. by Barry Moser. New York: Harcourt Brace Jovanovich, 1990.

An elderly Siksika Indian (Blackfoot) tells the story of how he came to be known as "He-Who-Loves-Horses" in this poetic story. The watercolor illustrations in shades of brown and yellow appear simple but are full of feeling.

Long ago the Blackfeet walked from camp to camp with only dogs to carry their possessions across the plains. One day they see strange beasts that they think are large dogs sent as a gift from Old Man, creator of all things. The children and adults are afraid, but not the narrator, the elderly Siksika Indian. He touches the beast, a horse, and soon learns how to care for and ride it. That's how the Piegan, "people of many horses," became leaders of the plains.

Young, Richard, and Judy Dockrey Young. "Skunnee Wundee and the Stone Giant," pp. 14-16, in **Favorite Scary Stories of American Children.** Little Rock, AK: August House, 1990.

Learn and tell this short, smoothly told tale from the Algonquin Indians.

When Skunnee Wundee, an Indian boy, is confronted by a Stone Giant who wants to eat him, he remembers that Stone Giants aren't smart and challenges it to see who can skip a rock furthest across the river. Skunnee Wundee hears Turtle call and convinces the giant that Turtle is a stone. He throws Turtle, who skips across the water then swims a long distance. Skunnee Wundee wins, and the giant, in anger, shakes himself into a thousand pieces.

Booktalks

Bernhard, Emery, reteller. **Spotted Eagle and Black Crow.** Illus. by
Durga Bernhard. New York: Holiday House, 1993.

Lots of dialogue and action, a story that flows well, and large, stylized
watercolor paintings are featured in this strong and finely crafted love story.

Spotted Eagle and his brother Black Crow love Red Bird. Black Crow
decides that Red Bird will want to marry Spotted Eagle, so he plots to get rid
of his brother. Black Crow convinces his brother they must war against the
Pawnee, who stole their best ponies on their last raid. Black Crow lowers
Spotted Eagle over the side of a cliff to get feathers from two young eagles for
them to wear on their war party. When Black Crow has lowered his brother, he
lets go of the rope and leaves. Trapped, Spotted Eagle goes without food for four
days, until a great eagle comes and accepts Spotted Eagle, who must promise
not to harm eagles. The great eagle brings food to Spotted Eagle, who shares
his meals with the eaglets in the nest with him. The eaglets grow and then
return Spotted Eagle to his home, where Black Crow has married Red Bird.
Spotted Eagle will not fight his brother because all men will be needed if the
Pawnee attack.

One day the Pawnee do attack. Soon only the two brothers are left. Black
Crow dies a warrior's death, but Spotted Eagle lives because he remembered
the wisdom of the Great Spirit and treated the young eagles as brothers.
Spotted Eagle gives thanks to the eagles and marries Red Bird.

Brother Eagle, Sister Sky: A Message from Chief Seattle. Illus. by
Susan Jeffers. New York: Dial Books, 1991.

Susan Jeffers trademark oversized, striking, and beautiful artwork serve
as a perfect visual counterpoint to the words of Chief Seattle, a Suquamish
Indian chief, who described his people's respect for the earth in a speech given
during treaty negotiations with white settlers in the 1850s. Chief Seattle's
words are as apt today as they were almost 150 years ago.

In this message Chief Seattle speaks eloquently of the sacredness of the
earth and the brotherhood between people, animals, and plants. He emphasizes
that we must treat the earth and everything on it with respect. He wonders
what will happen when men take over the land and cautions that whatever man
does to nature he does to himself.

Bruchac, Joseph. **The First Strawberries: A Cherokee Story.** Illus.
by Anna Vojtech. New York: Dial Books for Young Readers, 1993.

The creator made man and woman, and they married and lived happily
for a time. One day the man comes home from hunting, finds his wife picking
flowers instead of cooking dinner, and speaks harshly to her. Hurt and angry
because she wanted to share the beauty of the flowers with her husband, the
woman says she won't live with him and she walks away at a rapid pace.

The sun takes pity on the man, and, once he's sure the man is sorry for
his behavior, he decides to help the man. The sun shines and raspberries grow,
but the wife ignores them. The sun causes blueberries to grow, but the wife
ignores them, too. Finally the sun makes strawberries grow, the wife notices
them, and she stops to pick some for her husband. Finally, the husband catches
up with her and asks for forgiveness. She shares the strawberries with him.

To this day, when the Cherokee eat strawberries, they are reminded to always be kind to each other and that friendship and respect are as sweet as the taste of strawberries.

Goble, Paul. **Adopted by the Eagles: A Plains Indian Story of Friendship and Treachery.** Illus. by Paul Goble. New York: Bradbury Press, 1994.

Paul Goble's books are extensively researched, and here, as in many of his books, he includes references, a note explaining the thematic material, and the way the stories were told originally. Goble also includes a follow-up activity. His large paintings are bold and detailed in India ink and watercolor. His telling is dramatic, moving, and swiftly paced.

Two young men, White Hawk and Tall Bear, are Kolas, special friends who do and share everything and defend each other, too. Both young men love Red Leaf, and White Hawk plots to get rid of Tall Bear. He tells Tall Bear they must act on White Hawk's dream that they captured horses from their enemies. They travel far, but see no horse herds or camps. Instead, they see a nest with two young eagles on a ledge below them. White Hawk offers to lower Tall Bear so they can at least bring the eagles back with them. Once White Hawk lowers Tall Bear to the nest, he jerks the rope up and leaves Tall Bear to starve or fall to his death.

Tall Bear realizes White Hawk left him so he could marry Red Leaf. Then he prays to the Great Spirit. Instead of dying, Tall Bear is adopted by the eagle family. Soon, the young eagles want to fly from the nest, and they carry Tall Bear to his home. In return Tall Bear promises them gifts in the fall.

When Tall Bear returns home everyone is excited to see him because White Hawk said Tall Bear was killed by the enemy. White Hawk flees. The people want to follow and punish him, but Tall Bear stops them because White Hawk is his Kola.

In the fall, Tall Bear and Red Leaf marry. Tall Bear brings gifts of food to the eagles and says humans and eagles will always be relatives.

Goble, Paul. **Crow Chief: A Plains Indian Story.** Illus. by author. New York: Orchard, 1992.

Journey to a time long ago when Crows are white and people hunt buffaloes with spears and arrows. The Crow Chief hates people but is friends with buffaloes, so he always warns the buffaloes when the hunters are coming. The people are hungry because of this. Falling Star answers the people's prayers for help. He captures Crow Chief and makes him watch the people have a great feast so he'll know what it's like to be hungry. Falling Star explains that all must share and live like relatives.

Paul Goble's trademark striking and evocative illustrations accompany his meticulously researched and well-written myth.

Goble, Paul. **Her Seven Brothers.** Illus. by author. New York: Bradbury Press, 1988.

This retelling of a Cheyenne legend is as carefully crafted and illustrated as all of Goble's books.

Long ago a girl sews seven sets of clothing for seven men. She says there are seven brothers in the far north country she'll ask to be her brothers. They accept and adopt her. One day, several buffalo come and demand the girl. When the brothers refuse, all the buffalo stampede them. The little brother shoots an arrow, and a tree grows that he, his brothers, and the girl climb. When the young boy shoots another arrow, the tree grows to the sky, they climb it, and so become the Big Dipper.

Goble, Paul, reteller. **Iktomi and the Berries: A Plains Indian Story.** Illus. by author. New York: Orchard, 1989.

In words and paintings, Goble captures well the essence of Iktomi the trickster: sly but dumb, mischievous and lazy, always trying to trick others, ultimately tricking himself.

While hunting Iktomi complains that there's nothing to catch—no buffalo or prairie dogs (they're seen hiding from him). He decides to hunt ducks, goes to the water, sees berries instead, and jumps in to get them. Not until he's almost drowned does he look up and realize what he saw in the water was the reflection of the berries on the trees.

For another satisfying tale about Iktomi see Goble, Paul, reteller. **Iktomi and the Ducks: A Plains Indian Story.** Illus. by author. New York: Orchard, 1990.

Goble, Paul. **Love Flute.** Illus. by author. New York: Bradbury Press, 1992.

A special reader will be drawn to this story of a shy young man who can face enemy warriors but can't speak to the girl he loves. The young man sees others talk to the girl, is sad, and leaves camp. He shoots his arrow into the air, where it stays, points, and leads him. For four days the young man follows the arrow, which he knows is guided by unseen powers. The young man sleeps and when he awakens he sees two tall Elk Men who present him with a flute made by the birds and animals. Now the young man will be able to speak straight to the heart of the girl he loves.

This superbly told story from the Plains Indians is complemented by striking, detailed paintings. Author Goble provides extensive references for the text and for the drawings of the love flute.

Martin, Rafe. **The Rough-Face Girl.** Illus. by David Shannon. New York: G. P. Putnam's Sons, 1992.

Martin offers a well-written and touching version of an Algonquin Indian Cinderella story. Illustrator Shannon's artwork is striking and dazzling.

It is said that a rich, powerful, and handsome Invisible Being lives with his sister in the large wigwam of the village. Only the female who sees him can marry him. A poor man lives in the village with his three daughters. The two older sisters are cruel, call their younger sister ugly and "Rough-Face Girl," and force her to sit by the fire and keep it going. In this way her hands get burnt and scarred and her arms are rough and marred.

The two older sisters want to marry Invisible Being, but they can't answer the questions about Invisible Being that his sister asks. Rough-Face Girl also wants to marry Invisible Being. She has nothing fine to wear and people make fun of her, but she can see the Invisible Being and answer questions about him. Invisible Being's sister gives her fine clothing to wear, and when Rough-Face

Girl bathes in the lake her skin grows smooth and her black hair turns long and glossy. She marries Invisible Being and lives happily with him.

McDermott, Gerald, adapter. **Arrow to the Sun: A Pueblo Indian Tale.** Illus. by author. New York: Viking, 1974.

Vivid, bold blocks of color, particularly black and yellow, perfectly match McDermott's simple and moving adaptation of this Pueblo Indian myth.

The Lord of the Sun sends a spark of life to earth that travels to a pueblo, where it enters the house of a young maiden. In this way Boy comes into the world. When other children mock Boy and ask where his father is, he decides to find his father. Arrow Maker makes a special bow, and Boy becomes an arrow that flies into the heavens and travels to the sun. Boy must pass four trials and then is given the full power of the sun. Boy returns to earth and brings the Lord's spirit to the people.

Roth, Susan L. **The Story of Light.** Illus. by author. New York: Morrow Junior Books, 1990.

Dramatic, bold collage artwork in black, white, and yellow complement this well-told tale inspired by a Cherokee myth.

Readers are taken to a time when there was no sun, it was dark, and the animals couldn't see. The sun is on the other side of the world, and several animals try to get a spark of it but fail. Possum tries but singes his tail, and Buzzard ends up with a bald head. Everyone laughs when Spider offers to go because she is a small woman. She, however, succeeds by putting a small spark of the sun in a clay pot she made.

San Souci, Robert D., reteller. **The Legend of Scarface: A Blackfeet Indian Tale.** Illus. by Daniel San Souci. New York: Doubleday, 1978.

A young brave who is known as Scarface wants to marry the beautiful daughter of the chief, Singing Rains. When Scarface is goaded into asking her, she says she would marry him but she promised the Sun, Father of All, that she wouldn't. Singing Rains says she'll marry Scarface if she's released from her promise.

So begins Scarface's long, arduous journey to the Lodge of the Sun. He is treated like family by Morning Star, Sun's son; the Moon, Sun's wife; and the Sun. When Scarface rescues Morning Star from savage birds, Sun grants him a wish. He releases Singing Rains from her vow. The Sun gives Scarface a sign by removing his scar.

San Souci, Robert D., reteller. **Sootface: An Ojibwa Cinderella Story.** Illus. by Daniel San Souci. New York: A Doubleday Book for Young Readers/Delacorte, 1994.

San Souci's version of a Native American Cinderella tale is told in the best story-telling tradition (see Rafe Martin, **The Rough-Face Girl,** p. 170). This adaptation is richly told with dialogue that rings true and vivid descriptions. The full-page watercolors are painted in brilliant colors and offer a realistic depiction of the people, clothing, traditional designs, and landscape of a mid-eighteenth-century Ojibwa village.

An Ojibwa man, a widower, is raising his three daughters, who are supposed to share the work. The youngest girl, however, gets stuck with all the chores. Her older sisters are mean to her and call her Sootface. Young men laugh at Sootface because she has singed hair, stiff moccasins, and scraps for clothing.

Across the lake from the village lives a mighty warrior and his sister. No one sees the warrior because he is invisible. One day the warrior's sister tells the villagers across the lake that her brother will marry the woman who can see him. The chosen woman must say what the warrior's magic bow and bowstring are made of.

The women of the village try to guess the answer to the questions, but all fail, even Sootface's sisters. Then Sootface decides to try her luck. She dresses as best she can because her sisters won't let her borrow clothing. Everyone laughs at her, but Sootface goes, sees the handsome warrior, describes his bow and string, and is chosen. The warrior's sister braids Sootface's hair, gives her clothing and her beauty is revealed. The warrior calls her Dawn-Light. They are married, and everyone is happy, except her sisters, who must now do all the housework themselves.

Demonstration/Participation Activities

Bierhorst, John. **Lightning Inside You and Other Native American Riddles.** Illus. by Louise Brierley. New York: William Morrow, 1992.
    Bierhorst includes 140 riddles translated from 20 different languages, including those of the Comanche, Pawnee, Cherokee, and Huron tribes. Not all of these will be evident to children, but some fun and appropriate riddles are found on pp. 16, 19-20, 27, 34, 38, 40, 53, 57, and 72.
    The riddles are divided into categories, including "Natural World," "Animals," and "Things That Grow."

Blood, Charles L. **American Indian Games and Crafts.** Illus. by Lisa Campbell Ernst. New York: Franklin Watts, 1981.
    This book presents many simple activities derived from Native American culture. The description of each stick or hand game includes a list of equipment needed and an explanation of rules. Particularly easy games are "Playing a Stick Game," p. 6, and "Playing the Hand Game," p. 11. The crafts, "Making a Wall Hanging," p. 9, and "Sand Painting Without Sand," p. 12, have easy-to-follow instructions and are quick and simple for children to do.

Diehn, Gwen, and Terry Krautwurst. "Sand Painting," pp. 78-79, in **Nature Crafts for Kids**. Photos by Evan Bracken. Illus. by Rick Frizzell. New York: Sterling, 1992.
    In this version of sand painting you'll color white sand with powdered tempera paints before the program. During the activity each child will make a sand painting in a clear container. Few materials are needed, and the craft is fairly easy for most young children to do. Several suggestions are given for how to use the containers in creative ways.

Evert, Jodi. "Owner Stick," p. 41, in **Kristen's Craft Book: A Look at Crafts from the Past with Projects You Can Make Today.** Middleton, WI: Pleasant Company, 1994.

A stunning creation, this craft is time consuming and difficult for young children to make but perfect for you to demonstrate or for older children to do.

Gates, Frieda. "Eye-of-God," p. 30, and "Bowl Game," p. 40, in **Easy to Make North American Indian Crafts.** Illus. by author. New York: Harvey, 1981.

The author explains why and how Pueblo and Navajo weavers made this symbol. It's easy to demonstrate and not difficult for children to do, but it is time consuming. Show the children how to make the "Eye-of-God" then help each of them start their own, which they can finish at home.

The "Bowl Game" was played by most Native American tribes. It requires few materials and is extremely easy for children to play.

Hauser, Jill Frankel. "Colored Sand or Rice," p. 126, and "Sand Painting," p. 128, in **Kids' Crazy Concoctions: 50 Mysterious Mixtures for Art and Craft Fun.** Illus. by Loretta Trezzo Braren. Charlotte, VT: Williamson, 1995.

This book includes easy instructions for making colored sand or rice that you can provide the children with during the program. The sand painting activity is easy to do and requires few materials. The author explains how Navajo Indians made sacred designs with colored sand.

Hofsinde, Robert (Gray-Wolf). **Indian Picture Writing.** Illus. by author. New York: William Morrow, 1959.

You can turn this book into an activity. The author shows and explains Indian picture writing. Teach children some of the symbols. Have each youngster crumble brown paper from a paper bag to simulate leather and invite them to write picture symbols on the paper, perhaps creating a sentence with the words they learned.

Hofsinde, Robert (Gray-Wolf). **Indian Sign Language.** Illus. by author. New York: William Morrow, 1956.

The author uses words and illustrations to explain how to sign. Teach youngsters how to sign some of the words.

Kallen, Stuart A. "Totem Poles," pp. 26-27, in **Eco-Arts and Crafts.** Illus. by Vic Orenstein. Edina, MN: Abdo & Daughters, 1993.

Children enjoy making totem poles out of old logs. Few items are needed, and there are only two steps involved in this craft.

Kohl, MaryAnn F. "Sand Paintings," p. 29, and "Totem Pole," p. 91, in **Good Earth Art: Environmental Art for Kids.** Illus. by Cindy Gainer. Bellingham, WA: Bright Ring, 1991.

These crafts are easy for you to explain and demonstrate to children. Few materials are needed, and the steps are clear and straightforward. "Totem Pole" requires a large block of time, but it is fun and satisfying for children to do.

Liptak, Karen. **North American Indian Sign Language.** Illus. by Don Berry. New York: Franklin Watts, 1990.

Signs in this book are based on the sign language used by American Indians of the Great Plains. An excellent feature in this book are the line drawings that show what position fingers and hands should be in for each sign. For each word there is a written description of how to make the sign and a line drawing of the sign. A variety of practical signs and an index of signs are included.

Introduce children to some of the signs, then let them try them. Also, do some of the signs and invite the children to guess what they mean.

Penner, Lucille Recht. "Iroquois Strawberry Drink," p. 49, in **A Native American Feast.** Illus. selected by author. New York: Macmillan, 1994.

During the program show children how to make this delicious drink in a blender. You only need strawberries, water, and maple or brown sugar. (Check that none of the children are allergic to strawberries.)

Terzian, Alexandra M. **The Kids' Multicultural Art Book: Art and Craft Experiences from Around the World.** Illus. by author. Charlotte, VT: Williamson, 1993.

The following crafts can be found in the chapter on crafts of the "Native Americans of North American": "Plains, Magic Power Shield," pp. 18-19; "Northwest Coast, Animal Totem," pp. 30-33; "Northwest Coast, Storyteller Animal Mask," pp. 34-35; "Southwest, Zuni Hand Mask," pp. 38-39; and "Northeast and Woodlands, Sponge Painting Cut-Outs," pp. 40-43. Although these crafts are complicated, they are perfect to demonstrate or to do with children at the older end of the target group.

Chapter 14

Nonfiction Books:
A Show and Tell Program

The content and format of this program is different from the others in this book, but it is perhaps my favorite. When children attend this program I explain that I have become a "consumer snoop." I tell the children I have read many of the nonfiction books in the library's collection, particularly craft and activity books, titles that invite them to make or do something. I've judged the books on whether or not they are interesting and fun, have good illustrations or photographs, easy-to-follow instructions and inexpensive, easy-to-find materials. I then tell them that the books I'm going to show them are what I consider "best bets," titles that invite them to "Try This!"

This program requires careful planning, organization, and preparation ahead of time but is worth the effort because it is so satisfying and attention-grabbing. For each title, talk about the book briefly and then, depending on the text, either show samples of something you made from the book, demonstrate making something from the book, or invite the children to participate in an activity from the book. The titles cover a range of topics, including optical illusions, outdoor activities, photography, gardening, cooking, writing, sign language, word play, science activities, foreign language, drawing, and learning games.

The titles that follow meet all the criteria mentioned above. They give children an idea of the many things they can do with nonfiction books as a guide. You can, of course, take titles from the "Demonstration/Participation Activities" section of the other chapters in this book and use them.

For each title below I provide a descriptive annotation and then mention specific activities and state whether I show an already-finished project, demonstrate, or invite the children to participate. You'll probably want to select only one or two activities from each book because of time restrictions, but I offer several suggestions from each title.

To ensure this program runs smoothly, I place each book with its accompanying activity or item in a row on a table. I can then pick up each book in turn and talk about it without losing my train of thought.

Best Bets

Ancona, George. **My Camera.** New York: Crown, 1992.

Ancona's book is well organized and visually appealing. The author describes the use of a 35mm camera, gives advice on how to use the camera, and offers projects that introduce youngsters to composition, lighting, and taking action shots. Ancona takes children step-by-step from how to hold and steady a camera, where to stand depending on the type of shot desired, how to take photos from different angles, and how to use a telephoto lens. Ancona offers suggestions on what to take pictures of, including people, objects, and events. He explains how photographs can tell a story, offer a visual record of a trip, or be used to create a family history. He also shows youngsters how to make a book using photographs.

Once you've told the children about this book, take photographs of them using an instant camera so they can see the photos immediately. Use the camera to demonstrate some of the ideas Ancona offers.

Anno, Mitsumasa. **Anno's Math Games.** Illus. by author. New York: Philomel, 1987.

Anno's books are unique, creative, and appealing in text and illustrations. This title as well as two others in the series, **Anno's Math Games II** and **Anno's Math Games III,** offer original and thought-provoking puzzles, games, and activities that introduce math concepts.

In this title Anno invites children to look for differences in a series of items, to compare and classify. He encourages youngsters to put objects together and take them apart, which introduces the concepts of combinations, adding, and subtracting. Using playing cards, Anno invites children to find mistakes in a numerical series of cards. Anno introduces the characters Kriss and Kross, with whom the children can learn to compare height, length, even the number of beanbags two teams throw into baskets. There are activities on each page, and children probably won't realize they're working with mathematical concepts. They'll just know they're having fun.

Before the program make the five-piece Tangram found on pages 38-43. Show the children how to make some of the figures in the book using the Tangram. When the program is over, encourage the children to use the Tangram to make other figures from the book. You may want to make enough Tangrams for everyone who attends the program.

Carlson, Laurie, and Judith Dammel. **Kids Camp! Activities for the Backyard or Wilderness.** Illus. by Sean O'Neill. Chicago: Chicago Review Press, 1995.

You'll find one activity per page, each with a clear list of materials and step-by-step instructions. There are ideas for making clothes, camp gear, food, and crafts. The authors show how to set up a camp, make tents, and tie knots. Also included are fun games.

You can demonstrate how to make "Soap-to-Go," p. 27. You can show the children samples you've made of "Rock Collection," p. 86; "Twig Sculptures," "Twig Basket," "Tiny Twig Raft," p. 96; "Leaf Stencils," p. 109; or "Leaf Rubbings," p. 111. Or invite the youngsters to help you make "Great Gorp," p. 37; "Terrific Trail Mix," p. 40; "Wilderness Punch," p. 152; or "Cookies and Cream," p. 153.

Colen, Kimberly, comp. **Peas and Honey: Recipes for Kids (With a Pinch of Poetry).** Illus. by Mandy Victor. Honesdale, PA: Boyds Mills Press, 1995.

Colen's attractively packaged book, with soft illustrations in colored pencil interspersed throughout, includes easy-to-follow recipes, anecdotes, and poetry about food with a fond memory about food by each poet. You might like to do the tongue twister "Yellow Butter," p. 18, with the children; make "Peanut Butter," p. 29, or "Banana Mouse," p. 57, with the youngsters.

Editors of Passport Books. **Let's Learn Spanish Picture Dictionary.** Illus. by Marlene Goodman. Lincolnwood, IL: Passport Books/Division of NTC Publishing Group, 1991.

Other titles in this series introduce children to French, German, and Italian. The authors include words commonly taught in beginning Spanish classes, over 1,550 words. Children will see 30 large, colorful scenes relating to a specific topic from the classroom and home to the seasons and numbers. Items in each scene are labeled. Alongside each picture youngsters will find the words listed in English and Spanish with accompanying illustrations. My daughter Kate owns this book and turns to it again and again to look at the words and pictures.

Learn some of the words, if you don't know them already. During the program you can point to articles of clothing on yourself and the children and say their names in Spanish. If you prefer, you can point to different body parts and say what they are in Spanish.

Elliot, Marion. **Paper Fun for Kids.** (Step-by-Step series). Photos by James Duncan. New York: Smithmark, 1994.

Elliot includes an amazingly wide variety of decorations, projects, and gifts that can be made with paper. Children will find full-color photographs for each step in every activity and clear instructions. The instructions are in small type, but the photographs are so detailed that a child could do an activity from the photographs alone. The materials needed for each activity are listed and shown in small photographs.

Among the projects you might like to mention and show pictures of are "Painted Postcards," "Printed Wrapping Paper," "Spinner," "Calendar," "Rubber-Stamped Stationery," "Space Mobile," "Cowboy Face Mask," "Finger Puppets," "Jigsaw," "Photograph Album," and "Bookmarks."

Make one of the following crafts and show it to the children: "Woven Paper Cards," pp. 28-29; "Paper Chains," p. 32; "Sun and Moon Masks," p. 51; "Eye Masks," pp. 52-53; or "Magnetic Fish Game," p. 61.

Emberley, Ed. **Ed Emberley's Big Orange Drawing Book.** Boston, MA: Little, Brown, 1980.

Children will find step-by-step diagrams that add one detail in each successive picture and culminate in a finished drawing of a person or animal. Even I, who can only draw stick figures, can successfully draw the pictures in this book. Show the children some of the illustrations they can make, from pumpkins, carrot characters, and tigers to foxes, unidentified flying objects, and Halloween items. Then, show a drawing that you made using this book.

There are many other titles in this series, including **Ed Emberley's Drawing Book of Animals, Ed Emberley's Great Thumbprint Drawing Book,** and **Ed Emberley's Big Purple Drawing Book.**

Flodin, Mickey. **Signing for Kids.** Photos by author. New York: Perigree Books/Berkley Publishing Group, 1991.

It's easy to see why Flodin's book won the "Parents' Choice Award." **Signing for Kids** is well organized, comprehensive, and approachable. Flodin offers line drawings of hands doing the American Manual Alphabet. Then he introduces words in a variety of categories. For each word he provides a picture of a person's head and hands making the sign.

Some of the signs are easy to interpret. You can invite the children to guess the animal you are signing or to guess the snack from the sign you do. Teach the sign for "I Love You," or the first line of the "Happy Birthday Song."

Fyke, Nancy, Lynn Nejam, and Vicki Overstreet. **Great Parties for Kids: Over 35 Celebrations for Toddlers to Preteens.** Illus. by Chuck Galey. Charlotte, VT: Williamson, 1994.

Children like to be involved in their own party planning, and this is one of the most inviting party books I've ever read. The authors divide the parties into those for various age groups and occasions. Children will find ideas for inexpensive party favors, decorations, activities, and food. The author also includes reproducible party invitations. Appealing black-and-white illustrations are found throughout the book, and the text is in a nice format with four columns of writing flanked by sidebars.

Some of the activities you might like to mention include the "Recycling Relay," "Hula Hoop Pass," and "Sweat Suit Balloon Stuff." You might like to show children one of the party favors, a cookie cutter tied to a personalized wooden spoon, and a copy of the "Baseball-Birthday Party" invitation and the "Pirate Scavenger Hunt/Party" invitation. Among the crafts you can demonstrate or show the children are "Newsprint Hats," p. 19, and "Layered Sand Sculpture in a Jar," p. 39. Among the activities you can invite the children to do are "Copy Cat" and "Guess Who?" in the Zoo Party chapter; making bubbles with the "Bubble Formula," p. 29; and "Egg and Spoon Relay" and "Balloon Hop," p. 47.

Gans, Roma. **Rock Collecting.** Illus. by Holly Keller. New York: HarperCollins, 1984.

Gans's short and concise text is complemented by appealing, childlike illustrations, clear diagrams, and black-and-white photographs. Mention some of the facts that would be of interest to children, including what chalk and chalkboards are made of, how cement is made, and how and why volcanoes occur.

Show children how they can collect small rocks and store them in egg cartons, whereas larger rocks can be kept in cardboard boxes with dividers.

Kite, L. Patricia. **Gardening Wizardy for Kids.** Illus. by Yvette Santiago Banek. Hauppauge, New York: Barron's Educational Series, 1995.

This 220-page book in its red plastic spiral binder is chock full of information, activities, crafts, and games relating to fruits, vegetables, and herbs. Children will find indoor plant-growing experiments with food seeds. They can try tests at home to determine if all apples have the same number of seeds and if bean plants will grow in salted earth, for example. Someone might like to try the experiment that shows how water gets from a celery stalk into its leaflets.

Some of the tests take several hours or days, but they are fun and interesting to do. Children can do many of the activities by themselves; others require adult assistance. You can share interesting anecdotes from the book. Also, there are many crafts that children can make using this book: herbal bath water, herb bouquets, corncob dolls, flower eggs, perfumed oil, pomander balls, seed wreaths, totem poles, and Christmas trees.

You can show children how to play and then invite them to do "Pioneer Apple Games" and "Fortune Telling," p. 7.

Children can do another fun activity, "Does All Plain Popcorn Taste Alike?" pp. 136-37, in which the children can taste five different types of popcorn and rate them.

Lang, Susan S., with the staff of Cayuga Nature Center. **Nature in Your Backyard: Simple Activities for Children.** Illus. by Sharon Lane Holm. Brookfield, CT: Millbrook Press, 1995.

Children will find this book visually appealing. Each page is framed in a thin black outline and has a clean, uncluttered look. Watercolor illustrations blend nicely with the clear text. There are chapters and activities related to insects and worms, birds, backyard animals, seeds, plants, soil, air, and water. Many of the activities are intended to be done outdoors, like "Miss Ant: Don't Find Us—We'll Find You!" "A Bottle of Bugs," "Be a Human Scarecrow," "Footprint Fun," and "Pressed Flower Note Cards." Mention them to the children.

You can show the children "What Do Birds Like for Their Nests?" pp. 16-17, with actual samples of pinecones and a variety of items hanging from them that birds might use for their nests. You might like to show children a finished bird feeder or the materials to make the one found in "Making a Bird Feeder from Recycled Materials," pp. 18-19. You can prepare the materials before the program for "Making a Water Scope," pp. 44-45, and during the program show the children how to assemble the scope.

Maestro, Giulio. **Riddle Roundup: A Wild Bunch to Beef Up Your Word Power.** Illus. by author. New York: Clarion Books, 1989.

I like Maestro's format; it's very appealing. Each riddle is found at the top of the page and the answer is at the bottom. In-between is an oversize, cartoon-like illustration in gray, white, and shades of red that visually shows the answer to the riddle. The 62 riddles are based on different kinds of word play including puns, homonyms, and homographs.

Share some of the riddles with the children and have them guess the answers.

Morris, Ting, and Neil Morris. **Masks.** Illus. by Ruth Levy. New York: Franklin Watts, 1993.

The authors take this book one step beyond a craft book by including factual material for each mask and information on how, where, and in what time they were actually used. They include a map showing where around the world these masks were worn. Most of the masks require a large block of time and a number of materials to make. There are, however, comprehensive lists of materials required, clear directions, and inspiring color photographs of the finished masks.

Before the program make either the "Masked Ball," pp. 10-11 or the "Knight's Helmet," pp. 26-27. These are the easiest to make and probably the most appealing for your target group. Youngsters will want to make their own masks when you show them either of these.

Rankin, Laura. **The Handmade Alphabet.** Illus. by author. New York: Dial Books, 1991.

Author Rankin presents the manual alphabet used in American Sign Language. For each letter, children see a close up painting of a hand making the letter. Each signed letter holds, touches, or is linked in an imaginative way with an object that begins with that letter. For example, the hand signing the letter "A" holds asparagus while ribbon is entwined in the hand that signs the letter "R."

After you tell the children about this book and share some illustrations from it, sign a word that you've learned by using this book.

Tobey, David. **Free Stuff for Kids.** Deephaven, MN: Meadowbrook Press, 1996.
Many of you are probably familiar with this title that comes out in a new edition every year. Many weeks before the program, I send for items from this book that represent a cross-section of what you can get for free or for up to $1.00.

During the program I show the children the items I received. That always captures their interest and everyone wants to use the book to send for their own free items.

I also spend some time showing them postcards and explaining how to fill out and send them or letters and payment when required.

From the 1996 edition I'd show the "Chicago Bulls Fan Pack," "Jungle Stickers (from *The Lion King*)," "Enormous Erasers," "Dr. Seuss Postcards," and the "Bengal Tiger Pamphlet." I'd mention some of the other items youngsters can send for including "Bookmarks," "Scratch-and-Sniff Stickers," "Planet Stencils," "Bracelet Pens," and a variety of "Fan Packs" for basketball, football, hockey, and baseball teams.

Westray, Kathleen. **Picture Puzzler.** Illus. by author. New York: Ticknor & Fields Books for Young Readers, 1994.
This is a unique, fun participation book with striking visuals—optical illusions in full-color. The author includes impossible drawings, reversible pictures, tricky comparisons, and afterimages. Each illusion is clearly explained and cleverly demonstrated in an eye-catching illustration. The author uses clean lines for her varied illusions, many based on American folk art.

Most of the optical illusions are large enough to share with a group. Among the illusions you might like to share are 1) the many lines spaced close together that look like waves, 2) wagon wheels with circular lines that seem to move, 3) a man wearing a hat in which you must determine if the brim is longer than the hat is from top to bottom, 4) a picture that looks like a vase or two faces, and 5) a candleholder that seems to be made for three candles, but isn't.

Wilkes, Angela. **The Fantastic Rainy Day Book.** Illus. by Dave King. New York: Dorling Kindersley, 1995.
The packaging and format of this book is excellent and eye-catching. Equipment and materials required are listed and shown in color photographs. Each step in the craft is explained in text and shown in photos. First, tell the children about and show them photos in the book of some of the many interesting activities they can do: "Making Candies," "Junk Jewelry," "Gardens in Pots," "Beachcomber's Gallery," "Finger Puppets," "Kaleidoscope," "Making a Castle," and "Raggy Dolls."

Make ahead and show during the program one or several of the following: "Seed Collage" and "Painted Pebbles," p. 7; "Eye Patches," p. 12; "Movie Star Shades," p. 13; "Spinning Windmills," pp. 42-43; and "Making Binoculars," p. 48.

Chapter 15

Pumpkins

Read Alouds

Bang, Betsy, trans. and adapter. **The Old Woman and the Red Pumpkin: A Bengali Folk Tale.** Illus. by Molly Bang. New York: Macmillan, 1975.

Inspired by Indian folk art, the illustrations in shades of red, brown, and blue are full and rich, bold and striking, expressive with a sense of action. The tension in the story is tempered by the tale's humor.

On the way to visit her granddaughter an elderly woman is confronted, in turn, by a jackal, a tiger, and a bear. Each wants to eat the woman. She convinces them that she is just skin and bones now but once she returns from her granddaughter's home she'll be round and plump.

At her granddaughter's house the woman eats curds and curry until she is huge. She wonders how she'll get home safely. Her granddaughter puts her in a red pumpkin shell with some food, gives the pumpkin a push, and it rolls down the road. As the elderly woman tumbles she sings inside the shell. The bear and then the tiger hear the voice, kick the pumpkin, and then, curious, follow. When the jackal hears the singing he hits the pumpkin with a stick. It breaks open, the woman pops out, and the animals come running to eat her. The woman thinks quickly and says the strongest animal will eat her. While the animals fight over who is the strongest the woman creeps away until she returns home safely.

Cole, Bruce B. **The Pumpkinville Mystery.** Illus. by James Warhola. New York: Prentice-Hall Book for Young Readers, 1987.

Old-fashioned, quaint illustrations complement this delightfully told original story that reads like a folktale in the best oral tradition.

The tale is told by a narrator who offers an explanation for why faces are carved on pumpkins for Halloween. The dastardly councilmen in Turkeyville buy all the corn fields so everyone must buy feed for their turkeys from them. A scary-looking stranger wearing a hood and carrying a walking stick arrives in town. Only Hollis J. Goodbody and his wife Betsy welcome the stranger to their home. The stranger gives the Goodbodys seeds—magic seeds that grow into huge pumpkins. The townspeople use the pumpkins for food. Angry, the councilmen smash the pumpkins.

Hollis and Betsy move and plant more seeds. They build a town, and some of the people from Turkeyville move to the Goodbodys' town. Once again the councilmen plan to smash the pumpkins, but the hooded stranger scares them away. How he does that explains why pumpkins are carved on Halloween.

Hunter, C. W., reteller. **The Green Gourd: A North Carolina Folktale.** Illus. by Tony Griego. New York: G. P. Putnam's Sons, 1992.

This fast-paced, smoothly flowing tale with its pleasing rhythm and savory language is complemented by cartoonlike, action-packed, fluid, bright watercolors full of greens and browns and splashes of vivid colors and exaggerated facial expressions on the characters.

Up a holler and across a stream an old woman needs a new gourd dipper. Her gourds are green, not ripe, and she knows the saying that if you pick a gourd before it's ripe, it'll be bewitched. The woman, however, needs a dipper so she picks an unripe gourd. No sooner does she get the gourd home than it acts up, rolling around and jumping on everything, including her head.

The woman runs away with the gourd chasing her. A panther offers to help, but the gourd thumps it. The gourd whizzes through the air, humming like bees. Fox tries to help, but he's knocked down by the gourd. The woman is still running with the gourd in pursuit when a little boy offers her refuge in his house. Swiftly, the boy manages to jump on the gourd and squash it.

Johnston, Tony. **The Vanishing Pumpkin.** Illus. by Tomie dePaola. New York: G. P. Putnam's Sons, 1983.

A clever, original, and humorous story that bounces along with an appealing rhythm, the text is complemented by illustrations that capture well the faces and expressions of the people and creatures.

An 800-year-old man and a 700-year-old woman want to make pumpkin pie on Halloween, but the pumpkin they saved is gone. It's not in the house, and they decide it's been stolen. Outraged, the couple searches for the pumpkin. They meet a ghoul, a rapscallion, and a varmint, but none of them have the pumpkin. Each characters joins the couple because they'd like to share the pumpkin pie.

Finally, they find the culprit—a 900-year-old wizard who took their pumpkin and turned it into a jack-o'-lantern. The couple laments that they can't have pumpkin pie, but the wizard makes pie out of the insides of the pumpkin that they can all enjoy.

Mahy, Margaret. "The Pumpkins of Witch Crunch," pp. 45-56, in **Stuff and Nonsense.** Comp. by Laura Cecil. Illus. by Emma Chichester Clark. New York: Greenwillow Books, 1989.

In her tightly written story full of rich and expressive language, Mahy swiftly portrays character, introduces conflict, and builds suspense. The full-color and black-and-white watercolors capture the characters' personalities in their faces and the sinister appearance of the pumpkins with their sharp teeth, pointed noses, and vinelike hands.

Mr. Maverick-Mace is a crotchety man who covets his garden and thinks anyone who tries to peek at it really wants to steal his vegetables and flowers. One spring when he hears there'll be a shortage of pumpkins, Mr. Maverick-Mace decides to plant pumpkins. He doesn't like their straggly ways, but he would like to sell them and make a fortune.

Mr. Maverick-Mace makes a fatal mistake when he hears a voice, assumes it's his neighbor Mrs. Mehetibel, whom he doesn't talk to, and refuses to give her a cabbage when she asks. When he calls her an old witch she makes a cryptic comment that if he wants a witch, that's what he'll get. Now Mr. Maverick-Mace is alarmed and doubtful. Was that really Mrs. Mehetibel? Mr. Maverick-Mace's two immediate neighbors tell him how brave he was to talk like that to Ginger Crunch—Witch Crunch—Mrs. Mehetibel's twin sister.

Mr. Maverick-Mace pays no heed until strange things start happening in his garden. The pumpkin seeds turn blue, and when they grow, the pumpkins look like they have green arms and thousands of twining fingers. The pumpkins terrify the other vegetables in the garden, and they grow unnaturally fast. Mr. Maverick-Mace puts up with this because he wants to get rich from the sale of the pumpkins.

Finally, Mr. Maverick-Mace gets so upset, he threatens the pumpkins with his garden shears. They, in turn, terrify him by rustling and hissing and waving their arms like serpents. The pumpkins control the garden and hiss and lift their snaky arms whenever Mr. Maverick-Mace approaches them.

One night the pumpkins rush in the house at Mr. Maverick-Mace. His neighbors hear his cries for help and try to stop the pumpkins. It looks like the pumpkins will win, but Witch Crunch arrives and leads the pumpkins away.

Mr. Maverick-Mace's personality doesn't change, but he is polite to Mrs. Mehetibel and sends her vegetables.

McDonald, Megan. **The Great Pumpkin Switch.** Illus. by Ted Lewin. New York: Orchard, 1992.

Realistic paintings enhance this warm, personal, and satisfying tale. The story is narrated by an elderly man who is reminiscing about his youth with his grandchildren.

The day after a terrible storm the narrator and his friend Otto see wood from trees that have fallen. The boys accidentally saw the vine of the narrator's sister Rosie's pumpkin. Rosie was growing the pumpkin to earn Sunflower Girls' patches for her quilt. Released from the vine, the pumpkin bumps down the front steps and smashes. The boys need to replace the pumpkin before Rosie finds out.

The boys are saved by the Potato Man, Mr. Angelo, who gives them the biggest pumpkin he has on credit. Rosie sees the pumpkin and thinks it grew huge overnight. The boys find pennies stuck to the bottom of the butter churn, and Mama lets them keep 20 of them, enough to pay back Mr. Angelo.

Monfried, Lucia, comp. "The Pumpkin Giant," pp. 14-19, in **Diane Goode's Book of Scary Stories and Songs.** Illus. by Diane Goode. New York: Dutton Children's Books, 1994.

The story and the illustrations are a wonderful blend of humor and scariness.

Long ago there were no pumpkins, only a huge Pumpkin Giant who loved to eat children, especially plump youngsters. The king's daughter is so chubby, she has to be guarded constantly. A farmer and his portly son live near Pumpkin Giant's castle and tend a potato field. One day Pumpkin Giant approaches, and the farmer tries to hide his son behind him. When the giant comes too close, the farmer lobs a potato in his throat, the giant chokes, falls over, and his pumpkin head smashes.

The following spring there are Giant heads growing where potatoes once grew. Everyone worries that Giant bodies will grow, too, but they don't. Everyone forgets about the unusual crop except the farmer's son. He brings one of the Giant's heads indoors, cuts it, and eats it. Everyone thinks he'll die. The boy urges his parents to try a piece of Giant head. They do and find it tasty. The farmer's wife says it would be better cooked in a crust with eggs, milk, sugar, and spices. The pumpkin pie is delicious, so she makes them daily. One day the king rides by, smells the pies, tastes some, and is told the story behind the pie.

The king makes the farmer his head gardener, and the farmer's wife bakes pumpkin pies. The farmer's son and the princess eat the pies, and eventually they marry.

Ray, David. **Pumpkin Light.** Illus. by author. New York: Philomel, 1993.

Large, full-page, fluid artwork, predominately in shades of orange, blue, and brown, weave throughout this well-written story, which blends elements of fantasy, mystery, magic, and dreams. Note particularly the illustration of the young boy Angus rushing home against a swirling sky line bathed in blue night light.

Angus, who lives on a farm with his parents, loves pumpkins to eat and especially to draw and paint. Traditionally at Halloween Angus's father carves one pumpkin into a jack-o'-lantern, and his mother bakes a pumpkin pie. Angus runs a mile into town to gaze in the window of the general store all day and into the night, where the owner has jack-o'-lanterns throughout the shop. Angus draws the faces on the pumpkins.

The year Angus is 10 he's so busy drawing the pumpkins he forgets the time and runs home in the dark. His parents are angry, and Angus is sent to bed without a piece of pie and without hanging up his drawings.

Angus looks at the moon from his bed and imagines pumpkins floating across the sky to the old barn loft. Finally Angus falls asleep.

Angus finds himself in the barn loft. From there he sees his mother's pie on the windowsill, sneaks back, and steals it. He then hides behind the old scarecrow in the cornfield to eat the pie. The angry voice of the spirit in the scarecrow says Angus wasn't supposed to eat the pie, and he turns Angus into a little dog named Autumn. The scarecrow declares that every night he must go into the barn loft and guard a magic pumpkin until someone carves it and releases the power to change Angus into a boy again.

Angus's parents don't know what happened to him, but the little dog is always with them. At night, Angus/Autumn sleeps with his head against the magic pumpkin. Years pass. One Halloween Angus/Autumn hears his mother say she'll bake a pumpkin pie. He lures her to the barn loft where she finds the pumpkin.

Instead of making a pumpkin pie, Angus' mother carves a jack-o'-lantern, and, as she does, a light shines from inside the pumpkin. When she finishes carving, Angus turns into himself.

Angus senses a bright light. From his bed he sees his parents putting his drawings on the wall. The next day he eats pumpkin pie for breakfast.

Angus never stops drawing pumpkins, even when he is old. His favorite painting is of a dog sleeping in the glow of light from a pumpkin.

Ray, Mary Lyn. **Pumpkins: A Story for a Field.** Illus. by Barry Root. New York: Harcourt Brace Jovanovich, 1992.

The short text is deceptive because Ray's story is packed with meaning and emotion. There are many subtle messages about conservation of the land and what's really important in life. The tale is gentle, serious, and hopeful. The main character is a man who has a burning desire and conviction that helps him remain focused on his goal. The watercolor illustrations are compatible with the text—simply done but evocative.

A man lives across from a field that he loves and wants to buy rather than see it developed. The man doesn't have enough money, even when he sells almost all his possessions. He and the field discuss the possibilities and decide the man will grow pumpkins and sell them. The man rents airplanes, boats, and flying carpets to send the pumpkins worldwide. He calls kings and congresses, but many explain they wouldn't know what to do with pumpkins. The man realizes they don't know about pumpkin pie, pumpkin ice cream, and jack-o'-lanterns. So the man writes a tag for each pumpkin in different languages explaining their uses.

People from England to Thailand, from Egypt to Quebec, make jack-o'-lanterns, and the man has enough money to buy the field and some furniture. The man could plant more pumpkins and become rich, but he has all he wants.

Booktalks

King, Elizabeth. **The Pumpkin Patch.** Photos by author. New York: Dutton Children's Books, 1990.

Children in kindergarten will enjoy listening to this story, and youngsters in first grade and up will find this fun to read themselves. The text is succinct, and the crisp, full-color photographs taken from many views are visually appealing.

Children will see how pumpkins are grown—from preparing the soil and planting the seeds to watching the leaves and stems grow. They'll see the tendrils that appear on the vines, the flowers that bloom, and the bulbs beneath the flowers that are baby pumpkins. Pumpkins are shown turning from green to orange. An entire pumpkin patch is presented, and children see how the farmer takes the pumpkins to a stand. The final view shows children selecting their pumpkins.

San Souci, Robert D. **Feathertop: Based on the Tale of Nathaniel Hawthorne.** Illus. by Daniel San Souci. New York: A Doubleday Book for Young Readers, 1992.

A magnificent retelling of Hawthorne's tale, this work is illustrated with stunning, richly colored, and detailed paintings.

Mother Rigby, a powerful witch living in early New England, decides to make a scarecrow to keep birds away from her corn patch. The scarecrow's body is a meal bag, his head is a pumpkin, and he has rolling pin and wooden spoon arms. Mother Rigby gazes at her scarecrow in his threadbare breeches, worn silk stockings, and tri-cornered hat, decides he's too fine to stand in the field, and devises an elaborate joke.

Mother Rigby will get back at Judge Gookin, who always harasses her. She turns the scarecrow into a man and sends him to charm the judge's daughter, Polly. "Master Feathertop" impresses Judge Gookin and Polly, forgets that he's a scarecrow, and wants to marry Polly. Then he sees his scarecrow self in a mirror, remembers why he's there, and flees. When he confesses to Mother Rigby what happened, she laments that he has too much heart and turns him back into a scarecrow in the field.

Polly is drawn to the scarecrow. She also reveals her love of "Master Feathertop" to Mother Rigby. During a conversation Polly kisses the scarecrow's hand at Mother Rigby's urging and he turns into the human Master Feathertop. The couple is reunited.

Updike, David. **An Autumn Tale.** Illus. by Robert Andrew Parker. New York: Pippin Press, 1988.

Here's a special story, not action packed, but soft and sophisticated. The author creates a mood of enchantment and writes in a lyrical and descriptive style. The full-page, full-color paintings are in Parker's traditional style, sketchy and fluid. Recommend this book particularly to children in grade two and up.

A young boy, Homer, and his dog, Sophocles, have a magical adventure the night before Halloween when Homer takes the pumpkin he had carved from the bottom and places it over his head to make himself look like the moon.

In the glow of the full moon Homer sees the trees and bushes swaying, waving their branches like arms, and striding across the yard. An old elm brings Homer and Sophocles to the pond, where the trees gather every full moon to dance and play games. The elm introduces Homer and Sophocles as Mr. Pumpkin and his hound. Homer tries to explain he's a boy, but the trees don't believe him.

As the moon starts to sink, the trees head home. They must reach it before daybreak or they'll turn into firewood. Homer's pumpkin head is so heavy he can't run. An old apple tree that was left behind brings them home and slips its roots into the ground just before the moon fades.

Demonstration/Participation Activities

Brokaw, Meredith, and Annie Gilbar. **The Penny Whistle Halloween Book.** Illus. by Jill Weber. New York: Grove Weidenfeld/Grove Press, 1989.

You'll find many delightful crafts, games, and recipes to demonstrate or invite children to do. The authors include ideas on how to paint faces on pumpkins, how to use vegetables and toothpicks to create faces on pumpkins, and how to make character pumpkins.

"Pumpkin Toss," p. 63, is an easy game to share with children. You will have to prepare the pumpkins into which the children toss walnuts ahead of the program. Ideas are offered on how to keep score.

If you have access to an oven, you can follow the book's simple recipe for "Roasted Pumpkin Seeds" on p. 69.

Corwin, Judith Hoffman. "Jack-o'-Lantern Cookies," p. 47, in **Halloween Crafts.** Illus. by author. New York: Franklin Watts, 1995.

Before your program buy some cookies and then, following the simple instructions, make orange frosting. During the program children can spread frosting on the cookies and then use raisins or chocolate chips to make a face on each cookie.

Cuyler, Margery. **The All-Around Pumpkin Book.** Illus. by Corbett Jones. New York: Holt, Rinehart & Winston, 1980.

In this delightful book you'll find recipes, craft projects, and little-known facts about pumpkins. Cuyler explains the uses of pumpkins in history and stories, celebrations relating to pumpkins, and a history of the jack-o'-lantern.

There are many recipes, but most require a stove. You might like to demonstrate making "Pumpkin Health Shake," p. 74, and invite the children to try some.

You'll also find pumpkin jokes and games, including "Pumpkin Hunt," p. 90, which only requires construction paper pumpkins to play.

"Strip Lantern," pp. 86-87, requires few materials and is fairly easy for children to do if you have some of the items prepared ahead of time.

Gillis, Jennifer Storey. **In a Pumpkin Shell: Over 20 Pumpkin Projects for Kids.** Illus. by Patti Delmonte. Pownal, VT: Storey Communications, 1992.

Gillis' book is full of activity ideas that you might like to demonstrate or do with children. Using this text you can make a pumpkin seed necklace, a pumpkin painting, or a musical instrument.

Ross, Kathy. "Sock Pumpkin," pp. 8-9, in **Crafts for Halloween.** Illus. by Sharon Lane Holm. Brookfield, CT: Millbrook Press, 1994.

Clear line drawings, lists of materials, and step-by-step instructions make it easy for you to explain and do this craft with children. It's a bit messy, but simple and satisfying.

Smolen, Wendy. "Pumpkin Pals," pp. 160-61, in **Playing Together: 101 Terrific Games and Activities That Children Ages 3-9 Can Do Together.** Illus. by Jill Weber. New York: Fireside Book/Simon & Schuster, 1995.

Smolen explains clearly how, instead of carving jack-o'-lanterns, children can create pumpkin faces with a variety of materials. She also offers useful variations for different age groups.

Chapter 16

Rags to Riches

Read Alouds

Alexander, Lloyd. **The Fortune-Tellers.** Illus. by Trina Schart Hyman. New York: Dutton Children's Books, 1992.

Master storyteller Alexander has fashioned a literate, solid, and humorous tale of fortunes gained, adventure, and misunderstandings.

A young carpenter, unhappy in his work and wondering what else life holds for him, hears of a fortuneteller in a nearby town and goes to see him. The fortuneteller's answers say nothing and everything—they could apply to anyone. For example, he says the carpenter will be rich if he earns a lot of money and he'll be happy if he can avoid being miserable.

The carpenter leaves, but then returns because he has other questions. The fortuneteller is gone. Just then the cloth merchant's wife comes in, sees the carpenter, thinks the old fortuneteller has made himself young, and decides he must have great powers. She invites him to live rent free if he'll tell the family fortunes.

When the woman persists, the carpenter agrees, remembers the fortunes the real fortuneteller gave, and tells fortunes the same way. Soon neighbors want their fortunes told. His fame spreads, he grows rich, marries the cloth merchant's daughter, and lives happily.

The real fortuneteller, about whom the carpenter never stopped wondering, leaned over a balcony, lost his balance, tumbled down into a passing cart, plunged into a savanna, was chased by a lion, climbed a tree to escape, broke open a hornet's nest, was snatched by a giant eagle, dropped into a river, and was swept downstream.

This delightful story is set in Cameroon and is perfectly illustrated by award-winner Trina Hyman. Her richly colored artwork is exquisite, detailed, and expressive.

Anno, Mitsumasa, reteller. **Anno's Twice Told Tales: The Fisherman and His Wife and the Four Clever Brothers/by the Brothers Grimm and Mr. Fox.** Illus. by author. New York: Philomel Books, 1993.

Anno adheres closely to the original text in his rich tellings. His illustrations in watercolor and pencil are executed in his classic style, done with clean lines but challenging to the eye. The artwork is extremely appealing and draws you to look at it over and over.

In the first tale, when the fisherman heeds the pleas of a large fish he caught to let him go, the fish says he'll help the man. The fish is really an enchanted prince and can grant wishes. When the fisherman's wife hears of this she wants, in turn, a pretty house, a mansion, to be king, to be emperor, and then to be pope. All her wishes are granted until she wishes to be God. The fish then tells the fisherman to go home and his wife will be where she belongs—in their original little hut by the sea. (This is really a rags to riches to rags tale.)

In "The Four Clever Brothers" a poor farmer sends his four sons to seek their fortunes. Each goes his own way and vows to meet the others in four years. The first brother is taught to take things cleverly without being caught. The second brother meets an astronomer and learns how to use a telescope to see everything that happens on earth and in heaven. The third brother becomes a hunter's apprentice. At the end of his four years he's given a gun that can hit anything at which he aims. The fourth brother meets a tailor who gives him a special needle with which he can sew anything.

The brothers meet, return to their father, tell their stories, and show their skills. The father still can't decide which brother has done best, who is the most skillful and clever. Then word comes that a dragon has kidnapped the royal princess. Whoever rescues her can marry her. The brothers decide to save the princess, and with their skills they succeed. When the king says the brothers must decide who will marry the princess and they argue, the king decrees that none will marry her, but he'll make them princes and give each an equal portion of his kingdom.

Bender, Robert, reteller. **Toads and Diamonds.** Illus. by author. New York: Lodestar, 1995.

Kudos to Robert Bender for a witty, humorous, and satisfying retelling of this classic tale by Charles Perrault. Bender's artwork is unique and fascinating, bright and glowing, with an impressionistic effect.

The nasty widow Asphalta lives with her two daughters, Bleacha, who is just like her mother, and Merth, a kind, generous, and beautiful girl. Asphalta and Bleacha are jealous of Merth and treat her horribly.

One cold night Asphalta and Bleacha send Merth to fetch water from the well on the far side of the hill. Merth trips over a "log" that is actually a three-headed troll that asks Merth not to run from its ugly faces but to comb its matted hair and brush the moss off its noses. Merth does, and as reward the troll says whenever Merth sings, precious jewels will come out of her mouth. Merth sings her thanks and a diamond pops out.

Merth rushes home, and when Asphalta and Bleacha witness this good fortune, Asphalta tells Bleacha to go to the well, find out how to get the riches, too, so they can get what they deserve.

Bleacha resents going, grumbles, and kicks a big, soggy "log." When the same troll Merth met asks Bleacha to comb its hair and wipe the moss, Bleacha screeches and screams mean things at the troll. Calmly the troll says since Bleacha only says nasty words when she speaks, only slimy toads and other creatures will come out of her mouth. Bleacha tries to protest but a big toad comes out. Panic-stricken, Bleacha runs into the woods.

Just before morning Merth leaves her mother. She wanders and doesn't know what to do until she sings. Jewels come out of her mouth, and she goes to a nearby town where the people welcome her and build her a castle. They treat Merth like a queen. Merth lives there, singing her songs and enjoying and sharing her riches with the people.

Curry, Jane Louise. **The Christmas Knight.** Illus. by DyAnne DiSalvo-Ryan. New York: Margaret K. McElderry Books/Macmillan, 1993.

This is a beautifully crafted tale of a couple who go from riches to rags to riches, a story of kindness rewarded.

Sir Cleges and his wife Dame Clarys house and feed the homeless and downtrodden. Every Christmas they host a grand feast for all. After 20 years of generosity they are poor and their old neighbors ignore them. When King Uther holds a feast on Christmas Day, Sir Cleges and Dame Clarys are not invited.

In the morning of Christmas Day Sir Cleges is praying to the Christ Child under a bare cherry tree in his garden. When Sir Cleges says "Amen" a branch with green leaves appears on the tree and bright red cherries fall from it. Sir Cleges realizes it's a Christmas gift from God that he must take to King Uther. To get to the king he must promise the porter, usher, and steward one third of what he receives from the king. King Uther loves the gift and grants any reward, and Sir Cleges asks for 12 strokes of the king's staff, four each for the porter, usher, and steward.

There is a minstrel at the feast who sings an old song of the deeds of Sir Cleges, whom everyone thinks is dead. When Sir Cleges reveals who he is, King Uther dubs him the Christmas Knight and makes him lord of Cardiff Castle. There each Christmas Sir Cleges and Dame Clarys hold a feast for the poor, hungry, and homeless.

De la Mare, Walter. **The Turnip.** Illus. by Kevin Hawkes. Boston: Godine, 1992.

Full-page artwork in lush colors with intricate borders and somewhat surreal views (e.g., tilting candlepoles and characters with angular pointed chins and bulging eyes) complement this well-written, finely paced story.

Meet two half-brothers, one who is mean, evil, rich, and greedy. He hopes to be recognized by the king and made a nobleman. The other half-brother is a hard-working farmer who has little but is generous and happy. One evening when an elderly man asks the farmer for water, the half-brother gives the man a hearty meal.

The elderly man asks the farmer if he grows turnips, and when the farmer says yes, the man recites some incomprehensible words and leaves. A few months later the farmer discovers an enormous turnip on his land. It takes the farmer and his neighbors a day to dig it out and hoist it into a wagon.

The farmer takes the turnip to the king, who loves the turnip and likes the farmer. The king rewards the farmer with a wagon full of food. When he finds out more about the good farmer, the king makes him turnip provider for the whole royal family. Soon the farmer prospers, and everyone wants to buy produce from him. The farmer becomes rich and welcomes everyone to his home.

When the farmer's greedy half-brother hears of the farmer's good fortune, he sells most of his possessions, buys a beautiful ruby, and presents it to the king. The king knows about the greedy half-brother and decides to teach him a lesson. The king asks the half-brother what he'd like as a reward for the ruby, and the half-brother acts modest, hoping to get more. The king promises to send something he, the king, values greatly. The half-brother waits in anticipation for several days, when finally his reward arrives: It is a large slice of the farmer's turnip.

Demi. **The Empty Pot.** Illus. by author. New York: Henry Holt, 1990.

Suspense and tension hold children's interest in this beautifully written tale. The text is sparse yet rich and fulfilling. Feelings are deep, and the dialogue is satisfying.

Demi's watercolor artwork is delicate and fragile looking. Rendered in deceptively simple lines, the illustrations are gentle and sophisticated. Also note the diverse use of light.

The emperor is very old and needs to choose someone to succeed him as ruler. He decrees that all the children in the land must come to the palace and receive a special flower seed from him. At the end of the year whoever can show their best effort will succeed him.

Young Ping is sure he can grow a beautiful flower. He uses rich soil and tends it carefully, but nothing happens. The year passes quickly and the children rush to the palace with their beautiful flowers. Ping doesn't want to go, but his father convinces him that he did his best and that's good enough to present to the emperor.

At the palace the children show the emperor their grand flowers. When the emperor asks Ping about his empty pot, Ping explains what he did and that it was his best effort. The emperor declares Ping his successor. He explains that the seeds he gave the children had been cooked—none of them could grow. Only Ping was courageous enough to tell the emperor the truth. Ping receives the emperor's kingdom and becomes ruler of the land.

DeSpain, Pleasant. "The Listening Cap," pp. 19-20, in **Thirty-Three Multicultural Tales to Tell.** Illus. by Joe Shlichta. Little Rock, AK: August House, 1993.

Here's a delightful short story to learn and tell.

For her faithful visits to the shrine of a guardian spirit, a poor woman is rewarded with a listening cap. With the cap the woman overhears two robins and learns of a magpie tree that's in pain because it was cut down for the mayor's teahouse but it's roots weren't dug out. The mayor lies ill. The woman disguises herself as a doctor, convinces the mayor and his wife to demolish the teahouse and tend the maple. The mayor feels better, and the woman is given a bag of gold.

DeSpain, Pleasant. "The Magic Pot: A Story from China," pp. 49-50, in **Ready-to-Tell Tales: Sure-Fire Stories from America's Favorite Storytellers.** Ed. by David Holt and Bill Mooney. Little Rock, AK: August House, 1994.

The story line is one of my favorites (see Hong, **Two of Everything**, p. 197), and this version is perfect to share. Included are tips on how to tell the tale and sources for it.

A poor, hardworking woodcutter finds a large, old brass pot. He puts his ax in it, ties a strap to it and then around his waist and returns home. His wife is thrilled when she sees her husband with two axes. The couple soon realize that anything they put in the pot will double: one dinner becomes two, and a handful of coins tossed in doubles each time. Happy, the woodcutter dances with his wife, but she slips and drops into the pot. Now there are two of her. The wife makes her husband get in the pot so there are two of him. The two couples split their wealth and live side by side.

DeSpain, Pleasant. "The Princess Who Could Not Cry," pp. 47-49, in **Thirty-Three Multicultural Tales to Tell.** Illus. by Joe Shlichta. Little Rock, AK: August House, 1993.

You'll enjoy telling this short, original tale about common sense.

A princess cannot cry because of a spell placed on her. If the spell is broken only once, the princess will cry at the appropriate times. The king's advisers try everything but fail. A poor little girl who lives in the forest with her mother makes the princess cry; she teaches the princess how to peel an onion. The princess rewards the poor girl with land and gold.

Ducey, Gay. "Lazy Jack: A Story from England," pp. 43-46, in **Ready-to-Tell Tales: Sure-Fire Stories from America's Favorite Storytellers.** Ed. by David Holt and Bill Mooney. Little Rock, AK: August House, 1994.

You'll want to memorize and tell this delightful tale in which Jack, a lazy boy whose mother tells him she knows he can learn, is sent to find work. Each day he has a different job, receives different payment, and carries it home wrong, so that he loses or ruins it. In this version, each time he comes home his mother insists he can learn and tells him what to do with his payment next time. Of course, he carries the next payment home the way his mother explained for the previous payment and ruins it. Jack loses coins, has milk slosh in and ooze out of his pants' pocket, has cheese melt and stick to his hair, gets scratched by a cat, and drags meat in the mud. Finally, on Saturday, Jack works for the driver of a donkey train and is given a donkey. He remembers how his mother told him to carry the meat on his shoulders and does that with the donkey. On the way home he passes the house of a rich man who's daughter has never laughed. She just sits at the window and mopes. When the girl sees Jack carrying the donkey she giggles and laughs. The rich man had promised a fortune to anyone who could make his daughter laugh, so he gives Jack two bags of gold. Jack carries it home in his hands, and his mother says she knew he could learn. Jack and his mother are rich now and live in a nice house. Jack doesn't have to work and is addressed as Mister Jack.

Ellis, Elizabeth. "Jack and the Haunted House: A Story from the Appalachian Mountains," pp. 81-84, in **Ready-to-Tell Tales: Sure-Fire Stories from America's Favorite Storytellers.** Ed. by David Holt and Bill Mooney. Little Rock, AK: August House, 1994.

A great story to memorize and tell, this scary tale follows a poor fellow who becomes rich. The authors include tips for telling this tested yarn.

Jack and his mother are poor, so Jack must go into the world to seek his fortune. Jack asks for work at an inn. When he says that he's seeking his fortune, the innkeeper tells Jack if he can spend one night in the empty house on the hill that everyone says is haunted, the king will give Jack the house and its land.

Unafraid, Jack goes to the house with a bucket of beans and a hunk of cornbread the innkeeper gives him. He saves the food and moves carefully so he won't spill it. The doorknob is cold; the house full of cobwebs and shadows. Jack builds a fire in the fireplace and heats the food. A voice from inside the chimney says "I'm gonna fall!" Jack tells it to fall and be done. A pair of legs falls, sits in a rocking chair, and rocks it. Jack is more concerned about his beans spilling. He hears the voice again, he tells it to come, and a human body rolls out and fastens to the legs. Jack tells it not to spill the beans. Then two arms fasten to the body, and the body jumps up and runs around the room looking for its head. Jack offers to get the head, which was left in the cellar. Once the head is reattached, the Body says it's been haunting the house for seven years. Many people came to get his wealth, but only Jack helped him. He tells Jack where he buried his gold and that Jack can have it. Jack finds the gold and with his mother lives in the house happy, healthy, and rich.

Garner, Alan. **Jack and the Beanstalk.** Illus. by Julek Heller. New York: Doubleday Book for Young Readers, 1992.

Garner has penned a meaty, fleshed-out version of this classic tale. Garner's language is vivid and full of detailed imagery. For example, the giant doesn't just fall from the beanstalk; he swings and grabs at the beanstalk, looses his grasp, gets tangled in the beanstalk, then crashes. Garner includes many sensory details. Characters snuffle and sniff or caterwaul. The giant's wife doesn't just feed Jack, she serves him cold ham and a jug of buttermilk. The dialogue has an appealing old English sound, too.

Heller's full-page paintings are done in deep, rich, dark colors. His characters are larger than life, yet they seem real. Note the giant with his full red beard; the giant's wife, a buxom woman with kerchief and apron; Jack, a thin, wiry boy; and the beanstalk woven with twisting strands and leaves.

Hong, Lily Toy. **Two of Everything: A Chinese Folktale.** Illus. by author. Morton Grove, IL: Whitman, 1993.

Simply told and illustrated in uncluttered, bold watercolors, this is a delightful and witty tale.

Mr. and Mrs. Haktak are elderly and poor. Their garden provides them with food and some of the produce that they trade in the village for goods. One day while digging in his garden Mr. Haktak finds an ancient pot made of brass. He soon discovers that the pot duplicates everything that goes in. This is advantageous until Mrs. Haktak accidentally falls in the pot and there are two of her. Then Mr. Haktak falls in the pot and there are two of him. At first the Haktaks are upset, but the two couples become friends, live in houses side-by-side, and, with the pot, there is enough food and goods for them all.

Jarrell, Randall, trans. **The Fisherman and His Wife: A Tale from the Brothers Grimm.** Illus. by Margot Zemach. New York: Farrar Straus Giroux, 1980.

Of the many versions of this tale (for example, see Anno, p. 192) of riches gained and lost, this is one of my favorites. Award-winning illustrator Margot Zemach underscores the story with her oversize, expressive, lively watercolors outlined in thick black.

When a fisherman releases a talking flounder, his wife, a demanding, shrewish woman, insists her husband ask the flounder for a wish. The couple lives in a pigsty, and the wife wants a little cottage. The wish is granted. Not satisfied, the wife demands a big stone castle and then asks, in turn, to be king, emperor, and pope. Each time the fisherman asks the flounder to grant a wish, the seas grow darker and wilder. When the fisherman's wife demands to be like God, the mountains shake, houses and trees fall, and the flounder tells the fisherman to return home. There he finds his wife sitting in their original pigsty.

Kimmel, Eric A., reteller. **Boots and His Brothers: A Norwegian Tale.** Illus. by Kimberly Bulcken Root. New York: Holiday House, 1992.

A noted storyteller and fine illustrator have combined talents to bring to life this satisfying tale of kindness versus greediness, magic, and just rewards.

Three brothers set out to seek their fortunes: Peter and Paul, who are rough and rude, and kindly Boots. The brothers meet a beggar woman who tells them of a castle at the top of a mountain where a king lives, but whose light is blocked by an oak tree that covers the windows. The king has promised to pay his weight in gold to anyone who can chop down the tree. The king also wants someone to dig a well and fill it with water. The beggar woman then asks for help, but Peter and Paul push her aside.

Boots gives the woman a coin. For his kindness, the woman tells Boots the oak tree grows two wood chips for each one cut, the mountain is made of iron, and the nearest source of water is far away. She gives him some advice, and, by following it, Boots comes to have an ax that chops trees by itself, a spade that can dig anything, and a rippling stream in a walnut. He hides these items from his brothers.

Once at the castle, Peter and Paul try to chop down the tree, fail, and are chased away by the king's dogs. Boots succeeds with the tiny ax, spade, and walnut in chopping the tree, digging a well, and creating a stream. Boots receives his weight in gold, half the kingdom, and becomes the king's successor.

Kirstein, Lincoln, reteller. **Puss in Boots: Based on a Story of Charles Perrault.** Illus. by Alain Vaës. Boston: Little, Brown, 1992.

Sumptuous, detailed, realistic oversize paintings in deep watercolors capture well the ambiance of Europe in the seventeenth and eighteenth centuries. Faces are expressive and realistic. The telling is tight and well-paced, with some different "takes" on the original.

When the miller gets old, his sons force him to write a will in which the youngest boy, Robin, is left only Puss, the family cat. When the miller dies, Robin is lonely and Puss seems clever, so Robin follows his lead. Puss buys cowhide boots and a strong linen bag with long strings. He catches a pair of rabbits and presents them to the king as a gift from Robin. Then Puss has Robin pretend to be drowning in the pond, and while the king is rescuing him, Puss tricks an ogre out of his land and claims it as Robin's. In this way Puss leads Robin into marriage with the princess. Puss becomes prime minister.

McDermott, Gerald. **Tim O'Toole and the Wee Folk.** Illus. by author. New York: Viking, 1990.

From Ireland comes this sprightly tale with whimsical illustrations.

Tim and his wife Kate are so poor they have no food to eat. Kate sends Tim to find work, but there is none. While resting, Tim sees some wee folk, and because he sees them during the day, he can demand their treasure. The wee folk give him a goose that lays golden eggs. On the way home Tim stays at the McGoons' farmhouse. They exchange their goose for Tim's, and when he unwittingly returns home with the common goose his wife is angry. Tim confronts the wee folk and they give Tim a tablecloth that produces plentiful food. Again, Tim stays at the McGoons, and they switch tablecloths. Tim returns home, his wife is angry, and so is Tim. Again he returns to the wee folk, who tell Tim he was foolish to stay at the McGoons.

The wee folk have Tim leave a strange green hat where the McGoons will find it. When the McGoons tip the hat over, ten tiny men jump out and beat the McGoons on the legs. Tim demands his special goose and tablecloth. People from everywhere come to share in Tim and Kate's good fortune, but soon they tire of the crowds. The wee folk get rid of the masses, and Tim and Kate live happily and peacefully.

Meyers, Odette, reteller. **The Enchanted Umbrella.** (Based on a French Folktale). Illus. by Margot Zemach. San Diego: Harcourt Brace Jovanovich, 1988.

Told with an economy of words, this short, whimsical story moves swiftly and captures well the characters' emotions. Zemach's colorful yet soft and fluid watercolors highlight the many moods of this story, from sad and somber to fanciful and threatening.

Patou is an umbrella maker's assistant. They are family to each other; Patou cares for the man and does all his work when he is ill. The umbrella maker's greedy nephew does nothing. When the man dies, however, the nephew throws Patou out in the rain with a ragged umbrella he says his uncle left for Patou.

Soon Patou learns that the umbrella is magical. He is caught up in an incredible adventure until he comes to a land where people have never seen an umbrella. These people remember, however, that long ago kings owned umbrellas, so they crown Patou king and give him a house.

Perrault, Charles. **Cinderella.** Retold and illus. by Amy Ehrlich. New York: Dial Books for Young Readers, 1985.

For me, this is probably the definitive version of this tale. The telling is rich and the oversize illustrations are sumptuous and sparkle.

Perrault, Charles. **Puss in Boots.** Trans. by Malcolm Arthur. Illus. by Fred Marcellino. New York: Farrar Straus Giroux, 1990.

Translator Arthur captures well the clever and witty tone of Perrault's tale. Marcellino's large, full-color paintings in muted shades are drawn with an attention to detail. He captures landscapes and indoor scenes equally well.

When the miller dies, his youngest son isn't happy to receive only the family cat, Puss, until the cat speaks to the young man. Puss asks for fine boots and a sack. Puss captures several animals, presents them to the king, and says they're from his master the Marquis of Carabas. The cat knows when the king will be riding by the river with his daughter. He has the young man, "The Marquis of Carabas" stand in the river and as the king passes, Puss yells that his master is drowning. Recognizing the name, the king has his guards rescue the young man and provide him with clothing. The lad and the princess fall in love.

While the young man rides in the king's carriage, Puss runs ahead and tells the peasants and all the people he passes to say that the land belongs to the marquis. The land and the castle on it really belong to the richest ogre in the world. Puss tricks the ogre into turning himself into a mouse and then pounces on him. When the king and his entourage arrive at the castle, Puss welcomes them to the marquis' estate. The king offers his daughter in marriage to the marquis, and Puss becomes a great lord.

Philip, Neil, reteller. "Cinder-Stick," pp. 94-98, in **Fairy Tales of Eastern Europe.** Illus. by Larry Wilkes. New York: Clarion Books, 1991.

In this funny tale a wife tells her lazy husband to find work or leave. The man goes, but he meets a giant Div. The husband finds innumerable ways to convince the Divs that he is much stronger than they are. Finally, the Divs flee in fear, and Cinder-Stick takes the Divs' possessions and returns to his wife.

San Souci, Robert D., reteller. **The Talking Eggs: A Folktale from the American South.** Illus. by Jerry Pinkney. New York: Dial Books for Young Readers, 1989.

Adapted from a Creole folktale, this award-winning book begs to be read aloud. The language is rich and colorful, images are precise, the plot is well paced, the dialogue is pleasing to the ear, and the characters are three-dimensional. Realistic and fantastic elements are blended in a natural way. San Souci also does an excellent job of immediately drawing children into the story.

The stunning full-color artwork in watercolor and pencil by Jerry Pinkney is fluid and shows scenes from many views. The illustrator captures well the expressions and feelings of the characters. Pinkney conveys setting effectively and small details like the folds in a piece of cloth and the texture of a rug. He also does a remarkable job of blending realistic and fantastic elements. Note the illustration of the chicken house: you feel like you're in it, yet there's also a magical, misty quality to it, too.

Blanche, a kind girl, lives with her older sister Rose and her mother, who treat her shabbily. One day Blanche meets an elderly woman who supplies her with water. Blanche arrives home late, and her mother yells at and hits her. Blanche runs away and meets the old woman again, who takes her to her home. The woman tells Blanche not to laugh at anything she sees, and Blanche doesn't, not at the multicolored chickens, the two-headed cow with twisted horns, or at the woman when she removes her head.

The woman instructs Blanche to take home some eggs but only those that say "take me." As she approaches her house Blanche does what the woman told her: she tosses the eggs over her left shoulder. Treasures spill out of the eggs: jewels, coins, a pony, silk dresses, and a beautiful carriage. When Blanche brings these items home, her mother is sweet and finds out where the old woman's cabin is.

While Blanche sleeps, Rose is sent to get some talking eggs, too. Rose and her mother always spoke of acquiring wealth and moving to the city. Mother will steal Blanche's riches and together they'll go to the city and become fine ladies.

Rose sees the same elderly woman and demands to go to her cabin. There Rose laughs at the cow and the chickens. She complains about doing chores and when the woman removes her head, Rose grabs it and demands to know about the magic eggs. The woman tells Rose what to do, except she tells her to throw the eggs over her right shoulder. When Rose approaches home and tosses the eggs, snakes, toads, frogs, and yellow jackets pour from them. Rose runs hollering to the cabin and arrives angry, sore, and muddy.

Rose and her mother continue trying to find the cabin and the eggs but never succeed. Blanche goes to the city where she lives grandly but is kind and generous to others.

Schwartz, Howard, and Barbara Rush, retellers. "The Magic Sandals of Abu Kassim," pp. 45-52, in **The Diamond Tree: Jewish Tales from Around the World.** Illus. by Uri Shulevitz. New York: HarperCollins, 1991.

This tale, like the others in this collection, comes from an oral tradition and begs to be shared aloud—either read or told. The watercolor illustrations are vivid, in lovely colors.

A poor Turkish rag seller named Abu Kassim grows ever poorer when no one wants to buy rags. One day when Abu sits to eat his piece of bread, an elderly, tired-looking man passes by, and Abu offers him his bread. In repayment for his kindness the man grants Abu a special wish. Abu wishes for and receives a pair of new sandals. Soon Abu's luck changes; people buy his rags and Abu opens a shop where he sells fine clothes for low prices so even the poor can afford them. Over the years Abu grows rich, but he continues to share with the needy.

Abu always wears his sandals, but eventually they become ripped and cracked. Abu decides to get rid of them, but each time he tries, the sandals are returned to him. Abu decides to still wear the sandals because he realizes they were given to him by Elijah the prophet. Abu wears the sandals and enjoys good luck and fortune.

Booktalks

Climo, Shirley. **The Egyptian Cinderella.** Illus. by Ruth Heller. New York: HarperCollins, 1989.

Based on the tale of Rhodopis, this is one of the world's oldest Cinderella stories. There actually was a Greek slave girl, Rhodopis, who married the Pharaoh Amasis and became his queen. This tale is a blend of fact and fable. It's a satisfying telling with bright, colorful illustrations.

In the sixth century B.C. young Rhodopis is stolen by pirates and brought to Egypt, where she is sold as a slave. Unlike the Egyptian children, Rhodopis has blond hair and green eyes. The other servant girls call her names, tease, and boss her. One day the master sees Rhodopis dancing and feels she deserves a reward—slippers with toes gilded with rose-red gold for her bare feet. The other servant girls become more jealous. When the servant girls attend the Pharaoh's festivities they leave Rhodopis behind.

A hippopotamus splatters Rhodopis' slippers with mud, so she dries them on the river bank. A falcon takes one of the shoes and drops it in Pharaoh Amasis's lap. He regards this as a sign from the god Horus and commands that every maiden in Egypt try the slipper. None fit the small shoe. When the Pharaoh comes to the home where Rhodopis serves, the other servant girls try to squeeze their feet into the slipper but fail. The Pharaoh sees Rhodopis peering through the tall grass, asks her to try the slipper, and when it fits, asks her to be his bride.

Climo, Shirley. **The Korean Cinderella.** Illus. by Ruth Heller. New York: HarperCollins, 1993.

Heller's illustrations are based on research in Korea and are realistically detailed. Brilliant, bold colors splash across the pages. The people are stylized, but their clothing is accurate. The animals, plants, food, and buildings are carefully rendered.

Long ago in Korea when there were magical creatures, an old gentleman and his wife finally have a daughter, whom they name Pear Blossom. When his wife dies, the gentleman visits a matchmaker and he marries a widow who has a daughter, Peony. Mother and daughter are cruel to Pear Blossom. She must do all the chores and dress in rags. Her stepmother sets impossible tasks for her, but with the help of the animals Pear Blossom accomplishes them.

When Festival Day arrives, Pear Blossom must make all the preparations and can go to the festival once she weeds all the rice paddies. A kindly black ox does the task for Pear Blossom, so she sets off for the festival. On the way Pear Blossom removes one straw sandal to remove a stone. The magistrate comes along and in her confusion, Pear Blossom's sandal goes into the water. When the magistrate yells "stop" at his carriage bearers, Pear Blossom thinks he's yelling at her and she runs to the festival, where she watches and listens. There her stepmother and stepsister shout at her but are interrupted by the carriage bearers, who are looking for the person whose shoe they found. Pear Blossom's stepmother and stepsister think Pear Blossom is in trouble, but, no, the magistrate wants to marry her.

Haviland, Virginia, reteller. "Dick Whittington and His Cat," pp. 63-77, in **Favorite Fairy Tales Told in England.** Illus. by Maxie Chambliss. New York: Beech Tree Books, 1994.

When Dick Whittington's parents die and the villagers can't provide for him, he travels to London and is taken in by a kindly rich merchant, Mr. Fitzwarren. When one of Mr. Fitzwarren's trading ships prepares to sail, Dick learns that the custom is for the servants to share in the profits of the voyage by sending something to trade. All Dick has is his cat.

When the ship arrives at the coast of Barbary, the captain trades Dick's cat to the king, who wants to get rid of the rats and mice that are bothering him. The king pays ten times as much for the cat as for the rest of the cargo. When the ship returns to London the captain brings Dick his payment. Mr. Fitzwarren gives Dick the entire amount. Now Dick is rich. He dresses like a gentleman, eventually marries Mr. Fitzwarren's daughter, becomes Lord Mayor three times, and always shares his wealth with others.

San Souci, Robert D., reteller. **Sootface: An Ojibwa Cinderella Story.** Illus. by Daniel San Souci. New York: A Doubleday Book for Young Readers/Delacorte, 1994.

This adaptation is told with an economy of words, realistic dialogue, and vivid descriptions. The full-page, brilliant watercolors offer a realistic depiction of a mid-eighteenth-century Ojibwa village.

An Ojibwa man, a widower, has three daughters. The youngest girl does all the chores while her older sisters are mean to her and call her Sootface because of her singed hair and smudged face.

A mighty warrior, who is invisible, and his sister live across the lake from the village. One day the warrior's sister tells the villagers that her brother will marry the woman who can see him. The women of the village try to guess the answer to the questions that will prove they can see the warrior, but all fail, even Sootface's sisters. Sootface then decides to try her luck. She sees the warrior, is able to describe his bow and string, and is chosen to be his bride.

Demonstration/Participation Activities

Berger, Melvin, and Gilda Berger. **Round and Round the Money Goes: What Money Is and How We Use It.** Illus. by Jane McCreary. Nashville, TN: Ideals Children's Books, 1993.

On pp. 18-19 the authors list the names for money in different countries. For example, in Mexico people use pesos, in Japan they use yen, and in France there are francs. Turn this list into a matching game by listing the countries and then scrambling the names for the money. Invite the children to guess which country goes with which currency.

Burns, Marilyn. "Don't Fall for What Pops in First," pp. 75-76, and "The Ten Pennies Problem," p. 92, in **The Book of Think (Or, How to Solve a Problem Twice Your Size).** Illus. by Martha Weston. Boston: Little, Brown, 1976.

Set up several stations with these activities and invite small groups of children to solve them. In the first the challenge is to balance a quarter on the edge of a dollar bill. The author offers two possible solutions.

The second problem asks children to take a specific arrangement of 10 pennies (diagram included) and, by moving only three pennies, make them face the opposite way. Again the author offers an illustration that shows how to do this.

Remind the children that they're doing this for fun; it's not meant to be stressful. If they don't solve the puzzles, it's okay.

Maestro, Betsy. **The Story of Money.** Illus. by Giulio Maestro. New York: Clarion Books, 1993.

This book if full of ideas for activities to do. Like **Round and Round the Money Goes** (see Berger, above), author Maestro includes the names of money in other countries. You can use this information in a matching game in which the children guess which currency comes from which country. You can base another guessing game on this book: Create pairs of currency amounts, for example, 100 yen and $1.00, 1,000 pesos and $10.00, and let children guess which is worth more in each pair. Keep it light and fun.

Mandell, Muriel. "Bright as a Penny," p. 46, in **Simple Science Experiments with Everyday Materials.** Illus. by Frances Zweifel. New York: Sterling, 1989.

Invite the children to bring pennies to the program or supply them yourself. They'll be amazed to see how you can make dull pennies shiny by soaking them in lemon juice or vinegar. The author includes a short list of materials, easy instructions, and an explanation for why this activity works.

Sitarz, Paula Gaj. "Price Is Right."

There are several ways to play this game and children enjoy them all. You can display a variety of items familiar to children and invite them to guess the price of each. Whoever comes closest to the actual price wins. Another way to play is to offer two or three choices of prices for each item and ask the children to guess which is correct. A third way to play is to show pairs of items and to ask the children to guess which costs more. If you don't want to display the actual items, you can use illustrations and photographs from newspaper flyers and magazines.

Warner, Penny. "Price It Right," pp. 100-101, in **Kids' Party Games and Activities: Hundreds of Exciting Things to Do at Parties for Kids 2-12.** Illus. by Kathy Rogers. Deephaven, MN: Meadowbrook Press, 1993.

Warner offers a delightful game based on the TV game show in which children try to come closest to guessing the actual prices of a variety of items. Children enjoy this game a lot.

Wyler, Rose, and Mary Elting. "Hot Money" and "Penny Polish," p. 7, in **Math Fun with Money Puzzlers.** Illus. by Patrick Girouard. New York: Messner, 1992.

"Hot Money" is a clever trick in which you can convince children that you have the power to tell what penny they are concentrating on in a group of pennies. The author explains how this feat is possible. "Penny Polish" offers clear instructions for making dull pennies shiny and new looking.

Chapter 17

Scary Tales

Read Alouds

Ayres, Becky Hickox. **Matreshka.** Illus. by Alexi Natchev. New York: Doubleday Book for Young Readers/Delacorte Press, 1992.

A little wooden doll named Matreshka saves Kata's life when Kata becomes the prisoner of Baba Yaga the witch. Matreshka consists of five dolls, one inside the other. As Matreshka helps Kata escape from Baba Yaga and the situation requires a slightly smaller doll, the next one pops out.

There is much tension in this tale. Youngsters wonder if Baba Yaga will see the dolls and if she'll succeed in cooking Kata.

Illustrator Natchev conveys Baba Yaga's horrible and frightening appearance well. Baba Yaga has a bulbous, downward pointing nose with warts, small beady eyes, a wide wrinkled chin, and a mouth that reveals her gums and her few remaining teeth.

Baltuck, Naomi. "Red Lips," pp. 32-36, in **Crazy Gibberish and Other Story Hour Stretches: From a Storyteller's Bag of Tricks.** Illus. by Doug Cushman. Hamden, CT: Linnet Book/The Shoe String Press, 1993.

This is another excellent version of a traditional tale (see Horner, "The Mischievous Girl and the Hideous Creature," p. 211) in which the suspense builds until the unexpected ending releases the tension.

Jennifer moves to a big old house at the end of a long country road. To reach her attic bedroom she must climb a long dark stairway and walk down a long, dark hallway. The first night in her new room Jennifer awakens at midnight to the sound of scratching at her window. She sees a woman with a pale face, long black hair, bright red lips, and long red fingernails. When the woman asks Jennifer if she knows what she does with her lips and fingernails, Jennifer screams, pulls down the shade, jumps into bed, and pulls the cover over her head. The next night the same thing happens. On the third night the woman says she'll show Jennifer what she does, and she strums her index finger up and down between her lips and makes a silly noise.

This scary, funny, and clever tale is most effective when told rather than read. The author suggests actions for the teller to do with the story and includes story-telling tips.

Bauer, Caroline Feller. "The Hairy Toe," pp. 20-21, in **Halloween: Stories and Poems.** Illus. by Peter Sis. New York: J. B. Lippincott, 1989.

This is a short but effective story, that, if told correctly, will make children jump.

A woman finds a Hairy Toe while picking beans from her garden. That night while she's in bed the woman hears the wind moan and groan, and in the distance she hears a voice asking for its Hairy Toe. The woman hides under the covers. Her house creaks as if something is trying to get in. She hears the voice again, almost at the door. The woman pulls the covers over her head. She hears something slip in the door and creep across the floor. Then she almost feels "it" bending over her head. The awful voice repeats its question and the woman yells, "You've got it!"

Bodkin, Odds. **The Banshee Train.** Illus. by Ted Rose. New York: Clarion Books, 1995.

Noted storyteller Odds Bodkin creates immediate and non-stop tension and suspense in this eerie tale.

It's spring in the mountains west of Denver, Colorado, and the railroad men are nervous because the snow is melting fast and torrents of water are rushing down the mountain gorges. The men worry that bridges will be washed out. John Mercer, a train engineer feels uneasy about the Gore Canyon Trestle, which he is supposed to travel over that day. He knows that years ago the long wooden span over the Colorado River was washed out in heavy spring floods and the train engineer, driving in the fog, hadn't realized that the Gore Canyon Trestle was gone. His train plunged into the wild waters below.

As John Mercer and Michael O'Reilly, the fireman, travel alone on the train you sense the train rushing and want it to stop, especially with the knowledge that the same conditions of fog and rushing water exist on this trip toward Gore Canyon Trestle and beyond.

Suddenly, in Moffat Tunnel, John Mercer's throttle swings to the off position by itself. Then, without warning, the conductor's air whistle shrieks in Mercer's ear. He looks behind and sees the headlights of another train coming from the tunnel. Mercer fears being hit as the other train increases speed. He decides they'll go to a passing track in Tabernash to get out of the way. In Tabernash, however, a huge coal train is on the side track. Mercer and O'Reilly must continue into the mist and wet snow. O'Reilly asks about Gore Canyon Trestle. They should slow down, but Mercer can't. Suddenly, the throttle jumps from Mercer's grip and thunks off again. The engine brake iron flies back by itself and locks. The train grinds to a halt.

That's when Mercer and O'Reilly hear a chilling shriek and they see the train that was in pursuit traveling at 50 miles an hour. They see a banshee woman with red swirling face and white eyes racing along the cartops. The train doesn't collide with them because it's a ghost train, the train that plunged into the gorge years ago. Mercer and O'Reilly see the determined faces of the ghost engineer and the fireman and then the train is gone.

Mercer and O'Reilly's train comes to life and they get out of the train. The snow has stopped, the fog is lifting, and they see that Gore Canyon Trestle is gone. They realize that it was 20 years ago on that day that the other train went over.

This retelling of a banshee legend (brought by Irish immigrants who worked on the railroads in America) is illustrated in dark watercolors that evoke the cold, snowy, eerie, otherworldly look of the scene. The illustrator captures well the fear on Mercer and O'Reilly's faces.

Bunting, Eve. **Ghost's Hour, Spook's Hour.** Illus. by Donald Carrick. New York: Clarion Books, 1987.

This is a short but satisfying story that will appeal to children at the younger end of the target age group. The artwork is very atmospheric, dark, and full of shadows.

Jake is frightened one night by noises: his dog Biff's howling, the creak of his door, and the tree branches hitting his window. Jake goes to his parents' bedroom, but they're not there and Jake realizes there's been a power outage. As he climbs down the stairs Jake is further chilled by clatters and rattles, shuffles, and the sound of the clock booming. Then Jake sees a shapeless, bloblike white image. After scaring himself, Jake realizes what he saw was his and Biff's reflection in a mirror. Finally, he locates his parents in the dining room.

Bunting, Eve. **Night of the Gargoyles.** Illus. by David Wiesner. New York: Clarion Books, 1994.

Bunting's book is a striking, eerie mood piece. The text is poetic, told with a minimum of words, but it is precise and full of impact. The artwork done in black and white and shades of gray is haunting and spooky.

During the day the gargoyles stare unblinking from the walls of an art museum. At night they come to life, peer into the rooms of the museum, swing in the branches, and swoop to the water fountain. The night watchman hurries by the gargoyles in fear. The gargoyles, who dislike the humans who placed them high on roofs and ledges, scream at the watchman. As morning approaches the gargoyles return to their spots, projecting from the roof and eaves of the museum, until night comes again.

Cole, Joanna. "Bony-Legs," pp. 27-42, in **The Scary Book.** Comp. by Joanna Cole and Stephanie Calmenson. Illus. by Dirk Zimmer. New York: Morrow Junior Books, 1991.

Of the many stories about the Russian witch Baba Yaga, this is one of my favorites. It isn't overly long, but it's richly told. The author builds tension well and provides moments of humor, too. Dirk Zimmer excels at depicting scary scenes. His black-and-white illustration of Baba Yaga with pointy teeth, long bony fingers, warts, a crooked pointy nose, and scraggly hair captures her perfectly.

Cole introduces us to Bony-Legs (Baba Yaga) immediately. We see her running swiftly on her bony old legs, snapping her iron teeth, and waiting deep in the woods in her hut on chicken feet for children to pass so she can cook and eat them.

Sasha lives at the edge of the woods with her aunt and one morning is sent to borrow a needle and thread from a neighbor. Sasha takes bread and butter and a bit of meat. She comes to Bony-Legs's house. The gate to Bony-Legs's yard creaks, so Sasha greases it with butter. A skinny dog barks as she walks up the path. Sasha feels sorry for it and gives the dog her bread. Near the hut Sasha gives her meat to a mewing cat.

Sasha meets Bony-Legs and tells her what she needs. Bony-Legs orders Sasha to get into the tub so she'll be clean when she's cooked. Then Bony-Legs goes to get firewood and locks the door. The cat and dog to whom Sasha was kind give her a silver mirror and a wooden comb and help her escape.

Bony-Legs is angry when she finds Sasha gone. She asks the cat, dog, and gate why they were silent when the girl escaped, and they respond that Sasha was kind to them. When Bony-Legs runs after Sasha, the girl throws the mirror and it becomes a silver lake. Bony-Legs returns home, gets her tub, and rows it across the water. When Bony-Legs gets close to her, Sasha throws the comb and it turns into tall trees. Bony-Legs can't get around them, gives up, and returns to her hut. Sasha goes home.

DeFelice, Cynthia C. "The Dancing Skeleton," illus. by Ed Young, pp. 322-25, in **From Sea to Shining Sea: A Treasury of American Folklore and Folk Songs.** Comp. by Amy L. Cohn. Illus. by 11

Caldecott Medal and four Caldecott Honor Book artists. New York: Scholastic, 1993.

Here's a delightful, lively, and rhythmic telling of this classic tale, which is underscored with abstract artwork in shades of blue and white that swirl across the page.

When Aaron Kelly dies he refuses to stay dead and returns home to his wife. Eventually he dries up and becomes a skeleton. He rocks in a chair, clicking and clacking. A fiddler comes to "court" the widow, but it's difficult with Aaron there. One night Aaron asks the fiddler to play. Aaron dances so hard that one of his bones breaks off. When the fiddler and the widow realize Aaron's fast dancing will make him fall apart, the fiddler plays faster and faster until Aaron is a pile of bones. However, when Aaron's head talks to the fiddler, the latter flees. Aaron's widow returns her husband's bones to the grave and mixes them up so he can't get back together.

DeFelice, Cynthia C. **The Dancing Skeleton.** Illus. by Robert Andrew Parker. New York: Macmillan, 1989.

This book uses the same DeFelice telling as in the previous entry, but in this picture book version the illustrations are done by Robert Andrew Parker in his trademark lighthearted, "sketchy" watercolors. The artwork enhances the eerie quality of the tale.

DeSpain, Pleasant. "Ah Schung Catches a Ghost," pp. 59-61, in **Thirty-Three Multicultural Tales to Tell.** Illus. by Joe Shlichta. Little Rock, AK: August House, 1993.

This is a short and clever tale that is easy to memorize and tell.

When Ah Schung meets a ghost he outsmarts it by pretending that he, too, is a ghost. Ah Schung learns that what real ghosts fear most from humans is to be spit on by them. When the phantom changes himself into a horse, Ah Schung spits on him and has a serviceable horse for several years.

Forest, Heather, reteller. "Wiley and the Hairy Man," pp. 51-54, in **Wonder Tales from Around the World.** Illus. by David Boston. Little Rock, AK: August House, 1995.

Of the many tellings of this classic tale, this is one of the best. The language is rich and flavorful, and suspense is sustained throughout.

Wiley's momma warns him to beware the Hairy Man who lives in the swamp. One day Wiley meets the ugly Hairy Man, who has spit drooling over his huge teeth. Wiley quickly climbs a tree and Hairy Man starts to chop it. Wiley knows some conjuring, and he makes the wood chips reattach to the tree. Finally Wiley's dogs come and scare Hairy Man.

Wiley's momma tells him next time to trick Hairy Man into turning into various animals until he's small enough for Wiley to put in a sack and throw into the river. Wiley does that, but Hairy Man turns into the wind and blows out of the sack so Wiley must climb the tree again. Wiley tricks Hairy Man into making things disappear, including all the rope in the county. Now, his dogs, who were tied at home, can rescue him.

Momma says if Wiley can outsmart Hairy Man a third time, he won't bother Wiley again. Momma has a plan. She puts their pet pig in Wiley's bed. When Hairy Man comes asking for her baby, Momma says her baby's in the bed. Hairy Man protests that it's a pig, but momma says she didn't say what kind of baby she was giving him. Hairy Man is outsmarted and enraged, but he can't bother Wiley again.

Galdone, Paul, reteller. **King of the Cats: A Ghost Story by Joseph Jacobs.** Illus. by author. New York: Houghton Mifflin, 1980.

Children of all ages enjoy this traditional tale illustrated in Galdone's trademark oversized artwork. Here he uses dark, muted shades and gives the characters large, piercing eyes. In his telling Galdone builds suspense, mystery, and atmosphere well. The cats are eerie, especially the elderly couple's cat.

A gravedigger comes home late one night asking his wife who Tom Tildrum is. His voice and manner are so wild he frightens his wife and cat. The gravedigger tells his wife that he was digging Mr. Fordyce's grave when he fell asleep and was awakened by a loud miaow. He saw nine black cats carrying a small coffin. The gravedigger notices as he tells his story that his cat is very attentive and miaows whenever the gravedigger says the word "miaow."

The gravedigger says further that the cats stared at him and asked if he knew who Tom Tildrum was. If he did, he was to tell him that Tim Toldrum is dead. That's when the gravedigger's cat swells, exclaims that he, Tom Tildrum, is now King of the Cats, and disappears.

Galdone, Paul, reteller. "King of the Cats: A Ghost Story by Joseph Jacobs," pp. 3-7, in **Halloween: Stories and Poems.** Ed. by Caroline Feller Bauer. Illus. by Peter Sis. New York: J. B. Lippincott, 1989.

If you can't find Galdone's picture book version of this story (see previous entry), here's Galdone's text with imaginative and striking black-and-white illustrations made up of cross-hatchings by Peter Sis.

Galdone, Paul, reteller. **The Monster and the Tailor: A Ghost Story.** Illus. by author. New York: Ticknor & Fields/Houghton Mifflin, 1982.

Galdone's oversize artwork is always expressive and appropriate to share with a large group.

Trouble begins when the Grand Duke orders the tailor to make new trousers for him and insists that they must be stitched in the old graveyard at night because only then will the trousers give him good luck.

The tailor is afraid because strange things happen in the graveyard. He's sitting on a gravestone and sewing when the ground begins to tremble and a huge head pops up from the ground. The head speaks to him, but the tailor keeps stitching. Each time another body part appears the monster asks the tailor if he sees it, but the tailor just sews. The monster's chest appears, his long arms, his leg. Just as the creature pulls the other leg up, the tailor finishes stitching and runs. The giant chases him. The tailor reaches the castle, the Duke loves his trousers, the tailor is rewarded, and the monster is never seen again. The mark of the monster's fingers, however, remains on the castle wall.

Hirsh, Marilyn, reteller. "The Rabbi and the Twenty-Nine Witches," a Talmudic legend, illus. by author, pp. 47-68, in **The Scary Book.** Comp. by Joanna Cole and Stephanie Calmenson. New York: Morrow Junior Books, 1991.

Every month when the moon is full the people in a little village go home early and hide inside because that night 29 wicked witches fly shrieking over the village. When they do, strange things happen, babies cry, and everyone has nightmares. If it's raining on the night of the full moon the witches don't come. Many villagers live their lives without seeing a full moon.

Finally, an old grandmother decides she wants to see a full moon before she dies, and she asks her friend the wise Rabbi what to do. The Rabbi devises a plan, and the next night when it's raining, 29 brave but terrified men of the village, each with a long white robe stored in a clay pot with a tight cover, parade to the witches' cave. There the Rabbi, with the assistance of the men, tricks the witches outside, where they shrink to nothing in the rain. (The Rabbi deduced there was some reason they were afraid of the rain.) After that, the villagers enjoy every full moon.

Horner, Beth, adapter. "The Mischievous Girl and the Hideous Creature," pp. 106-109, adapted from American Folk Humor, in **Ready-to-Tell Tales: Sure-Fire Stories from America's Favorite Storytellers.** Ed. by David Holt and Bill Mooney. Little Rock, AK: August House, 1994.

Children love this tale that features a sassy, modern girl, a frightening creature, unexpected events, and a hilarious ending.

On three consecutive days a young girl does what she loves best: She scares her younger brother, grosses out her older brother, and gets her parents to say something impolite at the dinner table. Each night when she's in bed a hideous-looking creature with wild hair and two long noses with warts stares at her through the window. When the girl opens the window the creature asks her if she knows what it does with its long red fingernails and its big red lips. The girl doesn't want to know, slams down the window, and jumps under the bed. On the third night when the creature asks its question the girl is so annoyed she asks the creature what it does with its fingernails and lips. That's when the creature looks at her, smiles, puts its finger to its lips, and moves its finger up and down so its lips make a funny sound.

Howe, James. **Scared Silly: A Halloween Treat.** Illus. by Leslie Morrill. New York: William Morrow, 1989.

Meet Harold the dog, Chester the cat, Howie, a dachshund puppy, Bunnicula, an unusual rabbit, and the Monroes, the people who own them. Things turn scary one stormy Halloween night when the Monroes go to a party, the animals are left alone, the lights go out, there's a knock on the door, and a witch enters. She starts cooking a bubbling concoction, and the animals wonder if she's going to cook them. When the witch takes Bunnicula, the other animals rush into the kitchen, creating havoc. Just then the door opens and a skeleton, a gorilla, a mummy, and a monster enter. It's the Monroes in costume, and the witch, the animals learn, is really Grandma. She was making hot cider. The animals are still scared when they see Grandma holding a broom and she tells her family the flight was bumpy.

Bright, bold illustrations enhance this delightful story.

Johnston, Tony. **Alice Nizzy Nazzy: The Witch of Santa Fe.** Illus. by
Tomie dePaola. New York: G. P. Putnam's Sons, 1995.

Here's another splendid book by a fine author-illustrator team. In this
tale the Russian witch Baba Yaga has been transported (figuratively) to Santa
Fe, New Mexico. The artwork, in dePaola's trademark style is rendered in a
rich palette of colors that suggests the southwest. The scenes aren't realistic
(the hills are purple and mauve, the sky is salmon), but they are visually
appealing. The witch's house has masks and skull paintings on the walls. The
witch, Alice Nizzy Nazzy has black teeth; hair that consists of strings of chiles;
skin yellow like a squash; red, beady eyes; and a mouth like a zipper. One of
the most arresting illustrations depicts the shepherd girl, Manuela, when she's
frightened and her braids stick straight out.

Children are warned not to go near Alice Nizzy Nazzy, a mean witch who
lives in the desert in an adobe hut on skinny roadrunner feet surrounded by a
fence of prickly pear. When Alice Nizzy Nazzy mumbles special words or tickles
its feet, the hut carries her to naughty children whom she eats.

One day a little girl, Manuela, follows her lost sheep tracks to Alice's hut.
Manuela is scared, but she won't leave without her sheep. When the fence tells
her to leave, Manuela compliments it and the fence opens. The hut tells
Manuela to leave, but she compliments the hut and it opens the door. Alice,
with a huge horned lizard draped over her shoulder, welcomes Manuela. The
girl compliments the lizard. Alice insists that Manuela is naughty and puts her
in the cooking pot.

Manuela learns that Alice has run out of the tea that keeps her young. It
is made from the petals of the black cactus flower, but Alice can't find any. Just
as Alice lights the fire, Manuela shouts that she knows where the black flower
is. Manuela says she wants her sheep in return for the flower. Alice agrees, but
she has her fingers crossed.

Once the flower is found, Alice and Manuela return to the hut, but Alice
refuses to give Manuela her sheep and returns the girl to the pot. Alice tastes
the broth and finds it sour because Manuela **is** a good girl. When Alice flies off
in her mortar to find a naughty child, Manuela hops out of the pot. The moment
Alice whirls off, the spell is broken and the dirty pillows Alice kept in the hut
become Manuela's sheep once again.

Johnston, Tony. **The Soup Bone.** Illus. by Margot Tomes. San Diego,
CA: Harcourt Brace Jovanovich, 1990.

Johnston's well-written, smoothly flowing text is complemented by Margot Tomes's clean and crisp, scary and humorous illustrations in shades of
brown, gray, and white. Tomes pays careful attention to small details.

A lonely, little old woman is making soup, but it's too thin without a soup
bone. In her search for a bone she finds an entire skeleton who chases her,
enters her house, and starts eating her soup. The woman chases the skeleton
while wearing her dog Halloween costume, and the skeleton fears the "dog" will
eat him. Finally the woman and the skeleton promise not to scare each other
but to scare someone else together.

Leach, Maria. "I'm Coming Up the Stairs," pp. 57-58, in **Whistle in the
Graveyard: Folktales to Chill Your Bones.** Illus. by Ken Rin-
ciari. New York: Viking, 1974.

Leach builds suspense in this short tale of a young girl named Tilly who is afraid to go to bed because she'd been told some scary stories. One night Tilly hears a voice calling her name and saying it's coming up the stairs. Each night it tells Tilly where it is, and each night it is closer to her room, until one night the voice says it's standing by her bed. On the final night it says it's got Tilly.

Leaf, Margaret. **Eyes of the Dragon.** Illus. by Ed Young. New York: Lothrop, Lee & Shepard, 1987.

Leaf's satisfying tale is highlighted by sprawling pastel paintings in muted tones except for the dragon, which is vivid and bright.

The people who live in a small village in China have a wall built around their village because they fear wild animals and men. When the magistrate learns that his grandson marked the wall he is angry at first, but then realizes that the wall is rather plain. He decides that Ch'en Jung, the most famous dragon painter in the city, will paint a portrait of the Dragon King, who controls thunder and lightning and rain. Ch'en Jung agrees to paint the wall if he can paint the dragon in his own way.

When Ch'en Jung finishes, the magistrate complains that the dragon's eyes haven't been painted. The magistrate insists they be painted even when Ch'en Jung warns that it will be dangerous to do so. Ch'en Jung paints the eyes, says the villagers must live with the consequences, and leaves. Soon the dragon's eyes glow, the dragon moves, and it rises in the air. There is thunder and lightning, and the walls that surround the village crumble.

Low, Alice, comp. **Spooky Stories for a Dark and Stormy Night.** Illus. by Gahan Wilson. New York: Byron Preiss Visual Publications, 1994.

Alice Low has compiled a collection of some of the best and most beloved scary stories. The watercolors match each tale perfectly.

"Taily-Po," pp. 10-13, is an African American folktale retold by Stephanie Calmenson. One night a man who lives in a one-room cabin in the woods by himself has a creature fall down his chimney. When the creature's tail lands in the man's stew pot, the creature screams, which scares the man. He grabs his ax, swings it, and by accident chops the creature's tail. The man cooks the tail in his stew, eats it, and then falls asleep. After a short time the creature stomps on the roof asking for its tail. The man calls his dogs, who chase the thing into the woods. In the middle of the night the creature creeps down the side of the cabin and asks for its tail again. The man has his dogs chase the creature once more. Just before daylight the man is awakened by the creature scratching at the foot of his bed. The man tries to call his dog, but he can't make a sound. The creature wants his tail, and the man denies having it, so the creature turns him upside-down and shakes him until the tail falls out—whole. The man is never seen again.

"Wait Till Martin Comes," pp. 20-22. A man takes shelter in a deserted (and haunted) house when a storm threatens. During the storm the man sits reading. He looks up and sees a little gray cat sitting on the hearth. After awhile a big black cat appears. The cats ask each other what they'll do with the man, and they decide to wait until Martin comes. The man continues to read when a cat as big as a dog arrives, and then a cat as big as a calf. When the cats say again they'll wait until Martin comes, the man, fearing what size Martin will be, runs away.

"Wiley and the Hairy Man," pp. 48-55, is an African American folktale retold by Della Rowland. Wiley, whose mother always warns him about the Hairy Man who lives in the swamp, takes his dogs with him when he goes far and leaves them tied at home when he isn't going far. One day Wiley goes further and further. He doesn't have his dogs with him when he meets the hungry Hairy Man, who wants to eat him. Wiley must outwit the Hairy Man three times, and then the Hairy Man won't be able to bother him again. With the advice of his mother and the assistance of his dogs, Wiley does outwit the frightening Hairy Man.

"My Neighbor Is a Monster, Pass It On," pp. 58-61, by Eric Weiner. Here's a clever, eerie, and unique story in which Melanie watches her new neighbor Mr. Bartok move in and then tells Billy Walsh that Mr. Bartok is a monster and to pass on the message. The rumor spreads until it comes back to Melanie in a very different form. Now kids are saying that Mr. Bartok flies around his house like a giant bee, at dusk his hands turn into claws, and in the dark he grows fangs and sprouts fur on his head like a vampire bat.

The children's parents and the entire town hear the rumors and exaggerate them further. Melanie starts to believe the tales and decides she must know for sure. One dark and stormy night Melanie goes into Mr. Bartok's house. There's a bang, but when she realizes it's just thunder, Melanie laughs in relief. Then Mr. Bartok, the monster, flies into the room. . . .

"Rap! Rap! Rap!" pp. 108-112, retold by Jeanne B. Hardendorff. Suspense builds to an amusing ending in this story. Reginald Ewing Peabody is driving in the country when his battery dies and a storm ensues. Reginald seeks shelter in an empty house where all he hears is a faint rap coming from upstairs. Reginald follows the rapping sound to a door, up stairs to the attic, into a closet, to a box on a shelf. The rapping is coming from inside the box. When Reginald opens the box he finds a roll of wrapping paper.

"I'm Coming Up the Stairs," pp. 114-17, is an English folktale retold by Wendy Wax. Tilly begs her brother to tell her some of the spooky tales he heard at summer camp, especially the stories of the Creep Man. Herbie knows the stories will scare Tilly, but she insists. Herbie relates that the Creep Man lives on children's ear wax and sharpens his teeth on small fingernails. He continues that each year the Creep Man follows one child home from camp and stays for the winter. Rumor is that the boy the Creep man went home with the previous year never returned to camp the next year.

Tilly is scared now, Herbie is asleep, and her parents aren't home yet. Finally, Tilly goes to bed. Soon she's hears a creak and a voice telling her it's on the second step. The voice tells her step by step where it is; in the hall, at her door, in the bedroom, on her bed, until it shouts that it has Tilly.

"The Strange Visitor," pp. 118-20, is a Scottish folktale retold by Wendy Wax. A woman is spinning wool one night when she wishes for company. In comes a pair of broad feet. She keeps spinning and hoping for company when, in turn, short legs, thick knees, huge hips, wee waist, broad shoulders, long arms, huge hands, a small neck, and a huge head arrive. Each part attaches itself to the other to make one creature. Finally the woman speaks and asks the creature how each of its body parts came to have its shape. When she asks what the creature came for, it says it came for her.

"Boo!" p. 125, by Kevin Crossley-Holland. This is an extremely short but satisfying and clever story that is most effective when memorized and told.

Meet a girl who must sleep alone in an old house. She goes to bed early and checks that everything is secured, from the locks on the doors to the latches on the windows. She looks in drawers, under the bed, and in the wardrobe, then gets in bed and turns off the light. That's when a little voice says that's good, they're locked in safely for the night.

Mahy, Margaret. "Looking for a Ghost," pp. 79-88, in **A Tall Story and Other Tales.** Illus. by Jan Nesbitt. New York: Macmillan, 1992.

This wry and clever tale lets your audience get the joke before the main character does.

Sammy Scarlet goes to a tumbledown haunted house at the edge of the city to see the little ghost that supposedly lives there. Once there, Sammy meets Belinda, a mysterious little girl in a long, oversized dress. Sammy tries to discourage her from seeing the ghost because he says spirits can be horrible. Instead the girl encourages Sammy to enter the house. Belinda explains what the house looked like in the past, and she cleverly explains away how she knows this information.

Finally, Sammy leaves disappointed that he didn't see a ghost. After he goes, Belinda wonders if Sammy would recognize a ghost if he saw one, and then she disappears.

Mayo, Margaret. "The Halloween Witches," pp. 95-99, in **Magical Tales from Many Lands.** Illus. by Jane Ray. New York: E. P. Dutton Children's Books, 1993.

It's Halloween night and a coven of old witches has gathered in a cabin to tell tales. When a stranger knocks on the door, the witches call, "Who's there? Who-oo?" The stranger is hungry and cold, but the witches refuse to cook for him. Each time the stranger knocks, the witches ask who is there and refuse to feed him. Eventually the knocking makes the witches uneasy, and they decide to take a tiny piece of dough and cook it for the stranger. In the pan the dough swells and begins to fill the cabin until there's almost no room for the witches. The voice says that since the witches refused him, they will no longer walk. They're transformed into owls. The voice says now they'll live in a hollow tree. Even today they say "who-oo." On Halloween, however, they turn back into witches.

Monfried, Lucia, comp. **Diane Goode's Book of Scary Stories and Songs.** Illus. by Diane Goode. New York: Dutton Children's Books, 1994.

Several stories in this collection are good to share. The scary, sometimes humorous, artwork makes effective use of shading and exhibits expressiveness in the characters' eyes.

"Let's Go," p. 5, is an amusing, extremely short tale that's more effective when memorized and told. A family decides to move when the boggart that haunts the family becomes a nuisance. After loading their belongings on a wagon the family hears a tiny voice from the piled-up furniture saying it's ready to go.

In "Spooks A-Hunting," pp. 6-11, we learn that on St. Martin's Night, when the spooks go to the forest, humans must not look at them. Most people stay indoors with their curtains drawn. One curious woman peeks out her window and sees many strange sights until finally she laughs at an odd-looking goose. The goose pecks at the woman's fence, and the woman feels the pain in her left leg. The pain is still with her the next St. Martin's Night. The woman doesn't peek out then, and the goose says he'll take the hook out of the fence. The woman's pain disappears.

"My Big Toe," pp. 12-13, is short, amusing, and "icky." A poor elderly couple always has food to eat because they grow potatoes. One day the woman digs up what looks like a giant potato. She decides to surprise her husband with potato soup. That night in bed the couple hear a voice saying it wants it's big toe. When the husband gets up and sees something behind the kitchen table he's scared and jumps in bed. The woman goes to the kitchen and says she'll give whatever or whoever it is the rest of the potato soup if it will go away. After that night the woman never makes potato soup again.

In "Tain't So," pp. 22-25, Mr. Dinkins take ill and dies. The next day a neighbor passes by, sees Mr. Dinkins, and says he thought Dinkins was dead. Mr. Dinkins responds "Tain't so" to him and to everyone that comes by for the next few months. The townspeople hold another burial for Mr. Dinkins and have the tombstone engraved to say he is dead. When Mr. Dinkins sees the words he decides maybe he is dead, and no one hears from him again.

In "The Man Who Was Afraid of Nothing," pp. 26-31, four ghosts wager they can spook a fellow who they've heard is afraid of nothing. Each in turn appears to the man in the form of a skeleton and tries to pit him in a contest, but the man tricks them instead. The ghosts disappear when the sun rises, and everyone praises the man for his bravery. Just then a spider crawls on his sleeve, and he screams for someone to remove it.

The hero of "Dauntless Little John," pp. 38-41, is afraid of nothing. While traveling John discovers there are no rooms at the inn, and he is directed to a palace from which no one has come out alive. When John sits by the fireplace a voice asks if it should throw it down and John tells it to go ahead. A leg falls down. Things continue in this way. Another leg comes down, then an arm, another arm, the trunk of a body to which the arms and legs attach, and then a head that springs onto the body. John isn't afraid of the giant before him. The giant makes John go down a staircase with him to a stone slab. Beneath the slab are three pots of gold that they retrieve. The giant explains that the spell has been broken and body part by body part it goes back up the chimney. Little John is given one of the pots of gold and the palace that is never haunted again.

"Mr. Miacca," pp. 48-51, is the classic tale of young Tommy Grimes, who can sometimes behave very badly. One day, despite his mother's warning, he goes around the corner and Mr. Miacca pops him into his bag. He plans to eat Tommy, but Tommy's a bit tough so Mr. Miacca tells his wife to watch Tommy while he gets some herbs. Tommy talks to the wife and learns she likes to eat pudding, not just boy meat. Tommy says his mother makes a fine pudding and he'll be happy to get some, so she lets him go.

Tommy tries hard to be good, but he gets caught by Mr. Miacca again. This time Mr. Miacca puts Tommy under the sofa and sits on it while the pot boils. Getting impatient, Mr. Miacca tells Tommy to stick a leg out. Tommy sticks out a leg of the sofa which Mr. Miacca chops off and puts in the pot. While Mr. Miacca looks for his wife, Tommy runs home.

"The Green Ribbon," pp. 62-63, is a classic story in which a girl named Jenny and a boy named Alfred like each other. Jenny is like other girls except for the green ribbon she wears around her neck. Every time Alfred asks her why she wears the ribbon, Jenny says it isn't important and she'll tell him when the right time comes. They marry, they enjoy a happy life, and then, on her deathbed, Jenny lets Alfred untie the ribbon—and her head falls off.

Polacco, Patricia. **Picnic at Mudsock Meadow.** Illus. by author. New York: G. P. Putnam's Sons, 1992.

William fails to impress Hester at the annual Halloween picnic until he decides to do something daring. The picnic at Mudsock Meadow isn't far from the marsh, Quicksand Bottoms, which most people fear. Legend says the eerie lights that come out of the swamp at night are the ghost of Titus Dinworthy. William thinks the lights are caused by swamp gas.

During the picnic William hears a scream and sees a strange light coming from the swamp. Everyone except William runs away thinking it's Titus's ghost coming to get them. William runs to the light, leaps in the air, and lands in the slimy, gooey glowing gas, mud, and swamp water. The light goes out and William emerges wet, slimy, muddy, and glowing eerily. Everyone decides that William was brave and that he proved that the glow is caused by swamp gas. Now William is Hester's hero.

This original story is complemented by deep, rich watercolors that convey a sense of action and capture the expressiveness of the characters.

Polacco, Patricia. **Some Birthday!** Illus. by author. New York: Simon & Schuster, 1991.

The text is smoothly and swiftly paced and makes you want to know what will happen next. Polacco's warm and action-packed illustrations grab and hold the reader.

Patricia is scared and excited when, on her birthday, her father announces they're going to Clay Pit to photograph the monster at Clay Pit Bottoms. That night Patricia, her brother, cousins, and father go to the edge of the black, cold, deep water. Patricia's father describes the monster as ugly, mean, and slimy. He puts smelly cheese out to attract the monster. Soon they see something big in the water. Father says to run if it comes after them. The children hear snarling and growling and something big and awful smelling comes out of the water. The children scream and run home.

When Father returns later, he is soaking wet. He says the monster was a floating log and that he fell in the water when some bloodhounds found the cheese and fought over it. The mystery remains, and the children still wonder if there is a monster.

Powling, Chris. "The Oddment," pp. 31-37, in **Faces in the Dark: A Book of Scary Stories.** Comp. by Chris Powling. Illus. by Peter Bailey. New York: Kingfisher, 1994.

This unique, finely crafted, unsettling story is best shared with children in the upper end of the target age group.

A young boy has an "oddment," a ragged, soft, faded cloth that he carries with him. When he outgrows it he forgets it, but it always turns up in his bed in the morning. The oddment plays tricks on him, too. Finally the boy writes about the oddment for a school assignment. When the teacher suggests that the ending to the story could be that he mails the "oddment" to the other side of the world, the boy decides to really mail it—to Australia.

Three years later the boy receives a puppy, Spike, who always brings him treasures. One day he brings the boy a twisty, crusty piece of cloth, the boy's "oddment."

Riggio, Anita, reteller. **Beware the Brindlebeast.** Illus. by author. Honesdale, PA: Boyds Mills Press, 1994.

Birdie, a cheerful but poor old woman, does chores for the housewives of the village. They always urge her to leave for her home outside the village before dark because they fear the Dread Brindlebeast, who roams at night and changes into awful forms. On All Hallow's Eve, Birdie is hurrying home when she comes across a black kettle full of gold pieces. Birdie drags it toward her home, but when she glances at it the pot is now full of apples. Birdie continues and the apples become a pumpkin, then a jack-o'-lantern, and finally a huge monster, the Dread Brindlebeast. Birdie isn't afraid and simply remarks that the beast provided fun on her walk home.

Once in her house Birdie looks back and instead of a beast there's a little old fellow whom she invites in. They share a fine time talking and eating and he visits her often, providing food and wood. The villagers are still afraid of the Brindlebeast, but Birdie says nothing.

Oil paintings in fiery colors, some deep and dark, enhance this tale. The monster is frightening with its huge eyes, horns, and claws.

San Souci, Robert D. **The Hobyahs.** Illus. by Alexi Natchev. New York: Delacorte Press, 1994.

San Souci's telling of this spooky traditional tale begs to be read aloud. The refrains are musical and sensory. The illustrations have a European flavor, and the characters have appropriately exaggerated features and huge eyes.

A little orphan girl lives with an elderly woman and man in a house made of hemp stalks at the edge of a forest. The house is guarded by the man's five dogs: Turpie, Topie, Tippy, Tarry, and Tenny. Deep in the woods live the Hobyahs, furry creatures with pointed ears, sharp teeth, long tails, and claws. Each night the Hobyahs plot against the family, and each night one of the man's dogs barks loudest until the Hobyahs flee. Each morning the dog that barked the loudest is sent away. Finally, the man, woman, and girl are alone in the house, and the Hobyahs come, eat the couple, and take the girl to their cave in a bag.

The man's five faithful dogs hear the girl crying and hide in the bag in her place. When the Hobyahs open the bag the dogs gobble them. The girl and the five dogs build a new house and live happily ever after.

Torrence, Jackie. "The Golden Arm," pp. 134-35, in **Ready-to-Tell Tales: Sure-Fire Stories from America's Favorite Storytellers.** Ed. by David Holt and Bill Mooney. Little Rock, AK: August House, 1994.

I had the honor and pleasure of hearing and watching Jackie Torrence tell this tale. It was an incredible and unforgettable experience.

Every night a woman rubs her left arm and hand with a cloth because they are made of solid gold. She asks her husband to promise to bury her with her golden arm when she dies. When the woman dies, her husband decides he can use the golden arm to buy a new house, clothes, a wagon, and horses. He cuts off the arm and buries his wife without it.

The next night the wind is blowing hard, and the husband hears a voice asking who has her golden arm. The man thinks it's his imagination until he hears the voice again and closer, at the door. The man locks the door, takes the arm, and hides in the dark closet with it. The wind blows harder, and the door opens by itself. The man hears a voice coming across the room, and then the ghost of his wife grabs the golden arm and leaps out the window.

Yep, Laurence. **The Man Who Tricked a Ghost.** Illus. by Isadore Seltzer. New York: Bridgewater Books, 1993.

This is a longer version of the Chinese folktale "Ah Schung Catches a Ghost." (See p. 209.) The bold, realistically detailed full-page paintings are rich and exciting.

A brave man named Sung is not afraid of anything. One night he meets a ghost, a fierce warrior, on a dark and deserted road. Sung convinces the ghost that he, too, is a ghost. The warrior ghost reveals that he's going to Courtesy Town to teach Sung, a man who isn't afraid of ghosts, a lesson. The ghost says he'll kill Sung if he doesn't scare.

Sung finds out what the ghost plans to do to Sung and then tricks the ghost into telling him what ghosts are afraid of—human spit. Once a ghost is spat upon, it can't change its shape. Sung manages to lift the ghost and take him to the temple to have the priest destroy him. The ghost turns itself into a sheep, and Sung quickly spits on it so it remains a sheep.

Young, Richard, and Judy Dockrey Young. "Rap . . . Rap . . . Rap!" pp. 31-32, in **Favorite Scary Stories of American Children.** Little Rock, AK: August House, 1990.

In this wonderful version of a traditional tale, suspense is built effectively. The story is short enough for you to memorize and tell.

Shylock Bones, the greatest ghost detective, is called in by a lady who thinks her house is haunted. When Shylock Bones hears a rapping sound, he makes a thorough search of the woman's home: the basement, under the bed, in closets, and then in the attic. Tension builds as they get closer and closer to the sound, until they open drawer after drawer in an old chest of drawers and find—a sheet of wrapping paper.

Young, Richard, and Judy Dockrey Young. "Red Velvet Ribbon," pp. 61-63, in **Favorite Scary Stories of American Children.** Little Rock, AK: August House, 1990.

This short version of a traditional tale is more startling because of its brevity. When a lady who wears a red velvet ribbon around her neck marries a rich man, she won't let him touch the ribbon. When their child is a year old and the wife is napping, her husband gently removes the ribbon. The wife's head rolls off the bed and falls to the floor.

Young, Richard, and Judy Dockrey Young. "She's Got Me!" pp. 37-39, in **Favorite Scary Stories of American Children.** Little Rock, AK: August House, 1990.

A sassy girl and a polite girl are talking about an elderly woman who was buried that day. The sassy gal declares that the woman was a witch and she'd just as soon spit on and stick a fork in the witch's grave. When she arrives at the graveyard, long shadows fall on the pile of dirt on the grave. The girl spits on it, then feels something grab the hem of her dress. It pulls at her and looks like the bones of a hand. The sassy girl thinks the dead woman grabbed her, and she faints.

The polite girl hears the sassy girl's scream and with her father and brothers goes to the graveyard. The sassy girl is held down by her own fork. When they lift her she awakens.

Booktalks

Irving, Washington. "The Legend of Sleepy Hollow," retold by Della Rowland, pp. 24-36, in **Spooky Stories for a Dark and Stormy Night.** Comp. by Alice Low. Illus. by Gahan Wilson. New York: Byron Preiss Visual Publications, 1994.

This lengthy but excellent retelling of a classic tale uses contemporary language.

Ichabod Crane, a schoolmaster who is in love with Katrina Van Tassel, likes to tell and read ghost stories. Brom Bones, a huge man and a hero, loves Katrina and enjoys playing tricks on Ichabod. One evening Ichabod is last to leave a party at Katrina's house where ghost stories were told, especially about the local "Headless Horseman." Ichabod lingered to ask Katrina to marry him, but she refused.

Ichabod rides his pokey horse Gunpowder through the woods at midnight. He encounters the headless horseman, who throws his head at Ichabod. It hits Ichabod, and he falls from his horse. The next day there is no sign of Ichabod, only his horse, hat, and a shattered pumpkin.

Brom Bones marries Katrina. Often the story of Ichabod is told, and Brom always laughs at the part about the pumpkin.

Schwartz, Alvin, reteller. **In a Dark, Dark Room and Other Scary Stories.** Illus. by Dirk Zimmer. New York: Harper & Row, 1984.

This title is part of the I Can Read Book series, and the seven short stories are meant for children to read to themselves. Scary yet amusing pen-and-ink illustrations are interspersed throughout the book.

Children will enjoy the traditional tales "The Green Ribbon"; "The Teeth," in which a boy meets three men who have progressively larger teeth; the chant "In a Dark, Dark Room"; and the short song "The Ghost of John."

Wolkstein, Diane, reteller. **The Legend of Sleepy Hollow: Based on the Story by Washington Irving.** Illus. by R. W. Alley. New York: William Morrow, 1987.

Wolkstein's telling of this classic tale is finely crafted. Ichabod is portrayed as ridiculous and pitiful. Wolkstein carefully underscores the clues in this mystery in the jokes Brom Bones plays and in Ichabod's love of scary stories. The chase scene between the Headless Horseman and Ichabod Crane in the woods is particularly frightening. Alley's illustrations, done in watercolors, black ink lines, and cross-hatching, are expressive and almost surreal.

Poetry

Brown, Marc, comp. **Scared Silly! A Book for the Brave.** Illus. by author. Boston: Little, Brown, 1994.

Here Brown's trademark illustrations are scary yet humorous.

"What's That?" by Florence Parry Heide, p. 10, is about a horrible creature with seven slimy eyes that is creeping into the narrator's room.

"Absolutely Nothing," by Florence Parry Heide, p. 11, relates a boy's attempts to convince his parents that a dinosaur lives under his bed.

"Deep Beneath the Dark, Dark Sea," by Marc Brown, pp. 12-16, builds a great sense of anticipation as a young diver goes into the deep ocean to an old shipwreck where he has several frightening encounters.

"Witches Four," by Marc Brown, pp. 18-19, tells of some witches so creepy they even brush their teeth with spider paste.

"Witches' Menu," by Sonja Nikolay, p. 23, explains the many ways witches cook lizard.

"The Wendigo," by Ogden Nash, p. 28, is about a scary creature with slithery tentacles and blubbery lips.

"Monster Stew," by Judith Kinter, p. 31, reveals this recipe.

"One Hungry Monster," by Susan Heyboer O'Keefe, pp. 32-37, is actually about 10 monsters a young girl must get rid of.

"The Troll," by Jack Prelutsky, p. 38, is about a creepy creature who likes to grind and swallow people.

Heide, Florence Parry. "Beware of Rubber Bands," in **Grim and Ghastly Goings-On.** Illus. by Victoria Chess. New York: Lothrop, Lee & Shepard, 1992.

Chess's sinister illustration perfectly matches this creepy poem that takes a common, seemingly benign object and turns it into something scary.

The narrator warns that rubber bands were once worms and late at night they silently creep, ooze, and slither over you while you're in bed.

Monfried, Lucia, comp. **Diane Goode's Book of Scary Stories and Songs.** Illus. by Diane Goode. New York: Dutton Children's Books, 1994.

This outstanding collection also includes several scary poems.

"Someone," p. 20, tells how someone is knocking at the door, but the narrator sees no one.

"No One," p. 21, is a scary poem in which the narrator wonders who blew out the candle in the room.

"The Gobble-uns'll Git You Ef You Don't Watch Out!" by James Whitcomb Riley, p. 52, is a favorite with children.

"The Ghost of John," p. 53, is a short poem the children can learn and recite with you.

Prelutsky, Jack. **The Dragons Are Singing Tonight.** Illus. by Peter Sis. New York: Greenwillow, 1993.

Introduce children to a variety of dragons in this fine collection of original poems. There are nasty dragons, a girl with a dozen dragons, a thunder dragon, and a sick dragon who needs turpentine, phosphorus, and gasoline. Peter Sis's illustrations are colorful, lively, and imaginative.

Viorst, Judith. "That Old Haunted House," p. 53, in **Sad Underwear and Other Complications: More Poems for Children and Their Parents.** Illus. by Richard Hull. New York: Atheneum Books for Young Readers, 1995.

The child who is narrating this poem describes a terrifying, eerie, haunted house, and then says she or he would visit it again.

Songs

Cohn, Amy L., comp. "The Ghost of Tom," p. 330, in **From Sea to Shining Sea: A Treasury of American Folklore and Folk Songs.** Illus. by 11 Caldecott Medal and four Caldecott Honor Book artists. New York: Scholastic, 1993.

If children don't know this scary song, they'll learn it quickly because it's so short, and they'll want to sing it repeatedly.

Monfried, Lucia, comp. "A Ghostly Ballad," p. 36, and "The Worms Crawl In," p. 37, in **Diane Goode's Book of Scary Stories and Songs.** Illus. by Diane Goode. New York: Dutton Children's Books, 1994.

The children will enjoy both of these songs, and they'll probably already know the latter.

Demonstration/Participation Activities

Bauer, Caroline Feller, ed. "Spider on the Floor," pp. 48-49, in **Halloween: Stories and Poems.** Illus. by Peter Sis. New York: J. B. Lippincott, 1989.

Write this poem on a chalkboard or large piece of paper and do it in the form of a chant or echo verse with the children.

Brown, Marc, comp. **Scared Silly! A Book for the Brave.** Illus. by author. Boston: Little, Brown, 1994.

Brown has several activities that will appeal to a wide age range.

"Spooky Riddles," pp. 26-27. Share these riddles with the children. Be prepared to hear them groan (that's part of the fun).

"A Magic Chant," by Bobbi Katz, p. 27. Put the chant on a chalkboard or sheet of paper and invite the children to learn and recite it with you. The chant prepares them for anything that scares them. The words in the chant are fun to say.

"How to Scare Your Friends," p. 47. You'll need to prepare the items for this activity ahead of time. You can blindfold the children, ask them to shut their eyes, or do this in the dark. Combine food items and the children's imaginations to make them think they're handling body parts. For example, use peeled grapes for eyeballs. Brown's suggestions are the best I've seen.

Burr, Daniella. "The Goblin Effect," p. 19, and "The Great Mummy Wrap," p. 74, in **Don't Just Sit There! 50 Ways to Have a Nickelodeon Day.** Illus. by Steve Henry. New York: Grosset & Dunlap, 1992.

"The Goblin Effect" is a unique and fun activity in which children learn how to make and project a scary figure on a wall. Few materials are needed, and it's very easy to do.

For the second activity, you just need lots of space, rolls of toilet paper, and, for each team, one child who's willing to be wrapped like a mummy.

Cole, Joanna, and Stephanie Calmenson, comps. "Jokes and Riddles," pp. 106-121, in **The Scary Book.** Illus. by Dirk Zimmer. New York: Morrow Junior Books, 1991.

Share some of these varied riddles with the children. They are listed under a variety of headings and include riddles about ghosts, mummies, monsters, vampires, witches, and skeletons.

Cole, Joanna, and Stephanie Calmenson, comps. "Spooky Tongue Twisters," pp. 100-101, in **The Scary Book.** Illus. by Dirk Zimmer. New York: Morrow Junior Books, 1991.

These tongue twisters are challenging and fun. Write them on a chalkboard or large piece of paper and invite the children to try them.

Leach, Maria. "Dead Man Game," pp. 96-97, in **The Scary Book.** Comp. by Joanna Cole and Stephanie Calmenson. Illus. by Chris Demarest. New York: Morrow Junior Books, 1991.

In this classic game, objects that you say are body parts are passed from child to child in the dark. Leach's suggestions, combined with Marc Brown's, (see pp. 222 and above) make for a perfect version of this activity.

Morris, Ting, and Neil Morris. "Halloween Horrors," p. 16, and "Apple Horrors," p. 17, in **No-Cook Cooking.** Illus. by Ruth Levy. New York: Franklin Watts, 1994.

Prepare the small cakes for "Halloween Horrors" before the program. During the program the children can make horror faces on the cakes using the ideas the authors provide.

For "Apple Horrors," put the apples on skewers and prepare the icing before the program. During the activity, let the children ice and decorate their apples. The authors suggest many items to use.

Sitarz, Paula Gaj. "Skeleton Hangman."

Preparation before the program: Draw a skeleton or photocopy one from a book. Mount the picture on a piece of felt. Cut the skeleton into separate pieces: head, torso, arms, and legs. Select several book titles from the program for the children to guess. On a chalkboard, posterboard, or large piece of paper on an easel, place a dash for each letter in the title and slashes between words.

During the program: Invite the youngsters to guess letters in the titles one at a time. For each incorrect letter, place a piece of the skeleton on a feltboard. If the skeleton isn't assembled before the children guess the book title, they win. You win if the skeleton is put together before the youngsters guess the title. Keep the activity light and noncompetitive. Continue to play as long as the children are interested.

Warner, Penny. "Mummy Wrap," pp. 98-99, in **Kids' Party Games and Activities: Hundreds of Exciting Things to Do at Parties for Kids 2-12.** Illus. by Kathy Rogers. Deephaven, MN: Meadowbrook Press, 1993.

Warner includes the traditional and alternative ways to play this game. She also includes "Trouble-Shooting Tips."

Chapter 18

Tall Tales

Read Alouds

Arnold, Caroline. **The Terrible Hodag.** Illus. by Lambert Davis. New
    York: Harcourt Brace Jovanovich, 1989.
    This tale is based on stories the author heard at summer campfires in the
north woods of Wisconsin. The first Hodag stories were told in logging camps
over 100 years ago. Arnold's text has an undercurrent of scariness and fear.
The illustrations blend realistic details with other-worldly elements. The loggers' faces are eerily similar to each other. The boss man is sinister-looking
with his hat slung low over his eyes, small spiky-looking teeth, a signet ring
with a dollar sign on it, and a cigar he uses to point.
    In the far north woods the finest lumberjack, Ole Swenson, and the other
lumberjacks cut trees all day, but not at night. They fear the terrible Hodag, of
whom they've seen signs—huge footsteps and demolished clearings and bushes.
Then the mean and greedy boss says he wants the trees on the entire far hillside
cut or the men won't get paid. To accomplish this they must work at night, but
no one will go. Ole Swenson is out when darkness descends that night, and he
meets the Hodag with its giant teeth. But the Hodag is not hurtful. It doesn't
like the boss and is willing to help the lumberjacks. The Hodag uses its strong
tail to cut down all the trees. Ole Swenson doesn't tell the men who helped him.
    The boss still won't pay the men. Now he wants all the logs delivered to
the sawmill by Friday. Ole Swenson manages to accomplish this with the help
of the Hodag. Finally, Swenson tells the lumberjacks the Hodag has been
helping them. The lumberjacks ultimately decide not to be afraid of the Hodag.
Again the boss says he won't pay the men, but when he sees the Hodag, he's so
scared he drops the money bags and flees.

Cohen, Caron Lee. **Sally Ann Thunder Ann Whirlwind Crockett.**
    Illus. by Ariane Dewey. New York: Greenwillow Books, 1985.
    A perfect read-aloud, this book is also excellent for a beginning reader.
The illustrations are playful—full of action and humor. They are done with
simple lines in shades of brown, green, blue-gray, and yellow.
    Legend says that Sally Ann lived near the Mississippi River with her
husband Davy Crockett. She's a tough woman—wears a beehive for a bonnet,
can outclaw a mountain lion, and runs like a fox. Mike Fink also lives along the
Mississippi, and he's always looking for a fight. He can beat anyone except Davy
Crockett. Mike Fink likes to brag about his abilities, and one day Davy Crockett
tells Mike that he can't scare Sally Ann. Mike accepts the bet, but no matter
what he does he can't scare Sally Ann. She, however, flattens Mike Fink and
one night scares his teeth loose.

Day, David. **The Walking Catfish.** Illus. by Mark Entwisle. New York:
    Macmillan, 1991.
    The illustrations are vivid, stunning watercolors, fluid and expressive.
Illustrator Entwisle captures well the many moods of this story.
    The narrator of this tale is Lee Roy Jones. He tells the story of his friend
Hank Blizzard, who was the best teller of lies in Archie's Bottom. Hank and
Lee Roy were part of the River Rat Gang. They were pitted against the Road
Dog Gang in the Big Three Day Lie-Off. Woody Gunther is the judge of the
contest. The first day Woody listens to tales of mosquitoes so big they carry off

cattle and children, and stories of windstorms so fierce they blow the feathers off of chickens. After the first day a draw is declared.

At the end of the second day of the contest the Road Dogs are in the lead. That's when Hank tells his whopper of a tale. He describes a catfish that can walk out of the river and swallow several fishermen. The Road Dogs call Hank a liar, and now Hank has to prove his story—and he does. The Road Dogs lose points. But the Road Dogs aren't impressed, so Hank tells Tex, one of the Road Dogs, to meet him at the dock at dawn to see the monster catfish. What happens next is zany and confusing. When it's over, no one is sure what is true and what isn't.

The language in this story is rich and pleasing. For example, lies are described as "a heap of scorchin' hot lies that the paint is blistering on the store walls. . . ."

Day, Edward C. **John Tabor's Ride.** Illus. by Dirk Zimmer. New York: Alfred A. Knopf, 1989.

The author notes that there was a harpooner named John Tabor who, about 150 years ago, sailed from New Bedford, Massachusetts, on a whaling ship and spent 20 years at sea. On that voyage a young college graduate, who went as a seaman, kept a journal of his experiences. This story is based on the real John Tabor's yarns.

This is an enjoyable, fun adventure tale told with language that has a wonderful cadence and rhythm. Zimmer's distinctive illustrations are rendered in deep, rich color, pen-and-ink outlines, and cross-hatching. He captures well the atmosphere of each location in the story. The characters are caricatures, all with individualized and expressive faces. John Tabor is depicted with bright red hair and a long nose. The old man has a long beard (that looks like a stretched Brillo pad), pointy teeth, and piercing eyes.

John Tabor is a swaggering young sailor who's never been far from home or worked much. John complains constantly about everything. One night, while on deck, John sees a small man over 100 years old who asks John what kind of sailor he is. When John brags that he's a good whaling man, the old man, Old Tar Beard, rows John to a whale and makes John get on the whale's back with him. They speed to the Cape of Good Hope and into the South Atlantic Ocean, where the seas get rough. Finally, they glide through Taborstown's Main Street, scattering people until they bump against the town pump. John's joy at returning home is short-lived when Old Tar Beard puts John back on the whale and they continue their wide-ranging travels around the world. When they ultimately run ashore, John is flung off and the whale is gone. John pleads to return to his whaling ship. Old Tar Beard tells John if he wants to go whaling to do it and not complain—or Tar Beard will return. John becomes such a jolly whaler other sailors want to sail with him.

Fleischman, Sid. "February," from **McBroom's Almanac,** pp. 173-75, in **The Random House Book of Humor for Children.** Comp. by Pamela Pollack. Illus. by Paul O. Zelinsky. New York: Random House, 1988.

Here's a wacky and fun tall tale, or "whopper," told by Josh McBroom, owner of an amazing one-acre farm. Josh declares he's invented air conditioning. He calls it Winter Extract, and February is the last month you can get a supply of it.

When the wind outside has frozen solid, Josh and his 11 children saw chunks of frozen wind and store it in the icehouse. The McBroom's miserly neighbor Heck Jones comes by and says someone stole his left sock off the clothesline—his best black sock that had only three holes. Heck goes off and wears one sock all winter and into the summer.

When the hot summer days come, the McBrooms put a chunk of Winter Extract in their parlor. It thaws, generates a cool breeze, and then blows hard. One hot night when the McBrooms place another chunk of Winter Extract in the room and its breeze blows, Heck Jone's sock shoots across the room. The sock blows out the window and slips onto Heck's bare foot while he lies asleep in a hammock.

Helldorfer, M. C. **Moon Trouble.** Illus. by Jonathan Hunt. New York: Bradbury Press, 1994.

There's a pleasing rhythm to the dialogue and lots of action conveyed in the text and the illustrations. The artwork also captures the humor and incredible nature of the events that occur.

The first-person narrator sweeps you immediately into this tale set in the East, where people think Paul Bunyan is only a story—until the night the moon splashes into the river.

The Klank family can't determine what has fallen in the water until their neighbor Turpentine says it's the moon. The Klanks and their neighbors try about 100 ways to get the moon back in the sky, but all fail. Turpentine says they'll have to send for Paul Bunyan. Paul comes with his big blue ox Babe. Their first two attempts fail. Then Paul Bunyan goes to the North Pole, hangs on to the earth's axis, swings it until everything is upside-down and the moon rolls out of the river and into the sky. Paul then turns the earth right side up.

Hunter, C. W., reteller. **The Green Gourd: A North Carolina Folktale.** Illus. by Tony Griego. New York: G. P. Putnam's Sons, 1992.

This fast-paced, smoothly flowing tale with its pleasing rhythm and savory language is complemented by cartoonlike, action-packed, bright watercolors.

Up a holler and across a stream an old woman needs a new gourd dipper. Even though she knows if you pick a gourd before it's ripe it'll be bewitched, she needs a dipper, so she picks one of her unripe gourds. No sooner does she get the gourd home than it rolls around and jumps on everything.

The woman runs away with the gourd chasing her. A panther and fox offer to help, but they fail. The woman is still running with the gourd chasing her when a little boy offers her refuge in his house. Swiftly, the boy manages to jump on the gourd and squash it.

Isaacs, Anne. **Swamp Angel.** Illus. by Paul O. Zelinsky. New York: Dutton Children's Books, 1994.

This wonderful, original, lively tale is complemented by illustrations in an American primitive style. In dark hues, the illustrations are full of wit and a sense of action.

Young listeners will meet Angelica Longrider, born taller than her mother in 1815, able to build a log cabin at age two, and able to lift wagons out of a swamp for some pioneers when she's 12 years old. Angel becomes the greatest woodswoman in Tennessee. The people in Tennessee are preyed upon by

Thundering Tarnation, a thieving, strong, and scary bear. Many try to kill him, but all fail. Soon only Angel is left to tackle the bear. Everyone laughs, but Swamp Angel never gives up. She uses a tornado to bring the bear back after she tosses him in the air. They wrestle so much and stir up such dust the hills are still called the Great Smoky Mountains. They fight for three days and nights. By the fourth day they're wrestling in a lake. They even tussle in their sleep. Finally Swamp Angel is victorious.

Kellogg, Steven. **Johnny Appleseed.** Illus. by author. New York: Scholastic, 1988.

Steven Kellogg has done an excellent job of integrating the story of the legendary Johnny Appleseed and the real man John Chapman. He captures the human qualities of John the nature lover, the man who preceded the pioneers into the wilderness and prepared and planted apple orchards. Kellogg also provides much humor in relating the exaggerated tales that were told about Johnny Appleseed even during his lifetime. Children will sit enthralled as they hear about and see the wild tree-cutting contest Johnny had with a band of wild woodsmen. The accompanying double-page illustration is colorful, vivid, expressive, and full of action and detail.

Kellogg, Steven. **Mike Fink.** Illus. by author. New York: Morrow Junior Books, 1992.

Steven Kellogg has rendered lavishly detailed, wild, and action-packed illustrations to complement his equally exaggerated and humorous telling of the exploits of the famous tall tale character Mike Fink. Mike was a runaway at age two who just couldn't be held down. He grew up on the frontier and always wanted to be a keelboatman. His nemesis is Jack Carpenter, who, in a wrestling match, sends Mike flying into the Rocky Mountains. There Mike practices wrestling with grizzly bears. Mike returns to beat Jack Carpenter in a wrestling match, and soon everyone wants to best Mike, especially on the Mississippi River, where he is king of the keelboatmen. Mike's final race is against Captain Blathersby and his newfangled steamboat. Guess who wins.

Kellogg, Steven. **Paul Bunyan.** Illus. by author. New York: William Morrow, 1984.

The illustrations are amusing, and they almost explode off the page. The text is fast-paced, humorous, and over the top. Paul Bunyan is such a huge baby that he can pull trees out of the ground by their roots. Not everyone likes the ruckus Paul causes, so Paul's parents anchor him in his cradle in the harbor. His cradle stirs up high waves, so Paul's family is forced to move with him to the backwoods.

Paul races with deer and wrestles with grizzlies. He finds an ox under blue snow who remains blue, and Paul names him Babe. Together they are tremendous at logging and decide to head west with the best lumbering crew. Along the way they have incredible adventures, including meeting the underground ogres the Gumberoos and digging the St. Lawrence River and the Great Lakes. Paul's ax falls from his shoulder at one time, gouging a trench that becomes the Grand Canyon.

Kellogg, Steven. **Pecos Bill.** Illus. by author. New York: William Morrow, 1986.

There is so much to see in Kellogg's trademark illustrations, which are full of energy, outrageousness, humor, detail, and vibrant color.

As his family heads west, Pecos Bill is yanked overboard by a Texas trout nibbling on his fishing line, and a coyote nabs Bill from the water. Adopted by the coyotes, Bill learns their ways and romps with them until a guy named Chuck tells Bill he's a man, a Texan. Chuck tells Bill about the Hell's Gulch Gang, whom he says would be okay if they became ranchers. Bill sets out and impresses the gang by wrestling a rattlesnake and squeezing it into a rope. The gang makes Bill their boss. Texas cattle are ornery, but Bill invents cattle roping. After the cowboys and cattle tangle, the Gang decides to be cowboys, and after Bill tames a wild white stallion named Lightning, they become ranchers. Pecos Bill also meets Slewfoot Sue, who is his equal in every way.

Kellogg, Steven, reteller. **Sally Ann Thunder Ann Whirlwind Crockett.** Illus. by author. New York: Morrow Junior Books, 1995.

A sure-fire hit, this "rip-roaring" tale tells the story of Davy Crockett's wife from her birth to her marriage and life with the legendary Davy. The episodes are smoothly connected in a chronological story "life-line." The language is rich and savory. Kellogg's trademark full-color illustrations are humorous, raucous, detailed, action-packed, and expressive.

The saga begins about 200 years ago when the infant Sally dazzles her nine brothers by running to the top of a mountain and back while they're just starting their climb. By age one Sally beats the fastest runners in the state, and at age four she can flip the strongest arm wrestlers.

Ready for new challenges, Sally heads for the frontier when she's eight. For several years she lives with different animals and learns their habits. One winter it's so cold she hibernates near a warm grizzly. When the bear awakens ready to eat her, Sally Ann stuns him with her bright grin.

Eventually Sally Ann gets tired of living alone and one day she finds a man, asleep, his head stuck in a tree, with two eagles yanking out his hair for their nests. Sally Ann rescues and falls in love with the man, Davy Crockett, the most famous woodsman in the country.

When Davy mistakenly runs for Congress and wins, Sally Ann is left home alone while Davy goes to Washington, D.C. Sally has alligator troubles, but she kicks up a tornado and blows the gators away. When Davy returns and hears what Sally Ann did, he's so proud he brags about it. Mike Fink, a champion wrestler of people and alligators, doesn't believe the story.

Mike Fink decides to scare Sally Ann into revealing the story is a lie. He hides in an alligator hide. When Sally Ann sees the "alligator" she whips it until Mike Fink sails into the sky.

Kesey, Ken. **Little Tricker the Squirrel Meets Big Double the Bear.** Illus. by Barry Moser. New York: Viking, 1990.

The illustrations, full-color watercolors, capture the character of the animals in this tale perfectly: rabbit with a carrot in his ear, Sally Snipsister the Marten in her pink wrap and hands on hips, and Tricker the squirrel with huge eyes and buck teeth.

Kesey's text zips along in true story-telling style, with tall-tale sound and rhythm. For example, Kesey writes, "What in the name of sixty cyclones was that?" Author Kesey's words are precise, colorful, and perfect.

Big Double the bear eats what he wants, when he wants. He has "teeth . . . like stalactites in a cavern," and he wrecks havoc when he comes to Topple's Bottom. The animals try to escape Big Double. Charlie Charles the Woodchuck runs, Longrellers the Rabbit runs and jumps, but both are eaten. Each animal does what the one before did and adds one more maneuver, but all are eaten, except Tricker. Tricker, in a fabulous illustration of him wearing a baseball cap with a turtleneck, has been watching the action, and he thinks of a perfect way to outsmart Big Double and free his friends from inside Big Double.

Kroll, Steven. **Big Jeremy.** Illus. by Donald Carrick. New York: Holiday House, 1989.

Meet Jeremy, a friendly giant, who is helpful to his neighbors, the Terisons. He can plow their fields with a giant hoe in half an hour and build a cider mill in half a day. All is well until one summer evening Jeremy blows out the fire blazing from the Terisons' home but also blows some of the family out of sight. In his attempt to find the family, Jeremy puts his foot through the bridge. No one can cross the river, so Jeremy stretches himself across the water. Everyone's feet tickle his back and he loses his grip and they fall in the water. Jeremy gets down on himself, decides he is no longer a help, and settles on a mountaintop. Almost a year goes by when a man hikes up the mountain. It's Elwood Terison, and is he glad to find Jeremy. They need his help. A storm destroyed the farm, and all the relatives had to go to work in the city. Jeremy does return and helps restore the farm and return all the relatives to live there again.

Lester, Julius. **John Henry.** Illus. by Jerry Pinkney. New York: Dial Books for Young Readers, 1994.

This special, very poetic telling of the legend of John Henry is complemented perfectly by Jerry Pinkney's exquisite large-format, full-color artwork. Pinkney uses deep, dark colors and splashes of bright, vivid tones to create soft yet strong paintings. He conveys well John Henry's strength.

This is a refreshing story about the tremendously strong John Henry, who could chop an acre of trees after lunch and crush a huge boulder with his hammers. Henry works building the Chesapeake and Ohio Railroad through West Virginia. When the steam drill is invented, John Henry pits himself against it with a 20-pound hammer in each hand. They start on each side of the mountain to see who will get to the middle first. Henry wins, but dies. The story doesn't seem sad—it's so rich with John Henry's spirit and love of life.

McKissack, Patricia C. **A Million Fish . . . More or Less.** Illus. by Dena Schutzer. New York: Alfred A. Knopf, 1992.

McKissack's tale is rich and clever. The language is colorful, with a slow, easy style and cadence and expressive phrases. The artwork, in thick, bright paint, is splashy and fluid. The characters' faces are larger-than-life and very animated.

It's early morning and young Hugh Thomas is fishing on Bayou Clapateaux when Papa-Daddy and Elder Abbajon row up. The men say the bayou is an odd place, and they swap some outlandish tales.

When the men leave, Hugh Thomas catches three small fish. In the next half hour Hugh Thomas catches a million more fish of all sizes. As he heads home, Hugh Thomas must give a load of fish to the alligator who blocks his way. Hugh Thomas is continuing on the swamp path when he's confronted by an army of raccoons. Hugh Thomas must beat Mosley, the lead raccoon, in a jump-roping contest (the rope is a 20-foot snake) just to keep half his remaining fish. Hugh Thomas passes Mossland Mansion and throws part of his remaining catch to the waterfowl as tradition dictates. Almost home, Hugh Thomas is tricked out of all but three of his fish by his neighbor's cat, Chantilly. Hugh Thomas finally arrives at Papa-Daddy and Elder Abbajon's houseboat. When they comment on his fine catch, Hugh Thomas says he had a million more. When they ask if it really was a million, Hugh Thomas smiles, winks, says it was, more or less, and then tells the men his tale. Children will wonder long after the story's told if Hugh Thomas was telling a tall tale or if the events really happened.

Nolen, Jerdine. **Harvey Potter's Balloon Farm.** Illus. by Mark Buehner. New York: Lothrop, Lee & Shepard, 1994.

The illustrations are full page, sometimes double page, exaggerated, and at times surreal. Bodies and features are drawn larger than life, and Buehner shows views of scenes and people from a variety of perspectives.

This is a delightful tale of Harvey Potter, who grows balloons (on stalks) on his farm. He grows balloons in colors ranging from Bloomin' Blue to Jelly-Bean Black and in many shapes, from clowns to monsters.

Everyone except Wheezle Mayfield likes the field of balloons, so Wheezle calls the government to check on it. The government men in their white coats, hats, and gloves see nothing wrong and go away.

The narrator, a young girl, is curious to know how the farm grows, so one night she hides and watches. Harvey uses a conjure stick. He rises in the air, dances and prances, whoops and hollers.

In the morning there are the growing balloons. Harvey lets the girl take some. No one ever bothers Harvey again, but one day the young girl sails away in a big balloon Harvey grows for her, and she becomes a balloon farmer by her own methods.

San Souci, Robert D., collector and reteller. "Bess Call," pp. 13-18, in **Cut from the Same Cloth: American Women of Myth, Legend, and Tall Tale.** Illus. by Brian Pinkney. New York: Philomel, 1993.

Joe Call, who lived in Essex County, New York, until he died in 1834, was reported to be the strongest man in America. It's said that he had a powerful sister, Bess. In this tale Joe Call is constantly challenged to wrestle. One morning a man arrives from England. He has come to wrestle Joe, but when he sees Joe holding up a plow he decides to hire a trainer. Once he feels stronger, the Britisher returns to wrestle Joe, but this time he sees Joe lifting an oxen, and he goes into training again. The next time the challenger returns Joe isn't there but his sister Bess is. Bess isn't feeling well, but she usually wrestles when Joe's away. The Britisher laughs, thinking Bess is joking. This infuriates her, so she agrees to wrestle and tosses the man into a ditch. He's seen riding away as fast as he can.

Shepard, Aaron. **The Legend of Lightning Larry.** Illus. by Toni Goffe. New York: Charles Scribner's Sons, 1993.

Shepard's story is clever, original, and appealing for all ages. Goffe's cartoon-like pen-and-ink and watercolor illustrations are exaggerated and funny.

Lightning Larry arrives in the town of Brimstone, heads for the Cotton-mouth Saloon, asks for a lemonade, and gets in a tangle with Crooked Curt, a rustler and thief, part of Evil-Eye McNeevil's gang that's been terrorizing the town. Guns are drawn, and Larry zaps—lightning, a little bolt that hits Curt's heart and makes him pleasant. Evil-Eye's men start shooting, but Larry hits three more with lightning bolts, and they apologize and clean the mess. Evil-Eye is steaming, and he plots more dastardly deeds, but Larry's lightning thwarts his plans. Finally, there's a showdown, but how can Larry defeat seven men at once? No problem. Those reformed outlaws have lightning bolts in their guns. Before you know it, everyone's hugging, dancing, and drinking lemonade.

One of the most amusing parts of this book is the list of outlaw names, e.g., Dreadful Dave, Sickening Sid, Moldy Mike, and Gruesome Gus.

Shepard, Aaron. **The Legend of Slappy Hooper: An American Tall Tale.** Illus. by Toni Goffe. New York: Charles Scribner's Sons, 1993.

Goffe's watercolors perfectly complement Shepard's text in their exuberance, expressiveness, exaggeration, and humor. Meet Slappy Hooper, the world's biggest, fastest, bestest sign painter. He's seven feet tall and paints so fast you never see a brushstroke. Trouble comes to Slappy because his pictures are too true to life. Slappy paints a billboard for Eagle Messenger Service, but the eagle flies off the billboard and scares everyone. When Mr. Ray Sunshine from Sunshine Travel Agency hires Slappy to paint a billboard showing a man and woman on the beach sunbathing, the picture is so realistic that the snow on the ground melts, and soon people are sitting in bathing suits under the sign. Mr. Sunshine is angry because no one has the need to travel in winter now. Slappy tries to improve the situation by making the sun on the billboard too hot for them but that starts a fire. When Slappy tries to undo that mess, he creates more problems.

Slappy has just decided to throw his paint kit into the river when an angel in paint-splattered overalls stops Slappy and tells him he's from the Heavenly Sign Company and the Boss has a job for Slappy—painting a rainbow on Wednesday. Slappy botches that job, too, but it leads to his dream job.

Thomassie, Tynia. **Feliciana Feydra LeRoux.** Illus. by Cat Bowman Smith. Boston: Little, Brown, 1995.

Enjoy this fresh, original tale full of crisp images, rhythmic and vivid language, and featuring a strong, independent female character. The illustrations are colorful, humorous, fluid, and expressive.

Feliciana Feydra is Grandpa Baby's absolute favorite, but he still won't let her go alligator hunting with him and the male members of the family. It's not because she's female; he thinks the alligator would find her too delicious and sweet.

Once the men leave, Feliciana sneaks out with her pecan baby doll and paddles through the swamp until she faces the alligator. Grandpa and the boys are nearby, and when Grandpa tries to lasso the alligator, he's yanked into the swamp. Feliciana jumps in, distracts the alligator, and wedges her pecan doll in its mouth. Grandpa gets back in the boat and they catch the alligator. When they return home grandma thinks their story is a tall tale.

Wright, Jill. **The Old Woman and the Willy Nilly Man.** Illus. by Glen Rounds. New York: G. P. Putnam's Sons, 1987.

Glen Rounds captures well the flavor of Jill Wright's tale. His light illustrations, outlined in thick black, are funny. The exaggerated features of the characters are priceless, especially of the Willy Nilly Man with his long scraggly beard down to his knees, full of spiders, lizards, grease, and junk.

The old woman is tired of her shoes dancing and singing every night. Desperate, she asks the scary Willy Nilly Man for help. He agrees once she offers to bring him blackberry jam. But the Willy Nilly Man lies to her. Those shoes jump on her feet and she can't stop dancing. In her anger she makes blackberry jam, but she includes spiderwebs, black ink, paste, and a cat tooth. When the Willy Nilly Man swallows it in one gulp he gets a tremendous bellyache. First he's mad, but then he laughs because no one has gotten the best of him before. He decides to visit the old woman, and he promises that her shoes won't dance anymore.

Booktalks

Dewey, Ariane. **Laffite the Pirate.** Illus. by author. New York: Greenwillow Books, 1985.

This is a short book in five chapters with illustrations that spill over the pages and capture the mood of the text. With its brief chapters and short sentences, this book is perfect to suggest to young readers.

Author Dewey presents both myths and stories based on fact about Laffite, the pirate who aided the United States in the War of 1812 and then returned to his life as a pirate. Youngsters will read how Laffite outwitted the English, rode out a huge storm, and landed in Texas. The story also relates how Laffite supposedly buried his treasure in several locations. People have searched for Laffite's riches, but the treasure is allegedly protected by ghosts.

Dewey, Ariane. **The Narrow Escapes of Davy Crockett.** Illus. by author. New York: Greenwillow Books, 1990.

Dewey recounts many of Davy Crockett's adventures, each following swiftly one after the other. The exaggeration starts when Davy is eight and can pull a rainbow out of the sky. Davy even tangles with a bear. Some time later he's rescued by Sally Ann Thunder Ann Whirlwind when eagles have started making a nest in his hair. When Sally Ann and Davy marry, the exploits continue. Davy has to save himself from the open jaws of a boa constrictor, tangle with a rattlesnake, ride a streak of lightning, and sit atop an alligator going down Niagara Falls.

Emberley, Barbara. **The Story of Paul Bunyan.** Illus. by Ed Emberley. New York: Half Moon Books, 1994.

Snippits of Paul Bunyan's life are put together in an interesting and seamless way. Emberley's text has the sound of someone sitting and telling a story in an easy style. The striking, original woodcuts in brown and blue are strong and hearty.

Readers are introduced to a time when America consisted of forests and there were many mighty loggers and lumberjacks. Here they meet the biggest and strongest of these, Paul Bunyan. The episodes of his life are so outrageous they hold the interest of youngsters. They'll hear how Paul combed his long beard with an old pine tree and was so strong he could drive stumps into the ground with his bare fists. They'll also learn how Paul dug the Mississippi River in one afternoon and was so fast he could outrun his shadow.

Fleischman, Sid. **McBroom and the Great Race.** Illus. by Walter
Lorraine. Boston: Little, Brown, 1980.

This is one of several well-written, humorous tall tales about honest Josh
McBroom and his lying neighbor Heck Jones. Heck is always scheming of a way to
get Josh's one acre of remarkably fertile farm land in exchange for his worthless,
barren land. This time Heck fakes a fall, claims his leg is broken, stays with the
McBrooms, and drives them crazy with his demands. Finally, in desperation the
McBrooms decide that Josh should challenge Heck to a foot race. Heck will only
race if the prize is Josh's farm. Heck schemes and declares he's going to race on a
speedy Wyoming jackalope. He insists that Josh said a race, not a foot race. Josh
will have to ride Gertrude, his giant chicken. It's a wild race, and Heck cheats
throughout it. The suspense is incredible, but Josh manages to win.

Suggest other Sid Fleischman books about McBroom, including
McBroom Tells a Lie and **McBroom Tells the Truth.** These fast-paced
books are outrageous, funny, and full of exaggeration.

Glass, Andrew. **Folks Call Me Appleseed John.** Illus. by author. New
York: A Doubleday Book for Young Readers/Delacorte Press, 1995.

In a somewhat literary text that is still full of action, the author conveys
a sense of Johnny Appleseed's personality, his courage, and his humor. The oil
paintings are fluid and impressionistic. Characters' faces are expressive, especially their eyes. The landscapes are particularly well done.

Johnny Appleseed relates what happened when his half-brother
Nathaniel came to live with Johnny on the French Creek in northwestern
Pennsylvania. In the telling Johnny reveals a lot about himself. He has a close
relationship with the animals and the Native Americans. He is hardy and can
sleep in a hollow log. He paddles down the half-frozen Allegheny River with his
hand.

Johnny worries about Nathaniel as he goes to meet him, but he needn't
have. Nathaniel is safe with members of the Seneca tribe, who saved his life
and taught him how to hunt.

Lindbergh, Reeve. **Johnny Appleseed.** Illus. by Kathy Jakobsen. Boston: Little, Brown, 1990.

Lindbergh has written a beautiful text in verse, with pleasing rhythm.
His writing is descriptive and moving. Jakobsen's illustrations are detailed,
lively folk-art paintings. They are rich in brilliant colors and capture well the
landscape of the places the legendary character Johnny Appleseed visited.

Manes, Stephen. **Some of the Adventures of Rhode Island Red.**
Illus. by William Joyce. New York: J. B. Lippincott, 1990.

The unique tale of an original character, this story follows a little hero
with red hair who eats like a chicken, cock-a-doodle-doos, eats corn, and is
mighty strong. It isn't until well into the book that the young reader will learn
that Rhode Island Red, found in a farmyard and raised by Rhody the chicken,
is actually the lost child of Captain Sanford of Providence, Rhode Island. His
ability to reason and speak like a human yet communicate and relate to
chickens allows him to help some skinny chickens who are fed little by their
owner. Red also outwits a band of fox eager to eat the chickens. His further
travels result in many other adventures that are recounted in this book.

Osborne, Mary Pope. **American Tall Tales.** Illus. by Michael McCurdy.
New York: Alfred A. Knopf, 1991.

This collection of tall tales includes stories about Sally Ann Thunder Ann
Whirlwind, Johnny Appleseed, Stormalong, Mose, Febold Feboldson, Pecos
Bill, and John Henry. Especially worth recommending to young readers are
"Davy Crockett" and "Paul Bunyan." All of the stories are composites that
combine information from many sources. A bibliography for each hero is
included. The wood engravings add a nice touch.

Sanfield, Steve. **A Natural Man: The True Story of John Henry.**
Illus. by Peter J. Thornton. Boston: David R. Godine, 1986.

In this extremely well-written and illustrated book on the life of John
Henry, the text is poetic, expressive, and imbued with vivid imagery. The
black-and-white muted illustrations are moving. Author Sanfield not only
captures the legendary nature of John Henry, he captures his humanity.

Sanfield writes about John Henry's exploits. He relates, for example, how
a train was approaching where the track hadn't finished being laid, but John
Henry completed the job in time for the train to pass. Children will also read
how Henry traveled everywhere to drive steel with his wife Polly Ann and their
child. If John Henry couldn't do the job, Polly Ann did it.

Sis, Peter. **A Small Tall Tale from the Far Far North.** Illus. by
author. New York: Alfred A. Knopf, 1993.

The hero of this story may or may not have existed. He was a folk hero in
Czechoslovakia. Legend says that Jan Welzl made a dangerous journey from
central Europe to the Arctic regions in the late 1800s. He traveled by horse,
reindeer, and sled from a life of misery to a land of snow, ice, and great space.
Jan finds a mountain of gold to which he and everything else stick. Jan is
rescued by Eskimo hunters and nursed to health. They become friends, and Jan
learns how to survive in the harsh conditions. He in turn tries to help the
Eskimos. When gold diggers with guns come, Jan knows how to get them to
leave the Eskimos in peace. He'll show them the way to the golden mountain.

Small, Terry. **The Legend of John Henry.** Illus. by author. New York:
Delacorte Press, 1994.

Well written and sophisticated, this book is perfect for that special,
motivated reader. There is a wonderful rhythm and feel to the writing. Terry
Small's rich paintings truly shine in the musculature of the men's bodies, the
individualized faces, and the expressions. Without excessive detail, Small
captures the landscape, the moment, the scene. Terry also uses lighting effectively.

The contest of John Henry with his hammers versus the new Haley Drill
is a classic tale of human determination.

Demonstration/Participation Activities

Carlson, Laurie, and Judith Dammel. "Tall Tales in the Round," p. 160,
in **Kids Camp! Activities for the Backyard or Wilderness.**
Illus. by Sean O'Neill. Chicago: Chicago Review Press, 1995.

In a few sentences, the authors describe how to create tall tales with a group of children.

Sitarz, Paula Gaj. "Whoppers."

By presenting fill-in-the-blank sentences, youngsters get a chance to make up their own wild sentences that stretch the truth.

Once you've shared tall tales with a group of youngsters, you can invite them to invent their own "whoppers," or exaggerations, also known as "taradiddles" and "bouncers." Suggest that they let their imaginations run wild.

Before the day of the program put the following sentences, or others you invent, on a large posterboard, chalkboard, or large sheets of paper on an easel. If you prefer, you can type the sentences and make copies for each child.

You can do this activity with the entire group. Let several children offer endings for each sentence. If you prefer, you can give the children time to complete the sentences on their own and then share them aloud or hand in their responses to you and let you read them anonymously.

Following are sample sentences. The first one is done for you as an example:

1. Myra was so strong that she could lift **a 3,000-pound elephant with one finger.**
2. It snowed for so long that
3. The monster's teeth were so sharp that the monster could
4. Dan grew so rapidly that his head
5. During the storm, the wind blew so hard that it
6. It was so hot today that
7. When Lisa bit into the candy, it was so hard that
8. Tim ran so fast that
9. The bug was so tiny that
10. It was so dark outside, it was like
11. Amy ran so fast that
12. The picture in that book was so scary that I

Sitarz, Paula Gaj. "Whoppers or the Truth?"

In this participation activity invite children to determine if a short anecdote you read to them is the truth or a "whopper." Write the whoppers and the true anecdotes on separate index cards. Shuffle them. Read them aloud and ask the children to guess which are true and which are false. Continue as long as the children remain interested. I have included a sampling of "whoppers" I invented at the end of this entry. True anecdotes can be found in the books in the following list.

Eldin, Peter. **Amazing Pranks and Blunders.** Illus. by Kim Blundell. New York: Sterling, 1988. Eldin's book is a collection of anecdotes that describe a variety of humorous mistakes, pranks, and jokes. These incidents really happened, as improbable as they sound. I recommend for this activity "High Flyer," p. 64; "Dirty

Work," p. 65; "Be Prepared," p. 69; "Bungled Burglary," p. 75; "Most Embarrassing Locked Car," p. 87; "Opera Hang-Up," p. 92; and "Hi, There!" pp. 104-105.

Clark, Judith Freeman, and Stephen Long. **Scary Facts to Blow Your Mind.** Illus. by Skip Morrow. Los Angeles: Price Stern Sloan, 1993. I suggest using: "Killer Catfish," p. 2; "I Feel High!" p. 15; "Take a Walk on the High Side," p. 17; "I Dare You," p. 18; and "Asleep at the Wheel," p. 37.

Guinness Book of Trivia Records. Illus. by Bill Hinds. New York: Sterling, 1985. The following are true but unbelievable: "Endurance record for Ferris wheel riding," p. 25; "Endurance record for riding on roller coaster," p. 29; "Duration record for continuous swinging," p. 37; "The most prolonged continuous shower bath on record," p. 50; "The longest marathon merry-go-round ride on record," p. 55; "The largest pizza ever baked," p. 110; and "The longest recorded non-stop, rope-jumping marathon," p. 259.

Sobol, Donald J. **Encyclopedia Brown's Second Record Book of Weird and Wonderful Facts.** Illus. by Bruce Degen. New York: Delacorte Press, 1981. You'll find true statements on the following pages that will have children thinking: pp. 11, 28, 42, 54, 59, 65, 67, and 133. They range from the fact that young giraffes can grow up to half an inch per hour to the fact that humans and pigs are the only mammals that get sunburned.

Sample whoppers:

1. Moths and butterflies have eyes on their wings. These eyes help moths and butterflies see birds or other enemies who might be approaching. (Some moths and butterflies have markings on their wings that look like large eyes.)

2. Most people's hair grows about half an inch each month. Yet Jill Swanson of Derby, England, who lived in the 1800s had hair that grew three inches each month. She wore her hair in braids wrapped around her head.

3. Samantha Lewis holds the world's record for playing a piano nonstop. On May 22, 1952, when she was 15 years old, Samantha started playing the piano at eight in the morning and continued playing for 36 hours.

4. Dr. Seuss wrote many famous children's books, including **The Cat in the Hat** and **The Lorax.** His family revealed that he often wrote while wearing a pair of Mickey Mouse socks and a Mickey Mouse hat.

5. One of the unluckiest people is Jonathan Moore of Dartmouth, Mass. On December 9, 1978, Jonathan slipped on ice while getting the newspaper from his front porch. A few hours later while driving to the grocery store his car was hit when someone skidded on the ice. Jonathan and the other driver were not hurt but the left rear brake light on Jonathan's car was smashed. Three hours later he banged his thumb with a hammer while trying to hang a picture on his living room wall.

Chapter 19

Trickery and Tricksters

Included in this chapter are folktales and stories about trickery and tricksters as well as tales about characters who use their wits and outsmart others.

Many trickster tales are found in Native American stories. Refer to the chapter "Native American Tales" (pp. 155-74) for additional titles.

Read Alouds

Aardema, Verna. **Anansi Finds a Fool.** Illus. by Bryna Waldman. New York: Dial Books for Young Readers, 1992.

You'll find humor and expressive watercolors that capture the personalities of the characters in this Ashanti tale from West Africa.

Anansi, the spider, tells his wife, Aso, that he's going into the fishing business, but he's going to find someone else to do the work. Aso tells Laluah, who tells her husband Bonsu the news.

Bonsu decides he'll offer to fish with Anansi and trick Anansi into doing the work. Bonsu confuses Anansi by saying he'll cut the branches and Anansi can get tired for Bonsu. Anansi replies that he'll cut and Bonsu can get tired for him. Bonsu continues to confuse and trick Anansi until Anansi has done all the work.

Aardema, Verna. **Borreguita and the Coyote: A Tale from Ayutla, Mexico.** Illus. by Petra Mathers. New York: Alfred A. Knopf, 1991.

This is a delightful tale about Borreguita, "little lamb," who outsmarts a coyote determined to eat her. Borreguita first tricks Coyote by saying she'll eat clover to fatten herself and then Coyote can eat her. Coyote agrees, he leaves, and Borreguita flees. When Coyote confronts Borreguita a second time, the lamb tells Coyote she knows something that tastes better than her—cheese. She convinces Coyote to meet her at the pond that night and gets coyote to swim out to what he thinks is cheese in the water but is actually the reflection of the moon.

The third time Borreguita convinces Coyote to hold a mountain up with his feet while she runs for help. Coyote finally realizes he's been tricked again. The next morning Coyote springs out at Borreguita, but she again tricks Coyote and is never bothered by him again.

Aardema, Verna. **Rabbit Makes a Monkey of Lion.** Illus. by Jerry Pinkney. New York: Dial Books for Young Readers, 1989.

Illustrator Pinkney has painted expressive animals in his large-format artwork. Rendered in watercolor and colored pencil, the illustrations complement this well-told Swahili tale.

A honey guide, a bird, sings to Rabbit about a bees' nest in a calabash tree. While Rabbit and Bush-rat are in the tree collecting the honey, Lion growls from below and wants to know what they're doing eating his honey. Rabbit plots to trick Lion and manages to escape with Bush-rat.

The next day Rabbit returns to the tree, this time with Turtle. Again, Lion returns, and Rabbit plots to fool Lion a second time so he and Turtle can escape.

When Lion realizes Rabbit is behind these tricks he goes to Rabbit's house and lies in wait. Rabbit, however, sees Lion's tracks and devises one final trick. She convinces Lion that her house can talk and makes a fool of Lion. Lion decides that rabbits are just too hard to catch.

Aardema, Verna. **Who's in Rabbit's House?** Illus. by Leo and Diane
Dillon. New York: Dial Press, 1977.

This is a clever and sophisticated illustrated book. The brilliant, strong,
and spectacular full-color artwork incorporates elements of African art and
eastern and western theatrical traditions. The Dillons have created a fantastic
and magical world.

This Masai folktale is presented as a play, performed for fellow villagers
by Masai actors wearing animal masks. Hairstyles, costumes, jewelry, housing,
and the landscape are typical of the Masai. The masks are an invention of the
illustrators.

In the story, the masks change expressions. The opening pages of the book
set the scene, as expectant onlookers gather before a closed curtain. As the play
begins, the perspective shifts and the reader becomes the audience to this
performance.

Rabbit lives on a bluff overlooking a lake. One night Rabbit hears a big,
bad voice roar inside her house. It's The Long One, who eats trees and tramples
elephants. Rabbit wants to get into her house but doesn't know what to do.

Frog offers to help, but Rabbit rebuffs her, saying that Frog is too small
to do anything. Frog sits nearby to watch and listen.

Many animals offer to help, including Jackal, Leopard, Elephant and
Rhinoceros, but Rabbit doesn't like any of their suggestions. Frog offers her
help again, and this time Rabbit accepts.

Frog makes a horn that amplifies her voice. She announces to The Long
One that she's a spitting cobra who will squeeze under the door and spit poison
at the creature. Rabbit's door opens and out comes a terrified, long green
caterpillar. The caterpillar admits it was only playing a joke. The animals all
laugh, and The Long One inches away.

Alexander, Lloyd. **The House Gobbaleen.** Illus. by Diane Goode. New
York: Dutton Children's Books, 1995.

Lloyd Alexander is a superb storyteller, and this is an outstanding
original tale. The action is nonstop, the dialogue is riveting, and Alexander
develops characters more richly than most authors do in a short book.

Diane Goode's illustrations complement the text perfectly. She has a fine
sense of setting and detail, as seen in the landscape and the main character's
house. Goode shows detail, but her illustrations don't have a cluttered feeling.
She conveys characters well, too. The character Hooks has an appropriately
bulbous hooked nose, a jutting chin, and a greedy and nasty expression. Tooley
has exaggerated ears and features, unruly red hair, and patched pants. Gladsake, Tooley's smart cat, has a sharp, wary expression and expressive eyes that
match his intelligent and savvy personality.

Tooley always complains about his bad luck, although his cat, Gladsake,
points out that Tooley's luck is the same as everyone's. Tooley insists he needs
luck, and he tries to attract one of the Friendly Folk to his home by setting out
food. The next day Tooley finds a round-bellied little man eating the food, and
he feels lucky.

Gladsake advises Tooley to get rid of the man, Hooks, who says in essence
that once he's in he'll never be out, and once he's out, he'll never be back. Tooley,
however, insists that Hooks is one of the Friendly Folk. Tooley gives in to
Hooks's demands, convinced that his luck will come soon.

When day after day passes and Hooks's demands increase and he tells Tooley he never promised him luck, Tooley wonders why he's doing all this work. When Tooley tries to get rid of Hooks, the now rotund man reminds Tooley that once he's in, he's never out.

Tooley is frightened, but Gladsake tells him that he has a plan. They'll need a wheelbarrow with brambles, moldy cabbage, a bottle of vinegar, and a huge pot. Over the next several days, following Gladsake's plan, Tooley and his cat are able to convince Hooks that a Gobbaleen lurks in Tooley's house. When Hooks is good and jumpy, Gladsake bursts out of an iron pot, bares its teeth, puffs to three times its size, and yowls. Hooks is convinced the Gobbaleen has come. Hooks is so round that he rolls out the door while trying to flee. Gladsake remembers Hooks's words, "Once out, never back!" and knows they've tricked Hooks for good.

Baumgartner, Barbara, reteller. "The Grateful Snake: A Folktale from China," pp. 24-33, in **Crocodile! Crocodile! Stories Told Around the World.** Illus. by Judith Moffatt. New York: Dorling Kindersley, 1994.

This story begs to be read aloud. The plot is fast-paced and the tale has a good sense of justice finally served. One of the main characters, Zee, is foolish but appealing. He's naive, kind, and innocent. The colorful cut-paper illustrations have a three-dimensional effect. They offer different textures and are amazingly expressive. The artwork conveys a sense of emotion and action. The art is surprising and pleasing.

Long ago in China a mother, exasperated by her foolish younger son Zee, sends him with a sack of rice cakes to his brother Chu, who perhaps will hire him. Mother orders Zee not to return home until he can bring something of value.

Along the way to his brother Chu's, Zee sees a little snake, whom he feeds a piece of rice cake and then puts in his sack. Zee walks for days, giving bits of rice cake to the snake, who grows larger. Finally, there are no more rice cakes, and Zee tells the snake he can't return home until he has something valuable.

Zee, upon the snake's request, puts him in a river, where the snake turns into a beautiful dragon. He gives Zee a special horse from whose mouth three coins come when you say the magic words. Finally, Zee arrives at his brother Chu's house. When Chu says the horse must stay in the shed, Zee innocently tells his brother not to say the magic words. Of course, Chu does and the gold coins fall. The next day Chu gives Zee a different horse. When Zee returns home to show his mother, nothing happens and she considers her son foolish.

Zee tells the dragon what happened and this time the dragon gives Zee a magic rooster. Again Zee goes to Chu's house, spends the night, and foolishly reveals the secret of the rooster. Chu switches roosters, Zee returns home to show his mother this valuable possession, the rooster produces nothing, and Zee must leave again.

When Zee returns to the dragon he's given a magic stick that dances around him and tries to hit him when he says the special words. If he says "Teng" the stick will fall to the ground.

Zee finally realizes that his brother has been playing pranks on him and decides to use the stick to play a trick on Chu. As before with the horse and rooster, Chu says the stick must stay in the shed. As before Zee tells Chu the words he must not say. Again Chu says the words. The stick hits Chu's legs, but he doesn't know the words to make the stick stop. He yells for Zee, who says he'll make the stick stop if Chu returns Zee's horse and rooster. Chu agrees. Zee returns home, where he and his mother live peacefully and comfortably.

Bruchac, Joseph. "Rabbit and Fox," pp. 15-21, in **The Boy Who Lived with the Bears: And Other Iroquois Stories.** Illus. by Murv Jacob. New York: HarperCollins, 1995.

One full-page, colorful illustration with a tapestry look to it accompanies this clever tale. When Rabbit is startled by Fox he runs away. When he gets far ahead of Fox, Rabbit takes off his moccasins and tells them to run ahead and make tracks in the snow. Rabbit hides in the bushes and when Fox passes, he runs in the opposite direction. Fox finally catches up with the moccasins and realizes he's been fooled.

Fox backtracks and follows Rabbit's tracks until he comes to an old woman wearing a strange hat with two feathers sticking up from the top. The "woman" is really Rabbit in disguise, who tricks Fox, hits him on the head with a club, and runs away.

When Fox awakens he's even more determined to eat Rabbit. Again Fox follows Rabbit's tracks until he meets a medicine man who has a blanket wrapped around him and a strange cap with two feathers sticking out of the top. Again, Rabbit in his disguise tricks Fox into looking the other way, bops him on the head, and runs.

Fox awakens and follows Rabbit's tracks. Rabbit, in the meantime, comes upon an old rotten log with two sticks poking up from it. Rabbit hides in the bushes. When Fox sees the log with what look like two feathers, he decides it must be Rabbit. Fox eats what he thinks is Rabbit and feels ill. Fox decides maybe he doesn't like to eat rabbits, and he returns home. Rabbit runs away.

Cohn, Amy L. **From Sea to Shining Sea: A Treasury of American Folklore and Folk Songs.** Illus. by 11 Caldecott Medal and four Caldecott Honor Book artists. New York: Scholastic, 1993.

There are five stories about tricksters in this collection that you might like to share:

"Why Alligator Hates Dog," retold by J. J. Reneaux, pp. 46-49. Vivid and expressive artwork by Richard Egielski rendered in large blocks of bright watercolors blend well with this humorous tale. The sly, smooth dialogue is interspersed with Cajun words.

Long ago M'sieur Cocodril, the alligator, had the respect of all animals except for dogs, who loved to tease him. One day a dog, who was chasing a rabbit, falls in Cocodril's hole. The dog convinces Cocodril that he and the other dogs weren't teasing Cocodril, but, rather, inviting him to eat with them. Cocodril, who isn't very smart, follows the dog to his home and, when he arrives, is set on by the master and his dogs. Since then alligators have hated dogs. He's a lot smarter now, lying in wait for a dog to get too close.

"Brer Rabbit in Mr. Man's Garden," retold by Julius Lester, pp. 212-15. Lester's fine telling has rich dialogue and a fast-paced plot. The tale is complemented by award-winning illustrator Trina Schart Hyman's vivid and detailed artwork, which conveys characters precisely through their faces and stance.

Brer Rabbit loves lettuce and tricks his way into Mr. Man's garden through the man's daughter. After a week Mr. Man notices his lettuce is disappearing. His daughter asks him if he remembers telling Brer Rabbit that he had permission to take lettuce (that's what Brer Rabbit had told her.)

The next day Mr. Man catches Rabbit, tells Rabbit what he's going to do with him, and gets his whip. While Mr. Man is gone, Rabbit sings, tricks Mr. Man's daughter into letting him dance for her, and flees.

Brer Rabbit hears Mr. Man tell his daughter not to let Rabbit get at the peas. So, Rabbit dresses as Billy Malone and tells Mr. Man's daughter that he has Mr. Man's permission to take his sparrow grass. Brer Rabbit returns again in disguise and tricks the girl into letting him take peas.

When he returns a third time for peanuts, Mr. Man catches Rabbit in a box trap. Mr. Man vows he'll cook Rabbit. Brer Rabbit fools Brer Fox into taking his place in the box by saying he's being forced to eat lamb and doesn't want to. Brer Fox willingly takes Brer Rabbit's place with the promise of lamb in his mind. Once again Brer Rabbit tricks his way out of a tight situation.

"The Connecticut Peddler," retold by Maria Leach, p. 218. Trina Schart Hyman's classic, detailed, and vivid watercolors with pen-and-ink outlines enhance this delightful tale, which is most effective when memorized and told.

A peddler from Connecticut wants to spend the night at an inn in southern Virginia. The people are prejudiced against Yankee peddlers, but the innkeeper says the peddler can stay if he plays a "Yankee trick" on them before he goes.

In the morning the peddler folds the bed cover and puts it in his case. At breakfast he urges the landlady to buy some of his wares. She likes the bed cover—it matches one of hers—so she buys it. As the peddler drives off in his horse and buggy, he hears the innkeeper call that they didn't see a "Yankee trick." The peddler yells back that they will see the trick soon, and he continues driving out of town.

"Juan Bobo and the Buñuelos," retold by Lucía M. Gonsález, pp. 240-41.

In this short and witty story, Juan, a poor and foolish farmer, finds three bags of gold. Juan shows the riches to his wife, who knows they must belong to robbers. The gold must be kept a secret, but Juan can't keep confidences. His wife devises a plan to keep the gold and to keep her and Juan safe.

Juan's wife scatters fritters on the ground so her husband thinks it rained fritters. She convinces her husband that their donkey eats with its tail. When Juan tells everyone about the gold and three mean-looking men come looking for it, Juan honestly says he found the gold the previous day when it rained fritters and his donkey ate with its tail. The three men think Juan is crazy and leave. Juan's wife's trick worked.

"Brer Possum's Dilemma," retold by Jackie Torrence, pp. 249-51.

Ol' Brer Possum's kindheartedness gets him into trouble when, against his better judgment, he helps mean, evil Snake, who's stuck in a hole with a brick on his back. Suspense and tension build as each time Snake asks for help, Possum pauses to think if he'll assist Snake. Ultimately he does help him. Possum gets the brick off Snake's back, helps him out of the hole, and puts Snake in his pocket to keep warm. When Snake says he's going to bite Possum and Possum looks surprised, Snake reminds him that he knew he was a snake before he put him in his pocket.

dePaola, Tomie, reteller. **The Legend of the Persian Carpet.** Illus. by
   Claire Ewart. New York: Whitebird Book/G. P. Putnam's Sons, 1993.
   Bright, rich illustrations capture well the flavor of this folktale from Iran.

Kindly King Balash, beloved by his people, lives in Persia. His most prized possession is a diamond that sits on a special pedestal and fills the rooms around it with a million rainbows. The king trusts his people, and every afternoon he lets them come to see the beautiful light cast by the diamond.

One night a thief takes the diamond. His horse stumbles, the diamond crashes to the ground, and shatters. A boy named Payam finds the fragments among the rocks and shows the king where they are. King Balash wants to stay with the light, but he neglects his duties and the people decide they must act.

Payam, an apprentice in the Street of the Weavers, is commissioned to make a carpet as miraculous as the carpet of diamond pieces the king stares at day after day. Payam convinces the king to return for a year and a day. If, after that time, Payam doesn't fulfill his promise to fill the king's room with light and color, the people will live without a king. The king agrees.

With the help of weavers and dyers Payam finishes the carpet, and it is placed in the hall where the diamond stood. When the carpet is unrolled it fills the room with all the colors of the rainbow. Payam has managed to save the kingdom by using his wits and talent and tricking the king a bit.

dePaola, Tomie. **The Unicorn and the Moon.** Illus. by author. Parsippany, NJ: Silver Press, 1995.

DePaola combines pleasing and precise language and dialogue with fantastic-looking and evocative artwork executed in simple lines and blue, silvery white, and green watercolors.

Readers meet a beautiful but vain unicorn who likes to have the moonlight shine on her because that's when she looks best. One night the unicorn looks into the sky to find the moon and stand in its light, but she doesn't see the moon. The unicorn finds the moon trapped between two hills. When it was setting the moon didn't look where it was going and the two hills caught it. The hills want the moon to stay where it is so they can be beautiful.

The unicorn tramples over the hills to no avail. She tries to tickle the moon out of its trap, but that doesn't work. Then she enlists a griffin to frighten the moon free, but that plan fails, too.

Next, the unicorn goes to the alchemist, who tells her what to do. The unicorn pulls several round, shiny objects out of a bag and tosses them overhead. Now the sky is full of moons. While the hills try to catch some of these moons (actually mirrors), the real moon is able to escape. The unicorn keeps some of the mirrors just in case.

DeSpain, Pleasant. **Thirty-Three Multicultural Tales to Tell.** Illus. by Joe Shlichta. Little Rock, AK: August House, 1993.

There are several delightful tales about tricksters, trickery, outwitting others, and using your wits in this excellent collection of stories.

"The Tug of War," pp. 15-17, is a tale from Africa in which Tortoise tricks Elephant and Hippopotamus into a tug of war, which each thinks it's having with Tortoise. When Elephant and Hippopotamus tie, they each think they've tied with Tortoise and they have new respect for him.

"Alexander, the Dwarf and the Troll," pp. 25-27, is a folktale from Denmark. Alexander, a poor man, shares his meal with a tiny dwarf and is rewarded for his kindness. A huge troll wife suddenly appears and declares that the forest is hers and that she plans to eat Alexander. The troll wife gives Alexander three chances to outsmart her. With the dwarf's help Alexander is able on the last attempt to trick the troll wife.

"Ada and the Rascals," pp. 75-77, is a folktale from Holland. Johan is not very bright, but fortunately his wife is. Three rascals conspire to convince Johan that he's taking a horse to market instead of a cow so they can offer him a small amount of money for it. Ada thinks of a way to outsmart the rascals.

"The Devil's Luck," pp. 97-100, is a folktale from Hungary. A peasant crosses a bridge and is told by an old man that it's the Devil's Bridge. The Devil appears and directs the peasant to a specific house, where the man will meet his bride. When the couple marry and walk back over the bridge, the Devil appears again and gives them seven pigs as a wedding gift. The Devil vows to appear one more time with seven questions. If the couple answers the questions correctly they will enjoy seven years good luck. If they answer incorrectly they will endure seven years of suffering. The wife uses her wits to answer the questions correctly and outsmart the Devil.

DeSpain, Pleasant. **Twenty-Two Splendid Tales to Tell from Around the World: Volume One.** Illus. by Kirk Lyttle. Little Rock, AK: August House, 1994.

There are three stories about tricksters in this collection that you'll enjoy learning and sharing.

"Lindy and the Forest Giant," pp. 23-25, is a tale from Sweden. The lazy and cruel Forest Giant lives in a dark cave at the foot of Goat Mountain. Everyone in the valley must pay the giant a heavy fine to live in peace. If people are late with their payment, the giant throws boulders on their houses and barns. The villagers are afraid of the giant, except for a clever girl named Lindy. She decides to outwit the giant by challenging him to see who's stronger and tricking him into thinking she's mightier.

When her trick works and the giant says she can fish in the lake without paying him, Lindy says she wants the giant to pay back all he has taken from the villagers. The giant invites her into his cave, and Lindy knows he'll try to kill her during the night.

While the giant sleeps, Lindy places a log in her bed and hides. The giant gets up and chops the log, thinking it's Lindy. She swiftly tosses the log out and gets in the bed. When the giant sees Lindy, he's frightened. Lindy tells him all she felt was a little mosquito biting her during the night. The giant, afraid of Lindy's strength, gives her a large bag of silver coins and leaves the area.

"Reynard and the Fisherman: A French Tale," pp. 31-33. A fisherman who caught a string of fish and placed them in the back of his cart is guiding his horse Gigi home. Monsieur Reynard-the-Fox has seen this, runs ahead, lays in the road, and pretends to be dead. The fisherman is thrilled to see the fox, which he puts in his cart. As the fisherman continues home he thinks of the money he'll get for the fox's fur. The fisherman lets his imagination run wild, until he goes from imagining himself buying a cow to purchasing and selling a series of more costly items until he has a castle with servants.

During this time, Fox has been eating the fish. When he's done he tells the fisherman, who had been dreaming aloud, that he hopes the fisherman will share his wealth with Fox since Fox helped make him rich. The fisherman is shocked. Fox has fun with the situation. He runs off saying he must tell his mother he's dead. The fisherman shouts that Fox robbed him of his castle. Fox retorts that he thought he only robbed fish.

"The Man Who Was on Fire Behind: A Swiss Tale," pp. 47-49. In this short and satisfying tale the tables are turned on a trickster.

William enjoys playing tricks on his neighbors: locking chickens in people's clothes closets, placing goats on roofs. In the next village lives clever Greta, who has heard of William. One day, while Greta is making dinner over a wood fire, William arrives and asks for a drink of water. While Greta goes to the well, William snoops. He takes the largest chunk of beef out of Greta's kettle and puts it in his knapsack.

Greta returns and sees the steam and smells the beef in William's knapsack. She asks William to fetch more wood for her fire. While he's gone, Greta puts the beef back in the pot and replaces it with a smoldering piece of wood.

Walking home, William thinks the beef is good and hot and getting hotter. Then the neighbors yell and ask what's burning in William's coat and the seat of his pants. William jumps into the nearest pond where the water hisses and a mist rises from his backside. For weeks, the villagers tease William. He never tricks his neighbors again.

Frost, Heather, reteller. "The Tiger, the Brahman, and the Jackal," A Folktale from India, pp. 45-49, in **Wonder Tales from Around the World.** Illus. by David Boston. Little Rock, AK: August House, 1995.

Memorize and tell this humorous story that I have enjoyed telling for over 15 years. You can have a lot of fun with the jackal's confusion and the tiger's anger.

A poor Brahman is convinced by a fierce tiger to release him from his cage. Although the tiger said he wouldn't eat the Brahman, once free he says he will. The Brahman argues that it's unfair and no way to repay his kindness. The hungry tiger relents and says he won't eat the Brahman if they can find three things that agree with the Brahman that it's unfair.

A tree, an old buffalo, and a road have been poorly treated so they see nothing unfair in the tiger's threat. Then the Brahman explains the situation to an old jackal, but the jackal keeps confusing the facts of the story. The Brahman and the jackal return to the impatient tiger. The jackal still can't get the story straight and asks for a reenactment of the incident. When the tiger gets back in the trap, the jackal shuts the cage door and locks it. The jackal grins and says now he understands. The jackal and the Brahman continue down the road together.

Hamilton, Virginia. "How Jahdu Took Care of Trouble," pp. 18-25, in **The All Jahdu Storybook.** Illus. by Barry Moser. San Diego, CA: Harcourt Brace Jovanovich, 1991.

Jahdu, the trickster hero, is a creation of master storyteller Virginia Hamilton. Jahdu was born in an old oven beside two loaves of bread. The story is equally effective whether read or told.

Jahdu is heading south, but tumbleweeds are traveling north because they say Trouble lies south. Jahdu continues south anyway. He meets the giant Trouble, who wants Jahdu to get close to him so he can capture Jahdu and put him in the barrel attached to a hoop on his ear. In the barrel are many scared animals and humans Trouble has trapped.

Jahdu tricks Trouble into putting him in the barrel so he can help the animals and humans escape. Jahdu fools the giant, Trouble, into thinking his captives fainted. Trouble puts them in the mountain lake so they'll awaken. Jahdu then helps the animals hide in their natural habitats.

When Trouble returns, Jahdu stays out of his reach and flaunts the fact that he outsmarted Trouble. Trouble warns that he'll come after Jahdu again.

Hastings, Selina, reteller. **The Firebird.** Illus. by Reg Cartwright. Cambridge, MA: Candlewick Press, 1993.

The Firebird is one of the most famous Eastern European fairy tales. It was collected by the Russian folklorist A. F. Afanasyev. Here the telling is clean, understandable, and solid. Author Hastings builds tension throughout and underscores the tests and troubles the huntsman faces. She also highlights the fact that it is the huntsman's horse who at every turn uses its wits to enable the huntsman to meet his challenges. The stylized oil paintings in solid blocks of color, primarily browns and greens, are visually appealing.

The huntsman is the only servant the tyrannical king values highly. One morning, despite his horse's warning, the huntsman picks up a red and gold feather from the Firebird. When he brings it to the king, the tyrant commands the huntsman to capture the Firebird. The huntsman's horse advises him to ask the king for corn to spread over the open field. The next day when the Firebird pecks at the corn, the huntsman catches it.

The king is thrilled, but now he orders the huntsman to bring Princess Vasilisa to him so he can marry her. Again, the horse advises the huntsman, and he brings Princess Vasilisa to the king. The princess doesn't want to marry the king, so she declares that she must have her wedding dress that lies under a stone at the bottom of the sea. Again, the huntsman is ordered to get the dress or have his head cut off. Once again, the horse knows how the huntsman can secure the dress.

Vasilisa has another trick in mind. She says she'll only marry the king if the huntsman is bathed in boiling water. The huntsman is the king's favorite servant, but the king would rather marry the princess. This time the horse uses magic that results in the huntsman coming out of the cauldron as a young, handsome man. Seeing this miracle, the king wants to transform himself, so he plunges into the water—and boils to death.

The huntsman and the princess marry, and, by popular acclaim, the huntsman is crowned king. The huntsman never forgets he owes everything to his horse, who always and forever uses his wits to solve problems.

Holt, David, and Bill Mooney. "Is It Deep Enough?" pp. 114-17, an African-American story in **Ready-to-Tell Tales: Sure-Fire Stories From America's Favorite Storytellers.** Ed. by David Holt and Bill Mooney. Little Rock, AK: August House, 1994.

Youngsters love to join in on the catchy refrain in this clever and funny story. They enjoy the amusing rhymes by Rabbit, the repetition, the wonderful frog voices, and the colorful language. Possum's faked death scene is wild and wacky and fun. The story is most effective when memorized and told.

Ole Possum and his family love to eat frogs, but the frogs have gotten wise to them. Ole Possum's children are hungry and his wife is mad at him, so she sends him out to find frogs to eat. Rabbit hears Possum's tale, tells him to act dead, and says Rabbit will do the rest.

When the frogs hear Possum approaching they jump in the water. Rabbit convinces the frogs that Possum is dead and that they should bury him. The frogs dig a hole in the sand with Possum in the middle. Each time old frog asks if the hole is deep enough, Rabbit asks if the frogs can jump out of the hole. When they say yes, Rabbit says they should dig deeper. Finally, when the frogs say they can't jump out, Rabbit yells to Possum to get ready to eat.

Kimmel, Eric A., reteller. **Anansi and the Talking Melon.** Illus. by Janet Stevens. New York: Holiday House, 1994.

Children, particularly in kindergarten through second grade, will enjoy this well-told and humorous tale with appealing language and dialogue. Steven's classic, oversized, rich, full-color illustrations convey well the amusing animal characters.

Anansi the trickster spider is high in a thorn tree when he looks down and sees Elephant hoeing his ripe melons. Anansi loves melons but is too lazy to grow them himself. At noon, when it's very hot, Elephant goes inside. Anansi drops down from the tree and uses a thorn to bore a hole in the biggest melon. He squeezes in and eats until he's full and round. Anansi realizes that Elephant will soon return, but he's fat now and can't fit back through the hole. He'll have to wait until he's thin again.

Anansi gets bored and decides to make Elephant think the melon is talking. Excited, Elephant goes to tell the king about this amazing melon. On the way he meets Hippo, Warthog, Ostrich, Rhino, and Turtle, who don't believe the melon can talk until they hear for themselves. The animals all parade to the king.

When the animals place the melon before the king and tell him it talks, the king urges the melon to speak, but it doesn't. When the king calls the melon stupid, Anansi responds from inside the melon that he's not the one talking to fruit. The king is insulted and hurls the melon; it smacks into a tree and bursts into pieces. Anansi steps out, and, thin and hungry, he climbs a banana tree and eats.

Kimmel, Eric A. **Bearhead: A Russian Folktale.** Illus. by Charles Mikolaycak. New York: Holiday House, 1991.

You'll find much humor in this book, both in the text and the illustrations. Eric Kimmel is a fine storyteller, and he fills his story with captivating dialogue. He highlights the main character Bearhead's literal-mindedness and keeps you guessing as to whether Bearhead is foolish, or sly, or clever and deliberate. Charles Mikolaycak is an outstanding illustrator whose brilliant, large-format, and detailed paintings are rendered in a spectrum of vivid colors. Mikolaycak's witch is not traditional but depicted as a mortal with glasses askew, arched eyebrows, a topknot, and long, bony fingers.

A hardworking, childless woman finds and brings home a foundling who has a human body and a bear's head. She insists on keeping the child despite her husband's uncertainty. Bearhead grows to be a wonderful son. When his father is summoned by the witch Hexaba to be her servant, Bearhead goes in his place.

Bearhead follows Hexaba's instructions literally, so, for example, when she tells him to clear the table quickly, he tosses the table out the window. When she tells him to watch the lock on the door of her treasure house, Bearhead decides he can as easily watch the lock from indoors, so he rips the door off the building. Robbers come and steal Hexaba's treasures, but Bearhead only did exactly what she asked.

Hexaba sends Bearhead to collect 100 years rent from a goblin who lives in the lake. When the goblin refuses to pay and challenges Bearhead to a rock-throwing contest, Bearhead tricks the goblin out of a wagon full of gold and his hat. When Hexaba sees the goblin's hat and assumes it's the goblin coming for her, she hides under her bed and tells Bearhead to keep the money.

Kurtz, Jane. **Fire on the Mountain.** Illus. by E. B. Lewis. New York: Simon & Schuster Books for Young Readers, 1994.

In many ways this lyrical, beautifully told tale from Ethiopia reminds me of the story of David and Goliath. It's a tale of a child versus an adult, honesty versus cheating ways. Don't overlook this unique, strong, yet gentle tale. The illustrations are expressive and painted in earth-tone watercolors. The warm relationship between brother and sister is perfectly expressed visually. Especially beautiful is the painting that depicts the embrace between brother and sister. The close-up of the sister's face is realistic and warm looking.

Young Alemayu searches for his sister when his parents die. His sister is a cook in the house of a rich man, and Alemayu gets a job watching some of the cruel, rich man's cows. One day the master returns from town angry because he was insulted in the village. He declares that he is strong and brave; he once was lost in the cold mountains at night with only a mule. Honest Alemayu says that he often did that while watching his uncle's sheep. The master orders Alemayu to spend the night in the cold with only a thin covering. If he fails, Alemayu and his sister will be fired; if he wins they'll get four cows and a bag of money.

Alemayu succeeds, although the wind bites his feet and hands. He says that he watched a shepherd's fire on a mountain in the distance, dreamed of being warm, and that kept him going. The rich man says Alemayu lost because looking at a fire is like building a fire.

Alemayu and his sister, with the help of the servants, outwit the master at his own game. At mealtime wonderful smells come from the kitchen, but nothing is served. A servant pretends to play music. The help tell the master he's being served delicious food and listening to music. When the master asks who would believe that the smell of food can fill a man's stomach, Alemayu's sister responds, the same person who believes that looking at a fire can keep a boy warm. The next morning the master gives Alemayu and his sister the four cows and the bag of money.

McDermott, Gerald. **Zomo the Rabbit: A Trickster Tale from West Africa.** Illus. by author. San Diego, CA: Harcourt Brace Jovanovich, 1992.

McDermott's telling is deceptively simple and rich with rhythmic language. The artwork, in McDermott's trademark style, consists of brilliant paintings done in a patterned and graphic style with bold lines. The illustrations cover each double page completely. Children will revel in the large, glowing animals and the landscape.

Zomo, a clever rabbit, wants wisdom. When he asks the Sky God for wisdom, Zomo is told he must earn it by doing impossible tasks: He must get the scales of Big Fish, the milk of Wild Cow, and the tooth of Leopard.

Zomo beats his drum near the sea, and Big Fish dances until his scales fall from him. Zomo teases Wild Cow into running into a tree. When Wild Cow's horns get stuck in the tree, Zomo milks her. Zomo then spills some fish scales and milk on the hill where Leopard walks. Leopard slips, rolls down the hill, hits a rock, and his tooth pops out.

Zomo takes the three items to the Sky God and learns that wisdom consists of three things: courage, good sense, and caution. Zomo needs to remember these things because Fish, Cow, and Leopard can be seen chasing him. They're angry that Zomo tricked them.

O'Callahan, Jay. **Tulips.** Illus. by Debrah Santini. Saxonville, MA: Picture Book Studio, 1992.

It's exciting and wonderful to see master storyteller Jay O'Callahan's story published in an illustrated book. The artwork and text are full of humor and impishness—like the teller.

Every spring and fall, young Pierre visits his Grand Ma Mere in Paris, France. The servants don't look forward to Pierre's stay because Pierre loves to play tricks on everyone. He has tied the servant's shoelaces together, put the butler's keys in his oatmeal, hidden a toad in the gardener's boots, and hung the chambermaid's bloomers on the flagpole.

One fall Pierre decides to play a trick on his Grand Ma Mere for the first time. He plants the bulb for one black tulip among all the bulbs for red tulips. When he returns in the spring, Pierre bets Grand Ma Mere that the tulips won't all be the same as usual. Ah, but they are, they're all black. Grand Ma Mere knows how to play a trick on a trickster.

The next morning Pierre finds a grasshopper in his sock (from the gardener), flour on his hair brush (from the cook), a wet sponge in his shoe (from the butler), a golf ball in his cocoa, a lump of soap in his muffin, and a gold coin from Grand Ma Mere.

San Souci, Robert D., reteller. **The Brave Little Tailor (Adapted from the Tale by the Brothers Grimm).** Illus. by Daniel San Souci. Garden City, New York: Doubleday, 1982.

This fine telling of an appealing tale is complemented by expressive and dramatic illustrations.

When a spunky little tailor kills seven flies with one swat of his hand, he thinks he can take on anyone. The tailor embroiders "Seven at one blow" on his belt and goes into the world to seek his fortune. Soon he meets a giant who challenges him to squeeze water from a rock. The tailor tricks the giant by taking a soft cheese and squeezing much liquid from it. The giant challenges the tailor to throw a stone the farthest. The tailor tosses a bird in the air and it doesn't return. A third time the tailor tricks the giant, this time into thinking he carried the branches of a huge tree and jumped over the tree. Finally, at the giant's home, the tailor outwits and scares the giant.

The tailor comes to a king's castle. Hearing of the tailor's exploits, the king tells him that if he can get rid of the two ogres who terrorize his land, he'll give the tailor half his kingdom and his daughter in marriage.

The tailor finds the two ogres asleep under a tree. By tossing stones from above at one and then the other ogre, the tailor leads each ogre into believing the other ogre is hitting him. The ogres fight with each other until they expire. Seeing this, the king wants the tailor to catch a ferocious unicorn. Using his wits and tricks, the tailor accomplishes this feat, too, and the king gives him all that was promised.

Watkins, Yoko Kawashima. "Monkey and Crab," pp. 37-44, in **Tales from the Bamboo Grove.** Illus. by Jean and Mou-sien Tseng. New York: Bradbury Press, 1992.

Monkey tricks Mother Crab and her children out of their rice ball by offering them a persimmon seed in exchange that he says will grow and bear fruit. The persimmon grows into a tall tree and blossoms rapidly, but the Crabs can't climb the tree to reach the fruit. Monkey offers to climb the tree and drop the fruit to the Crabs. Once in the tree, however, Monkey eats the best persimmons and drops unripe ones to the Crabs. One fruit hits Mother Crab's back and she faints.

When Mr. Mortar hears the little Crabs crying he comes to them and Monkey flees. The Crabs tell Mr. Mortar of Monkey's deeds, and he enlists Mr. Bee and Mr. Chestnut to help teach Monkey a lesson. Mr. Chestnut hides in Monkey's fireplace, Mr. Bee hides by the water jar, the Crab children under the porch, and Mr. Mortar on the roof.

Monkey struts home. Once the fireplace heats, Mr. Chestnut pops out and burns Monkey's forehead. Mr. Bee stings Monkey, Mr. Mortar jumps on him, and the Crab children pinch Monkey's body. Monkey begs forgiveness of Mother Crab and mends his ways. The trickster has been outsmarted.

Booktalks

Brusca, María Cristina, and Tona Wilson. **Pedro Fools the Gringo and Other Tales of a Latin American Trickster.** Illus. by María Cristina Brusca. New York: Henry Holt, 1995.

Author Brusca has retold 12 of the short, amusing tales about Pedro Urdemales, a popular trickster from Latin America. The stories are interconnected, with Pedro fooling many of the same individuals from story to story. The collection is entertaining and cleverly written. Pedro is an appealing character who tricks people who, in many instances, seem to deserve it because they are greedy and foolish and often rich and powerful. The stories move swiftly and could be read by youngsters in second grade and up.

Among his pranks, Pedro tricks a priest out of his horses twice. He tricks two gentlemen out of 1,000 gold coins by convincing them he has a magic pot. Some time later he fools the same men out of 5,000 pesos by convincing them he has a money tree to sell. Pedro even tricks the Devil.

Thurber, James. **The Great Quillow.** Illus. by Steven Kellogg. New York: Harcourt Brace, 1994.

This delightful, clever, original, and well-written story has been newly illustrated by Stephen Kellogg. The artwork is colorful, expressive, detailed, and captivating. The illustrations sprawl over the pages and offer surprising and different perspectives. For example, the giant's huge head looms from the left corner of a page. The story's hero, Quillow, looks a bit like Albert Einstein. He wears clothing that is too small and has wild, white hair.

Hunder, a huge, ferocious giant, makes outrageous demands of the people who live in the town where a toymaker named Quillow works. The town council grumble about Hunder's demands, but they do his bidding. Every day the baker, candlemaker, cobbler, blacksmith, and candymaker use their time and the town's resources to give Hunder three sheep, a pie baked with 1,000 apples, a huge chocolate, a new jerkin, a pair of boots, a house, and a story to amuse him. Quillow, whom the townspeople tease as fanciful, is quiet when the town council meets and rejects every possible plan to rid themselves of Hunder. Every day, however, Quillow works in his toyshop making eight-inch high blue toy men. Each day he also tells Hunder a tale.

Quillow's plan is to convince Hunder there is a disease that once affected another giant's mind. Quillow lists the symptoms of the ailment and enlists the townspeople's assistance to make Hunder think he has the disease. The first symptom is Hunder will only hear the word "woddly" when people speak. The townspeople say only that word to Hunder. Quillow tells Hunder not to worry because he doesn't have the second symptom: all the house chimneys will turn from red to black. That night Quillow has the people paint all the chimneys black. Hunder is fearful, but Quillow says Hunder hasn't seen the blue men yet. If he sees them, then he should run to the sea and jump. During the time Quillow has built Hunder's fear, he's been making little blue men in his toyshop.

That night while Hunder sleeps Quillow places the blue men around Hunder. The next day when Hunder stamps his feet, the blue men jump around him. Quillow, when asked, says he didn't see the blue men, but Hunder seems to be shrinking. Hunder jumps in the middle of the sea.

Yep, Laurence, reteller. **The Shell Woman and the King.** Illus. by Yang Ming-Yi. New York: Dial Books for Young Readers, 1993.

Author Yep transports children to the Kingdom of the Southern Han (during the 900s) in China. The kings of that time were reported to be cruel and extravagant. Yep's telling is well written, swiftly plotted, and uses rich dialogue. He uses an economy of words to tell this attention-holding tale, which features a strong female character. The artwork, done in watercolor and ink, captures the mood and atmosphere of the story and offers fine detail in the setting and clothing.

A man named Uncle Wu meets, falls in love with, and marries an orphan girl named Shell. The girl comes from the sea and can change herself into a large seashell. Eventually, the cruel king hears about Shell and decides he won't be happy until Shell becomes his queen. The king puts Uncle Wu in his dungeon and demands that Shell either become his queen or give him three wonders. The king demands things he's sure will be impossible for Shell to find.

Shell easily locates the first two objects, hair from a toad and the arm of a ghost. The king's third request is for a bushel of luck. Shell soon returns with a large black dog that she says will bring the king luck if he feeds it fire. The king says he won't release her husband, he just won't kill him. He also has Shell seized. Then the king orders the dog be fed fire. Immediately the dog starts spitting flames until the king is surrounded by fire. Shell points out the king didn't say what kind of luck he wanted. Shell and Wu flee on the dog's back. There is nothing left of the king.

Young, Ed. **Little Plum.** Illus. by author. New York: Philomel, 1994.

From China comes this clever and finely crafted tale of a tiny hero who uses his wits and tricks to best the lord of the city. The illustrations in deep, dark pastels are expressionistic and evocative.

An elderly couple's wish to have a child, even if it's only the size of a plum seed, is granted. Overjoyed, the couple name their son Little Plum. He never grows larger but is able to do anything because he can get where no one else can.

Hard times come to the villagers. When the tax collectors from the city come to collect payments of grain and they find none, the lord of the city sends soldiers to beat the villagers and take their possessions.

The villagers don't know what to do, but Little Plum says he can get everything back. Using his wits and intelligence Little Plum gets into the lord's walled city and locates his people's stolen animals. Guards are asleep outside the door of the barn. Through trickery and cleverness Little Plum releases the animals, and while riding in a mule's ear, he leads the animals home.

Angry, the lord sends his soldiers to exact revenge against the villagers. Little Plum tells the soldiers he is responsible for what happened, and they chase him. Little Plum is too fast to be hit and he slips out of chains. Then Little Plum climbs on the lord's whiskers and when the soldiers try to hit Little Plum with their staffs, they beat the lord instead. The lord orders the soldiers to stop. He realizes he's been defeated and returns to his walled city.

Demonstration/Participation Activities

Eaton, Deb, and others, eds. "Eye Foolers," p. 7, and "Clip Trick," p. 38, in **Games and Giggles Just for Girls.** (American Girl Library). Illus. by Paul Meisel. Middleton, WI: Pleasant Company, 1995.

Share the visual illusions in "Eye Foolers" with children and ask them the related questions. They'll be surprised how tricky these illusions are.

Scientists can't explain why "Clip Trick" works, but it does. All the youngsters will want to try this activity. All you need is a dollar bill and two paper clips. There's a diagram and short, clear instructions that explain how to do this quick trick.

Lewis, James. "Balancing Act," p. 60-61. **Measure, Pour and Mix: Kitchen Science Tricks.** Illus. by Steve McInturff. Deephaven, MN: Meadowbrook Press, 1990.

The trick is to balance a potato on the point of a toothpick. Demonstrate and set up stations so small groups of children can try this activity. Few materials are required, and the steps are easy and few.

Penrose, Gordon. "Bubble, Bubble," pp. 14-15, "Finger Fun," pp. 18-19, and "Bag Boggle," pp. 22-23, in **More Science Surprises from Dr. Zed.** Ed. by Marilyn Baillie. Photos by Ray Boudreau. Illus. by Tina Holdcroft. New York: Simon & Schuster Books for Young Readers, 1992.

All the youngsters in your group will want to try "Bubble, Bubble." The first trick is to make raisins dance, and the second is to make spaghetti swim. These activities are easy and require few materials.

In "Finger Fun" two tricks will keep the children wondering. They'll put their finger in water and have it come out dry. They'll also stick a finger in water and make pepper run away from their fingers. Few materials are needed for these quick activities.

A sink, plastic sandwich bags, and pencils are all children need to try the last trick, "Bag Boggle."

Chapter 20

Wind, Kites, and Balloons

Read Alouds

Caduto, Michael J., and Joseph Bruchac. "Gluscabi and the Wind Eagle,"
p. 67, in **Keepers of the Earth: Native American Stories and
Environmental Activities for Children.** Illus. by John Kahionhes
Fadden and Carol Wood. Golden, CO: Fulcrum, 1989.

This is an Abenaki tale from the Northeast Woodlands. Gluscabi can't
paddle as strong as the wind can blow, so he decides to stop the wind. Gluscabi
succeeds, but once the wind stops, Gluscabi learns that the wind also brings
some good with it that he had not realized. He decides to free Wind Eagle.

Calhoun, Mary. **Jack and the Whoopee Wind.** Illus. by Dick Gacken-
bach. New York: William Morrow, 1987.

Calhoun's story (which could also be included in the program on tall tales)
is raucous and action-packed with full-color, exaggerated illustrations.

Jack lives on a farm in Whoopee, Wyoming. Jack doesn't mind a breeze,
but the wind is so strong it has blown most of his farm away and made his
chickens bald. When that wild wind humiliates Jack's dog Mose, Jack decides
to stop the wind. He uses a huge fan to shove the wind back, has everyone gather
blankets to create a wind sock that will capture the wind, and uses blankets to
create a huge curtain as the wind tries to come through Windy Gap. These and
several other schemes don't work. That's when Jack realizes that he can't stop
the wind but that he can find something useful for it to do.

Evans, David. "Maui's Kite," pp. 33-37, in **Fishing for Angels: The
Magic of Kites.** Illus. by Adele D'Arcy. Toronto: Annick Press, 1991.

This story flows well and is effective if memorized and told.

Long ago in Hawaii young Maui is inspired to make a beautiful, carefully
constructed kite. With the help of his friends, Maui carries the kite to the
Keeper-of-the-Winds. Upon Maui's request the Keeper, a wise old woman,
releases the gentle breezes that send the kite soaring over the trees and the
sea. Then the Keeper says the winds must be respected, and she returns the
soft breezes to the gourd where they are held.

Maui, not content for long, wonders how much higher his kite can fly. The
next day Maui and his friends return to the Keeper, and Maui asks for the gourd
that contains the Four Great Winds. The Keeper refuses, but Maui chants the
words that bring forth the winds. The Keeper tries to put a lid on the gourd,
but the wind knocks the gourd from her hands. When the kite goes into the
clouds Maui calls the winds back, but he can't control them. The winds rage
and send the kite sailing away. Finally the Keeper coaxes the screaming and
howling winds into the gourd. Disgraced, Maui finds himself alone. With
nothing to do, he makes a small kite, flies it, studies the movement of the kite
in the sky, and can soon foretell the weather. At first the people ignore Maui
when he predicts that it will rain or be stormy. Eventually the people rely on
his predictions and learn how to use kites for the same purpose.

Fleischman, Sid. "February," from **McBroom's Almanac,** pp. 173-75, in **The Random House Book of Humor for Children.** Comp. by Pamela Pollack. Illus. by Paul O. Zelinsky. New York: Random House, 1988.

In this wacky tall tale, Josh McBroom, owner of an incredible one-acre farm, declares he's invented air conditioning, or Winter Extract. When the wind outside has frozen, Josh and his 11 children saw chunks of the frozen wind and store them in the icehouse. When the hot summer days come, the McBrooms put a chunk of Winter Extract in their parlor. It thaws, generates a cool breeze, and then blows a cold gust.

Gray, Nigel. **A Balloon for Grandad.** Illus. by Jane Ray. New York: Orchard, 1988.

Sam is unhappy when his red balloon with silver stars floats out the open back door and rises above the buildings. The wind grabs the balloon, but Father assures Sam that the balloon is traveling to visit Grandad Abdulla. The balloon sails high over mountains, across the sea, over the desert where falcons and hawks try to tear it, to an island by a river, where Grandad, who lives in North Africa, finally holds it in his hand.

Lamorisse, Albert. **The Red Balloon.** New York: Delacorte Press, 1956.

Author Lamorisse wrote this classic fantasy tale based on his movie version of **The Red Balloon,** and the book includes photographs from the film. Through Lamorisse's skillful writing, children empathize with the main character, Pascal, and they feel the tension and conflict between Pascal and his principal, mother, and a gang of boys. The photographs show fascinating views of Paris, France, and feature lots of action.

In Paris, Pascal, a young boy and an only child, is lonely until he finds a red balloon tied to a street lamp, unties it, and has it follow him everywhere. They become friends and are inseparable. This friendship gets Pascal into trouble but offers him moments of joy, too. When a gang of boys steal the balloon and Pascal rescues it, a chase ensues until Pascal is surrounded by the boys and they burst his balloon. In an incredible final scene, balloons fly to Pascal from all around, they twist their strings into one strong rope, and Pascal holds on to be lifted into the sky.

Lies, Brian. **Hamlet and the Enormous Chinese Dragon Kite.** Illus. by author. Boston: Houghton Mifflin, 1994.

This book reminds me of Bill Peet's amusing picture books; the animal characters appeal to young children, yet the story is lengthy, funny, and delightful. If you have children at the younger end of the target age group, read this book aloud. If most of the children are at the older end of the target group, present it as a booktalk. The color illustrations sprawl across the pages and are full of action. The dialogue, characters, and action blend well and offer a good time.

Hamlet is an impulsive, adventure-seeking pig, and his best friend is level-headed Quince, a porcupine. Quince tries to talk Hamlet out of buying a kite and then out of buying a fierce-looking Chinese dragon kite because he's sure something will go wrong, as it always does for Hamlet.

Hamlet doesn't listen to Quince. He flies the kite on a windy day and is soon lifted into the sky. While Quince worries about him, Hamlet has an exciting adventure involving eagles and a cow.

Mahy, Margaret. "Kite Saturday," pp. 21-25, in **A Tall Story and Other Tales.** Illus. by Jan Nesbitt. New York: Macmillan, 1992.

It's Kite Saturday and children are taking their kites into the hills to fly them. Joan, however, doesn't have a kite, she can't make one, and there's no one to help her. Joan's mom gives her a silver coin to buy a treat and ease her disappointment. Joan sees an elderly woman sitting near a straw basket with a sign that says "Lucky-Dip. Wishes and Dreams." Joan trades her coin, reaches into the basket, and a bundle pushes its way into her hand. When Joan opens the package in the hills as the woman instructed, a beautiful kite unfolds. The kite carries Joan in the air, over the sea, and then lands.

Munsch, Robert. **Millicent and the Wind.** Illus. by Suzanne Duranceau. Toronto: Annick Press, 1984.

Munsch's text is a short, delicate fantasy about young Millicent, who lives on a beautiful mountain top. Unfortunately, the nearest children live three days away in the valley. Since there are no children to play with, Millicent plays with and talks to the wind.

Millicent and her mom hike to the valley for supplies. There the children are curious about Millicent, but when she tells them the wind is her friend, they make fun of her. It's then that a gusty wind swoops in and lifts the red-haired boy who insulted Millicent. The children run away.

Back at home Millicent asks the wind to find her a friend to play tag. The wind fulfills Millicent's wish.

Nolen, Jerdine. **Harvey Potter's Balloon Farm.** Illus. by Mark Buehner. New York: Lothrop, Lee & Shepard, 1994.

In this fanciful tale Harvey Potter grows balloons of all types and colors. Harvey's farm is temporarily in jeopardy when Wheezle Mayfield calls the government to check this unusual crop. The government men examine the farm but find nothing wrong.

The narrator of this story, a young girl, is curious about the farm, so she watches one night and learns that Harvey uses a conjure stick to grow his field. One day, when the girl wants to leave town, Harvey grows a huge balloon that carries her off to a new life where she becomes a balloon farmer.

Ober, Hal, reteller. **How Music Came to the World.** Illus. by Carol Ober. Boston: Houghton Mifflin, 1994.

In this ancient Mexican myth, Sky God and Wind God meet and bring music to the world. Sky God declares that it's too quiet on earth because there's no music. Sun has all the singers and music makers, and he won't share. Sky God wants Wind God to get the music.

With the help of Sky God's servants, Wind God arrives at the House of the Sun. There he sees golden flute players, blue wandering minstrels, and white lullaby singers. Sun tells the musicians not to speak to Wind God, but Wind God whips up thunder and lightning. In fear, the musicians go to Wind

God, who brings them to earth. There they play and sing, and eventually the people sing and play, too.

The text flows swiftly, the dialogue is rich, the tale is told with an economy of words, and tension builds well. The bold, vibrant, full-color artwork is done in large designs in shades of red, orange, yellow, green, and blue. The illustrations are cut-out oil pastel drawings.

Purdy, Carol. **Iva Dunnit and the Big Wind.** Illus. by Steven Kellogg. New York: Dial Books for Young Readers, 1985.

Kellogg's illustrations are wild, swirling, detailed, motion-filled watercolor paintings.

Take youngsters back in time to meet Iva Dunnit, a pioneer woman with six children who uses wit and strength to survive alone on the prairie with her family. Iva's not afraid of anything. She's battled a prairie fire, saved little Iris from a pack of wolves, and outwitted a thief.

In this tale Iva gets stuck outdoors in the raging Big Wind. While checking on the chickens, the Big Wind lifts her petticoats and sails her to the barn. Iva removes her petticoats and climbs the roof, with the chickens tied to her corset strings, to check on a loose flap of roofing. The wind blows the ladder away and Iva is left hanging from the roof. Iva instructed the children to stay indoors, but ultimately they rescue their mom.

Reddix, Valerie. **Dragon Kite of the Autumn Moon.** Illus. by Jean and Mou-sien Tseng. New York: Lothrop, Lee & Shepard, 1991.

Both illustrators were born and raised in Taiwan, and this familiarity is revealed in their touching, realistic renderings of indoor and outdoor scenes set in Taiwan.

Tad-Tin and his grandfather have always made, flown, and then released a kite on Kite Day. In Taiwan it is a custom that Kite Day occurs during the ninth month of the year, six days before the rising of the full moon. Tradition says that if a kite is set free at the end of the day and burned when it falls to earth, it will carry all a person's troubles away.

This year Tad-Tin's grandpa is ill and can't finish making the kite. Tad-Tin makes the tough decision to fly the big dragon kite his grandfather made for him when he was born. Alone at night Tad-Tin takes his treasured kite and uses all his strength to make it fly. Tad-Tin cuts the string and wishes all misfortune away. When Tad-Tin returns home, his grandfather is starting to feel better.

Tunnell, Michael O. **Chinook!** Illus. by Barry Root. New York: Tambourine Books/William Morrow, 1993.

In this humorous yarn, one episode swiftly follows another, the language is rich and colorful, and the illustrations are larger-than-life, soft, impressionistic, and full of sensory imagery.

Annie and her brother Thad, who have just moved from the East, are trudging through knee-deep snow to ice skate on the lake. They see a rowboat with a dark lump and a potbellied stove in it on the frozen water. As Annie and Thad approach the lake an old man explodes from the dark lump, waving his arms wildly. Quickly he gets the children in the boat and introduces himself as Andrew Delaney McFadden. Andrew, or Andy, explains that he's ice fishing in a rowboat because when a Chinook, a warm wind, comes in winter it causes an immediate thaw, and a granddaddy Chinook is as hot as a furnace.

Andy explains that once he was ice fishing when he saw Horace McRae in his sleigh trying to stay ahead of a Chinook. The front sled runners were in snow and the back runners were sinking in mud, that's how fast the Chinook was melting the snow. Andy was running across the ice when the Chinook caught up with him and he fell into the hot water. Ever since, Andy takes his rowboat when he's ice fishing.

Andy tells of other Chinooks, including one where the horses that were standing on extremely high snow were suddenly dangling from the church steeple when a Chinook blew through town.

Thad and Annie head for home after listening to Andy's stories. When they look back at Lake Turnabout it's suddenly covered in thick fog that is rolling toward them.

Vaughan, Marcia, and Patricia Mullins. **The Sea-Breeze Hotel.** Illus. by Patricia Mullins. New York: HarperCollins, 1992.

No one wants to stay at the Sea-Breeze Hotel, situated on a cliff, because it's so windy for 11 months of the year. Young Sam, grandson of Henry the handyman, unwittingly helps the hotel become a desirable spot when he makes a kite one day. The staff of the hotel thinks it's a great idea, and between them they make a butterfly kite, a box kite, and a dragon kite. People begin to notice the kites and come to join the fun. The staff makes many kites, and soon people come from near and far to fly kites. No one complains about the wind anymore, and the hotel is constantly busy.

Wade, Alan. **I'm Flying!** Illus. by Petra Mathers. New York: Dragonfly Books/Alfred A. Knopf, 1994.

At first look this book appears too young for the target age group, but there's a sophistication in text and illustrations that makes it appropriate for young school-age children. The artwork matches the text perfectly; it's surreal like a child's fantasy, full of humor and interesting expressions on the characters' faces.

A young boy lives surrounded by other small houses and wonders what the rest of the world is like. When the boy's friend, Mr. Witherspoon, gives him a box of weather balloons and a tank of helium, he sends up everything he doesn't like, from his math book and toothbrush to his teacher and his mean cat. Once the boy starts he can't stop.

The next day the boy ties 16 balloons to an old lawn chair, and, armed with soda, candy, and other necessities, he flies into the clouds, through a storm, past eagles, and airplanes. When Carl, a seagull he befriends, picks at the balloons, they start to pop. A flock of seagulls ensure the boy lands gently—on a tropical island where he finds everything he originally sent up, even his teacher. The boy forgets about home until a balloon arrives with a sign asking him to return.

Yolen, Jane. **The Emperor and the Kite.** Illus. by Ed Young. New York: Philomel, 1988.

Ed Young's illustrations are unique. He lends a subtle flavor of China. His paintings consist of thick lines in a variety of rich colors. On some pages he uses single colors, often browns or greens, and he uses white space effectively.

In ancient China the emperor has four sons to whom he pays great attention, three daughters whom he loves greatly, and a tiny daughter, Djeow Seow, who is ignored and spends most of her time playing with her kite. Every day a monk recites a poem to Djeow Seow about her kite.

Evil men plot against the emperor and place him in a sealed tower in the middle of a wide, treeless plain. The men take over the kingdom; the emperor's sons and daughters flee the land. Unseen, Djeow Seow builds a hut not far from her father. Using her kite she sends a basket of food to her father daily. One day the monk walks by and recites his poem about her kite, but he changes the last line. The new words reveal to Djeow Seow how she can save her father—by flying her kite to his small window. The rescue is exciting, as is the defeat of the evil men. And once the emperor is restored to his thrown, he no longer ignores Djeow Seow or neglects anyone.

Booktalks

Bellville, Cheryl Walsh. **Flying in a Hot Air Balloon.** Photos by author. Minneapolis, MN: Carolrhoda Books, 1993.

Bellville's book is for children at the older end of the target group. She grabs readers by relating her experiences with hot air ballooning as a passenger and ground crew member in a text that is not complex but is satisfying. Bellville explains terms in a clear and concise manner. She describes the sport, from flight preparation to dismantling the balloon, and includes information on ballooning organizations and hot air balloon flight schools. The photographs are bright, sharp, stunning, and complement the text well. Bellville includes a glossary, a labeled diagram of a hot air balloon, and an index.

Branley, Franklyn M. **Tornado Alert.** Illus. by Giulio Maestro. New York: Thomas Y. Crowell, 1988.

Here's one of the many solid titles in the series Let's-Read-and-Find-Out Science Book. The text is clear, interesting, covers one main concept per page, and explains the topic thoroughly. The illustrations are uncomplicated and appropriate.

Author Branley immediately draws children into the subject with a description of a tornado from development to destruction. Within the factual material, Branley builds drama as the tornado grows and strikes. Children learn how tornadoes form, what they look like, and where they occur. Youngsters will learn what happens during a tornado, what type of damage tornadoes cause, and what precautions they can take during a tornado alert or warning.

Coerr, Eleanor. **The Big Balloon Race.** Illus. by Carolyn Croll. New York: Harper & Row, 1981.

This is an I Can Read Book for beginning readers. The story is based on the Myers family. Mr. Myers was an inventor and a balloon maker who made balloons for his wife, the aeronaut Carlotta, an expert and popular balloonist in the 1880s. The Myers' daughter Ariel became a balloonist, too.

This story is about a balloon race in which Ariel falls asleep in the basket of the balloon and her mother lifts off without noticing Ariel. Since the balloon and ballast are meant for one passenger, problems arise. Mother and daughter get caught in a wet cloud, they lose ground, and when they find a faster stream of air below them, they almost hit a church steeple. Finally they land in a lake, but Ariel doesn't give up. She quickly thinks of an unorthodox way to win the race.

Dorros, Arthur. **Feel the Wind.** Illus. by author. New York: Thomas Y. Crowell, 1989.

This is a soundly written title in the Let's-Read-and-Find-Out Science Book series. The watercolors are inviting and the diagrams are clear.

Author Dorros explains plainly what wind is, what makes it, and ways the wind blows. He explains the importance and uses of wind and includes an experiment that shows the strength of wind.

Fleischman, Sid. **McBroom and the Big Wind.** Illus. by Kurt Werth. New York: W. W. Norton, 1967.

This is a short, fast-paced, funny, over-the-top tale. The watercolors, which use a limited palette of hues, matches the text perfectly in action and humor.

Josh McBroom describes in a series of anecdotes how windy it can be on the prairie. He explains that a breeze is a wind that carries a cow. A strong draft is how Josh describes the wind that ripped off their new shingle roof and the nails that held them, then swept both to shingle every gopher hole in the next county.

A big wind creates such a draft that it sweeps the 11 McBroom children up the chimney and sends them flying along with timber wolves and a bear. Josh McBroom must throw a rope to his children and then drag them home like balloons on a string.

Gibbons, Gail. **Catch the Wind: All about Kites.** Illus. by author. Boston: Little, Brown, 1989.

Author-illustrator Gibbons draws young listeners and readers into her nonfiction book about kites by introducing them to Katie and Sam, who visit Ike's Kite Shop to buy kites for a kite festival. In conversation with the children, Ike tells Katie and Sam a bit about the history and uses of kites and describes a variety of kites to them, from box kites to delta kites. Ike also explains what types of materials are used to make kites. Sam and Katie buy their kites and go to the kite festival, and there readers see and hear how to fly kites. Gibbons includes instructions on how to make a flat kite, how to launch a kite, and how to bring it down.

McKissack, Patricia C. **Mirandy and Brother Wind.** Illus. by Jerry Pinkney. New York: Alfred A. Knopf, 1988.

This book is delightful, sensitive, and humorous, with sprawling, fluid, somewhat impressionistic watercolors.

Mirandy's going to enter the local dance contest known as the junior cake-walk and she'd like to dance with Brother Wind. Mirandy's heard that if you catch Wind, he must do as you wish. A clumsy boy named Ezel would like to be Mirandy's partner, but Mirandy suggests Ezel ask Orlinda to dance with him.

Mirandy tries a variety of tricks to catch the wind, but when she does, and she recalls how the girls teased Ezel, she changes her wish. She realizes that Ezel is her friend, and she wishes, instead, that he become a good dancer.

Morgan, Paul, and Helene Morgan. **The Ultimate Kite Book.** New York: Simon & Schuster, 1992.

This book is geared to children older than the target group, but it's perfect to show children at the beginning of the program. It's a large-format book with striking full-color photographs of a variety of kites. Show children traditional, flat, fighter, delta, soft, paper, plastic, and stunt kites. They'll be amazed by how many types of kites there are.

San Souci, Robert D. **The Snow Wife.** Illus. by Stephen T. Johnson. New York: Dial Books for Young Readers, 1993.

An apprentice woodcutter takes shelter in a hut during a snowstorm and a young woman appears to him. She promises not to harm the young man, but he must promise never to speak of her.

Later, on the road, the young woodcutter meets a lovely woman, Yuki, whom he marries. One night he tells her the story of the charming lady who appeared to him during the storm. The woman was Yuki. Because he broke the promise Yuki changes into the Woman of the Snow and disappears. The woodcutter's search for Yuki takes him to the shrine of the Wind God, who lives on the peak of Bitter Mountain. On the way he is challenged by Mountain Man and the horrible Mountain Woman. Eventually the woodcutter reaches the Wind God and pleads for Yuki's return.

Demonstration/Participation Activities

Carlson, Laurie. "Paper Bag Kite," p. 136, in **EcoArt! Earth Friendly Art and Craft Experiences for 3- to 9-Year Olds.** Illus. by Loretta Trezza. Charlotte, VT: Williamson, 1993.

This is an easy kite to make at the end of a program or before the program to show the children. The only materials you need are a large paper grocery bag, a pencil, tape, string, scissors, and a hole punch.

Dorros, Arthur. "Weather Vane," in **Feel the Wind.** Illus. by author. New York: Thomas Y. Crowell, 1989.

Each child will find it easy to make this craft. You'll find the instructions clear and concise.

Drake, Jane, and Ann Love. "Fly a Kite," pp. 98-99, in **The Kids' Summer Handbook.** Illus. by Heather Collins. New York: Ticknor & Fields, 1994.

Demonstrate making this kite for youngsters and invite them to check out this book and try creating the kite at home. The instructions are clear, and it isn't difficult or too time consuming to do, but practice ahead of time. It does require a number of materials.

Erickson, Donna. "Make a Tornado in a Jar," p. 38, in **More Prime Time Activities with Kids.** Illus. by David LaRochelle. Minneapolis, MN: Augsburg Fortress, 1992.

This extremely easy demonstration requires only a clear plastic jar, blue food coloring, and liquid dishwashing detergent. By shaking the filled bottle in a certain manner you can simulate a tornado. If time allows, invite the children to create the tornado, too.

Hetzer, Linda. "A Sled Kite," pp. 109-10, in **50 Fabulous Parties for Kids.** Illus. by Meg Hartigan. New York: Crown, 1994.

This is another good kite to make ahead of time to show the children, or if your schedule doesn't allow, show the book and the page on which the directions are found.

Kohl, MaryAnn, and Jean Potter. "Wind Catcher," p. 40, in **Science Arts: Discovering Science Through Art Experiences.** Illus. by K. Whelan Dery. Bellingham, WA: Bright Ring, 1993.

This is a delightful project, and if your schedule allows, it's perfect for youngsters to do, also. The materials are very basic, and the nine steps involved are easy.

MacLeod-Brudenell, Iain. "Flying Fish," pp. 14-15, in **Animal Crafts.** Photos by Zul Mukhida. Milwaukee, WI: Gareth Stevens, 1994.

You'll find easy-to-follow instructions for making a carp kite.

Mandell, Muriel. "Blowing Up a Balloon with a Lemon," p. 53, in **Simple Science Experiments with Everyday Materials.** Illus. Frances Zweifel. New York: Sterling, 1989.

After you demonstrate this easy but amazing activity, give the children an opportunity to make a balloon inflate over the top of a bottle with lemon and baking soda. The instructions are brief and clear.

Potter, Jean. "Tornado Mix," p. 29, in **Nature in a Nutshell for Kids: Over 100 Activities You Can Do in Ten Minutes or Less.** Illus. by author. New York: John Wiley & Sons, 1995.

Each child in the group can do this short and easy activity. Few materials are required.

Richards, Roy. "Windmills," p. 49, and "Kite," p. 52, in **101 Science Tricks: Fun Experiments with Everyday Materials.** Illus. by Alex Pang. New York: Sterling, 1991.

The first activity is a simple version of a pinwheel that children can do fairly quickly without much assistance if you demonstrate while they are making theirs.

The kite is easy to demonstrate or for children to make with you. The only materials required are a trash bag, two dowel rods, and a ball of string. There are only three steps involved in making this kite.

Robins, Deri, Meg Sanders, and Kate Crocker. ". . . Kite," p. 39, in **The Kids Can Do It Book.** Illus. by Charlotte Stowell. New York: Kingfisher Books, 1993.

This kite is probably too complex for children to make during the program, but easy enough for you to demonstrate quickly. All you need is a piece of thin cardboard, masking tape, nylon thread, paper squares, a needle, and scissors. If you prefer, make this kite before the program and simply explain how you made it. You may inspire some budding kite enthusiast.

Sparks, Karen Unger, and others. "Blow Up a Balloon," p. 134, and "Go Fly a Kite," p. 222, in **Brownie Girl Scout Handbook.** New York: Girl Scouts of the U.S.A., 1993.

Children never cease to be amazed by this first simple activity. You need a small bottle into which you pour vinegar and a small balloon into which you pour baking soda. When you place the mouth of the balloon over the bottle and the baking soda falls and interacts with the vinegar, the resulting chemical reaction causes the balloon to inflate.

You'll find a clear list of materials and direct instructions to make the kite. If program time allows, this is a kite youngsters can make.

Van Cleave, Janice Pratt. "Paper Hop," p. 46, in **Janice Van Cleave's 200 Gooey, Slippery, Slimy, Weird and Fun Experiments.** New York: John Wiley & Sons, 1993.

This short and easy activity requires few materials and can be done by each child in your program or class.

Walter, F. Virginia. "Flying Fish Kite," p. 7, and "Pinwheels," p. 22, in **Fun with Paper Bags and Cardboard Tubes.** Illus. by Teddy Cameron Long. New York: Sterling, 1992.

You don't need too many materials to make the flying fish kite. The line drawings complement the clear directions on how to make the flying fish. Have all the materials cut and painted before the program and then demonstrate how to assemble the pieces.

"Pinwheels" is a unique and fun activity. Although there aren't many steps involved and common materials are used, I would only show the children this book and the page with the line drawings and instructions because one of the steps, putting shellac on the brown paper, requires time to dry.

Warner, Penny. "Homemade Hurricane," p. 105, in **Kids Holiday Fun: Great Family Activities Every Month of the Year.** Illus. by Kathy Walters. Deephaven, MN: Meadowbrook Press, 1994.

This extremely easy activity requires few materials but takes about 20 minutes to do. Have enough materials so small groups of children can do this together while you demonstrate it.

Chapter 21

Word Play and Name Games

Read Alouds

Abbott, Bud, and Lou Costello. "Who's on First?" pp. 312-13, in **From Sea to Shining Sea: A Treasury of American Folklore and Folk Songs.** Comp. by Amy L. Cohn. Illus. by 11 Caldecott Medal and four Caldecott Honor Book artists. New York: Scholastic, 1993.

Children find this classic comedy routine hilarious. The key to making this successful is to do it with another adult and to practice several times before your presentation. The skit is fast paced, and timing is everything. Turning words into proper names causes total confusion.

Lou Costello is confused when Bud Abbott tells him the names of the men on the St. Louis baseball team they're going to play. "Who" is on first base, "What" is on second base, and "I Don't Care" is the shortstop.

Betz, Adrienne, and Lucia Monfried, comps. "Bendemolena," pp. 20-27, in **Diane Goode's Book of Silly Stories and Songs.** Illus. by Diane Goode. New York: Dutton Children's Books, 1992.

Be sure to share this traditional American tale's comical illustration, with its appealing cats, and the whimsical borders around the text.

Bendemolena lives in a noisy house with her brother and sister cats and a continuous stream of visiting cousins and friends. She decides to put a shiny pot on her head that blocks out the noise. Bendemolena likes the quiet so much she decides to wear the pot all the time.

A friend of Mrs. Cat is sick, so she takes Bendemolena with her to run errands and Bendemolena's siblings stay home to clean the house and prepare supper. Mrs. Cat sends Bendemolena back and forth to tell her siblings what mother wants done. Because Bendemolena has a pot on her head, she doesn't hear what her mother says and mixes up the words. When Bendemolena's mother says to tell her siblings to put the fish on to bake, Bendemolena tells them to put soap in the cake. All afternoon Bendemolena runs back and forth with incorrect information. She tells her siblings to iron the meat, sew clothes on the clock, and put a horse in the sink.

When mother returns home the kittens are sure she'll be pleased because they think they've done what she wanted. Mrs. Cat realizes what has happened, looks at her smiling children, and can't stay angry. She puts holes in Bendemolena's pot so her ears can stick out, and she places the pot back on Bendemolena's head.

Betz, Adrienne, and Lucia Monfried, comps. "Master of All Masters," pp. 60-63, in **Diane Goode's Book of Silly Stories and Songs.** Illus. by Diane Goode. New York: Dutton Children's Books, 1992.

Amusing and wacky illustrations add to the flavor of this short, hilarious story. If you have time, memorize and tell it.

In this classic English tale a young girl hires herself out as a servant to an old gentleman. The master has his own names for things, which the girl must learn. She's a quick study and soon learns, for example, that a bed is a barnacle, pantaloons are squibs and crackers, fire is hot cockalorum, and water is pondalorum.

That night the girl wakes up the master to tell him something important. She uses his words. Invite the children to guess what the girl means.

Birdseye, Tom, reteller. **Soap! Soap! Don't Forget the Soap! An Appalachian Folktale.** Illus. by Andrew Glass. New York: Holiday House, 1993.

This funny tale is accompanied by amusing and expressive illustrations.

Plug Honeycut, who lives in Sassafras Hollow, North Carolina, is so forgetful he can't remember his name. His mother, however, loves him, has faith in him, and sends him to the store to buy soap. Plug keeps repeating what he must buy until he meets a woman whom he frightens and causes to fall in the creek. When she says she's a mess, that's the line Plug keeps repeating when he comes upon a boy tangled in the brambles with a basket of cracked eggs on his head. The boy thinks Plug is calling him a mess and throws Plug in the thorns. The boy says Plug's in a fix now, and that's the phrase Plug repeats. Plug meets a man who's had a tree fall on his truck. He hears Plug's words about being in a fix and makes Plug cut the firewood and load his truck.

Plug continues this way for some time, repeating the phrase the previous person he met said and getting in trouble with the next person he meets because of it. Finally, he innocently insults the mayor's wife, who says she should wash his mouth out with soap. That's when Plug remembers what he's supposed to buy. Plug returns home and gets a bath. From then on he never forgets anything his mama tells him.

Calmenson, Stephanie, reteller. "The Viper Is Coming," pp. 69-72, in **The Scary Book.** Comp. by Joanna Cole and Stephanie Calmenson. Illus. by Chris Demarest. New York: Morrow Junior Books, 1991.

At first scary, then funny, this story should be memorized and told for optimum impact.

A lady is home alone when the phone rings and a voice says that it's the viper and he's coming to see her. The phone goes dead and the lady is shaken. Downstairs in her house the buzzer rings and the strange voice repeats its message. The phone rings and the viper says he's on the first floor and will soon be there. He calls from the second and third floors, and the lady gets more terrified until there's a pounding on her door. When the lady asks who it is, the voice says it's the viper and he's come to "vipe her vindows."

Gwynne, Fred. **A Chocolate Moose for Dinner.** Illus. by author. New York: Prentice-Hall Books for Young Readers, 1976.

A little girl overhears her parents talking and visualizes something quite different from what they mean. Children love these funny homonyms. The full-color and exaggerated illustrations work well with the text.

When Mommy says she had a chocolate mousse for dinner her daughter pictures a moose made of chocolate dining with her. When the girl overhears on television that a man held up a bank, the girl visualizes a man lifting a bank with one hand. You can read this book straight through or pause and ask the children what they think the author actually means.

Gwynne, Fred. **The King Who Rained.** Illus. by author. New York: Windmill Books/Wanderer, 1970.

Here's another of Gwynne's collections of amusing homonyms accompanied by large, uncluttered, childlike artwork. Of the books in this series, the homonyms in this title are most easily understood by children.

The young narrator hears her father say there are forks in the road and she imagines dining forks on the highway. When she hears her mom say she has a frog in her throat, the girl pictures a frog peeking out of her mother's mouth.

Gwynne, Fred. **A Little Pigeon Toad.** Illus. by author. New York: Simon & Schuster, 1988.

Youngsters will enjoy this collection of homonyms and figures of speech that are twisted and given entirely different interpretations than the one intended. The illustrations work with the text to create word and picture jokes. You can give the children time to guess what each pun really means.

One example: When a girl's daddy says tennis rackets should be taut, the girl pictures tennis rackets in student desks while she stands at the chalkboard and teaches them.

Gwynne, Fred. **The Sixteen Hand Horse.** Illus. by author. New York: Prentice-Hall Books for Young Readers, 1980.

Gwynne depicts a young girl's visual images of what her parents are saying. The illustrations work in conjunction with the short text to create word and picture jokes. Examples from this collection include the following: The young narrator hears her daddy say Uncle Arthur runs a plant, and she pictures him running with a plant on a leash. When the girl hears that someone lives in an eerie house, she visualizes a house with ears all over it.

Kimmel, Eric A. **Anansi and the Moss-Covered Rock.** Illus. by Janet Stevens. New York: Holiday House, 1988.

The well-known trickster Anansi the Spider comes across a strange moss-covered rock and soon learns that if you say the phrase, "strange moss-covered rock," you fall down asleep for an hour. Anansi lures the animals of the jungle to the rock, gets them to say the phrase, and while they're asleep takes whatever food he wants from them.

Little Bush Deer watched this in hiding. Bush Deer tricks Anansi back to the rock and gets Anansi to say the special phrase. While Anansi sleeps, Bush Deer and the other animals go to Anansi's house where they take back the food Anansi stole from them. When Anansi returns home the food is gone.

Langley, Jonathan, reteller. **Rumpelstiltskin.** Illus. by author. New York: HarperCollins, 1991.

Langley gives this traditional tale his own personal touch. The main character is a strong female, subtly developed. Langley's artwork envelops almost every page. His watercolors are lighthearted, sprightly, delicate, expressive, and humorous.

The miller likes to tell tall tales, and he especially likes to boast about his clever daughter Ruby. His stories are silly, and his neighbors simply laugh at them. One day, however, the king hears the miller's tales and decides that since Ruby is so clever, she can spin straw into gold. If she doesn't spin the straw into gold, Ruby will be fed to the Royal Crocodiles. A little man appears and spins the straw on the first day for a necklace and on the second day in return for her ring. On the third day the little man says he'll spin the straw into gold once again in exchange for Ruby's first baby when she's queen. Ruby assumes she'll never be queen so she promises.

When the king sees the gold a third time, he asks Ruby to marry him. Since he doesn't mention being thrown to the crocodiles, Ruby agrees. They are happy together and happier still when their first child is born because Queen Ruby forgot her promise.

The little man, however, returns for the child. He relents and gives Ruby three days to guess his name. If she does, the man will release her from her promise. Luckily, on the third day a messenger relates to Ruby that he heard a strange little man singing a song and saying his name. Ruby gives this female messenger a bag of gold.

When the little man returns Ruby says his name and he disappears in a puff of smoke. Ruby is a good, well loved queen. Shortly after she has another child, it is decreed that Ruby and her children will rule the country. The king is left to count his treasure. One day, after a long life, the king, while carrying a heavy sack of gold, accidentally falls into the Royal Crocodile Pool and is never seen again.

Lottridge, Celia Barker, reteller. **The Name of the Tree: A Bantu Folktale.** Illus. by Ian Wallace. New York: Margaret K. McElderry Books, 1989.

Lottridge's gentle telling is complemented by illustrations in soft, light pastels that capture the landscape of the plains and jungle and the look of the animals.

Long ago in the land of short grass the animals were hungry because there had been no rain and no grass had grown. The animals decide to cross the great flat plain until they come to something to eat. Only Lion, king of the animals, remains in the jungle.

After many days the animals come to an extremely tall tree with a bounty of fruit on it. None can reach the fruit. Old Tortoise recalls a story about the tree and its delicious fruit. To reach it they must know the name of the tree and it's the king, Lion, who knows its name. Gazelle runs over the plain to the jungle where Lion tells him the tree's name is Ungalli. Gazelle trips in a hole on the way back and forgets the name. Elephant then gets the name from Lion, but on his return trip he steps in a rabbit hole and when he gets out, he can't remember the name.

A young tortoise offers to go and says he knows how to remember. The other animals think he's too young, small, and slow. Tortoise, however, even though he's hungry and tired and falls in the rabbit hole, remembers the name of the tree.

When the animals say "Ungalli" the branches of the tree bend so all the animals can reach the fruit. The animals eat and chant the name of the tree so they won't forget it.

Mahy, Margaret. "Tom Tib Goes Shopping," pp. 49-55, in **Tick Tock Tales: Twelve Stories to Read Around the Clock.** Illus. by Wendy Smith. New York: Macmillan, 1993.

Light and amusing illustrations are found throughout this comical story.

Young Tom Tib can do many things well, but he has a difficult time remembering what his mother wants him to buy when she sends him to the store. Tom might get an umbrella instead of bread or an elephant instead of vinegar. Tom's mother gives him one more chance and tells him a rhyme to help him remember to buy a pot of honey.

On the way to the shop Tom meets a bear with a can stuck on his nose. Tom recites the rhyme his mother told him, but the bear tells Tom a verse more appropriate to the situation. Then Tom meets a man who is growing roses. When the man tells Tom to smell the roses, Tom recites the rhyme the bear told him, which is inappropriate to this situation. The rose grower tells Tom a rhyme he should have said.

Tom continues this way, saying the rhyme the previous person told him to the next person he meets and being told it's inappropriate, then being told a new verse. By the time Tom arrives at the store he wonders if he can remember the rhyme his mother told him. Tom recites the rhyme the last person told him and, fortunately, it also suggests a pot of honey. Tom, by luck, brings the right item home.

Parish, Herman. **Good Driving, Amelia Bedelia.** Illus. by Lynn
    Sweat. New York: Greenwillow Books, 1995.

Literal-minded Amelia Bedelia, the intrepid maid to the Rogers family, needs to review her driving skills, and her boss, Mr. Rogers, agrees to accompany her while she practices. Amelia Bedelia's interpretation of Mr. Rogers' instructions results in mishaps for the characters and fun for the reader or listener.

When a cow with large horns looks in the car and Mr. Rogers tells Amelia to "push on the horn," Amelia pushes on the cow's horn instead of the car horn. Mr. Rogers later tells Amelia to look for a fork in the road, but Amelia says she doesn't see any forks or spoons.

When the car gets a flat tire and they don't have a spare or a jack, Mr. Rogers walks toward town to get help. While he's gone, a man with a tow truck comes. Amelia asks if he's Jack and he says he's John, but she can call him Jack. When "Jack" asks if Amelia has a spare tire, she says she wish she did because she'd give it to him.

Parish, Peggy. **Amelia Bedelia and the Baby.** Illus. by Lynn Sweat.
    New York: Greenwillow Books, 1981.

This title is one in a series of titles about Amelia Bedelia, the Rogers family's literal-minded maid. Amelia Bedelia constantly does things wrong because she does word for word what she's told to do, not what is meant.

Here Amelia Bedelia is asked to babysit at the Lane's house. Amelia has never taken care of a baby, but Mrs. Lane leaves a list of instructions. When the baby, Missy, cries Amelia reads that she should give Missy a bottle. This sounds dangerous to Amelia because the bottle might break, so she gives Missy a can and a box. When a neighbor hears the baby crying she prepares a bottle, and Amelia is amazed by this bottle that doesn't break.

When Amelia gives Missy a bath she refers to the list. It says to use baby powder. Amelia showers herself with the powder and thinks how nice it was of Mrs. Lane to think of her. Amelia does many other things topsy-turvy, but everything turns out fine.

Rattigan, Jama Kim. **Truman's Aunt Farm.** Illus. by G. Brian Karas. Boston: Houghton Mifflin, 1994.

With his unique, refreshing, and colorful artwork, illustrator G. Brian Karas depicts scenes from different angles and portrays characters with somewhat cartoonlike faces. Karas' illustrations perfectly complement author Rattigan's witty and original story.

A boy named Truman receives a birthday present from his Aunt Fran—a card he must mail to receive free ants for the ant farm he's always wanted. Finally, his gift comes, but instead of receiving ants, Truman gets aunts, many of them who hug him, pinch his cheeks, and pat his head. There's a line of aunts outside his house with knitting, banana bread, and magazine subscriptions.

When Truman writes to Aunt Fran and she doesn't give him useful advice on what to do with the aunts, Truman decides he wants them to be good aunts, so he'll start an aunt farm and train them. He has the aunts outside blowing bubbles, flying kites, and finding birds' nests. The aunts are happy and clever, and they play, sing, dance, and talk just enough. Aunt Fran keeps sending aunts and Truman has over 200 of them. He doesn't have room for them all so he puts up a sign advertising his Aunt Farm and offering aunts free to good homes.

Boys and girls come, each with a specific preference. One child wants an aunt who knows jokes and stories, whereas another wants an aunt who's a good cuddler. The children watch the aunts do headstands, roller skate, and do cartwheels. These aunts listen to the children, and they don't pat heads or pinch cheeks.

Each child finds the perfect aunt, but Truman is sad—something is missing. The next day a package arrives and inside is his Aunt Fran, with whom he spends a special day.

Sage, Alison, reteller. **Rumpelstiltskin.** Illus. by Gennady Spirin. New York: Dial Books for Young Readers, 1990.

Exquisite, detailed, magical illustrations in deep, rich colors with a European, old-world flavor complement this wonderful, well-written version of the classic tale by the Brothers Grimm.

In this telling the miller's wife suggests that if the king thought the miller was someone special maybe he'd visit them, want to use their mill, and they'd become rich. With this idea, the miller goes to the king and says his daughter can spin straw into gold. The king's reaction is not what the miller expects. The king wants the daughter brought to the palace. If she succeeds in the task, the miller will be richly rewarded. If she fails, her head will be cut off. The miller tries to backpedal and say he made up the story, but the king stands firm.

The miller's daughter, Rose, is horrified. When the king meets Rose he is surprised at her grace and courage. The guards feel sorry for her. As in other versions, the little man appears three times and spins the straw into gold in exchange for Rose's ring, necklace, and promise of her first born. The third time even the king hopes Rose succeeds because he realizes he could never find a richer or more beautiful woman.

Rose and the king marry and have a baby. Rose forgets the little man and his promise, but he returns a year later. He demands the child, but when Rose cries, he relents and gives her three days to guess his name. On the third day the king goes hunting, returns and tells Rose about a little man who sang a squeaky little song. Rose now knows his name, and when he returns she sings his song. Rumpelstiltskin stamps his foot through the floor, gets his beard tangled in the splintered wood, and, with a scream, vanishes.

Vernon, Adele, reteller. **The Riddle: Based on an Old Catalan Story—El Rei I El Carboner (The King and the Charcoal Maker).** Illus. by Robert Rayevsky and Vladimir Radunsky. New York: Dodd, Mead, 1987.

Striking, vivid, and stylized artwork blends with this clever, witty tale from Spain.

The king loses his way while hunting in the forest and eventually comes upon a charcoal maker. The worker realizes the king is before him and provides what little food he has. The king is surprised when the charcoal maker says that he earns no more than 10 cents a day but that it's enough. With this money he can pay back a debt, save for his old age, and still have something left over to throw out the window. The king is surprised, but the man explains. The debt paid is to his mother, whom he supports the way she used to care for him. He provides for his son, whom he hopes will care for him when he's old. He has to provide a dowry for his daughter, and that's like throwing money out the window.

The king loves the charcoal maker's riddle. Now the king wonders if the ingenious man is also honest and trustworthy. The king asks the man to keep the riddle a secret until he's looked upon the king's face 100 times. Then the charcoal maker shows the king the way back to the main road.

At the palace the next day, the king presents the riddle to his court. He declares that whoever can answer the riddle first will be made First Counselor of the Kingdom. Many try to answer, but can't. One courtier finds the charcoal maker and asks what the answer is. The charcoal maker won't reveal the answer until the courtier gives him 100 coins.

The courtier returns to the castle and answers the riddle. The king has the charcoal maker brought before him and says he feels the man is dishonest. The charcoal maker replies that he did what the king asked. He didn't give the answer to the riddle until he saw the king's face 100 times—on each of the 100 coins the courtier gave him. The king realizes the charcoal maker is right and clever and so he gives him three bags of gold.

Wood, Audrey. **Elbert's Bad Word.** Illus. by Audrey and Don Wood. New York: Harcourt Brace Jovanovich, 1988.

Short, sassy, sophisticated illustrations with people who look like caricatures highlight this original and appealing story. The bad word is cleverly personified, at times looking like dust with a creepy face or displaying a glowing mouth and eyes, hair, and long limbs with hands.

Elbert hears a bad word at a garden party. When the word floats in the air, Elbert grabs it and puts it in his pocket.

Chives the Butler tries to balance several trays of eggs and drops them on Madame Friatta's gown. Madame in turn spills her spritzer on Sir Hilary's bald head and Sir Hilary throws his croquet mallet in the air. When the mallet lands on Elbert's big toe, he opens his mouth to scream, but the bad word springs out. Everyone is shocked.

Elbert's mother makes him clean the bad word out of his mouth, but while he scrubs his tongue, the bad word sits on Elbert's shoulder and snickers. Elbert knows something needs to be done. He runs to the gardener, who is also a wizard. The gardener gives Elbert strong words that will help him express how he feels without saying a bad word. The gardener mixes the strong words in a batter and has Elbert eat the resulting cake. The ugly word shrivels.

Elbert returns to the garden party and more mishaps occur. When Sir Hilary's croquet mallet lands on Elbert's big toe again, everything stops and everyone looks at Elbert. When Elbert shouts, words like "zounds," and "my stars" come out of his mouth. Everyone is relieved and Elbert is happy. The bad word scurries down a dark hole and disappears.

Zelinsky, Paul O., reteller. **Rumpelstiltskin: From the German of the Brothers Grimm.** Illus. by author. New York: E. P. Dutton, 1986.

Zelinsky's version of this classic tale is accompanied by striking full-color, oversized, detailed illustrations in deep, rich colors. The characters' faces are extremely expressive.

Booktalks

Barber, Antonia. **Catkin.** Illus. by P. J. Lynch. Cambridge, MA: Candlewick Press, 1994.

Catkin is written in the finest oral tradition. Barber's text has a literary quality; it uses almost "old-fashioned" language. The language is poetic and full of imagery. Lynch's artwork, breathtaking watercolors, match the text seamlessly. Note the play of light and shadow in the illustration that depicts the little girl with red-gold curls playing with Catkin in a field of multicolored wildflowers. Note, too, the close-up of the Wise Woman's hands, realistic hands in which you can see veins and muscles. Children will find many visual pleasures in this book.

Catkin is given by the Wise Woman to the farmer and his wife, who have one child, a baby girl named Carrie, whom they treasure. The Wise Woman tells Catkin to watch over the little girl because she has seen that danger awaits Carrie.

One day Carrie is left to nap under Catkin's watchful eye while the girl's mother gathers blackberries. Catkin eventually gets restless and follows a butterfly. When quiet suddenly descends and is followed by music from deep in the hill, Catkin realizes the Little People will parade by Carrie. He runs to her, but it is too late. The Little People have taken Carrie and left a changeling in her place.

The Wise Woman directs Catkin to rescue Carrie, but warns him not to drink from the Little People's water of forgetfulness and never to reveal his name. If he does, the Little people can keep him forever.

The Lord of the Little People is confident he can outwit the cat. He challenges Catkin to solve three word riddles to free Carrie. Catkin easily guesses the answers to the first two riddles. He's faced with a dilemma when he realizes the answer to the third riddle is his name. If he speaks it, Carrie goes free, but Catkin will be held forever.

Catkin does reveal his name, but the Lord of the Little People is torn. If the child goes free, his Lady will be sad. If Catkin remains, Carrie will be unhappy. If both go free, the Lord and Lady will be lonely. It is the Wise Woman who solves the dilemma.

DeGross, Monalisa. **Donovan's Word Jar.** Illus. by Cheryl Hanna. New York: HarperCollins, 1994.

The younger children in your group will enjoy having someone read this title to them, whereas the older youngsters will enjoy reading this book themselves. It's a short, delightful chapter book with large print, wide margins, and soft, warm illustrations rendered in graphite pencil.

Donovan has an interesting collection: He collects words. He keeps them on slips of paper in a big glass jar. When the word jar fills Donovan doesn't know what to do. He wants to put more words in the jar, but he doesn't want to give up any of the words he has.

Donovan visits his grandma, who lives in a senior citizens' apartment building. She enjoys sharing Donovan's words with him and says she knows other people in her building would enjoy his words. Donovan doesn't mind if others see his words, but he doesn't want to give them away.

Many of grandma's neighbors are in the lounge, where an argument is in progress. Donovan gives them the word "compromise," and the people resolve their problem. Then, Donovan goes back upstairs because he forgot to ask his grandma to dinner. He leaves his word jar in the lounge. When Donovan returns to the lounge his grandma's neighbors are animated and excited, not quiet and listless. Each of them had taken a word from the jar that is meaningful and helpful to him and makes him feel better. They have taken all of his words, but Donovan sees the words have led the people to talk to each other.

Donovan's grandma gives him his grandfather's cigar jar to collect more words. He decides it will be fun to fill the jar and then find ways to give the words to others.

Hurwitz, Johanna. **The Adventures of Ali Baba Bernstein.** Illus. by Gail Owens. New York: William Morrow, 1985.

Children at the upper end of your target group will enjoy this humorous and finely crafted story.

David is tired of his name. There are four Davids in his third-grade class. He'd like an exciting name. David decides on the name Ali Baba when he reads **The Arabian Nights** for a book report assignment. David insists everyone call him Ali Baba and is sure his life will now be filled with adventures.

David is involved in several situations that he thinks will be exciting, but all turn out uneventful. He thinks one of his neighbors is a jewel thief and learns instead that he's an 82-year-old former opera singer. David thinks he can turn a frog into a princess by kissing it, but nothing happens. He's sure his friend's sister has been kidnapped, but she just got out of her crib and is sitting behind a curtain in the living room.

Finally, David remembers all the David Bernsteins he saw listed in the phone book. For his ninth birthday he gets his parents' permission to invite all the David Bernsteins to his party. Seven of the 17 people attend. They range in age and profession and are all happy to be named David Bernstein because they feel unique.

Lear, Edward. **Daffy Down Dillies: Silly Limericks.** Illus. by John
    O'Brien. Honesdale, PA: Caroline House/Boyds Mills Press, 1992.

Share some of Lear's nonsense verses when you tell your group about this
book. Show the wildly outrageous, varied, surreal watercolor illustrations with
their pen and ink cross-hatching that splash across the pages.

Mention some of the characters the children will meet if they read these
limericks: the man with the nose like a trumpet, the girl who wears a wig and
rides a pig. Also cite some of the situations and settings: a person who eats
gruel and mice, a man with birds perched on his nose.

Moser, Barry. **Tucker Pfeffercorn: An Old Story Retold.** Illus. by
    author. Boston: Little, Brown, 1994.

Moser sets his solid retelling of the classic tale **Rumpelstiltskin** in the
American South. His artwork is stunning, fluid, and dark.

A group of miners are swapping stories when Jefferson Tadlock tells a
crazy tale about a young widow, Bessie Grace Kinzalow, who has a little
daughter Claretta. Jefferson says the woman can spin cotton into gold. Rich
and mean Hezakiah Sweatt wants to see for himself. Bessie Grace tells Mr.
Sweatt the story is a tall tale, but he locks her in a shed with spinning wheels
and cotton and takes her child.

An odd little man appears to Bessie and spins the cotton into gold thread.
Sweatt returns the next day with five bales of cotton. Again the little man does the
work and again refuses any payment. He says some day he'll take something. A
third time Mr. Sweatt demands Bessie spin the cotton, and a third time the little
man helps. He also helps Bessie escape with her child. Mr. Sweatt is gone.

One night the little man returns and demands her daughter, Claretta.
When Bessie refuses, the man says he'll return in two days and give her three
chances to guess his name. That night, by chance, Bessie overhears the man
sing his name. When the man returns Bessie says his name, and he has a fit
and splits in two.

Parish, Peggy. **Amelia Bedelia and the Surprise Shower.** Illus. by
    Barbara Siebel Thomas. New York: HarperCollins, 1995.

Many children are familiar with Amelia Bedelia, whose literal-mindedness
leads to hilarious adventures. Amelia works as a housekeeper for the Rogers
family. This book is a newly illustrated edition of one of the original titles in this
series.

Amelia Bedelia hears from her cousin Alcolu that Mrs. Rogers is giving a
surprise wedding shower for Miss Alma. Amelia wonders why Miss Alma can't
give herself a shower. When Alcolu must prune the hedges, Amelia shows him
how to stick prunes on the shrubbery. Mr. Rogers instructs Amelia to scale and
ice the fish for the shower, so Amelia puts the fish on a scale and then ices them
with chocolate frosting.

Mrs. Rogers asks Amelia to run over the tablecloth with an iron. Amelia
puts the cloth on the floor, holds the iron in her hand, and runs on the
tablecloth. The preparations continue in this wacky way.

When Miss Alma and the guests are seated outside, Amelia and Alcolu
appear in bathing suits. Amelia throws the gifts at Alma, and Alcolu turns the
garden hose on for Alma's shower. Everyone is angry until Miss Alma laughs
because she thinks the situation really is funny.

Pfeffer, Susan Beth. **The Riddle Streak.** Illus. by Michael Chesworth. New York: Henry Holt, 1993.

Pfeffer's amusing short story perfectly captures the competitive spirit between siblings.

Amy Gale is tired of losing every game to her brother Peter, who is two years older. She wants to be better than him at something. Amy's friend Maria and her grandfather tell Amy some riddles. Peter knows the answers to the riddles Amy learns. Then, Amy gets the new **Riddle Encyclopedia** from her school library. Peter reads it, too. Finally, Amy finds a way to start her own winning streak—a riddle winning streak. Amy invents her own riddles, which the whole family thinks are clever, even Peter, who can't guess the answers.

Poetry

Carroll, Lewis. "Jabberwocky," pp. 10-13, in **Owls and Pussy-Cats: Nonsense Verse,** by Edward Lear and Lewis Carroll. Illus. by Nicki Palin. New York: Peter Bedrick Books, 1993.

The language is playful and original in "Jabberwocky," and the accompanying illustrations combine realistic faces on the characters with a surreal creature and settings. The weird, but appealing, artwork has many details to enjoy.

Children will relish words, which include "manxome foe," "uffish thought," and "whiffling through the tulgey wood." The characters include the Jabberwock and the frumious Bandersnatch.

Lansky, Bruce, comp. **A Bad Case of the Giggles: Kid's Favorite Funny Poems.** Illus. by Stephen Carpenter. Deephaven, MN: Meadowbrook Press, 1994.

Lansky includes several amusing poems that involve word play. Children will enjoy hearing the following:

"Pick Up Your Room," by Mary Ann Hoberman, p. 16. Everything a boy's mother says to him has double meanings.

"Your Nose Is Running," by Jeff Moss, p. 17. A child thinks it's wonderful when he learns his nose has feet.

"English Is a Pain! (Pane?)," by Shirlee Curlee Bingham, p. 39. The young narrator laments the many homonyms in the English language, which make spelling words difficult.

"Ned Nott," by Anonymous, p. 86. This is a clever tongue twister that children may want to learn and say with you.

"Betty Botter," by Anonymous, p. 87. Children love this classic tongue twister.

"Alphabet Protest," by Calvin Miller, p. 88. Find out what would happen if Congress passed a law that changed "K's to "B's and "B's to "K's.

"I Thought a Thought," by Anonymous, p. 90. Here's another clever tongue twister.

Lear, Edward. "The New Vestments," pp. 26-27, in **Owls and Pussy-Cats: Nonsense Verse,** by Edward Lear and Lewis Carroll. Illus. by Nicki Palin. New York: Peter Bedrick Books, 1993.

Colorful language, a story in rhyme, and surreal artwork are found in this comical verse.

A man who lives in the kingdom of Tess creates and wears an original outfit. The hat is made of a loaf of bread, the waistcoat and trousers are pork chops, the coat is made of pancakes, and his cloak consists of green cabbage leaves. The man walks a short way when beasts, birds, and boys rush him and demolish his outfit. Cows eat his cloak, apes seize his girdle of biscuits, pigs tear off his stockings and shoes, and birds eat his hat. The man decides never to wear clothes like that again.

Nash, Ogden. **The Adventures of Isabel.** Illus. by James Marshall. Boston: Little, Brown, 1991.

Marshall's hilarious illustrations, in which characters have exaggerated faces and expressions, sprawl across the pages of this funny, well-known verse.

Feisty Isabel easily defeats a variety of threatening creatures. When a huge bear says he'll eat Isabel, she washes her hands, straightens her hair, and then eats the bear. When a wicked witch threatens to turn Isabel into an ugly toad, Isabel turns the witch into milk and drinks her. When a dream says "Boo" at her, Isabel wakes up and fools the dream.

Prelutsky, Jack. **Something BIG Has Been Here.** Illus. by James Stevenson. New York: Greenwillow Books, 1990.

Children will enjoy the tongue twister, "Twaddletalk Tuck," p. 64, and the puns in "I Wave Good-Bye When Butter Flies," pp. 80-81.

Rosen, Michael, comp. **Walking the Bridge of Your Nose.** Illus. by Chloë Cheese. New York: Kingfisher Books, 1995.

Rosen has assembled a fun collection of humorous poems, limericks, riddles, and other word play. The artwork that sprawls over the pages is playful, done in vivid colors, and complements the text. Parts of this book, especially the last half, are more appropriate for children in grades three and up, but there's lots to share with younger children.

"The Cow," by Jack Prelutsky, p. 11, is a long tongue twister in rhyme.

"Oodnadatta," by Ronald Oliver Brierley, p. 14, has fun with silly names.

The section "Nonstop Nonsense" includes stories that never end. Children love them.

You'll find different takes on familiar nursery rhymes, including "Old Mother Hubbard" and "Hickory, Dickory, Dock" on pp. 18-19.

Demonstration/Participation Activities

Baltuck, Naomi. "My Aunt," pp. 60-61, in **Crazy Gibberish and Other Story Hour Stretches: From a Storyteller's Bag of Tricks.** Illus. by Doug Cushman. Hamden, CT: Linnet Book/The Shoe String Press, 1993.

This stretch is a chant in which the children echo what you say (or you can sing it). The children also mirror your actions. Once they do a motion, they continue to do it even after the next one is added, until they're doing five things at once.

Baltuck, Naomi. "Traditional Riddles from Many Lands," pp. 115-18, in **Crazy Gibberish and Other Story Hour Stretches: From a Storyteller's Bag of Tricks.** Illus. by Doug Cushman. Hamden, CT: Linnet Book/The Shoe String Press, 1993.
　　Invite the children to guess the answers to these clever and thought-provoking riddles that come from a variety of lands, including Russia, Algeria, India, and Siberia.

Buck, Nola. **Creepy Crawly Critters and Other Halloween Tongue Twisters.** Illus. by Sue Truesdell. New York: HarperCollins, 1995.
　　Zany and detailed illustrations in vivid colors complement these refreshingly clever and fun tongue twisters.
　　As you share some of these tongue twisters, show the accompanying illustrations. Invite the children to say the twisters with you.

Cohn, Amy L., comp. "The Fox, the Goose, and the Corn," p. 259, in **From Sea to Shining Sea: A Treasury of American Folklore and Folk Songs.** Illus. by 11 Caldecott Medal and four Caldecott Honor Book artists. New York: Scholastic, 1993.
　　Tell this short and intriguing riddle to your audience. Invite the children to offer possible solutions to it before you reveal the answer.

Cohn, Amy L., comp. " 'Twas Midnight," p. 229, in **From Sea to Shining Sea: A Treasury of American Folklore and Folk Songs.** Illus. by 11 Caldecott Medal and four Caldecott Honor Book artists. New York: Scholastic, 1993.
　　Recite this short rhyme and then ask the children to point out what the impossibilities are in the story.

Cole, Joanna, and Stephanie Calmenson, comps. **Six Sick Sheep: 101 Tongue Twisters.** Illus. by Alan Tiegreen. New York: Morrow Junior Books, 1993.
　　Children enjoy these tongue twisters. Select some to put on posterboard and invite the children to try them. The tongue twisters are arranged by category. You'll find tongue twisters about food, twisters with the "S" sound, two- and three-word twisters, tongue twister stories, and even a tongue twister game.

Cole, Joanna, and Stephanie Calmenson, comps. **Why Did the Chicken Cross the Road? And Other Riddles Old and New.** Illus. by Alan Tiegreen. New York: Morrow Junior Books, 1994.
　　Use this book for a change of pace in your program. Select riddles that appeal to you and those you think children will get. The riddles are divided by type, from animal, elephant, and spooky riddles to noisy, Mother Goose, and silly-billy riddles.

Drake, Jane, and Ann Love. "Can Cord Phone," p. 111, in **The Kids'
  Summer Handbook.** Illus. by Heather Collins. New York:
  Ticknor & Fields/Books for Young Readers, 1994.
  It takes a bit of time to make this more sophisticated phone out of cans,
but it's perfect to demonstrate to the children.

Fraser, Betty. **First Things First: An Illustrated Collection of Sayings (Useful) and Familiar for Children.** Illus. by author. New
  York: Harper & Row, 1990.
  You can turn this collection of familiar proverbs into a game by saying a
proverb, showing the children the humorous illustration that accompanies it,
and then inviting them to guess what the proverb means. Continue to do this
with other proverbs for as long as the children seem interested.

Hall, Katy, and Lisa Eisenberg. **Batty Riddles.** Illus. by Nicole Rubel.
  New York: Dial Books for Young Readers, 1993.
  Share some of these riddles about bats with the children and give them
time to guess the answers. Some will make them laugh, others will make them
groan. When you share the answer also show the accompanying illustration
(they're wacky and colorful).

Hartman, Victoria. **The Silliest Joke Book Ever.** Illus. by R. W. Alley.
  New York: Lothrop, Lee & Shepard, 1993.
  Pick and choose a variety of jokes to share with the youngsters, and let
them try to guess the answers. You'll find jokes about food, animals, gruesome
things, and technical objects. Share the lighthearted, whimsical, and humorous
watercolor artwork that accompanies the riddles.

Hilton, Joni. "Fill in the Blanks," p. 121, and "Tell a Funny Story in a
  Round," p. 131, in **Five Minute Miracles: 373 Quick Daily
  Discoveries for You and Your Kids to Share.** Illus. by Matt
  Wawiorka. Philadelphia: Running Press, 1992.
  In the first activity select or invent a short story, but leave out the nouns when
you read it to the youngsters. Invite the children to supply the nouns as you go along.
  In the second activity, you and your audience can create a silly story by
having each person in turn add a sentence to an initial sentence.

Hurwitz, Johanna. **A Word to the Wise and Other Proverbs.** Illus.
  by Robert Rayevsky. New York: Morrow Junior Books, 1994.
  Share some of the proverbs in this collection with youngsters, show the
accompanying stylized, eye-catching illustrations and ask the children what
they think each proverb means. Do several or all of them.

Kneen, Maggie, comp. **Too Many Cooks . . . : And Other Proverbs.**
  Illus. by Maggie Kneen. New York: Simon & Schuster, 1992.
  The book's 23 proverbs are accompanied by lighthearted, whimsical
illustrations. Let the children offer guesses about what the proverbs mean. The
proverbs include "Look before you leap" and "Don't count your chickens before
they hatch."

Koontz, Robin Michal. **I See Something You Don't See: A Riddle-Me Picture Book.** Illus. by author. New York: Cobblehill Books/Dutton Children's Books, 1992.

This is a clever picture book version of a popular guessing game. Read each riddle to the children without showing them the accompanying illustration. See if anyone can guess the riddle without the visual clue. If necessary, show the illustration. The answers are included on the last page (in case you have trouble guessing them).

Maestro, Giulio. **More Halloween Howls: Riddles That Come Back to Haunt You.** Illus. by author. New York: Dutton Children's Books, 1992.

The riddles in this collection are actually funny, as are the illustrations. There are riddles about witches, vampires, skeletons, and other Halloween creatures.

Milord, Susan. "Create a Rebus," p. 67, in **Hands Around the World: 365 Creative Ways to Build Cultural Awareness and Global Respect.** Illus. by author. Charlotte, VT: Williamson, 1992.

Using the clear and concise instructions included in this book you can guide children in writing their own rebus messages.

Mohr, Merilyn Simonds. "Hangman," pp. 272-73, in **The Games Treasury: More Than 300 Indoor and Outdoor Favorites with Strategies, Rules and Traditions.** Illus. by Roberta Cooke. Shelburne, VT: Chapters Publishing, 1993.

You'll find clear instructions for playing this classic word-guessing game.

Mohr, Merilyn Simonds. "Twenty Questions," p. 260, in **The Games Treasury: More Than 300 Indoor and Outdoor Favorites with Strategies, Rules and Traditions.** Illus. by Roberta Cooke. Shelburne, VT: Chapters Publishing, 1993.

Clear and detailed instructions are provided for playing this well-known question-and-answer game. The author also includes excellent variations on this game.

Most, Bernard. **Zoodles.** Illus. by author. New York: Harcourt Brace Jovanovich, 1992.

In this collection of riddles the answers are a combination of two animals. When you see each answer, you'll be surprised at how well the two animal names blend. The large and uncomplicated illustrations depict the fanciful combination animals.

The creatures you'll see include a kangarooster, a zebram, a flamingoat, and a crabbit.

Nims, Bonnie Larkin. **Just Beyond Reach and Other Riddle Poems.** Photos by George Ancona. New York: Scholastic, 1992.

Like many books of this type, Nims's title looks simple but is really aimed at school-age children who can solve the riddles. Here, the riddles are in the form of short poems. The riddle appears in large type on the right page. The interesting and sharp photograph of the answer is on each left page. Share some of the riddles with the children and invite them to guess the answers. Some are easier than others.

Rees, Ennis. **Fast Freddie Frog and Other Tongue-Twister Rhymes.** Illus. by John O'Brien. Honesdale, PA: Caroline House/Boyds Mills Press, 1993.

Author Rees offers a collection of tongue twisters and tongue-twister rhymes that he has created. Most of them have been adapted from characters and situations found in folklore. Write some of these on posterboard or a chalkboard and invite the children to do them with you. These tongue twisters are not your usual, familiar ones. They are fresh and fun and will appeal to today's children.

Rounds, Glen. **I Know an Old Lady Who Swallowed a Fly.** Illus. by author. New York: Holiday House, 1990.

There are many illustrated versions of this nonsense verse, but I particularly like Glen Rounds's rugged, rough, and other-worldly looking illustrations. You can share this with the children as a chant or as a song.

Schwartz, Alvin, comp. **A Twister of Twists, a Tangler of Tongues.** Illus. by Glen Rounds. New York: J. B. Lippincott, 1972.

This is a great and classic collection of tongue twisters that you can invite children to do. Some will be familiar, like "Peter Piper" and "Betty Botter," whereas others will be new to the youngsters. Some of the twisters are phrases, some are sentences, and others are stories or limericks. Make sure you practice these before you share them. Some are quite tricky. Schwartz even includes tongue twisters in other languages with pronunciations keys and translations.

On p. 111 you'll find a succinct explanation on how to create tongue twisters. You might want to give the children time to write some original twisters.

Shannon, George. **More Stories to Solve: Fifteen Folktales from Around the World.** Illus. by Peter Sis. New York: Greenwillow Books, 1991.

Shannon, George. **Still More Stories to Solve: Fourteen Folktales from Around the World.** Illus. by Peter Sis. New York: Greenwillow Books, 1994.

Shannon, George. **Stories to Solve: Folktales from Around the World.** Illus. by Peter Sis. New York: Greenwillow Books, 1985.

These three outstanding collections offer extremely short stories, each with a mystery or a problem for the characters and the listeners to solve. Solutions are given for each. Share one or several of these with youngsters and give them time to guess the answers.

Sitarz, Paula Gaj. "Book Talk Bingo."

This activity requires some preparation before the program: Make original bingo boards. Use an 8 1/2-x-11-inch piece of paper or posterboard. Draw a 6-x-6-inch square on it. Divide into nine equal 2-inch squares. In each square, type or print the title of a book with which you think the children will be familiar, or a title from the program. Prepare a separate board for each child. Each bingo board must have the titles in a different placement and not all boards will have the same titles. On small squares of paper, type the book titles found on the bingo boards. Cut color construction paper into circles slighter smaller than the 2-inch squares on the bingo board. Cut enough circles for the children to cover the book titles on their bingo boards.

During the program: Give each child a bingo board and colored "cover" squares. Place the small squares of paper on which you've typed the book titles in a bowl or other container. Pull one paper at a time, read the title, and instruct the children to cover the title when they hear it. If you have a group in which some of the children can't read, have older children help them during this activity.

The first child to get three book titles in a row across, down, or diagonally wins. If time allows, tell the children a little about each title. Play once or several times, depending on the youngsters' interest and the time available.

Terban, Marvin. **Eight Ate: A Feast of Homonym Riddles.** Illus. by Giulio Maestro. New York: Clarion Books, 1982.

Lighthearted illustrations accompany this collection of original riddles in which the answers are homonyms. To use with a group of children, ask the riddle, show the illustration, and then reveal the answer. Some of the answers include "foul fowl," "bare bear," and "sees seas."

Terban, Marvin. **Mad As a Wet Hen! And Other Funny Idioms.** Illus. by Giulio Maestro. New York: Clarion Books, 1987.

Author Terban explains over 100 idioms and divides them into a variety of categories. He explains that idioms are sayings with hidden meanings, expressions that don't mean exactly what the words say. The accompanying illustrations are funny.

To use this as an activity, say the sentence that includes the idiom and see if, in context and with the illustration, the children can guess what it really means. The idioms include "It's raining cats and dogs!" "She laughed her head off," and "Sister is blowing her top."

At the end of the book the idioms are listed alphabetically. You can say a few of the idioms and invite the children to draw what images they suggest when taken literally.

Terban, Marvin. **Superdupers! Really Funny Real Words.** Illus. by Giulio Maestro. New York: Clarion Books/Houghton Mifflin, 1989.

This is one of the best and most interesting in this series of books about words for youngsters. Author Terban explains the meaning of over 100 nonsense words, including words with two, three, and four syllables that rhyme, words that almost rhyme, and words that are created by repeating a word.

There are several ways to use this book as a game. You can say the word, read the sentence it's used in, and invite the children to guess the meaning of the word. Or you can write a list of these words and a jumbled list of the definitions and invite the children to match each word with its definition. You can also provide children with a definition and ask them to select from a list of possible words the one that means the same as the definition. For example you could say "a soft stuffed animal" and the answer would be "fuzzy-wuzzy," or you could say "something very secret" and the answer would be "hush-hush."

Warner, Penny. "Gossip," pp. 150-51, and "Rewrite," pp. 186-87, in **Kids' Party Games and Activities: Hundreds of Exciting Things to Do at Parties for Kids 2-12.** Illus. by Kathy Rogers. Deephaven, MN: Meadowbrook Press, 1993.

The author offers clear instructions on how to play the classic game "Gossip," which gets everyone laughing. She also offers alternative ways to play.

In "Rewrite," Warner offers several ways to create your own homemade versions of the popular game "Madlibs."

Author, Editor, Illustrator Index

289

Title Index